CLMBEC

FIRST STEPS

LOCAL AGENDA 21 IN PRACTICE

MUNICIPAL STRATEGIES
FOR SUSTAINABILITY AS PRESENTED AT
GLOBAL FORUM 94 IN MANCHESTER

Printed on
recycled paper

London : HMSO

Manchester
making it happen

Manchester City Council would like to thank the following Local Authorities, International Organisations, The British Council and the many individuals who have generously contributed both their time and financial support towards the organisation of the International Local Agenda 21 Conference at Global Forum '94.

Our thanks for financial assistance to

East Sussex County Council
Conference Interpretation • Headsets

Lancashire County Council
Conference Interpretation

Kirklees Metropolitan Borough Council
Delegates Bags • Conference Catering

Avon County Council
Seminar Organisation • Conference Catering

Bristol City Council
Seminar Organisation

City of Cardiff
Conference Interpretation

Mendip District Council
Translation of Conference Papers

City of Glasgow District Council
Translation of Conference Papers

Local Government International Bureau
Seminar Organisation • Interpretation • Conference Catering

Leicester City Council
Seminar Organisation • Interpretation • Conference Catering

In conjunction with

UK Local Agenda 21 Committee

Local Government Management Board

United Towns Organisation

IULA
International Union of Local Authorities

CEMR
Council of European Municipalities and Regions

ICLEI
The International Council of Local Environmental initiatives

The British Council

Association of Metropolitan Authorities

I would like to thank the many individuals and local authorities who have in some way contributed to this book, either by way of supplying written or photographic material, in conversation, or through reviewing parts of the earlier drafts. In particular I owe a large measure of gratitude to Maggie Bosanquet for her critical and thoughtful comments and editorial assistance which has improved much of the text and to Nick Jacob and Janet Hyde for proof reading assistance.

I would like to thank the following for permission to reproduce copyrighted material : Sustainable Seattle, International Council for Local Environmental Initiatives and the Swedish Association of Local Authorities.

I also extend thanks to The Environmental Picture Library Ltd and Manchester Communication Service, without whose efforts this book would not have appeared and to Interlingua for their translation services.

It is also appropriate to thank all those involved in organising and supporting the International Local Authority Local Agenda 21 Conference held in Manchester 27 June - 1 July 1994 : members of the International Local Authority Steering Group and especially ICLEI, Manchester City Council members and personnel and in particular Cllr Arnold Spencer, Dr Ted Kitchen , Janet Heron, Julie Barnes, Kirstine Hogg and individuals Alisia Tomalino and Dr John Whitelegg. In addition to the speakers to the conference the following individuals involved in workshops and other sessions are thanked for their valuable contributions : Professor Colin Fudge, John Craddock, Ann Maggee, Sneha Palnitkar, Bret Willers, Adelina Auguste, Aydam Erim and Jane Morris.

The views presented in the individual papers do not necessarily coincide with those of the editor, Manchester City Council or the other local authorities and associations who have supported this publication.

Many of the papers are based upon transcripts of speeches delivered to the conference and of translations of written and spoken contributions. An attempt has been made to retain as much of the original text as possible. However, any incorrect contextualisation of ideas incurred in the translation, recording and editing process is regretted.

Stella Whittaker
Editor

CLHBEC

Contents

List of Contributors   v

Figures   vii

Editors Notes   ix

SECTION 1   THE MANCHESTER REPORT   1

SECTION 2   LOCAL ACTION FOR SUSTAINABILITY   9

SECTION 3   INTRODUCING LOCAL AGENDA 21   15

SECTION 4   NATIONAL LOCAL AGENDA 21 CAMPAIGNS   27

SECTION 5   LOCAL AGENDA 21 INITIATIVES   45
             LOCAL AUTHORITY CASE STUDIES

SECTION 6   LOCAL AGENDA 21 IMPLEMENTATION   71
             DEBATES AND KEY ISSUES

SECTION 7   INTERNATIONAL FRAMEWORKS FOR LOCAL AGENDA 21 IMPLEMENTATION   81

SECTION 8   THE WAY FORWARD   105
             WORKSHOPS AND FINAL REPORTS

SECTION 9   LOCAL AGENDA 21 IN PRACTICE   125
             WORKSHOP PAPERS AND CASE STUDIES

SECTION 10   LOCAL ENVIRONMENTAL MANAGEMENT, SEMINAR REPORTS AND CASE STUDIES   207
             • Integrated Economic and Environmental Development at the Local Level
             • Designing for Sustainable Cities, Access, Mobility and Public Transport
             • International Links and Sustainable Development
             • Integrated Sustainable Energy Strategies for Urban Areas

             LIST OF DELEGATES   229

             INDEX   243

LIST OF CONTRIBUTORS

Foreword
Cllr Arnold Spencer, Chair of Environmental Planning Committee
Manchester City Council
Towards a More Sustainable Manchester
Dr Ted Kitchen, City Planning Officer, Manchester City Council

Welcome Address
Cllr Graham Stringer, Leader Manchester City Council
Local Action for Sustainability
Professor Chris Baines, Independent Environmental Broadcaster

Introduction by Conference President
(and Local Authority Case Study Six)
Ms Beate Weber, Lady Mayor Heidleberg, Germany

What is the Local Government Response to Local Agenda 21?
(and Implementing the Local Agenda 21 Mandate,
Local Agenda 21 Implementation and the International
Framework)
Jeb Brugman, Secretary General, International Council for Local
Environmental Initiatives
Local Agenda 21 and the United Nations
How Local Agenda 21 Fits into the UN Process.
Zehra Aydin, Department of Policy Co-ordination and
Sustainable Development, The Commission for Sustainable
Development, UN
Local Authorities and Agenda 21
How Local Authorities are Responding to the Challenge
Mr Paulo Maluf, Mayor of Sao Paulo, Brazil

National Local Agenda 21 Campaigns
Case Study One - Australia
Bernie Cotter, Project Manager, Australia's Local Agenda 21
Programme
Case Study Two - The United Kingdom
Cllr John Harman, Leader Kirklees Metropolitan Council, UK
Case Study Three - Japan
Saburo Kato, Senior Executive Director, ICLEI Japan & Director of
The Global Environment Programme, Japan Environment Agency
and Member of the Japan Local Agenda 21 Panel
Case Study Four - Columbia
Edgard Moncayo, Director, Mision Siglo XX1, Bogota

Local Agenda 21 Initiatives
Local Authority Case Studies
1. Hamillton - Wentworth, Canada
Mr Jim Thoms, Commissioner of Planning and Development &
Dale Turvey, Commissioner of Transportation and Environmental
Services, Regional Municipality of Hamilton and Wentworth
2. Cajarmarca, Peru
Luis Guerrero Figueroa, Provincial Mayor, Municipality of
Cajamarca
3. Chaing Mai, Thailand
Ms Maey-Ing Amarangkul, City Clerk, Phuket Municipality &
formerly of Chaing Mai Municipality
4. Gothenburg, Sweden
Ms Kerstin Svenson, City Commissioner for the Environment,
Gothenburg City
5. Harare, Zimbabwe

Mr Charles Tawengwa, Mayor of Harare City Council
6. Aalborg, Denmark
Mr Kaj Kjaer, Mayor of the City of Aaborg

Local Agenda 21 Implementation
Involving Young People and Marginalised Groups in Local
Agenda 21
Mexican Popular Youth Organisation

The International Framework
The ICLEI Model Communities Programme
Dr Pratibha Mehta, Director, Local Agenda 21 Model
Communities Programme, ICLEI
Proposals by "The Group of Four" for Implementation of Local
Agenda 21, "From Rio 92 to Istanbul 96"
Alain LE SAUX, Scientific Director, World Association of Major
Metropolises
Networking and Local Agenda 21
Marcelo Nowerzstern, Director of Programmes in Latin America,
United Towns Development

Workshops and Final Reports
1. Creating a Community Base for Planning Local Agenda 21
 New York, US, Mendip, UK, Canada and Japan
2. How to Set up an Environmental Action Programme
(John Craddock, Director, Muncie Water Quality Bureau, Muncie,
Indiana, US)
Wellington, New Zealand, Sao Paulo, Brazil and Kanagawa,
Japan
3. Environmental Information Gathering and Interpretation
(Sneha Palnitkar, Director, All India Institute for Local Self
Government, Bombay, India)
Lancashire, UK, Africa and Australia
4. Local Economic Strategies for Sustainable Development
(Bret Willers, Environment Strategy Co-ordinator, Cardiff City
Council, UK)
California, USA, Graz, Austria and Coventry, UK
5. Sustainability Indicators
(Aydam Erim, Council Member Cankaya, Turkey)
The European Commission, Seattle, USA and the UK
6. An Ecosystems Approach to Urban Environmental
Management
(Roger Levett, Environment Team Leader, CAG Consultant, UK)
Gothenburg, Sweden, ICLEI, the UK and The Swedish Association
Local Authorities)

Where Do we Go from Here?
Margarita Pachenco, Environmental Studies Institute, National
University of Columbia
Priorities for Action
Cllr Louise Ellman, Leader Lancashire County Council

Local Environmental Seminar Reports and Individual Case
Studies

Integrated Economic and Environmental Development at the
Local Level
(Jane Stevens, Environment Co-ordinator, East Sussex County
Council, UK)
East Sussex, UK & Haute Normandie, France
Designing for Sustainable Cities - Access, Mobility & Public
Transport
(Dr John Whitelegg, Ecologica UK)
Gijs Kuneman, Co-ordination, European Federation for Transport
and Environment
Charles Kunaka, Centre for Transport Studies, Zimbabwe
European Practice - Amsterdam, Zurich and Copenhagen
Bristol, UK & Adelaide, Australia
International Links and Sustainable Development
(Vernon Smith, Local Government International Bureau, UK)
Integrated Sustainable Energy Strategies for Urban Areas
(Centre for Sustainable Energy, Bristol)

LIST OF FIGURES

Section	Figure	Title	
4	1	The Six Key Areas of Action in the Local Agenda 21 Process (UK Local Agenda 21 Steering Group).	
4	2	Details of the Six Action Areas for the Local Agenda 21 Process (UK Local Agenda 21 Steering Group)	
4	3	Latin American and Caribbean Growth in GNP (CEPAL produced by Mision Siglio XXI, Colombia)	
4	4	Production/Distribution Structure for GNP. World Bank produced by Mision Siglio XXI,Colombia	
4	5	Rural-Urban Transition(1938-2000) in Colombia. (Produced by Mision Siglio XXI, Colombia).	
4	6	Rates of Demographic Growth, Annual Average (1780-2000) Colombia. (Provided by Mision Siglio XXI, Colombia).	
4	7	Estimated Specific Rates of Fertility in the Country (1964-1969) (1978-1983) (1998-2003), Colombia. (Produced by Mision Siglio XXI, Colombia).	
4	8	Urbanisation Rate Columbia 1938 - 2025 (Provided by Mission Siglo XXI, Columbia)	
5	9	Hamilton-Wentworth Sustainable Community Initiative (Hamilton and Wentworth, Canada).	
5	10	Environmental Policy Statement (UEGP, Thailand).	
5	11	Urban Environmental Action Plan Formulation Process (UEGP, Thailand).	
5	12	Actors in Urban Environmental Management (UEGP, Thailand).	
5	13	Structure/Personnel/Budget (UEGP Thailand).	
5	14	A Good Management System (UEGP Thailand).	
5	15	The Structure of Each Guideline Topic (UEGP, Thailand)	
7	16	Strategic Services Planning. A Framework For Local Agenda 21 (ICLEI). Stages and Processes	
7	17	Strategic Services Planning. Indicators for Performance Evaluation and Feedback.	
7	18	Strategic Services Planning. A Framework for Local Agenda 21 - (ICLEI)	
7	19	Service System Map - Resource Inputs and Investment (ICLEI)	
7	20	Service Issues Map (ICLEI)	
7	21	Service System Auditing (ICLEI)	
7	22	Service System Audit Record Sheets	
		A	Resource Inputs and Investments
		B	Parameters (Infrastructure, Regulations, Procedures, Customs, Norms).
		C	Service Programs and Operations
		D	Service Users and Beneficiaries
		E	Service By-Products (Wastes, Social, Economic and Environmental Impacts) (ICLEI)
7	23	Identifying Partners (ICLEI)	
7	24	Community Priority Setting (ICLEI)	
7	25	Selecting Consultation Methods (ICLEI)	
7	26	Defining Target Communities (ICLEI)	
7	27	Informing Communities About The Planning Effort (ICLEI)	
9	28	Local Agenda 21 Programme - Mendip District Council (Mendip District Council, UK)	
9	29	Steps Towards 'Kankyo Jichitai' - Environmentally Orientated Municipality (All Japan Prefectual and Municipal Workers Union, Japan)	
9	30	Construction of the Environmental Ordinance (Kawasaki City)	
9	31	Kawasaki City Environmental Master Plan (Kawasaki City, Japan)	

9	32	Environmental Elements of Kawasaki City Environmental Master Plan (Kawasaki City, Japan)	9	49	Indicators of a Sustainable Community - Master List (Sustainable Seattle, USA)
9	33	Contents of Specific Indicators of the Objectives - Kawasaki City Environmental Master Plan. (Kawasaki City, Japan)	9	50	The Sustainable Seattle 1993 Indicators of a Sustainable Community (Sustainable Seattle, USA)
9	34	State of the Environment (SOE) Audit; What Is It? (Lancashire County Council, UK)	9	51	Wild Salmon Returning to their Home Stream (Sustainable Seattle, USA)
9	35	Why Did We Audit? (Lancashire County Council, UK)	9	52	Ecosystem Approach Access, Mobility and Transport Issues Table
9	36	What Did We Audit? (Lancashire County Council, UK)		A	Master Grid
				B	Physical Ecology Table
9	37	State of the Environment (SOE) Audit: What Does It Cover? (Lancashire County Council, UK)		C	Human Ecology Table (CAG Consultants, UK)
9	38	Environmental Data (Lancashire County Council, UK)	10	53	Bristol Energy and Environment Plan (Centre for Sustainable Energy, UK)
9	39	Environmental Components - Air (Lancashire County Council, UK)			
9	40	Environmental Change and Conditions (Lancashire County Council, UK)			
9	41	Environmental Indicators (Lancashire County Council, UK)			
9	42	Lancashire Environmental Forum (Lancashire County Council, UK)			
9	43	What Does LEAP Do? (Lancashire County Council, UK)			
9	44	How Do We Produce LEAP? (Lancashire County Council, UK)			
9	45	Using Environmental Information To Create A Local Agenda 21 Programme (Lancashire County Council, UK)			
9	46	Eco-profit Graz - Program (City of Graz, Austria)			
9	47	Materials, Waste and Emissions - Old Technology (Automobile Spraying) (City of Graz, Austria)			
9	48	Materials, Waste and Emissions-New Technology (Automobile Spraying) (City of Graz, Austria)			

EDITOR'S NOTE
STELLA WHITTAKER CONFERENCE DIRECTOR, INTERNATIONAL LOCAL AUTHORITY PROGRAMME GLOBAL FORUM '94

SENIOR LECTURER, URBAN POLICY STUDIES, EDGE HILL UNIVERSITY SECTOR COLLEGE, LANCASHIRE UK

Global Forum'94 was the official follow-up to Global Forum'92 held at the Earth Summit in Rio de Janeiro Brazil. In June 1994 over 1,000 delegates from over 50 countries of the world gathered in Manchester to discuss "Cities and Sustainable Development" . The fundamental concept of inter-sectoral negotiation first developed at Rio was followed at Global Forum'94 - business, local government, non-governmental and trade union representatives met together for the first time. Thus people involved and active at the local level were drawn together with regional and international experts for a truly global view.

Alongside Global Forum'94 local authorities held a four day International Local Authority Programme. The event was supported and co-organised in a unique collaboration between representatives from UK local authorities and their associations and international local authority associations. Over 145 local authorities from over fifty countries gathered in Manchester. More than thirty case studies were presented from individual municipalities who with their local communities are taking their first steps on Local Agenda 21 and six of the world's most prominent international agencies reported on their Local Agenda 21 programmes. The two day International Local Agenda 21 Conference was also accompanied by four separate seminar programmes.

Local authorities all over the world are starting to translate the global sustainability agenda - Agenda 21 - into local action. In fact in the words of the conference president Beate Weber, Lady Mayor of the City of Heidelberg:

" National Agenda 21 is not complete without Local Agenda 21."

The global nature of the response signifies the level of international interest and commitment to Agenda 21 since the Earth Summit in 1992. This has made it possible to find examples from every corner of the world of local as well as regional, national and international efforts which could be included in this publication.

Any consideration of Local Agenda 21 would be incomplete without including a definition of sustainability. A widely used definition of sustainable development was given in the Brundtland Report, "Our Common Future" by the World Commission on Environment and Development, 1987. *"...ENSURE THAT DEVELOPMENT MEETS THE NEEDS OF THE PRESENT WITHOUT COMPROMISING THE ABILITY OF FUTURE GENERATIONS TO MEET THEIR OWN NEEDS"*

The Commission followed the definition with this formulation *"the concept of "needs", in particular the essential needs of the world's poor, to which overriding priority should be given".* By presenting a global perspective of the Local Agenda 21 process it is the primary aim of these papers to reinforce these aims.

In their Local Agenda 21 local authorities are adopting very different approaches based upon their individual, cultural, institutional and environmental circumstances, but they all share an approach which involves attempts to evolve a holistic, cooperative and integrated approach to municipal environmental management. This forges or builds upon partnerships with the local communities they serve (involving the community in the widest sense - business, trade unions, interest groups, individuals, agencies etc). Additionally Local Agenda 21 requires municipalities to encourage the community itself to participate in setting its own priorities.

Manchester City Council

Conference delegates

The variety of style and content of the collection of papers presented in this document reflects the range of approaches being adopted worldwide. It is the intention to retain this sense within the document to give the reader an idea of both the diverse and the shared direction in which local governments are progressing. It would be fair to say that the papers collected together for this publication represent some of the best practice in the world today. Manchester City Council, the host local authority for Global Forum 94, worked closely with international local authority associations, and in particular the International Council for Local Environmental Initiatives, to invite local authorities working in a variety of innovative ways to share their experience with others. Many of these authorities are involved in ICLEI's Local Agenda 21 Model Communities Programme, an action research project involving over 20 municipalities from all of the different regions of the world to develop a planning framework for Local Agenda 21. For the first time case studies from many regions of the world are presented together in one document. In some cases the information is being published for the first time.

It is the aim to provide here a unique and essential guide to Local Agenda 21 specifically from a local government perspective, which will be of use not only to those looking for an introduction to the subject but also for municipalities with advanced environmental programmes who are dealing with the complexities of the Local Agenda 21 process. The various authors explain how they have taken the first steps in their community on Local Agenda 21, building on their experiences to explore essential factors and concerns. Local authorities following in their footsteps will be able to learn from their mistakes and build upon their successes. It is hoped that individual local authorities will be inspired by the examples given and that this book will be used to demonstrate to other local authorities and local communities, as well as national and international governments and agencies, what can be done.

As Kerstin Svenson, City Commissioner for the Environment, City of Gothenburg states : *"We are only starting our work with Local Agenda 21. Our ambition and our hopes are high. And we don't intend to lower them!"*

The concept of sustainability is in itself very complex. Local authorities across the globe are faced with the task of putting this concept into operation and a key question is where to make a start. Local Agenda 21 requires municipalities to look at social and economic as well as environmental aspects and to do this in a manner which is truly participatory, dynamic and interactive. The Local Agenda 21 mandate therefore presents municipalities with an onerous task.

Cities now face the task of balancing the competing aims of addressing local service demands on the one hand and global and system-related issues on the other hand. There is such an obvious and major conflict between these sets of demands that it is often hard to see how they can be reconciled within the confines of traditional municipal duties and powers. Jeb Brugman, Secretary General, ICLEI and other contributors shed light on questions that arise for local authorities as they develop their Local Agenda 21 based upon their experiences of working with, and in, local authorities all over the world. How can marginalised groups be involved in the participatory process? What is the relationship between statutory plans and a Local Agenda 21 vision document? How to focus on local needs whilst addressing the whole breadth of Agenda 21?

Manchester City Council
Ms Macy Ing Amarangkul, Thailand

Case studies include Colombia's National Local Agenda 21 Campaign run by Mision Siglo XX1 in Bogota who initiated a multi-sectoral programme involving municipal departments, central government agencies, major business groups and numerous universities and research institutions. Thirty two district studies were undertaken. Distinct agendas for each district were developed and these agendas directly input into the Social Priority Development Plan for Metropolitan Bogota. (Section 4) In the Regional Municipality of Hamilton and Wentworth, Canada, work began in 1990 to create a Local Agenda 21 called "Vision 2020" with a process of consultation and input from more than 1,000 citizens. The municipality is now creating mechanisms for implementation, including an annual public reporting process, development of sustainability indicators and the formal integration of Vision 2020 priorities into the annual municipal budget process. (Section 5) A Local Agenda 21 effort has also been carried out in the highland Province of Cajarmarca in Peru where a Provincial Sustainable Development Plan ties economic growth and quality of life improvements to ecosystem management. Six consultation fora were held covering education; natural resources and agriculture; employment; cultural heritage and tourism; urban environment, and women, family and population. Multi-sectoral development strategies have been created which will be implemented through signed inter-institutional agreements. (Section 5) In 1992 seven Thai cities joined together in a project to develop and apply environmental planning guidelines for community-priority setting on environmental issues. Stakeholder groups were established with municipal support to engage residents and the different sectors of the community. Specific projects are now being funded to address the identified priorities. It is within this framework that Chaing Mai municipality have begun to develop their own unique Local Agenda 21(Section 5).

Posters which can be reproduced as training materials, have been compiled from the workshop debates to guide readers through the key elements of Local Agenda 21 - creating a community base for planning a Local Agenda 21, setting up an environmental action plan, environmental information-gathering and interpretation, local economic strategies for sustainable development, sustainability indicators and the ecosystems approach to urban environmental management. These guidelines are based upon the experiences of both workshop speakers and conference participants. It is not the aim of this collection of papers to present a global method for implementing Local Agenda 21 which can be applied to any municipality regardless of size or circumstances, but rather to provide advice and information tailored specifically to local authorities on how they might acquire the capability to develop their own Local Agenda 21.

Some of the very latest tools and techniques being developed and tried out globally are presented and discussed, such as eco-balancing in environmental protection and physical planning which is being tried out in Sweden, the ecosystems approach to urban environmental management being piloted in a number of cities by the OECD in its Ecological City Project, community - mapping exercises both in India and Mendip in the UK, 'Eco-Feedback' - the municipal trade unions environmental management plan for local government in Japan, Wellington's 'Sustainable City Strategy - Local Agenda 21', Hamilton and Wentworth's 'Vision 2020' document, Kawasaki City's "Fundamental Environmental Ordinance", Lancashire's Green Audit I and II, 'Eco-Profit Graz' - a municipal project which attempts to put into practice the concept of profit from pollution prevention. Guidance on useful techniques such as round-tables, rapid urban environmental assessment and sustainability indicators are also presented. Although the use of techniques and tools such as roundtables and indicators are relatively new to the majority of municipalities there is a wealth of experience in some countries, for example Sustainable Seattle have been at the forefront of developing and using indicators and Canadian municipalities have been using roundtables for many years. Their accumulated experience is presented in these papers.

It is paradoxically true that for many the very globalizing of vision required by sustainability can mitigate against the implementation of the essential processes at lower scales. There are considerable problems for local authorities in tackling global and development issues which are often seen to be largely outside of the traditional responsibilities of local government. The original intentions of the concept of sustainability in restructuring North /South relations on a more equitable basis and eradicating poverty, as several speakers to the conference point out, is in danger of being overlooked especially by local authorities from more developed nations. For instance Ms Maey-Ing, Thailand, states that if the environment was considered at all it was a low priority issue. Priorities are split between what is referred to in Thailand as a 'Brown' and a 'Green Agenda'. The former takes overriding priority and deals with basic and essential issues such as water supply, public health and waste management and the latter with issues such as traffic management and green spaces - the kind of initiatives more closely related to the priorities of the environmental agendas of more developed nations. Combatting poverty is the central theme of environmental work in Harare, Zimbabwe; actions to tackle malnutrition, migration, housing shortages, disease and declining economic growth take priority. As Alioune Badiane, Regional Coordinator for the Africa - Urban Management Programme, sponsored by the World Bank, stresses in his paper on UMP in Africa, one of the greatest threats to sustainable human and economic development comes from the downward and mutually reinforcing spirals of poverty and environmental degradation which are endangering current and future generations in developing countries, and especially in Africa.

Many of the contributors make reference to the ecological footprint of their city, town or region. This analysis and imagery provide not only a more user-friendly methodology for calculating and ultimately communicating the concepts of sustainability but also begins to build global linkages into the thinking of municipalities. So often the compulsion for change, particularly in the more developed world, has been dominated by the desire to improve the quality of life for the inhabitants of an individual city or region. There has been considerable focus to date on creating cities for people and on improving the quality of life in cities which are compact, aesthetically pleasing, cleaner, greener and quieter as well as more effective in economic terms. The case studies selected for this publication, however, aim to progress the debate about what could constitute a sustainable community beyond this view by presenting a truly global perspective. Often local governments engage in the processes of consultation, planning and report preparation and ultimately produce programmes for recycling, pollution reduction strategies and traffic management believing that they have achieved sustainability. Evidence presented here questions how a municipality can know whether it is achieving sustainability through a set of individual programmes.

What is clear from these papers is that Local Agenda 21 involves much more than pulling together existing projects and plans. It also involves much more than traditional urban environmental management. Many local authorities have viewed Local Agenda 21 as an 'umbrella'-type initiative in which existing schemes can be collected together and packaged. Some municipalities however are recognising Local Agenda 21 as a means to enable people to work together in the community in a totally different way. This view is stressed by Zehra Aydin of the United Nations Commission for Sustainable Development who suggests that Local Agenda 21 can make sustainable development a truly global process of environmental governance whereby local authorities and other actors become pivotal in facilitating transparency and accountability. Indeed Saburo Kato, Director of the Global Environment Programme, Japan Environment Agency, suggests that Local Agenda will be a milestone towards the objective of giving local government and non-governmental organisations an important role in national state diplomacy.

The International Local Agenda 21 Conference

Manchester City Council

The capacity of local government therefore to deliver Local Agenda 21 is likely to be determined much more by their ability to adopt new interactive and dynamic ways of governing their local communities. Good examples are presented in this document from local authorities like Gothenburg in Sweden, Cajamarca in Peru, Heidelberg in Germany, Lancashire in the UK and Kawasaki in Japan, which are all embarking on innovative participatory processes to get people to work on a blue-print for their own future.

These local authorities are experimenting with new forms of partnership, consensus building and community priority setting working towards a process which could be termed 'environmental governance'.

SECTION ONE
THE MANCHESTER REPORT

THE MANCHESTER REPORT

FOREWORD
Cllr Arnold Spencer, Chair Environmental Planning Committee,
Manchester City Council

TOWARDS A MORE SUSTAINABLE MANCHESTER
Dr. Ted Kitchen, City Planning Officer, Manchester City Council

FOREWORD
Councillor Arnold Spencer,
Chair, Environmental Planning Committee, Manchester City
Council

The Local Authority Key Sector component of Global Forum '94 was the first time that the world's local authorities had been given the opportunity since the Rio Summit to get together and discuss progress towards the achievement of more sustainable cities, and particularly the major part within this that local authorities can play and in many cases are playing. It was very gratifying for us as organisers that local authority representatives came to Manchester for this event from all the corners of the world. Conference registrations were right at the capacity of the available accommodation, which not only made the event a success but also illustrated how eager the world's local authorities had been for an opportunity like this. As always is the way with events of this kind, much valuable interchange took place outside the formal sessions, many useful contacts were made which will go on being useful when MANCHESTER in JUNE 1994 is but a (hopefully pleasant) memory.

Metrolink in the City of Manchester

The feedback we got from this was most encouraging, and if the event has stimulated the development of thinking about sustainability in the world's cities, Manchester City Council will be pleased to have had the opportunity to make such a contribution. Whilst of course everybody has worked hard during the four days of the event as a whole, many people also took the opportunity to see something of the city and its surrounding area, and it was interesting to hear that many people's images of a grimy industrial city disappeared in the face of what they saw. Modern Manchester is a bustling city with a rich architectural heritage and a great feeling of vitality, and whilst changing people's perceptions is a long job, we hope that many of our visitors took away with them much more positive images of the city than those with which they arrived. Of course, we too are grappling with the problems of urban sustainability just like everyone else, and hopefully our experiences contributed positively to the International Local Authority Programme. We certainly learned much from listening to and talking about the experiences of others; and are already translating the knowledge gained into action.

The real proof of all this, however, is in what happens afterwards. It was clear from all the exchanges at the International Local Authority Programme that, across the world, we will all need to speed up on the delivery of Local Agenda 21 if the Rio target of 1996 is to be achieved. But if this recognition is not followed by action to this end, the recognition itself will mean little. This is why we thought it was important to get out a good record of what happened during those four days in Manchester in June 1994, and to do it in such a way as to make it accessible to a much wider audience than the conference delegates. We hope that this volume inspires and provokes, as well as standing as a record of the event itself for those who came to it. Stella Whittaker's role as editor of this volume has been critical in this, and special thanks go to her for undertaking this task.

Finally, no event of this kind can take place without a great deal of effort by a lot of people. On behalf of the City Council, therefore, I would like to thank the organising team, our sponsors, the speakers, the staff on the days of events who acted as stewards and as helpers, the translators, the catering staff and our Conference President, Mayor Beate Weber; they all contributed in large measures to the success of the event. Last, but not least, however, I would like to thank the conference delegates, not merely for coming, but for giving so freely of their time and their experience so that we had as stimulating an exchange worldwide as the 100 year old town hall has seen throughout its life. Particularly to those who came from afar, I hope they felt that their journey was worthwhile, and I hope they also feel that they will always be welcome in Manchester.

TOWARDS A MORE SUSTAINABLE MANCHESTER

Dr Ted Kitchen, City Planning Officer Manchester City Council

Manchester's ecological footprint has been a large one, ever since the earliest days of the Industrial Revolution. As the world's first major industrial city, Manchester prospered on the back of transport and technological innovations which turned it within a relatively small number of years from a town to a major city, and then to being the hub of one of Britain's largest conurbations. In all of this, Manchester impacted on the world not just in terms of its trading activities but also in its role as a place where ideas were in ferment. In the 19th century in particular, continuing rapid industrialisation and urbanisation were accompanied by the development of a radical tradition that was to have a civilising effect not just on the forces that were making Manchester progress but also nationally and internationally. In the 20th century, whilst the make-up of all of this has changed, it remains the case that Manchester is genuinely a global city, with responsibilities to match. This was one of the reasons why the City was proud to have the opportunity to host Global Forum'94.

Of course, being the "shock city" of the Industrial Revolution brought with it a whole series of problems for future generations to tackle. The best examples here are probably:

✪ A legacy of much very poor housing, with inadequate space and construction standards and only a bare minimum of facilities (and sometimes none at all).

✪ A concentration of heavy manufacturing Industry and the problems (such as contaminated land) that its operations brought.

✪ Very poor air quality, as a result of both industrial and domestic fuel consumption.

✪ Very poor water quality, as the City's rivers were used as dumps for untreated sewerage and industrial wastes.

Manchester - host to Global Forum '94

The consequences of all of this were becoming obvious to many 19th century social reformers and novelists, and the work of radical writers and speakers in drawing attention to the unacceptable living and working conditions and the effect on people's health were vitally important in bringing about change not just in Manchester but many other parts of the world as well. Much of this thinking was devoted to the question of the role of Governments (Central and Local) in tackling these problems. The second half of the 19th century saw a stream of legislation enacted in Britain to give local authorities the powers to begin to tackle these problems, and the birth of the modern local authority in Britain can really be traced to this period. Indeed, the very major role of the local authorities, both in tackling directly many of the worst problems of industrialisation and in regulating many of the activities of industry and of developers grew as a result of the experiences of cities like Manchester. This is therefore another reason why the City was so keen to see a gathering of the world's local authorities as part of Global Forum 94.

The speed with which the major legacies of the Industrial Revolution could be tackled was a very variable commodity, which illustrates many of the difficulties associated with the notion of sustainability. The four examples given above illustrate this point very well:

✪ The problems caused by the legacy of poor housing were the main priority of the City Council in the period immediately following World War 2. Very broadly, over the two decades from the mid 1950s to the mid 1970s the City Council demolished about 100,000 houses and built about 80,000 within the boundaries of the City, the balance being attributed to overspill because it was not possible to redevelop satisfactorily at historic densities. In its own way, this was as radical a change as had been the initial wave of house building during the Industrial Revolution; and just as with that previous period it brought its own problems with it. Much of the housing stock constructed during that period remains sound, but it also introduced into the City multi-storey blocks and industrialised building methods which have not always stood the test of time and have not always been popular with their occupants. As a consequence, much of the City Council's housing programme today is devoted to tackling the worst of these problems.

✪ The problems caused by the adverse consequences of traditional manufacturing industry were also, in many ways, closely linked with the City's sources of wealth. The desire to deal with these adverse consequences has thus been tempered by a desire to retain and, if possible, to improve the economic base of the City, at a time when in any event the economies of British Cities have been experiencing very major structural change and their citizens as a consequence have seen major and prolonged periods of unemployment.

✪ The move to clean air has been one of the success stories of the postwar period, with the whole of the City of Manchester now being covered by Smoke Control Orders. This happened gradually over this period, but has now created a situation where not only the health of the City's population has improved as a consequence but also it has been possible to clean years of accumulated grime from Manchester's buildings to reveal them in their true, rich colours. The issue in recent years, has been returning in a different form, however, and today the greatest air quality problems (particularly in areas of concentrated activity, such as the City Centre) are caused by road traffic. One of the greatest challenges facing the City today is the need to come to terms with man's (and woman's) love affair with the private car, without destroying the economic base of the City in the process. Clearly, investing in a good quality public transport alternative is critical to this, and whilst in Britain, in recent years, it cannot really be said that we have found effective ways of meeting this need, the recent opening of Metrolink in the City is at least part of the solution here.

Can recycling facilities

✪ There has probably been least progress with dealing with problems of water quality, mainly because it is clear that for water pollution to be eradicated the problem needs to be tackled at source. Although much has been done (for example, in the treatment of raw sewerage), there are still many industrial pollutants in our water courses as a result of long-standing operations which predate modern controls. What certainly has been a success story, however, is the bringing of clean drinking water long distances into the City from the Lake District.

All of these things might be taken to show that the City has been in the sustainability business for a long time, and in a sense that is very true. There is, in this sense, nothing new about the concept of sustainability. There are, on the other hand, four cautionary points from these experiences which need to be remembered if the current drive towards sustainability is to be successful:

✪ Many of these programmes have taken a very long time to achieve, and sometimes the process of trying to do too much too quickly in one generation, can cause problems for subsequent generations, as the housing example illustrates.

✪ The programme really needs to be seen to be inter-related, and thus to be part of a coherent whole, whereas in most cases, and for most of their lives, they have been pursued as free-standing initiatives. The problems of trying to cope with the economic consequences of long-standing industrial practices based upon the exploitation of the environment for the dumping of waste products illustrate this very well.

✪ Technology cannot always be relied on to solve problems (see for example, the failure of industrialised housing in Britain), and often brings problems of its own, as is dramatically illustrated by the rise in private car ownership and usage in the 20th Century.

✪ People's values and aspirations change over time, and programmes are very difficult to implement without contemporary support. As an example, the thrust for clean air in the second half of the 20th century has commanded widespread support (much more, apparently, than the thrust for clean rivers and canals once the problems of providing clean domestic water had been overcome), but one form of air pollution is now being replaced by another as rising wealth has led to a massive growth in car ownership and usage, without it yet being clear that people will accept major curbs on this freedom for environmental reasons even when it can be shown that one person's freedom is another person's problem.

Manchester illustrates all of these lessons very well, and thus as hosts to Global Forum '94 our hope was that people from all over the world would feel that our experiences were of value to them. Our experience in trying to tackle sustainabillty in a holistic way is, however, a very recent phenomenon, and this actually makes us much more like the majority of cites in the world than are the acknowledged brand-leaders in this field. Openly acknowledging that Manchester could not yet claim to be a sustainable city, the City Council wanted, nonetheless, to respond positively to the imperatives that emerged from Rio in 1992. Its role as host City for Global Forum '94 undoubtedly gave impetus to this process. It therefore began from some very simple principles:

✪ That sustainability is about the balance between environmental, economic, social and community concerns, rather than just being about environmental/ecological matters.

✪ That what the Council does in this field needs to be related to its broad policies and aspirations for the City, many of which (for example, re-populating the inner city) are in any event four square with sustainability concerns, but some of which may raise challenges to proposals emerging from the new emphasis on sustainability which will need to be faced up to.

✪ That the Council wants to be seen to be doing things itself, which are tangible evidence to the outside world that it is taking sustainability seriously. In particular, the belief was that we could not offer the leadership within the rest of the community that is envisaged as part of the Local Agenda 21 process without being seen first to be getting our own house in order.

✪ That the absence of a 'state of the environment' report, or its equivalent, should not be seen as a barrier to action, although clearly this is something that needs to be addressed during the Local Agenda 21 process if we are to get to the position of being able to measure progress from a baseline. Many of the things that need to be done to move towards sustainability are obvious from the daily experiences of living and moving around in the City, however, and thus the absence in many cases of sophisticated analysis of them need not be seen as an inhibitor on starting to get things done.

Promoting cycling in the city

If there is a good dose of Manchester pragmatism in these four principles, there was an even larger dose in the process of getting to the point where 100 action points (the Manchester 100) were identified and action on many of them instigated. From a standing start, having been asked by the City Council in May 1993 to take the lead on sustainability matters, the Environmental Planning Committee and the City Planning Officer had got to the position by October 1993 of being able to recommend the 100 action points to the City Council. The basic approach had two stages to it; an internal brain-storming stage, where about 50 points were identified within the Planning Department in consultation with the Chair of the Committee, and then a process of challenging other committees and chief officers to comment on this first list and to add to it, which in fact resulted in its being doubled. In practice, the Manchester 100 has been sub-divided into 11 clusters, for ease of presentation to the outside world and of monitoring. These clusters are:

Air and Water Quality
Citizens Challenge (basically, grants and awards schemes)
Council Challenge (basically, internal work to review policies and procedures)
Energy Saving
Landscaping
Litter
Publicity
Recycling
Economic Development
Transport
Technology

Whilst these were 100 action points identified at a particular point in time, the commitment to action that they were seen as representing was a continuous thing which would not disappear as each point got ticked off. Thus, the first annual monitoring report in October 1994 showed good progress with about 40% of these initiatives, which both made the point that even this is an agenda which will take some time to work through fully and illustrated the need within a twelve month period to begin the process of looking for a sizeable number of replacement initiatives. It is important that this is seen in these terms, however, not only because we do not wish the Manchester 100 to become the Manchester 10 within a relatively short space of time but also because no matter how good the brainstorming and how active the response to the challenges of 1993, a set of initiatives taken from these processes at one point in time could only be scratching the surface of what needs to be done to make Manchester a more sustainable city.

Like almost everywhere else, if Manchester is to achieve the Rio target of having a Local Agenda 21 Statement in place by the end of 1996 it will have to move much faster in the second half of this period (from Global Forum '94 onwards) than it did in the first half from Rio to Global Forum. Taking these things seriously in its own actions, and being seen to be doing so, was the first essential step in doing this as far as the City Council was concerned. Local Agenda 21 Statements are essentially about the kinds of commitments that key stakeholders in the City are prepared to make, and if the Council wished to offer a lead in this (a role for Local Authorities that was envisaged at Rio as being the norm) then it would have to take a lead in making commitments to action. That having been said, it is also important to acknowledge that the Council is not in control of the Local Agenda 21 process and should not be trying to take control of it. This balance between on the one hand offering a lead and on the other hand not taking control is a difficult one, especially for local authorities used in much of their everyday lives to a 'consult and decide' model of decision-making. Nonetheless, the spirit of Agenda 21 is that it is about consensus-building around commitments to action, and the City Council believes that is has an important enabling role to play with many stakeholders in encouraging them to see Agenda 21 in this light and to play their full part in it as a consequence. This will undoubtedly include facing up to some of the preconceptions that some of these stakeholders have of the City Council!

The regeneration of Castlefield, Manchester

It is very early days in the Local Agenda 21 process in Manchester as yet, and certainly far too early to be making progress reports on how all of this is going. What we can say, however, is that an important part of this is learning as we go along from our own and from other people's experiences, and the exchanges that took place during the International Local Authority Programme and the contacts that were made during those few days in Manchester in June 1994 are already proving very valuable to us.

SECTION TWO
LOCAL ACTION FOR SUSTAINABILITY

The United Nations Conference on the Environment and Development (the Earth Summit) held in Rio in 1992 and its follow on event Global Forum '94 warned that people had to change many of the ways in which they did business and lived or the world would face unacceptable levels of human suffering and environmental damage.

˙ UNCED in 1992 it is an obligation of national govern-
ˉmulate a national sustainable development plan or
Agenda 21. Local government has a key role in
ᵉcific commitments are highlighted in both
ˋle Human Settlements" and Chapter 28
ıapter 28 of Agenda 21 presents local
ıdate to produce a Local Agenda 21 for
their area by 1996.

ıons on the conservation and management of
trengthening the role of 'major groups' and the
ꞁplementation are presented in Agenda 21 which
ᴜver 150 programme areas and over 2,509 separate
ᴜvities. Agenda 21, like Local Agenda 21, is not a legally
binding document but it has considerable influence.

A key problem is how to put the concept of sustainability into operation and to move from ideas and papers to environmental policy responses. There is no single answer or set of policies to be applied equally. There are however a number of principles which could be used to guide activities in a sustainable direction.

LOCAL ACTION FOR SUSTAINABILITY

WELCOMING ADDRESS
Councillor Graham Stringer, Leader of Manchester City Council

LOCAL ACTION FOR SUSTAINABILITY
*Professor Chris Baines, Independent Environmental Advisor,
Writer and Broadcaster*

WELCOMING ADDRESS
Councillor Graham Stringer, Leader of Manchester City Council

"Can I start by welcoming all delegates to Manchester Town Hall and to the Local Authority Agenda 21 Conference. My name is Graham Stringer and I am the Leader of Manchester City Council. We are delighted in Manchester at the end of Global Forum '94 to be holding this Local Agenda 21 Conference. It is appropriate that Global Forum '94 and this conference is half way between the Earth Summit which took place in Rio in 1992 and Istanbul in 1996 where the City Summit will take place with the Habitat II Conference.

I am particularly pleased to welcome 400 delegates to this Conference, including 30 mayors and leaders of Local Authorities and representatives of 150 other Local Authorities. I think this is a recognition that Local Authorities around the world are taking Agenda 21 seriously. Certainly in Manchester we are well on our way to implementing the process of Agenda 21, a complicated process of involving local organisations from different sectors in the community and getting their commitment to participate in Agenda 21 and arrive at proposals on how the success of Agenda 21 is going to be measured. That process is one of partnership and it is the way that Manchester, and I, believe that many delegates who have been in Global Forum view the way forward. None of us have final and complete solutions to the problems that are facing our cities, our Local Authorities and the world, but we know that we are more likely to come to conclusions and solutions to those problems if we work in partnership. That partnership must involve first of all the community, it must involve business, it must involve Trade Unions and non-statutory groups involved in the environment. In that way we can share the expertise from all those different sections of the community and I believe that sharing and the partnership approach will be a theme which runs through this Conference as the different experiences and expertise of different Local Authorities represented in this hall are shared.

In Manchester we take our commitment to the environment seriously. We have to, we are the world's oldest industrial city and we face many of the consequences of the 18th and 19th century industrialisation and pollution. We are moving towards solutions - for example you will see on the streets of Manchester what was two years ago the first on-street new tram system in this country, built for the first time in 80 years.

We in Manchester are taking the environment seriously because we believe that creating sustainable cities is the way forward for the future. Certainly in this country during the past 30 or 40 years cities have been seen as a problem. I believe, the Local Authority in Manchester believes, that cities in actual fact are part of the solution. Producing blueprints, producing agendas to create sustainable cities is in all our interests and I believe that this Conference, as well as the Global Forum Conference is part of that programme and progress."

LOCAL ACTION FOR SUSTAINABILITY
Professor Chris Baines, Independent Environmental Advisor, Writer and Broadcaster

If we really are to help the Earth get better, and achieve a comfortable quality of life for all the people of the world, then sustainability must be deeply rooted in every local neighbourhood. Success can only come through active participation from all corners of the community, with individuals and organisations playing to their own particular strengths. Ambition, resourcefulness and co-operation are the key, and in local authorities there is a ready-made mechanism for raising expectations, and co-ordinating all of a local community's resources. Local authorities obviously vary from place to place, but there are several substantial ways in which they can be influential.

1. As a major consumer of resources.

In many communities, the local authority is by far the biggest employer of staff, and consumer of resources. Certainly in the UK, the local council is usually a larger organisation than any of its individual local industries. As a consequence, policies which improve efficiency, reduce waste and supply the other objectives of sustainable development internally, really do make a significant direct contribution. Every local authority must get its own environmental house in order.

2. As a force for change in the market place

As the biggest corporate consumer of goods and services in the town or city, a local authority can exercise considerable influence over its suppliers. Clear buying policies which demand high performance from others in the supply chain, and emphasise the cradle-to-grave approach to product appraisal can achieve an effect which will extend way beyond the boundaries of the local community.

3. As a role model for other organisations

There is an urgent need for well researched and well documented examples of improved environmental practice. Within any local authority's structure, it is possible to find subdivisions to serve as parallels for any individual or organisation in the surrounding community, and there is great value in passing on the local authority's practical experience as an inspiration to others. Some of that experience may be highly technical; market-testing the energy efficiency of new technology for example, or changing accounting systems to accommodate long term environmental costs. The most difficult task of all though, is to make improved environmental performance an integral part of the culture of any organisation, and the more enlightened local authorities are recognising that. They are beginning to develop methods of recruiting grass roots support from everyone within their realm, and there are parallels in the more enlightened commercial companies too. Passing on successes in this area of environmental motivation is invaluable, since this provides the framework for long term, sustainable change, and rarely requires large capital investment.

4. As providers of information

The environment in which we live is immensely complex, and most of us are subjected to a constant flood of information. Few organisations or individuals have the facility to filter out the relevant facts, and local authorities have a role to play as translators, editors and educators. In the UK at least, that role has generally been accepted with regard to children in schools, and to "the general public" at a domestic level. Increasingly though, there is a recognition that providing easy access to emerging information is a key role for local authorities in their support of the local commercial community and non government organisations too.

5. As providers of enabling services

Many of the improvements in environmental performance can only be achieved collectively. Such diverse things as reduced dependence on the car, recycling of ozone depleting refrigerants, conserving ecological integrity of urban green networks and a host of other desirable objectives are simply not attainable by individuals on their own. Local authorities have many opportunities to provide the strategic framework within which all of us can then improve our personal environmental performance. Even large organisations still rely on central provision of such services as public transport, development control, waste management and education.

6. As networkers

If all members of the community are to contribute to improved environmental sustainability, then there is a need for far greater co-operation and partnership. Within many local authorities there is at last a realisation that compartmentalised, tunnel-visioned management cannot possibly address the complexities of the environment, and internally at least, new ways of collaborative inter-departmental working are beginning to emerge. However, the real progress will come through creative collaboration between individuals and organisations traditionally separated into different sectors. The commercial and voluntary sectors need to combine forces within the public sector if the full resource base of any community is to be realised, and local authorities have a valuable role to play as match-makers. They should be able to bring together all kinds of complementary resources in order to achieve greater sustainability through co-operation.

7. As consensus builders and lobbyists

The framework for increased sustainability needs to change at national and international level. Local authorities should be one important means by which the hopes and aspirations of local people can be projected upwards. Here in the UK there is a constant cry for more sustainable strategies from national government for energy use, food production, waste management, transport, and a host of other resource related issues. At an international level, there is growing concern, for instance, that the G.A.T.T. world trade philosophy and the Rio sustainable development philosophy are mutually exclusive, and that policies on world peace-keeping and foreign aid owe more to short term commercial considerations than to human rights or equity. Local authorities must be one of the more accessible means by which local concerns for sustainability reach the world stage.

Conclusion

At Rio we saw world-wide endorsement of the need to live in harmony with the Earth's resources: to strive for improved human health and happiness without stealing from the future. That is a very tall order which requires breathtaking changes. Somehow, we know we must translate the global dream into practical reality, and to do that, everyone must play their part. Already there are many encouraging initiatives around the world, at every scale from individual households to multi-national corporations, and the good news is that wiser use of the world's resources can actually bring tangible local benefits, from improved corporate profits to healthier food.

Most people have an environmental horizon which is very local - the end of the street or the top of the next hill. Sustainability has first to make sense at that neighbourhood level, if it is ever to reach global proportions - and local authorities are undoubtedly the means by which most of us will start to make Rio a reality.

SECTION THREE
INTRODUCING LOCAL AGENDA 21

In this section of this book Agenda 21 and the Local Agenda 21 mandate are explained more fully. It is important to note that although the concept was born only three years ago at the United Nations' Earth Summit in Rio in 1992 Local Agenda 21 has already captured the imagination of many. However as a relatively new term and policy area there are many inconsistencies both in the ideology and practical application of Local Agenda 21 which will be examined by international expert speakers who are involved and active at the international level. The local government response to Agenda 21 and the Local Agenda 21 mandate are examined along with a report on how local Agenda 21 fits into the United Nations process.

Work is only just beginning to be done to examine the framework for application and implementation of what is in essence a very complex policy area. As local authorities are asked to produce a Local Agenda 21 for their area by 1996, there is an urgent need for such an analysis of the Local Agenda 21 process.

INTRODUCING LOCAL AGENDA 21

INTRODUCTION BY CONFERENCE PRESIDENT
Ms Beate Weber, Lady Mayor of Heidelberg, Germany

IMPLEMENTING THE LOCAL AGENDA 21 MANDATE
WHAT IS THE LOCAL GOVERNMENT RESPONSE TO
LOCAL AGENDA 21?
Progress report from Jeb Brugmann, Secretary General ICLEI

LOCAL AGENDA 21 AND THE UNITED NATIONS
HOW LOCAL AGENDA 21 FITS INTO THE UN PROCESS
Zehra Aydin, Major Groups Focal Point, Division for
Sustainable Development, Department of Policy Coordination
and Sustainable Development, DPCSD, United Nations.

LOCAL AUTHORITIES AND AGENDA 21
HOW LOCAL AUTHORITIES ARE RESPONDING TO THE
CHALLENGE.
Paulo Maluf, Mayor of Municipality of Sao Paulo, Brazil

INTRODUCTION BY CONFERENCE PRESIDENT
Ms Beate Weber, The Lady Mayor of The City of Heidelberg, Germany

We are the ones to act! It is the city and the local authority where the people first have to practice responsible thinking and action. It is here that they start to participate in the decision-making process - informing themselves and getting the proper knowledge so that they can react adequately to the environmental challenge.

If the cities raised interest in environmental questions like energy saving, waste management, sustainable use of resources and the biosphere, our citizens will not really need to interfere in political action on a regional, national and global basis. It is here too however that the contradictions between speeches and actions of the people and the governments, between so called "green speak" and responsible action, will be unmasked.

If governments sign Agenda 21, if they commit themselves to the aims of reducing carbon dioxide and other trace gas emissions that are endangering our atmosphere, it becomes obvious on the ground that something is wrong, if the same government still favours the users of cars by providing tax incentives and reductions for car commuters and does not give the same advantage to those walking or using public transport systems to get to work!! Local authorities will then be limited in their efforts. It is also here at the local level that people have to decide on their appropriate behaviour on waste management by making, for example, the right decision on not to buy packaged or wrapped goods or non-returnable bottles. It is here where pupils have to learn about food chains and about the necessities of protecting species in the local forests. If you do not raise the awareness here and state that responsibility for the local neighbourhood is necessary then you will never get global awareness.

When we started in our "Action Against Global Climatic Change" in Heidelberg two years ago we gave our posters the provocative title "Rio has negotiated Heidelberg acts".

We had a twofold aim :

- Firstly to challenge national and international government policies and to push for the formulation of common and binding declarations.

- Secondly to push people in Heidelberg to act together in their own town, in their own living environment, to work towards global change because global agreements must have local consequences.

A city forms the closed environment for thousands or millions of people. Everything that is done here - working, living, transport, tourism; each activity has its own effect on the environment, not only in the town but also regional, national and often effects on more distant borders.

Our city problems are not new. In antiquity there were rules to for instance get rid of waste, but there is something new in our time, now we have to deal with urbanisation. With the growing number of people in the world there is increased movement into the towns which is becoming a severe problem and is overburdening our natural resources. The United Nations estimate that there will be about 93 cities with more than five million inhabitants by the year 2025, eighty of which will be in the Southern hemisphere.

It has been known for a long time, this is not a recent phenomenon, that it is imperative for cities to act. This is especially important in North America and Europe as their urban areas are mainly responsible for the world's released environmental pollution.

Chapter 28 of Agenda 21 that was adopted in Rio in 1992 provides us with aims and measures to be urgently undertaken. It is not easily understandable why the important role of the cities was not properly stressed from the beginning. Here knowledge of the role of cities and administrations has to be raised, leading to proper political decisions, local budgets have to be properly audited for us to be able to fulfil the tasks ahead and legal decisions at other levels have to be prepared and pushed to support and not contradict local action as is so often the case.

Many cities and many of them in Europe have started to act basing their work on a wide-ranging knowledge about local needs and opportunities. They have already taken their first steps towards sustainable development drawing up local action plans. These initiatives, like the European Charter for Sustainable Cities and Towns signed in Aalborg in May this year, may be deemed to be uncompetitive however they are comparable to the aims of many other local authority groupings and initiatives on the environment If humankind has reached a decisive turning point in its history, as it is warned in the preamble to Agenda 21, if we find ourselves at the beginning of a new global society which will be fundamentally different from today's society, indeed as the world after the industrial revolution was from the one before it, then we can only reach a secure and positive future if we act in a global partnership and accept the challenges together. This is equally valuable for all nations as well as for the European Union.

Our task is to take the right environmentally sound track towards an improvement in the quality of life in our so called "biosphere" town. Our responsibilities have grown enormously as the effect of our actions on the environment are becoming clearer. We all know that adequate environmental protection must be holistic and cross border, not only do we need national agreements but also ones that are between departments in administrations and this is a difficult task as we all experience in our day to day operations. Everybody must be made to feel responsible for the environment, this cannot remain the green playground for some "eco-freaks". Environmental protection must be part of all decision-making in all political areas - like finance, economy, transport, energy, agriculture, city planning, land use and so on.

Since elected to office three and a half years ago we have taken some important decisions in Heidelberg. These initiatives are detailed in a later presentation to this conference.

As a city's problems are of a practical rather than theoretical nature, then we get clear signals of nature's stress. This must force us to think about strategies and to act accordingly. Agenda 21 will and can only be successful together with Local Agenda 21. Let us draft the framework of local action in this conference but let us also shape the picture which is to appear within this frame. Let it be clear and precise, not ill-defined and vague, because that is what all citizens expect from us and what future generations will demand.

To come to the end and back to the start. The environment needs individual actions and they need information to act. Our task is to provide this information to allow and to enhance public participation. That is why environmental protection is the crucial challenge for an emancipated and democratic society.

IMPLEMENTING THE LOCAL AGENDA 21 MANDATE
What is the Local Government Response to Local Agenda 21
Jeb Brugman, Secretary General, International Council For Local Environmental Initiatives.

"I am going to start by saying that this is a very important event and I want to thank Manchester City Council for taking the leadership to organise it. This is the first international gathering following up on the Local Agenda 21 mandate from the Earth Summit. We tend to think about events being important by the quantities of people involved in them or by the social status of people involved, but what I would like to put forward is that I think this is an important event because of the quality of the people involved. It is also important because of the quality of the commitment you have shown by taking the little mandate presented to you by the Earth Summit, a small remembrance of local government by the international community, and translating it into something very meaningful in your communities. I shall give a brief report on what has happened with this mandate.

I would like to put it into context. In May, the United Nations Commission on Sustainable Development had its second meeting and one of the major themes to be discussed at that meeting was human settlements. However I have to report to you that local government was not really included in the discussion. Local government representatives did introduce some proposals at that meeting. For instance we proposed that the secretariat of the Commission, which is represented here and which does support the involvement of local government in the process, should prepare a special report on how local government is following up on the Earth Summit. However, the representative from China said that doing such a report would be an intrusion on their national sovereignty. We also put forward a proposal that Local Authorities and their national associations are critical partners in human settlements management but the representative from Belgium protested and said that the Local Authorities and their Associations are not critical partners. Most governments had nothing to say about Local Authorities at all when they talked about human settlements. I say this not to be negative, but to point out that we still have a long way to go.

It is typical of the Earth Summit process that Agenda 21 itself forgets about local government. The chapter about solid wastes talks about non-governmental organisations and private business, but it does not mention local government once. The chapter in Agenda 21 on Human Settlements Management refers 17 times to the activities and roles of international institutions, 17 times to the private sector, 14 times to non-governmental organisations and community-based organisations and refers only 9 times to local government. The chapter on Fresh Water Management and Sewage Treatment refers twice to local government and I know why, because at the last minute a US government representative thought that this was a ridiculous situation and introduced some appropriate wording as an after thought.

There are two reasons why local government is not given much regard in the international discussions on sustainable development. One is because we do not represent ourselves there well and in a forceful way. I would urge you to give more impor-

tance to this when you think about your involvement in sustainable development. The second reason is that recognition of local government by national governments, and the club of nations we call the United Nations, is very controversial and is something we are going to have to push very hard in the next years if Local Agenda 21 is going to be meaningful.

However, we do have this mandate. If we go through the chapters of Agenda 21 and we look for the words 'local government' we rarely find them, but then we come to chapter 28 and there are two pages about local authorities. This basically says that by 1996 it is expected all local authorities in the world will mobilise a process with their communities and come up with an action plan on how this document Agenda 21 in its entirety will be implemented at a local level. When it talks about resources for that process, it talks about giving the UN agencies a million dollars, but does not specify what money will be given in support of local authority activities.

So that is where we stand in the international context, where do we stand locally?

Locally, I am very happy to say that in spite of all of this there are more than 300 local authorities that have established serious Local Agenda 21 processes since 1992 and these campaigns are taking place now or just getting started in over 29 countries, including Finland, Norway, Sweden, Denmark, UK, The Netherlands, Germany, Poland, Austria, France, Portugal, Papua New Guinea, Japan, Australia, New Zealand, Peru, Ecuador, Brazil, Columbia, El Salvador, USA and Canada.

You would think that to have something like this started in such a short period of time there would have to be a great organising effort, but in fact there has been very little. All of this activity is the result of commitment and your leadership and of course the pressure of your citizens on you, as local leaders, to do something about Local Agenda 21. Only in May, the European Commission with the International Council for Local Environmental Initiatives (ICLEI) and the City of Aalborg, held a European Conference to launch the European Campaign for Sustainable Cities and Towns and that conference established a Charter for European Cities which commits the signatories to doing Local Agenda 21. I am happy to say that, in just one month, 60 cities signed the Charter and made that commitment. At that conference the Danish Environment Minister announced that they will be establishing a national Local Agenda 21 campaign, joining the UK, Sweden and Finland as other European countries that have established such national campaigns. Also at that conference, The Netherlands and Austrian governments in informal discussions expressed their intentions to do the same.

National campaigns with the formal involvement and approval of national governments and national local government associations are also being explored in Zimbabwe, in South Africa, in India and Australia, New Zealand and in Japan. So the response to our little mandate and Agenda 21 has been quite enthusiastic and I think that its impact on your local activities and local policy making are also quite important. It is because of the extent of the response that the UN system is now beginning to listen and in particular I am pleased that the secretariat, the

staff who are organising the 1996 City Summit - the UN
Conference on Human Settlements, which will take place in
Istanbul in 1996, have decided that they will include Local
Agenda 21 as a major input into the City Summit. So we have
this conference as a way to exchange experiences with one
another, to make sure that we are sharing the methodologies
and talking about the challenge of meeting the Local Agenda 21
mandate. But we are also here to make sure that by 1996 we
have a strong voice in the City Summit and that our Local
Agenda 21 activities are given full consideration by the UN and
indeed are given continued support for the rest of the century."

LOCAL AGENDA 21 AND THE UNITED NATIONS - HOW LOCAL AGENDA 21 FITS INTO THE UN PROCESS
Zehra Aydin, Major Groups Focal Point, CSD Secretariat, Division for Sustainable Development
United Nations Department for Policy Co-ordination and Sustainable Development, New York

(In this presentation brief statements on the UN process on the role of Local Authorities and Local Agenda 21 in this process and a brief response to the previous statements particularly that of ICLEI on the Local Agenda 21 process are provided.)

The UN Process

The United Nations process under focus here is the process of implementing, monitoring and coordinating the agenda for sustainable development; Agenda 21.

Agenda 21, is an extensive work program that member States of the United Nations adopted, by consensus at the Earth Summit, in Rio, in 1992. It contains over 150 programmes and 2509 activities. Its realisation requires an enormous amount of political and financial commitment and a broad simultaneous coordination of activities at the local, national and international levels.

Agenda 21 is not a perfect document. As numerous scholars have already demonstrated, Agenda 21 has many internal contradictions and, at times, it lacks practical clarity. These add to the difficulties in its implementation. However, it is also a revolutionary document for several reasons. Firstly it is the only globally agreed and recognised starting point to prepare the global community for the environmental and developmental challenges and responsibilities that lie ahead. Secondly, it makes an unprecedented opening for the involvement of people under the concept of "major groups" which is composed of nine groups in civil society (1). By distinctively recognising the essential role and contribution of major groups to the implementation and evaluation of sustainable development activities, Agenda 21 makes achieving sustainability a duty and responsibility for everyone rather than limiting this responsibility to a specific inter-governmental body or to the policies of national governments.

The global coordination and monitoring of activities that implement Agenda 21 takes place in the UN under the guidance of a newly created UN Commission: The Commission on Sustainable Development (CSD).

The CSD is located in New York and has a small Secretariat of less than two dozen people. The Secretariat services the CSD's annual meetings which last two weeks. The results of the CSD sessions are reported to the Economic and Social Council of the United Nations.

(1) These nine groups include Women, Children and Youth, Indigenous People, Non-governmental Organisations, Workers and Trade Unions, Local Authorities, Business and Industry, Scientific and Technological Communities, and Farmers. The role and contribution of these major groups are specifically addressed in the 10 chapters of Section III of Agenda 21. In

addition, throughout the rest of Agenda 21's 30 chapters, specific roles and contributions are ascribed to specific major groups.

The CSD was created by the UN General Assembly not as a new UN Agency, a think-tank or as a legislative body, its first and foremost mandate is to coordinate the implementation of Agenda 21 at the global level and motivate a similar coordination process at the national and local levels.

The emphasis on coordination has an important advantage. It makes sustainable development an integral approach to all the international and national institutions rather than leaving Agenda 21 implementation to one institution or agency alone. Moreover, coordination also emphasises efficient and effective use of existing capacities; an approach that is consistent with the spirit of the sustainable development concept. The CSD coordinates the implementation of Agenda 21 primarily through a global reporting and evaluation exercise. This exercise follows a thematic programme of work and set of guidelines adopted by the CSD in the first session in June 1993. The reporting exercise depends on the inputs from three main spheres of Agenda 21 implementation: the international agencies, the national governments and the organisations of civil society.

All levels of the reporting process are required to actively involve local, national and international "major group" organisations. Thus, Governments who provide information to the reporting process are asked to consult with national and local "major groups".

The international level of reporting is organised through Task managers, which are UN Agencies that have a particularly strong technical expertise on a given theme. For example, Habitat was the Task manager for human settlement issues. For the national process, Governments are sent information about the themes and the reporting guidelines. Each Government then sets up mechanisms to collect the national information. The recommended national process, according to the Rio discussions, is to create national councils or commissions for sustainable development. This mechanism, where it is in place, appears to be the best practice.

A simultaneous and essential part of the reporting process is what is known as the inter-sessional meetings. There are two types of inter-sessional meetings: those that are organised and sponsored by National governments and those that are organised by the CSD Secretariat. The inter-sessional meetings help bring experts, rather than political people, together to focus on the annual themes. In the past year for example, the Governments of Sweden, Norway, France, and Denmark organised inter-sessional workshops on the themes of toxic chemicals, consumption patterns, freshwater and health. A number of Governments also organised joint inter-sessional meetings. For example the Governments of Columbia and the United States cooperated to hold a workshop on transfer of environmentally sound technologies. Similarly, the Governments of Japan and Malaysia jointly organised a seminar on financing Agenda 21.

Role of Local Authorities and Local Agenda 21:

Local Authorities are recognised as a major group in Agenda 21. Like other "major groups", local authorities are recognised on the basis of their distinct contributions, strengths and potentials in sustainable development.

Local Authorities have numerous strengths. At the risk of over-simplifying them, I will mention only a few. Local authorities are close and more accessible to the communities they serve than are national governments and international organisations For a mayor, local problems are not just other people's problems but also hers/his. The mayor and the administration are people who have rooted personal ties to their communities which makes them more open and accessible to the communities they serve. This in turn increases partnership potential and forms a basis that allows for the trying out of new approaches and ideas.

Furthermore, Local Authorities, at least in some countries, have a degree of independence in terms of economic decisions, legal options and resource allocations. Countries may take years to decide on environmental standards or on new initiatives. A city on the other hand, can pass a locally applicable pollution standard or try out new ideas for waste management, or initiate local education programmes without having to wait for a national programme to be initiated. Local authorities also provide an official and structured link between the local communities and the national governments as well as between the people of local communities and the communities of other cities. Through international organisations, Local Authorities also provide a link between their communities and the UN process.

Perhaps the most important strength of local authorities lies in the fact that they are the administrative structures at the level where things are actually done. International agreements are useful and national policies are meaningful because of their wide consensus building effect. However, agreements and policies have led to tangible processes which almost always start at the local level. This simple reality makes Local Authorities the engines of implementation at a fundamental level. While Local Authorities motivate, undertake and generate sustainable development action at the local level, the Local Agenda 21 process provides a common framework through which global goals are translated into local actions. The Local Agenda 21 process helps adapt the global and general objectives to the local conditions, needs and priorities; to turn them into locally implementable action and lead to progress in the overall achievement of sustainable development goals.

This link is more than an instrument of implementation. For example, the Local Agenda 21 process generates or maintains the same level of commitment and involvement that was reached at the Earth Summit. It keeps the memories of Rio alive by involving people in projects and activities that they can relate to on a daily basis while also feeling connected to a global objective. Furthermore, Local Agenda 21 processes, through action and participation, enabling the kind of intellectual shifts Agenda 21 requires. These shifts are stronger than a negotiated global agreement because they are directly relevant to the everyday lives of the communities.

Local Agenda 21 is a tool not only for achieving better environments but also greater social cohesion. This is not insignificant considering one of the most pressing problems is the continuous loss of mutual trust and cohesion in the modern social settlements. As we feel more disconnected from each other we are less able to communicate and cooperate with each other. According to the 2050 project of the Brooking Institute in the United States, sustainable development is the only emerging hope to regain the social contract that has led to the present modern social structures. It is an ideal that has an enormous moral and ethical hold on each individual. Thus, according to some, the environment movement could in fact be the only hope for the human race to find a new layer of social connection, regrouping people as communities rather than self-interested and self-survival seeking alienated pockets of humanity. This cohesive effect of the environmental movement needs to find local applicability and the Local Agenda 21 is a brilliant initiative in this sense.

The linkage to the UN process is at two levels. First is the straight-forward information generation process that feeds into the global monitoring and review process. Through organisations of Local Authorities, the UN receives valuable information on how the local implementation of Agenda 21 is processing. In the CSD Secretariat we feel the information from Local Authorities' organisations is not a substitute or a part of the national reporting process but one that qualitatively enhances it.

This leads to the second level of linkage between the UN process and the Local Agenda 21 process. This is the issue of increasing the accountability and the transparency of the global process. The "major groups", including Local Authorities, are the balancing factors to facilitate a transparent and accountable system; in other words making sustainable development truly a global environmental governance process. Information generated through local processes helps the global process have a better perspective in looking at the national and regional achievements as well as problems. This has a direct effect on the value and strength of the Commission's decisions and its feedback to the countries. Thus, Local Authorities, as well as other "major groups" have two ways to influence the national processes: one from within the country and the other through the process in the CSD.

A related contribution of Local Authorities and Local Agenda 21 to the UN process is in terms of increasing the overall peer pressure to which the CSD process depends for success. When case studies show that cities have achieved better waste management, better transportation systems, have reduced pollution and increased community participation, this has a demonstration effect not only for other cities but to the countries and the global community. This demonstration effect is the most needed message of hope that people around the world need to hear, including the diplomats at the United Nations. Local Authorities, and Local Agenda 21 processes they embrace, help push the national and international efforts further.

Without these initiatives, Agenda 21 is likely to remain at an abstract level with fewer and fewer people finding it relevant. As the memories of Rio and the Earth Summit fade we need to replace the memories with local and tangible initiatives that keep Agenda 21 alive. Local Agenda 21 initiatives are doing that by generating commitment from local communities.

Have Local Authorities had an effect on the CSD so far? Yes. We received very useful inputs from numerous national local authorities' organisations as well as similar organisations at the international level such as the International Council for Local Environmental Initiatives. These inputs were integrated in both the report on "major groups" and the relevant sectoral reports prepared for the second session of the CSD that took place last month. One outcome of active participation of Local Authorities in the reporting and review process at the CSD was the decision of the Commission asking for case studies to further illustrate the role of local authorities in implementation of Agenda 21. These case studies will be presented to the third session of the CSD next year. The case study requested by the CSD is likely to increase the CSDs Secretariat's active collaboration with local authorities' organisations.

As the Secretariat of the CSD, we are allowed to work closely with a broad set of actors of civil society than is possible for other organisations. Unlike many other inter-governmental international bodies, the CSD Secretariat does not require an organisation of civil society to obtain formal status before it can make an input to the CSD's work. The Agenda 21 review process is open to all sectors of society and the Secretariat actively encourages everyone to be part of the reporting and monitoring process. In fact, many NGOs who have been working with UN bodies feel the CSD is one of the most open processes in the UN system. Both the CSD and its Secretariat firmly believe that sustainable development is not in the domain of international agencies and national governments alone but equally in the domain of the people and their representatives, such as Local Authorities. But people and their organisations need to continuously claim their place in this process as rightfully theirs. Local Authorities have already made great contributions in helping their communities to make this claim locally and nationally. As part of the Secretariat I look forward to being of service to all of you in helping bring your messages to the international arena.

Response to ICLEI's report on the state of Local Agenda 21

One theme of ICLEI's statement made by Jeb Brugman was the limited number of references to Local Authorities in Agenda 21. Numbers are there to indeed show that the role of local authorities is mentioned fewer times than say the role of women or NGOS. In fact, in some thematic chapters of Agenda 21 the role of local authorities is left out even though the logic of the theme would have required a greater emphasis on the role of this particular major group. For example, one expects to find many more references to the role of local authorities in the land related chapters (Chapters 11-16 concerning land management, forests, sustainable agriculture, biodiversity and desertification). There are also instances when the on-going contributions of local authorities could have been recognised by Agenda 21.

However, designing the future strategies of a major group on the basis of the numbers of references to its role in a programme of action would be undermining the clearly recognised

place of that group in sustainable development. If Agenda 21 refers to NGOs 100 times it does not mean NGOs have 100 activities to undertake and it stops there. In other words, the role of a "major group" is not determined by the number of times the group is mentioned. Rather than counting the explicit references, it may be more productive to find the inherent opportunities for partnerships and design activities accordingly. We in the Secretariat are authorised to encourage and enhance the role of each major group and therefore are ready to help bring your activities and contributions under the spotlight at the international level.

Another theme of ICLEIs report here was the contradiction of labelling local authorities as a "major group" which many understand as the non-governmental sector. Local authorities are often elected local government and are, to some, more governmental than non-governmental entities. The underlying conflict is a structural and political one and will need time to resolve.

In the meantime, it might be useful to look into the advantages that come with being classified as a "major group". I believe that being a "major group" enables local authorities to participate in Agenda 21 process as a distinct group rather than being absorbed into the Governmental sphere. As a "major group", local authorities are able to make statements, submit inputs and undertake activities that are recognised independently of the statements, or inputs made by the country delegations in the CSD. Being considered as a distinct group gives you a greater chance to influence decisions as your inputs act as a balancing factor to that of the international organisations and national governments. This is the whole point of emphasising "major groups" inputs: to balance and enhance the transparency and accountability of the international and national processes towards sustainable development. In fact, the greatest strength of the CSD is the transparency in which it has to operate because Agenda 21 requires the Commission to take equally into account the experiences of civil society as it does the experiences of Governments and inter-governmental bodies. Thus, being a "major group" enhances your position in the overall sustainable development process not reduces it.

As I mentioned earlier, the CSD Secretariat is fully committed to the letter and spirit of accountability and transparency that Agenda 21 expresses. Our role includes helping organisations of civil society to bring their constituencies' concerns to the international arena. We believe that without the inputs and involvement of major groups we will not achieve the proper accountability and transparency that is essential to implementing Agenda 21. Without your influence as Local Authorities in particular, and that of "major groups" in general, the international community is not likely to maintain the pressure that is necessary to achieve the commitments made at the Rio Earth Summit.

HOW LOCAL AUTHORITIES ARE RESPONDING TO THE CHALLENGE

Mr Paulo Maluf, Mayor of Sao Paulo, Brazil

"The city where I was born, Sao Paulo, is probably the second or third largest metropolitan area in the world. In the census of 1890 about 100 years ago it was a very small city of about 20,000 inhabitants. Immigration from Portugal, Italy, Japan, Spain, the Middle East countries, Japan, Korea, China and from all parts of the world over 100 years transformed Sao Paolo from a very small village of 20,000 people to a village of 10 million people. The metropolitan area has grown even larger and where there were cities of 20,000 and 30,000 people 25 years ago, they are now reaching half a million. The metropolitan area of Sao Paulo today is about 17 to 18 million people. People can easily imagine the problems we have, but very honestly I think psychologically speaking that the Mayor must not see a problem as a problem, but as a challenge which gives motivation and stimulation.

The city is growing and is constantly being upgraded. We have many rich people, as we are the largest industrial city, the biggest financial city in Latin America and have the largest University in Latin America, but we also have the highest number of poor people in Latin America .

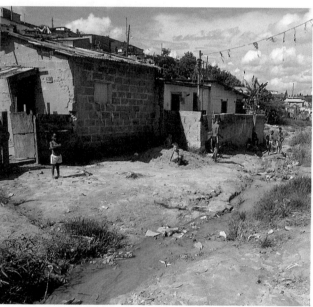

Slums in Sao Paulo - home to 1 million people

Rob Franklin, EPL

So, we created the Secretary of Green and Environmental Issues to promote a better quality of life in our city. Imagine how many tons of garbage we produce in the city of Sao Paulo - 12,000 tons daily, must be collected and separated into paper, plastic, glass, metal. We must make fertiliser of the organic garbage and the rest we must burn in incinerators using the latest technology producing zero pollution. Under this programme that is not a problem - it is a challenge. We are investing $700 million over the next 3 years in the city to make Sao Paulo the biggest and cleanest city in the world.

Sao Paulo too, because of the very rapid growth has few green areas and this year we have plans for the biggest city reforestation in all the world. Our plan in the next summer from December to February is to plant 2 million trees in the city.

We hope to plant them by mass production and using local labour.

We also have the problem in the city of air pollution caused by the exhaust of cars, automobiles, trucks and buses. Twenty-five years ago 50% of air pollution came from chimneys and 50% from cars but since then the numbers of cars has increased in the city from 500,000 to 4 million so that consequently cars now account for 90% of the pollution in the city. So we are adding 20% of ethynol alcohol to all our gasoline which gives almost zero pollution so that today although we have 8 times more cars in the city than 25 years ago, our air is much cleaner. We have a law that buses in the city cannot use diesel. In 8 years time all the buses in the city will be electric, or run on natural gas.

We are also involved in another very large project. The city with the State of Sao Paulo is cleaning all the water extracted from the two major rivers in the city. This will amount to $2.4B of investment in 10 years time.

We are also carrying out a big education and schools campaign. If you invest money but do not educate the children in the culture of preservation then your investment will be wasted. So in all our municipal schools, where we have about one million pupils, we are giving lessons on conservation and preservation. Teaching pupils how to take care of the green areas, how to plant fruit trees in gardens and how to take care of the trees they have planted on the school grounds.

We also have a very large water research programme in the city. Imagine how much water we need to provide for 17M people - we need over 70 cubic metres of clean water per second. If you don't have clean water available near the city then you must go and try to get water from 50, 60, or 70 kms from the city, making it economically absolutely impossible to finance. So we are trying to keep all our sources of water very clean and we are investing, not only in cleaning the water, but investing too in the people that live near the water sources encouraging them not to put sewage into what will eventually become theirs and other people's drinking water.

The city of Sao Paulo in these ways is changing. It is today one of the cleanest cities in the world, the gardens are very well cared for, the air is not so polluted, the quality of life has been upgraded. As I told you, we have problems, but as I said we consider these as challenges.

One further challenge we face concerns the one million people who are living in slums, 10% of our city's population. What are we are doing about this? We are involved in an unusual programme to get rid of these slums. Instead of taking out the people, we are involved in site re-urbanisation. We are constructing 4 storey buildings on the cleared sites so that for instance on 10,000 sq metres of slum area you can construct enough buildings in 2,500 square metres and you can leave 7,500 square metres for gardens, schools, football fields and other sports areas or facilities. I want to end my contribution by making a proposal. I propose that under the coordination of our Secretary of Green and Environmental Issues we create a commission in Sao Paulo to coordinate the implementation of the Agenda 21. I think this is a practical way in which we can contribute to the resolution of these and other problems."

SECTION FOUR

NATIONAL LOCAL AGENDA 21
CAMPAIGNS

"Governments and citizens at the local and national levels are taking the United Nations mandate for "Local Agenda 21s" very seriously. Campaigns are beginning or underway in more than 20 countries. These efforts are producing new tools and innovative approaches for municipal environmental management, urban services provision and development policy. The International Local Agenda 21 Conference was the first opportunity since the 1992 Earth Summit for local officials world-wide to share their Local Agenda 21 experiences" Jeb Brugman, Secretary General, ICLEI

According to international experts more than 300 local authorities globally have a Local Agenda 21 process in 28 countries (UK, Finland, Norway, Sweden, Denmark, The Netherlands, Germany, Poland, Austria, France, Portugal, Palestine-West Bank, Turkey, Uganda, Zimbabwe, South Africa, India, Thailand, Papua New Guinea, Japan, Australia, Peru, Ecuador, Brazil, US, El Salvador, Columbia, Canada) and national campaigns are in operation in the UK, Japan, Australia, Sweden, Denmark, Finland, The Netherlands and Austria. All this activity demonstrates how far and fast the global commitment to Local Agenda 21 is growing.

National campaign representatives from four countries report in these papers on the progress being made in their part of the globe on both national Agenda 21 and Local Agenda 21 programmes.

NATIONAL LOCAL AGENDA 21 CAMPAIGNS

CASE 1 – AUSTRALIA

Bernie Cotter, Project Manager, Australia National Local Agenda 21 Programme and Convenor, of Australia's National Local Government Environment and Resource Network

CASE 2 – THE UK

Cllr John Harman, Leader, Kirklees Metropolitan Council

CASE 3– JAPAN

Saburo Kato, Senior Executive Director, ICLEI Japan, Director, Global Environment Program, Japan Environment Agency and Member of Japan Local Agenda 21 Panel.

CASE 4 – COLOMBIA

Edgard Moncayo, Director, Mision Siglo XXI, Bogota.

CASE 1 - AUSTRALIA

AUSTRALIA'S NATIONAL LOCAL AGENDA 21 PROGRAM
MANAGING FOR THE FUTURE: A LOCAL GOVERNMENT
GUIDE
PART OF A LOCAL AGENDA 21 PROGRAM FOR AUSTRALIA
Mr Bernie Cotter Local Agenda 21 Program Manager
Convenor, National Local Government Environment Resource
Network
Vice - President, Municipal Conservation Association of
Australia

BACKGROUND

Australia has three levels of government; a central Federal
Government, eight state or territory governments and nearly 900
local authorities. The responsibilities of local authorities, or
councils, vary from state to state but generally speaking they
generate local policy, provide services and give development
approvals. Local authorities range in size of population from
Brisbane City Council with 800,000 residents to small councils of
a thousand and range in area from a few square kilometres to the
shire of East Pilbara, occupying an area the size of England.

Environmental management is a shared responsibility in Australia.
However, both the designation of responsibilities and co-operative
arrangements are complex. Local governments are established by
the state government but are not entrenched in State Constitutions.
State governments have important legal powers under the
Australian Constitution and have their own laws but have
insufficient revenue raising powers. The Federal Governments
have limited constitutional legal powers but adequate taxing
powers which are used to influence states' roles and more
recently to provide local government financial assistance.

Recently, to assist in establishing a clearer way to effectively
manage the environment, all spheres of government have signed
an inter-governmental agreement on the environment which
attempts to foster a co-operative approach, a better definition
of roles and a reduction in intergovernmental disputes. This has
produced more certain decision-making and environmental
protection. In addition, over recent years a number of initiatives
and programs have been launched which provide assistance to
local environmental decision-making.

Local governments have traditionally reflected the types of
organisations found at state and federal level with separate
departments for different services. All local authorities in
Australia are to varying degrees experiencing significant change,
with amalgamations, corporatisation, competition for service
delivery and a growing expectation from the community for
more effective and responsible environmental management.

Local councils have always had to respond to the needs of their
local community and the legislative demands of their state
government. Now they are also being seen as a crucial part of
regional initiatives. The Federal Government sees them as
delivering more in terms of national policy and now each is
being linked to international policy through Agenda 21 and
other declarations agreed at the federal level.

LOCAL AGENDA 21 IN AUSTRALIA

The Local Agenda 21 program in Australia has been pioneered
by the Municipal Conservation Association (MCA). As an
innovative and focused group, they have been involved in local
strategy development and community-council partnerships since
1988. The Victorian State Government, responding to the
recommendations of the Australian National Conservation
Strategy and World Conservation Strategy of 1980 (and 1991)
introduced a Local Conservation Strategy Program which was
based at the municipal level and sought to introduce locally
developed and relevant environment strategies. To date, over
60 strategies have been developed and assisted by the MCA.

With this background the MCA saw the development of Local
Agenda 21 as an extension of that initial work. Building upon
the experience of the last six years, the MCA have recently
completed an introductory booklet and guide for local authorities
in Australia. The process of developing the guide has been
participatory and has reflected the types of interest groups
needed to undertake a Local Agenda 21 process. By the very
nature of the process the consultation sessions sought assistance
from local authorities, community groups, trade unions, youth
groups and women. As an example, workshop and information
sessions were held in each state from which a first draft guide
was produced. This work was further refined by a steering
committee and two reference groups before being re-tested in
four further national workshop sessions. The draft guide was
provided to over 500 further people to review and make comments before it was edited and finalised. It takes the form of a
discussion of the background concepts of Agenda 21 and a step
by step guide for local governments to follow or adapt. But the
writing of a guide and its promotion by a focused group is really
the easy part. Having it accepted and adopted by local authorities
and their associations is another matter, especially given the
turmoil and restructuring in councils today.

Based on our experience, it is also evident that environmental
strategies will remain marginalised until embraced by municipal
leaders, even when the benefits appear obvious. In the
Australian Local Agenda 21 initiatives we have tried to make
the process just as attractive to the economic or community
services department as to the environmental services sections.

This program attempts to capitalise on both the opportunities of
local authorities undergoing change and their own perceived
needs to develop a more integrated approach to planning and
decision-making. Furthermore, it tries to use the synergy of a
myriad of existing and new projects and techniques which are
already familiar to local councils, rather than trying to just
introduce new ones. In this way the application of Agenda 21
principles to normal programs, new planning strategies and
corporate plans, together with any daily activity of councils, is
promoted.

To do this effectively the Local Agenda 21 material examines
the issues of economic necessity, environmental imperatives,
and community demands to give a positive case for change
from unsustainable practices. It argues for a change to
"management systems" to ensure all planning and policy
making is integrated. The focus is on long term outcomes and

involvement of all sectors of the community. It provides benefits like:

✪ reducing the need for major trade-offs between environmental sustainability, social welfare and economic viability;

✪ improving the efficiency of council operations and service delivery;

✪ providing opportunities for attracting new more "future orientated" industry;

✪ involving those often dis-enfranchised from decisions about their future;

✪ achieving sustainable pricing policies and mechanisms;

✪ providing greater certainty to residents and developers;

✪ focusing on the long-term as well as the immediate term;

✪ providing a basis for monitoring progress towards sustainability;

✪ assisting in creating sustainable jobs.

To be effective the program recognises the need for effective management systems. These would be required to:

✪ initiate effective training systems for council operations;

✪ establish an open information system and education strategy;

✪ develop a strategic and participatory decision-making system;

✪ assess the approvals system against stated sustainability goals;

✪ ensure that the budgetary system considers full social as well as economic costs;

✪ develop pricing and charging systems that are equitable and examine the life cycle of products;

✪ encourage the transfer of technology, knowledge and experience.

Each of these then forms part of the required 'on the ground' actions which involve:

✪ eco-system maintenance/repair;

✪ sustainable use of resources;

✪ promotion of sustainable economic development;

✪ health improvement for the community;

✪ quality of life improvements for all;

✪ improving access to adequate services, sustenance or amenities;

✪ providing meaningful employment;

✪ ensuring security and safety;

✪ community service development;

✪ preserving cultural heritage;

✪ advocacy and creating strategic partners for all actions.

CAN AUSTRALIA MEET ITS OBLIGATIONS?

To turn to the question of whether we can achieve the aims set for 1996; Australia can achieve them! Australia has a unique opportunity. It is a politically progressive country which has attempted to discharge its international responsibilities and has taken a leadership role in many global programs. The community is comparatively affluent, well educated, well informed and aware of many issues with consistent and comprehensive media coverage which is able to report on and encourage effective management at all levels.

Australia is enthusiastic and able to pick up on new ideas. Agenda 21 is intergovernmental in nature and it's implementation is a shared task for all governments and communities and not just the responsibility of local government. Agreements made across all levels of government have the opportunity to ensure a positive approach. In general, we have had enormous success in developing local strategies to implement national or international programs. An example is the Local Conservation Strategy approach - the response to the World Conservation Strategy. Building upon these earlier successes there is a continuing trend of growing interest in Agenda 21 at all levels. The Federal Government is also committed to its National Ecologically Sustainable Development Program. However, it currently lacks an effective method of delivery. There are also positive local community responses and local environmental initiatives which indicate the pioneering work of 'Clean Up' days, landcare and catchment management initiatives and many other examples of local responsibility and action.

Good communication and exchange mechanisms are basic requirements in the co-ordination of a national or global program, like Agenda 21. Australia is a continent well connected with basic communications systems and now with the introduction of information exchange systems, both human and technical, we ensure we learn from each other and exchange what we know (which is a primary part of Chapter 28). Further-more because of Australia's large land mass and our relative isolation from the rest of the world, we have also focused on the effective use of electronic communication systems. When this is linked with the wealth of information from the environmental databases that have been developed and are being refined, a strong combination results.

Australia can also succeed because it will consider its responsibilities very carefully and make every effort to complete them. As a nation, we understand that to effectively take our place within both our own region and the world generally, we should "make good" our declarations. The occasions at which we should report, whether it is at an event like Global Forum, or to the Commission for Sustainable Development, are important in checking our resolve and achievement.

Australia's Local Agenda 21 program should also build upon other initiatives. This means using the opportunities offered by new planning schemes, the restructuring of local councils or amalgamations with other councils, or legislative requirements (such as a local state of the environment report or a regional economic strategy). Such programs could, if co-ordinated with activities at other government levels, combine to assist in developing effective local strategies. Finally, local authorities need to undertake a local process because it is this process which will deliver the integrated benefits for all departments. All this can be delivered at a time when resources are tight yet community accountability is high.

It will not be an easy process, regardless of the great number of benefits outlined here. The process of a more direct democracy and a genuine openness to work with the community will be resisted in many areas. People will deny the long term benefits for the short term profits as they always have. What makes this program the more likely to succeed than ever before is its global nature and its universal application. A local Agenda 21 process in Australia should be recognised as basically good governance and good long term planning. Further work is needed on providing effective networks for sharing information, education and awareness to promote the message. Development of a local sustainable development "network" to motivate local authorities and other spheres of governments and the establishment of a "funding trust" drawing upon the resources of the whole community to promote the work in its initial stages are needed. Training and monitoring are also important both to see how far we have come but also to examine how far we still need to go.

Finally, there are some concerns that have yet to be tackled at the local level. The first is the limited recognition of the role that Australian local authorities can play in directly assisting developing world or southern communities. While we provide aid at the Federal Government level, little is done between individual local authorities. The use of 'sister city' relationships and the "twinning" of local authorities should be further examined. Secondly, the work of the Municipal Conservation Association in pioneering the Local Agenda 21 program has been positive but the major local government associations in Australia have yet to effectively take up either the Local Agenda 21 initiative, or more generally co-ordinated environment management programs (and this is so despite their membership of ICLEI and IULA).

It has been suggested that Australia has both borrowed ideas from other countries and also developed unique approaches. For those still developing a program, I would encourage other countries to collect, combine and adapt information from various global programs and individual countries to assist in your national and local initiatives. This process of learning and adapting should be continuous and will become greatly enhanced as more local authorities begin, complete, review and share their experiences.

Australia's Local Agenda 21 Program has been funded by the Federal Department of the Environment, Sport and Territories with work undertaken by the Municipal Conservation Association (MCA). The MCA also currently manages Council Net an electronic information service. It provides support and assistance to members through training sessions, a national newsletter and environmental management manuals.

CASE 2 - THE UK LOCAL AGENDA 21 INITIATIVE
Councillor John Harman Leader of Kirklees Metropolitan Council, West Yorkshire
Vice-chair and environment spokesperson for the Association of Metropolitan Authorities.

Many local authorities in the UK have already taken major steps towards achieving Local Agenda 21 and it is seen as a way to bring together and mutually strengthen, an authority's commitments to the environment, to local economic and social development and to local democracy. Many components of the Local Agenda 21 process are already in place within local authorities and the key is to recognise old and new measures as part of this new sustainable development agenda, linking global and local issues. Local Agenda 21 is where all these components meet.

In the UK the 6 local authority associations have set up a joint Local Agenda 21 Steering Group representing industry, trade unions, the voluntary sector, women's organisations and higher education as well as local government. The Local Government Management Board was asked to coordinate and drive Local Agenda 21 on their behalf and have appointed a Local Agenda 21 Project Officer to work with all the UK local authorities. The Steering Group are organising conferences and Round Table groups on aspects of sustainable development at a local level, publicising guidance notes and representing the interests of local government in national and international policy, for example making contributions to the National Sustainable Development Strategy, the European Commission and the United Nations Commission for Sustainable Development.

The UK Local Agenda 21 Initiative sets out six key action areas, (Fig 1), in which work needs to be undertaken to achieve an effective Local Agenda 21. The first two areas are actions which need to be followed through within the local authority itself, while the other four areas require action in, with and for the wider community. Local Agenda 21 means actively involving the local community in working together towards sustainable development. Local authorities should create and facilitate opportunities for action to achieve this partnership approach. Each of these six key action areas is outlined below, indicating the variety of work involved. (Fig 2)

MANAGING AND IMPROVING THE LOCAL AUTHORITY'S OWN ENVIRONMENTAL PERFORMANCE.

Developing a corporate commitment from both members and officers to working towards sustainable development is an essential starting point for a successful Local Agenda 21.

Staff training and awareness raising on environmental issues is also necessary to give local authority officers the understanding and confidence to progress these issues within their own work. Environmental Management Systems such as the European Eco-Management and Audit scheme (EMA) or British Standard 7750 can provide a structured framework for the local authority to identify and act on its major environmental impacts. Environmental management systems allow targets to be set, responsibilities and resources to be allocated and monitoring and reporting processes to be established.

Each service function's decision making process also needs to take account of the environmental consequences of their work practices in their own and in other areas.

Budgetary processes within local authorities need to be flexible enough to provide money for supporting environmental work, which will often lead to future savings. While local authorities are coming up against increasing governmental pressures to cut finances and the need to make year on year financial savings, providing a central fund for environmental work is very important as it is one of the most effective ways of resourcing positive environmental action. There is also a need to integrate environmental policy and practice initiatives into mainstream service budgets, so that they are not seen as an add-on function, only to be tackled when 'spare' money is available. A strong argument for this is that undertaking environmental work supports local economic activity and can play an important part in local regeneration. For example, spending on energy conservation can be targeted to reduce fuel poverty which has a knock-on effect on health and creates jobs in energy installation.

INTEGRATING SUSTAINABLE DEVELOPMENT AIMS INTO THE LOCAL AUTHORITY'S POLICIES AND ACTIVITIES.

A local authority can improve its own direct effects on the environment through good environmental (or 'green') house-keeping - such as energy conservation measures and ensuring that all purchasing of supplies is environmentally responsible.

All the policies and services carried out by a local authority will have effects on the environment. Some of the most vital areas to target for improvement are outlined here:

✪ Land use planning has to take account of Planning Policy Guidance, issued by the government, which now encourages local authorities to promote sustainability through the planning system. Policies can seek to promote development which reduces the need to travel, encourage energy efficient patterns of development and protect habitats and landscape, including urban open land.

✪ Transport policies and programmes can take a broader view to encourage a move away from car use towards public transport, cycling, walking and seek to reduce the need to travel.

✪ Economic development sections within local authorities need to be aware of the concepts of sustainable development and should encourage environmentally responsible businesses, stressing the economic benefits which can arise from environmental improvements - such as reduced energy and waste bills and, ultimately, the avoidance of costly fines for non-compliance.

✪ Environmental criteria can be included in tender documents, provided they are not 'anti-competitive' and relate to the goods or services being bought (rather than the suppliers' other activities).

✪ Housing Services can refurbish buildings to high standards of energy efficiency, promote grant schemes for insulation and draught proofing and provide energy advice for tenants.

THE 6 KEY AREAS OF ACTION IN THE LOCAL AGENDA 21 PROCESS

1   Managing and improving the local authority's own environmental performance

2   Integrating sustainable development aims into the local authority's policies and activities

| ACTION WITHIN THE LOCAL AUTHORITY |

3   Awareness raising and education

4   Consulting and involving the general public

5   Partnerships

6   Measuring, monitoring and reporting on progress towards sustainability

| ACTION IN THE WIDER COMMUNITY |

UK Local Agenda 21 Steering Group, 1994

Fig. 1

DETAILS OF THE 6 ACTION AREAS FOR THE LOCAL AGENDA 21 PROCESS

Managing and improving the local authority's own environmental performance	Integrating sustainable development aims into the local authority's policies and activities	Awareness-raising and education	Consulting and involving the general public	Partnerships	Measuring, monitoring and reporting on progress towards sustainability
Corporate commitment	Green housekeeping	Support for environmental education	Public consultation processes	Meetings, workshops and conferences	Environmental monitoring
Staff training and awareness raising	Land use planning	Awareness-raising events	Forums	Working groups/ advisory groups	Local State of the Environment reporting
Environmental management systems	Transport policies and programmes	Visits and talks	Focus groups	Round Tables	Sustainability indicators
Environmental budgeting	Economic development	Support for voluntary groups	'Planning for Real'	Environment City model	Targets
Policy integration across all sectors	Tendering and Purchaser/provider splits	Publication of local information	Parish Maps	Partnership initiatives	Environmental Impact Assessment (EIA)
	Housing services	Press releases	Feedback mechanisms	Developing-world partnerships and support	Strategic environmental assessment
	Tourism and visitor strategies	Initiatives to encourage behaviour change and practical action			
	Health strategies				
	Welfare, equal opportunities and poverty strategies				
	Explicitly 'environmental' services				

UK Local Agenda 21 Steering Group, 1994

EPL V. Miles

Traffic congestion is now a part of urban life in the UK

Council strategies also need to take account of the environmental effects and interactions of the services provided and commitments made. For example:

✪ Strategies for tourism should encourage 'green tourism' which encourages the use of public transport and enhances and protects the natural environment.

✪ Strategies for health, welfare, equal opportunities and poverty can recognise the links between economic, social and environmental deprivation and address the problems as a coherent whole.

Lastly, those services of a local authority that include explicitly 'environmental' work, such as landscaping, maintenance of parks and gardens, countryside management and waste collection of disposal can all ensure that sustainable development aims are expressed through their strategies and work programmes.

AWARENESS RAISING AND EDUCATION

To play an active role in the Local Agenda 21 process, local people need to know about the issues of sustainable development and to become aware of the impact their own lifestyles have on the environment. Awareness-raising activities must try to reach all sections and all age groups within the community and can include:

✪ Support for formal environmental education through schools and colleges;

✪ Programmes of visits and talks to local voluntary groups;

✪ Awareness-raising events, which get the environmental message across in a fun and informal way, highlighting the opportunities for practical action and behaviour change.

In addition, it is important to provide published information, ensuring that local people can find out about key environmental problems and events, the most significant pressures on their local environment and what their local authority is doing for the environment.

CONSULTING AND INVOLVING THE GENERAL PUBLIC

To ensure Local Agenda 21 plans truly reflect the needs and views of the whole of a local community it is necessary to open up the decision-making processes of a local authority and ensure representatives from all key local sectors can plan their part in the democratic process of drawing up a Local Agenda 21. Public consultation mechanisms should be set up aiming to cover the whole community. Two examples of consultation mechanisms are:

✪ Environmental Forums, where a range of organisations and individuals can discuss and propose solutions to environmental problems.

✪ Focus Groups of small numbers of people who share a common interest (for example, people without cars) can discuss and provide views on specific local issues which can be fed into the main consultation process.

Other ways of determining the views of local people on their area's environment include techniques such as 'Planning for Real' - where expert facilitators work with a group to try out different approaches to real life planning problems, and Parish Map projects, where people produce a visual map of the things they value in their local community and its surroundings.

Practical projects involving feedback mechanisms can also be useful tools. For example, EcoFeedback is a project designed to raise energy awareness in the community, which has been run by a number of local authorities in the UK. EcoFeedback aims to make householders more aware of the energy they use at home, helping them to use energy more efficiently, so protecting the environment and lowering fuel bills. Global Action Plan is another project being promoted to UK local authorities, which helps people become more aware of the environmental consequences of their lifestyles, through information and feedback.

PARTNERSHIPS

A successful Local Agenda 21 must involve partnerships with the local community. As well as the consultation mechanisms described before, there will often be a need for more formalised meetings on environmental issues. These may take the form of traditional seminars, conferences and working groups, but one specific type of partnership group worth highlighting is a Round Table. This Canadian concept sets up a standing body of partners - not a one-off meeting - composed of senior representatives of local and/or central government, business and environmental interest. Round Tables are non-hierarchical - that is the people involved are equal partners and no one partner may dominate or 'own' the meetings. Round Tables are not just discussion groups, they are consulted by decision making bodies and are often asked to propose policies, guidance and initiatives.

A series of cross-sectoral Round Table groups have been set up by the Local Government Management Board to look at a range of issues seen as central to the Local Agenda 21 process. The Round Tables are producing a set of guidelines for sustainable development in seven areas:

✪ Community Participation
✪ North/South Linking for Sustainable Development
✪ Greening the Local Economy
✪ Education and Awareness-Raising
✪ The Transport/Planning Interface
✪ Green Purchasing and Compulsive Competitive Tendering, CCT
✪ Sustainability in Rural Areas

The resulting guidance notes are being circulated to all UK local authorities to be used in developing Local Agenda 21 programmes.

Another example of partnerships that are working is the UK Environment City Model, now running in four British cities, which encompasses many of the elements of partnership working groups and consultation mechanisms that have already been mentioned. The Environment City model includes the establishment of eight specialist working groups, with representation from the local authority, local business and the voluntary sector. Specialist working groups, each tackling a specific environmental issue, plan, put forward and monitor environmental policies and practice. The use of specialist working groups is a feature of many Council environmental strategies throughout the UK.

Partnerships should not be exclusive to the local, or even national area. There is much to be gained by encouraging

"Sustainable Lifestyles " - Local Authorities can raise awareness and highlight opportunities for behaviour change

international partnerships between local authorities such as twin towns, friendship and working links, to increase the sharing of knowledge on sustainable development. In particular partnerships with towns and cities in developing countries can provide good opportunities for information exchange. Towns in developing countries may benefit from accessing skills and resources in the 'developed' world, while sharing the lessons learnt from dealing with common problems, including urban deprivation and pollution. In Europe we can learn to appreciate the environmental dilemmas posed by the conflict between the need to create economic development, whilst being asked to preserve natural resources by countries who have already largely destroyed their own long ago. Such partnerships could be a real learning ground for developing a meaningful and practical approach to sustainability.

MEASURING, MONITORING AND REPORTING ON PROGRESS TOWARDS SUSTAINABILITY

To work towards sustainability, it is necessary to know and understand how our actions are affecting the environment and so threatening sustainability. Defining, collecting and sharing information about the environment must therefore form an important part of the Local Agenda 21 process.

The production of local State of the Environment reports, as well as providing data on the physical environment of an area, can include the views and values of the local community. State of the environment reporting should not be seen as a one-off exercise but should include processes for continually monitoring and updating the information base.

For sustainable development to be a coherent policy objective it is necessary to try to measure what progress is being made towards it. Sustainability indicators are measurable features which inform us whether we are becoming more or less sustainable. The UK National Sustainability Indicators project was commissioned by the LGMB and contracted to a consortium of consultants comprising Touche Ross Management Consultants, the United Nations Association Sustainable Development Unit and the New Economic Foundation, supported by a steering group of local authority officers and members.

The work has involved developing a framework for measuring sustainability at a local level using specific indicators.

The framework is currently being tested and refined in practice by six pilot authorities and four 'shadowing' authorities, all of whom are being assisted by consultants for a six month study. Each pilot and shadow authority will choose a selection of indicators, from the overall framework, which aim to provide baseline measurements to reflect aspects of our lifestyles which need to be changed in order to achieve a more sustainable society. Measuring changes from the initial 'benchmark' should provide tangible proof of changes in the quality of life.

The pilot and shadow authorities will set up or build upon existing community involvement processes and raise awareness of sustainable development in their communities. Each of the pilot/shadow authorities will need to assess:

✪ the relevance of chosen indicators in practice at the local level

✪ whether chosen indicators provide information for personal empowerment as well as information for action at the authority level

✪ how best to achieve cross-sectoral discussion and community participation in reporting on the indicators

✪ opportunities to link the indicators with other programmes, both within and outside the local authority's sphere of influence

Other more established ways of reporting on environmental issues include the Environmental Impact Assessment (EIA) of proposed projects or developments which allows environmental issues to be considered but comes too late in the decision process to look at alternatives. Once a proposal has been put forward (for example to build a new road) the assessment will only be able to suggest how to relieve environmental impacts (such as landscaping works) rather than taking a broader view of the issue (which might have shown no need for the road in the first place).

Strategic environmental assessment of plans and policies can also be carried out. This will ensure that consideration is given to alternative ways of achieving objectives before any specific projects are put forward.

THE LOCAL AGENDA 21 PLAN

As we have seen, the Local Agenda 21 process should start from a commitment to sustainability and should involve progress in each of the six key areas of action outlined above. All six areas need to be addressed at the same time - running in parallel, not in sequence.

The UK guidance on Local Agenda 21 is asking each local authority in the UK to produce, as a minimum, a local strategy or action plan for sustainable development - The Local Agenda 21 Plan - and a short report outlining its progress in the six key areas, by the end of 1996.

The published document should be short, clear and accessible and should identify the main sustainability issues and aims for the area. It should also contain explicit objectives for both the state of the environment and for indicators of the quality of life in the area. The document should also state which organisations or sectors will take what actions (and by when) to work towards these objectives and how performance and achievements will be assessed. Finally, the document should also set out a review process for the whole programme.

CONCLUSION

In conclusion, the consolidation of environmental considerations into all local authority policy making and practice, combined with creating effective partnerships with people from all sections of the community will make real progress towards the development of Local Agenda 21, leading communities forward into a more sustainable future.

CASE 3 - JAPAN

Mr Saburo Kato, Director, Global Environment Programme,
Japan Environment Agency, Director ICLEI Japan, and member
Japan Local Agenda 21 Panel

"It is my pleasure to be able to report to you what is happening in Japan, with regard to the formation, implementation and preparation of national Agenda 21, and also Local Agenda 21. Basically, I would like to report to you, two things, one is the efforts or actions taken by national government, and secondly, the response of local governments in Japan.

In response to the Agenda 21 itself, in December last year, just six months ago, the government of Japan came up with Agenda 21 for Japan, it is called "National Action Plan for Agenda 21". This was compiled by all parties and peoples concerned in the equal collaboration. Of course, I will not go into details of the national Agenda 21 itself, but let me introduce some of the underlying philosophies which might be of interest to you. The first philosophy I would like to emphasise is that we are committed to making extensive efforts to construct a society which will allow sustainable development, a society with a reduced load on the global environment, and enhanced public awareness which is needed to change people's lifestyle to one which is, of course, more environmentally-friendly. The second philosophy I would like to emphasise is that we are committed to actively participating in, and contributing to, the creation of an effective international framework with regard to the conservation of the global environment, including financial mechanisms. The third philosophy I would like to emphasise is that we are committed to making efforts to promote environment related technology development and contributing to the capacity building of developing countries to address environmental problems through providing appropriate and well-planned Official Development Assistance (ODA), including the promotion of technology transfer. The fourth philosophy I would like to emphasise is that we are committed to ensuring international co-operation for observation, surveillance, and research which relate to the conservation of the global environment. The fifth point I would like to emphasise is the commitment to enhancing the level of effective co-operation among major constituents of society, including the Central Government of course, local authorities, business and non-governmental organisations.

With these philosophies in mind, an action plan was formulated about a half year ago, and in Chapter 28 just like Agenda 21 itself, there is a government commitment to assist local governments to formulate Local Agenda 21. Namely, in our Chapter 28 it is said that government will provide assistance for measures regarding voluntary and independent environmental conservation activities by local authorities. The government will also actively provide assistance to the activities of local authorities in the field of sustainable development, including assistance for the establishment of a Local Agenda 21, which gives due consideration to the specific characteristics of the individual localities, and commendation for local authorities who have shown remarkable results in environmental conservation. Thirdly, the government will provide assistance for international co-operation on the local government level, by such means as providing information to local authorities and their people in developing countries. Fourthly the government will further apply the experience and "know-hows" of local authorities to inter-governmental co-operation.

In accordance with the decisions made which were embodied in this action plan, the Environment Agency began to set up guidelines for Japanese local governments to formulate a Local Agenda 21 for themselves. In fact, the Environment Agency set up a study group which was composed of representatives of local governments, university professors and independent researchers, like myself. They met several times to formulate sensible guidelines for Japanese local governments on Local Agenda 21. Fortunately, just one week ago, the recommendations were formulated and the Environmental Agency have now adopted and published their recommendations, 'A Guide to Local Agenda 21' and, of course, this is rather a lengthy document perhaps for me to explain fully, but I would like to mention some of the major points which might be of interest to you. For instance, let me give you one example, in Japan the term "Agenda" itself is a little difficult for us to understand. For English speaking people, the term agenda may be easy to understand, but not for us, "agenda"? is rather difficult to translate and understand. Of course 21 is easy to understand, it relates to the 21st Century. So we have had to explain what "agenda" means, and additionally and perhaps more importantly, of course in Japan a number of local governments, prefectural governments and municipalities, have already formulated a variety of environmental management programmes and they are implementing such programmes. Then what would be the relationship between Local Agenda 21 and their existing environment management programmes? Such questions should be answered.

EPL J. Hilmes

Constructing a more sustainable society where the traditional meets the modern - Local Agenda 21 at work in Japan.

In the case of Japan we have, in a sense, two levels of local government - one is the prefectural level - we have 47 prefectures in Japan, and the other is the municipal level - we have some 3,300 municipalities, cities, towns and villages. Therefore we have had to provide guidance in regard to the hierarchy of the different levels of local government, on the formulation and implementation of Local Agenda 21. I am very happy to tell you that, already, five prefectures have formulated a Local Agenda 21 and also, as far as I know, four other local governments are in the process of formulating a Local Agenda 21 for their citizens. I sincerely hope that the guide, we, the Environment Agency, have produced for formulating a Local Agenda 21 will help many other local governments in Japan to formulate their Local Agenda 21 and to address the issue of sustainability. In

this connection I am quite happy to repeat the words spoken the President of the conference, the Lady Mayor of Heidelberg, to the effect that National Agenda 21 is not complete without Local Agenda 21. I do think her words are very important and, at the same time, I would like to fully support what was said by Jeb Brugmann, to the effect that local government should be more widely and strongly represented at major international meetings, to address the fate of humanity. I have a feeling that the era of national state diplomacy is coming to an end. I feel that local governments as well as NGO's should be given more opportunities to play a very, very important role, and in this connection, I do think Local Agenda 21 will be a milestone towards that objective."

CASE 4 - COLUMBIA
Mr Edgard Moncayo, Director, Mision Siglo XXI, Bogota

"I am from Colombia and am the manager of a non-governmental organisation which carries out research applied to regional urban subjects, including, of course, the subject of environmental management at the local and regional level.

First of all, some general points about Colombia to remind you of Colombia's position in the world and its general features from an economic, demographic and political point of view. Colombia is right on the equator and is a tropical country. However, the great majority of the country's cities, at least 90% of the cities and 90% of the population, are located in the Andean Region of the country. Columbia is a country which has all the bio-regions or natural ecosystems imaginable. It is a region dominated by the presence of three mountain ranges which go through the country from south to north. There is a vast and practically unpopulated area which consists of the country's eastern plains, with vast jungle areas, a coast on the Atlantic stretching 1,000 km and a coast on the Pacific which runs for another 1,000 km or so. There are human settlements in all the country's regions but they are concentrated mainly in the Andean area. Although Colombia is a tropical country, 90% of the population have to live in heated accommodation because they live at heights between 1,000 m and 2,500m.

To summarise, the great majority of the country's urban centres are located in this Andean area which occupies more or less only a third of the area of the country - almost two thirds of the country is practically unpopulated. The largest urban centre is the capital, Bogota, which as I will be explaining later is the city which has taken the lead in subjects of urban environmental management and applying the principles of Local Agenda 21. There is also the country's second city, Medellin, to the north of Bogota, the third city is Cali , on the Pacific coast, and the fourth city is Barranquilla, on the Atlantic coast. These four cities account for three quarters of the national economy and also at least three quarters of the country's total population.

I would like to offer some indicators, which are set out in Figs 3 and 4. to show the economic role which Colombia plays as I believe that, to a great extent, the environmental problems of the cities arise from the nature of the economic activity which is carried out in them. Colombia is a relatively industrialised country, some 32% of the gross national product can be attributed to the industrial sector. Its growth rates have been relatively high by Latin American standards, at least in the last few years, with growth rates from 1989 to 1994 which have not been below 2%, and inflation levels which have been steadily decreasing since 1991, now at approximately 20%.

As a result, Colombia is classified by the indicator which is calculated by the United Nations Human Development Agency, as a country of intermediate development. In terms of human development, Colombia holds 68th place in a league which includes 160 of the worlds major countries. Its level of social development is slightly higher than that normally associated with this level of economic development. In the last 20 years, the accumulated growth of Colombia has been 53.9, the highest in Latin America, that is at least among the large and medium size countries. Perhaps this is the only indicator in which we

rate higher than Brazil. The level of the participation of the industrial sector in the gross domestic product is around 32%.

As in almost all the other countries in Latin America and many developing countries, Colombia has experienced a rapid process of urbanisation and a rapid rural-urban transition. In the 1930s, 30% of the people lived in the cities and the remaining 70% in the countryside. Today, the situation has reversed; almost 70% live in the cities and the remaining 30% in the countryside and it is anticipated that, around the year 2000, this process will have been further consolidated and the country will have attained urbanisation rates close to 80%. (Fig 5).

Moving on to the pressures which the process of urbanisation places on urban environmental conditions. It should be noted that at the same time as this rural - urban transition, the country was also experiencing a rapid population transition; over this period the population growth rates have fallen from the 7% or 8% which were characteristic of the 1970s, to less than 3% at present. The accompanying Figs. 7,8, and 9, show how, due to the reduction in population growth rates, there is also a tendency towards reduced urban growth because of the effect on the growth of the population in cities. These diagrams also illustrate the phenomenon of population transition and the very significant reduction in the rates of births.

This is sufficient to place the country in geographic and economic terms and to try and derive, from this, some implications from the point of view of cities' environmental problems. There are at least three other phenomena to which I would like to draw attention; these are three structural processes which are moulding the features of the country's urban transformation and the features of the environmental problems which are arising within cities. The first of these structural trends which has taken place in the country over the last ten years is a very much accelerated and very deep process of decentralisation, not only from the political and administrative point of view, but also from the fiscal point of view. At present, all of the state governors at regional level and all of the 1,000 mayors corresponding to Colombia's 1,000 local authorities are chosen by direct popular election. Most of the functions and duties related to infrastructure, services delivery, basic education and also environmental matters have been transferred either to the mayors or to the state governors. This places the local authorities as the main actors in urban environmental management.

However, at the same time as this decentralisation process took place, the country adopted, 10 years ago now, a development model which is in line with many other Latin American countries based on what we will call the principles of economic neo-liberalism. The State is reducing its size and cutting down its intervention in the planning and general management of the economy. At the same time, there has been a process of economic "opening-up" in an effort to link the country more actively to the flow of international trade and, paradoxically, this has brought with it - as has happened in other Latin American countries - a reduction in social expenditure. The efforts needed to meet foreign debt commitments, and the efforts to concentrate investment in the industries which are to be made more efficient and more productive, has brought, as a result, an appreciable reduction in social expenditure. Eight years ago, social expenditure accounted for 40% of the central government's total expenditure and it is now scarcely 28%. So, at the same time as more responsibilities, more duties and more functions are being transferred to local government, the resources which the central State is transferring to local government are decreasing. This is despite the fact that participation of central government investment in the local and regional territories has increased from 0.5% to 2%. The first key point I would like to make is that there is little hope of successful environmental management and there will not be a greater role for local authorities in handling environmental problems if this process is not accompanied by the allocation of more resources. Generally, then, macro-economic policies go against greater transfer of resources to local authorities.

In Colombia, the handling of cities' environmental problems has developed in a way which is more or less characteristic of other Latin American countries. A preoccupation with environmental problems initially started in rural aspects, in the handling of natural resources, forests and water. The first institutions and legislation relating to the environment which emerged in the country were very much linked to the handling of these issues and had very little emphasis on urban environmental policies. This situation has however improved. Major pieces of legislation which concern urban matters have included measures to address environmental problems. It is increasingly being demanded that programmes relating to housing and to the infrastructure of domestic public services should have very explicit environmental components. This process, and these institutional and regulatory developments culminated in components of the new constitution, which Colombia adopted in 1991, setting out the right to a healthy environment as a fundamental right of every citizen. A series of principles for community participation in dealing with environmental problems, setting local government as the main

party responsible for urban environmental management were adopted resulting from the constitution of 1991, at the end of 1993, and the Ministry for the Environment was set up. A national environment system which includes, apart from the Ministry, an inter-ministerial council and a series of regional corporations which are the bodies responsible for carrying out national environmental policies at the regional and local level have been established. So each region and each municipal group, will have one of the 34 regional corporations.

I will now refer to the process of Local Agenda 21 in Colombia. After considering the presentation made by others the first consideration I would like to make is that in Colombia there is not, as in England or Australia or Japan, a national policy responsible for pushing forward and giving guidelines on Local Agenda 21. The majority of the initiatives which have been taken, even in the case of Bogota, which is a city which has advanced considerably in this process, are initiatives taken by a variety of bodies and not the government. These initiatives have been advanced by non-governmental organisations, advanced research centres and universities, to the point where practically all of the 12 initiatives which I have recorded to be in progress in Colombia have emanated from protagonists rather than the actual governments. This shows the need to undertake a much more aggressive campaign of awareness raising at all levels which has to start with the national government itself, if we are to push forward the Local Agenda 21 process.

In Bogota a process has been carried out which I think may be what we could call a model process, at least in the Latin American context. This model process has followed four defined stages: firstly, the formation of a body entrusted with management of the environment in the city; secondly the adoption of an urban environmental management plan; thirdly, the definition

Fig. 3

LATIN AMERICA AND CARRIBEAN GROWTH IN GNP									
(America Latine y el Caribe Crecimiento del Producto Bruto Interno)									
(% ON BASIS OF 1980 VALUES AND PRICES)									
	Tasas anuales de variación							Variación acumulada		
	1987	1988	1989	1990	1991	1992	1993	1981-90	1991-93	1981-93
America Latina y el Caribe	3.2	0.8	0.9	0.3	3.8	3.0	3.2	12.4	10.3	22.7
Paises exportadores de Petróleo	2.7	2.0	0.1	4.1	4.5	3.3	1.2	15.1	9.3	24.4
Bolivia	2.6	3.0	3.2	4.6	4.6	2.8	3.0	1.2	10.9	12.1
Colombia	5.6	4.2	3.5	4.0	1.9	3.6	4.5	43.6	10.3	53.9
Ecuador	4.8	8.8	0.2	2.0	4.7	3.3	1.5	20.4	10.0	30.4
México	1.9	1.2	3.3	4.4	3.6	2.6	1.0	17.9	7.2	25.1
Perú	8.0	(8.4)	(11.5)	(5.6)	2.1	(2.7)	6.5	(11.4)	5.8	(5.6)
Trinidad y Tobago	(4.6)	(3.3)	(0.5)	2.2	1.8	(0.6)	(1.0)	(19.6)	0.1	(19.5)
Venezuela	3.8	5.9	(7.8)	6.6	10.2	6.9	(1.0)	4.2	16.6	20.8

Source: CEPAL

of environmental priorities at the level of each of the 20 districts into which the city is divided and, finally, and this is a job in which we are co-operating, the organisation of a bank of environmental projects, using a geographical information system, to simplify management and investment in the 250 priority environmental issues which were identified for Colombia.

I would like to summarise in four points and that is, firstly, that although the main actors in environmental management , as has been highlighted repeatedly here - are the local authorities themselves, there must be a clear inter-relationship between their actions and the actions of the national government. Macro-economic policies and national policies may well nullify the efforts which are made at the local level, for example policies which reduce social expenditure or transfers and resources available for local areas. Secondly, in countries such as Colombia, an explicit urban policy is needed which attempts to make up for the wastage which arises from the overall processes of urbani-

extensive environmental diagnosis with less emphasis on initiatives and plans of specific action."

Fig 4

PRODUCTION/DISTRIBUTION STRUCTURE FOR GNP
(ESTRUCTURA DE LA PRODUCCION
DISTRIBUCION DEL PRODUCTO INTERNO BRUTO)
(% 1965-1990)

SECTOR	1965	1990
AGRICULTURA	27	17
INDUSTRIA Manufacturas	27 19	32 21
SERVICIOS etc.	47	51

Source: World Bank

sation and economic development. This could be along the lines of the regional fund which exists in the European Economic Community, something which does not exist in Colombia. Thirdly, what is needed is a more aggressive, and more sustained effort with regard to pushing forward the process of Local Agenda 21 in Colombia. The local authorities are not sufficiently familiar with this process and, as I have said, the majority of the initiatives have been taken by non-governmental organisations. I must mention that there is a city, a small city with a population of 100,000, which is called Buga, which has been chosen by ICLEI as one of around 20 cities in the world for the model communities programme, which is exemplary in the field of environmental management. Finally my last point relates to the fact that the majority of the work in Colombia has been done by research centres, universities and non-governmental organisations which has meant that it has been work of a theoretical nature. Greatest emphasis has been given to the research stage and to the preparation of very specific and very

Fig 5

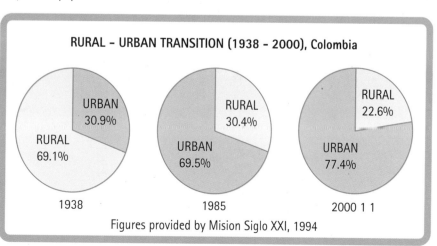

RURAL - URBAN TRANSITION (1938 - 2000), Colombia

1938: URBAN 30.9% / RURAL 69.1%

1985: RURAL 30.4% / URBAN 69.5%

2000 1 1: RURAL 22.6% / URBAN 77.4%

Figures provided by Mision Siglo XXI, 1994

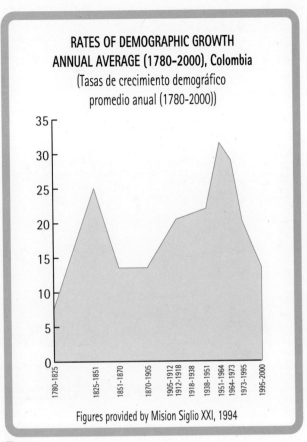

RATES OF DEMOGRAPHIC GROWTH ANNUAL AVERAGE (1780-2000), Colombia
(Tasas de crecimiento demográfico promedio anual (1780-2000))

Figures provided by Mision Siglio XXI, 1994

Fig. 6

URBANIZATION RATE COLOMBIA 1938-2025
(Tasa de Urbanizacion Colombia 1938 - 2025)

Figures provided by Mision Siglo XX1, 1994

Fig. 8

Fig. 7

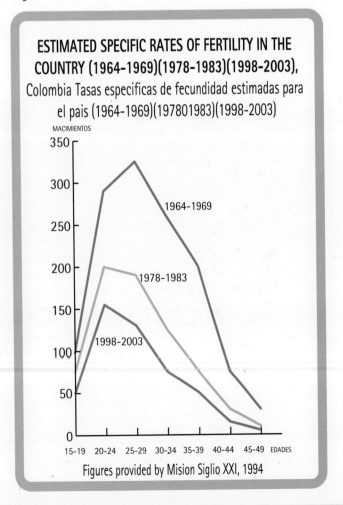

ESTIMATED SPECIFIC RATES OF FERTILITY IN THE COUNTRY (1964-1969)(1978-1983)(1998-2003),
Colombia Tasas especificas de fecundidad estimadas para el pais (1964-1969)(197801983)(1998-2003)

Figures provided by Mision Siglio XXI, 1994

"Local Agenda 21 can be seen as a way to bring together and mutually strengthen an authority's commitments to the environment, to local economic and social development and to local democracy. Many components of the Local Agenda 21 process may already be in place within a large number of local authorities and the key is to recognise old and new measures as part of this new sustainable development agenda, linking global and local issues meet" (Cllr J Harman, UK)

Local authorities are beginning to define their own sustainability strategies for the local level and in some cases a Local Agenda 21, focusing on initiatives that they themselves can influence through their statutory powers, responsibilities and enthusiasm. Local Agenda 21 can be approached in a variety of ways, for instance local authorities can initiate the process themselves or they can choose to co-ordinate community interest. It need not be a plan that can be put down on paper but it can be a process that is ongoing in a community. The six local authority case studies presented here give a good representation of the kind of initiatives that local authorities globally are undertaking.

LOCAL AGENDA 21 INITIATIVES
LOCAL AUTHORITY CASE STUDIES

1. HAMILTON - WENTWORTH, CANADA

Mr Jim Thoms, Commissioner of Planning and Development &
Mr Dale Turvey, Commissioner of
Transportation/Environmental Services, Regional Municipality
of Hamilton and Wentworth

2. THE CAJAMARCA, PERU

Luis B Guerrero Figueroa, Alcalde Provincial, Municipalidad de
Cajamarca

3.CHAING MAI, THAILAND

Miss Maey-Ing Amarangkul, City Clerk, Phuket Municipality
and formerly of Chaing Mai Municipality

4.GOTHENBURG, SWEDEN

Ms Kerstin Svenson, City Commissioner for the Environment,
Authority of Gothenburg

5.HARARE, ZIMBABWE

Mayor Charles Tawengwa of Harare City Council

6.HIELDELBERG, GERMANY

Ms Beate Weber, Lady Mayor of Heidleberg

7.AALBORG, DENMARK

(Including a report from the European Conference on
Sustainable Cities and Towns)

Kaj Kjaer, Mayor of the City of Aalborg

1. HAMILTON - WENTWORTH, CANADA

BUILDING A SUSTAINABLE COMMUNITY
HAMILTON-WENTWORTH'S
SUSTAINABLE COMMUNITY INITIATIVE

*Mr. Jim Thoms, Commissioner of Planning and Development &
Mr Dale Turvey Commissioner of Transportation &
Environmental Services, Regional Municipality of Hamilton-
Wentworth, Canada*

INTRODUCTION

Under the broad umbrella of sustainable development,
Hamilton-Wentworth has initiated various actions which are
changing the method of business in local government. A new
focus has been developed which is moving the Region towards
decisions that will help create a sustainable community.

Formally initiated in 1990, our sustainable community project
has been an ongoing effort for over four years. This project has
seen over 1,000 citizens become involved in a variety of activities
leading to the development of a community vision and a broad
strategy for making the vision a reality.

The focus of our talk today is to give you an overview of our
sustainable community initiative and where the project is heading
over the next few years. But before we get into the project we
would like to briefly describe Hamilton-Wentworth.

THE REGIONAL MUNICIPALITY OF HAMILTON-WENTWORTH

Located at the western end of Lake Ontario, Hamilton-Wentworth
is a community of just over 450,000 people. We are located
approximately 100 kilometres from Niagara Falls and about 75
kilometres west of Toronto.

Our region is part of the larger urban agglomeration called the
Golden Horseshoe. Running along the shore of Lake Ontario
this urban area encompasses almost 6 million people.

As the upper tier of Ontario's two tier municipal government
structure, Regional Council is responsible for providing water
and sewerage, major roads, public transit, police, social services,
public health services, economic development, and regional land
use planning. Our Region covers a large geographic area of over
270,000 acres and includes both a major urban concentration
and almost 100,000 acres of farmland. In the past the local
economy was dominated by manufacturing, in particular steel
production, which is concentrated here around the harbour.
However, over the last 10 years a change has occurred as the
steel industries restructure and reduce their labour force. The
largest employment areas are now in the service sector, with
the health care and research sector becoming one of the largest.

Although the perception of our community is one of smoke-
stacks and industry, it is also an area of many natural features.
The Niagara Escarpment which has been designated as a world
biosphere runs directly through the centre of the urban area.
Large tracts of Carolinian forest have been protected by the
local conservation authority, while in the rural areas there
remain almost 12,000 acres of wetlands.

Our community is a place with great diversity, opportunities,
and challenges. Like most North American cities our urban area
continues to sprawl further into the rural areas as more people
move away from Toronto. The local economy is going through
some very significant changes. Manufacturing will
no longer be the dominant employer in the Region. How our
community is dealing with these and other challenges is the
purpose of our talk.

WHY THE SUSTAINABLE DEVELOPMENT PROJECT?

The major reason why we embarked on the initiative started
with discussions around the development of the Region's capital
budget. There was a general feeling amongst members of the
management team that more comprehensive criteria were needed
to evaluate budget decisions. There was no corporate plan or
vision to guide decisions about what projects should be included
in the budget.

At the same time two of the Region's major long range planning
documents, the Official Plan for land use and the Economic
Strategy were coming due for review. Preliminary investigations
suggested that many directions were never achieved because of
a lack of overall community support. If new plans were to be
developed, it was recognised that they needed to be based on
community values and desires.

These were the three major reasons for starting the sustainable
community initiative. Essentially our goal has been to implement
a process which would lead to a community consensus about
the future of the Region and create partnerships for making
that desired future a reality.

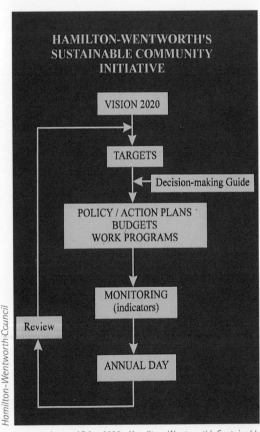

*Vision 2020 - Hamilton-Wentworth's Sustainable
Development Plan*

A CITIZENS TASK FORCE

The first step towards this goal occurred in 1990 with the creation of a citizens task force on sustainable development. This group was given the mandate to explore the concept of sustainable development and to develop, in cooperation with its fellow citizens, a future vision for the community.

When selecting the members for the task force we followed the round table model and tried to achieve a balance of different views and backgrounds. Eighteen members were selected with backgrounds in areas such as agriculture, health services, environmental groups, labour, business and industry. Members were selected not solely for their backgrounds but also because it was felt they would see a broad rather than narrow perspective when dealing with issues.

To ensure that no one interest dominated it was agreed by the members at their first meeting that all decisions would be a consensus.

Although the involvement in the project varied between members, and some resigned because the commitment was greater than anticipated, the overall success of the project is a direct result of the energy of these people. During their two and half year mandate they attended in excess of 70 meetings, forums, discussion groups, and other events. Everyone made an effort to carry the ideas back to their own organisations and increase awareness about competing values and the need for sustainable development. All of them made trade-offs to ensure that the final report kept the three components of sustainable development in balance; these being the environment, the economy and social and health factors.

BUILDING A COMMUNITY VISION

To develop a true community vision the Task Force implemented one of the most extensive community out-reach processes ever done by a municipality. Although the Task Force controlled the process, it was developed in consultation with an advisory committee made up of professionals from local agencies such as the Social Planning Council, and the District Health Council. The process embraced the following statement from the Brundtland Commission, "the creation of a sustainable community requires the widespread support and involvement of an informed public and of non-governmental organisations and industry".

The first phase of the public out-reach process focused on collecting community values. In the fall of 1990, seven town hall meetings were held, attended by around 150 people. Participants were led by Task Force members through a discussion designed to identify which issues were of concern to the community. In the meetings, people were asked to answer four questions. These were:

1) What do I like about life in Hamilton-Wentworth?
2) What detracts from life in Hamilton-Wentworth?
3) What should be done to improve life in Hamilton- Wentworth?
4) What values should guide development in Hamilton-Wentworth?

Although town hall meeting are an easy way to reach people, we felt that mechanisms were needed to reach people who would normally not attend a public meeting. An invitation was made to community organisations to hold small focus group discussions. Through this tool, citizens such as people living in emergency shelters, seniors, and the non-English speaking community had the opportunity to express their views. Their discussions were facilitated by student volunteers from the local university and were guided by the same four questions. Although the focus groups' process was probably the best way to create broader involvement, it was a relatively time consuming process. Only eighteen group discussions were completed whereas the original goal was to do fifty.

To foster community ownership of the project we organised eight vision working groups. Chaired by a Task Force member and involving an additional 35 citizens, these groups were mandated to prepare a report outlining visionary directions in an assigned topic area. The eight topic areas were selected by the Task Force and based on the major issues identified in the town hall meetings.

Hamilton–Wentworth Council

Blue box recycling programme serving 150,000 homes

Once these groups had completed their reports we held a major all-day community forum. At the forum the working groups presented their reports and listened to the comments from participants. The forum was an opportunity for all citizens to present their thoughts on a future vision. The crowd of over 250 people was enthusiastic but did criticise us for having too many speakers and not providing enough opportunity for people to contribute their views.

After the forum each working group revised its report, and presented it to the task force. With this, the task force had completed the first phase of its public outreach process. As you might imagine they had a large number of ideas and the challenge they now faced was to develop a consensus and present these thoughts in a concise form.

Because of the diversity of backgrounds, constructing a consensus took almost six months which was four months longer than planned. However, they did reach a consensus and developed Vision 2020 which reflects the identified issues and values of

Hamilton-Wenrworth Council

Combined sewer overflow tanks eliminate sewage problems in the Harbour

the community. This statement was eventually adopted by Regional Council as a guide to all future decision making. The vision statement is only four pages in length and when it was first released, many people in the community reacted in a negative manner. Both the media and about fifty citizens informed the Task Force that they felt the vision was not enough for one and half years of effort. This reaction suggested that we had created high expectations but more importantly had failed to effectively communicate what a vision statement is and that the Task Force was in fact still working on the detailed action needed to make the vision a reality.

The final phase of the outreach process was the identification of action needed to implement the vision. It was in this phase that an effort was made to involve as many outside agencies and staff from other regional departments as possible, in order to begin the process of building partnerships for implementation.

We organised 8 working groups called implementation teams and asked these teams to develop a report identifying the decisions necessary to make their assigned topic area of Vision 2020 a reality. The implementation teams differed from the original vision working groups, in their membership. They were made up of Task Force members, former volunteer vision working group members, regional staff and representatives from possible implementing agencies. For example, the team responsible for natural areas consisted of former working group members, representatives from the four local conservation authorities, and community groups like the naturalist club. Through these changes in membership it was hoped that the recommended actions would be based on what could be reasonably achieved and more importantly a commitment would be developed for undertaking the recommended actions.

As with the working groups the efforts made by these 70 plus participants went beyond expectations. The final reports were both well researched and prepared documents. An unexpected benefit was a lowering or breakdown of some of the traditional mistrust between the public and bureaucrats. A better understanding was developed about the direction of Vision 2020 by the bureaucrats and the public developed a better appreciation of some of the limitations of Regional Government's mandate.

To allow wider community input the task force hosted another all day community workshop. At this forum, participants, in small group discussions facilitated by implementation team members, discussed their ideas for action. Taking people's comments from the last forum, this workshop had no public speakers and consisted solely of small working group discussions. The focus of the day was on listening, not speaking.

After the community workshop, the task force again faced the challenge of building a consensus on what actions should go into their final report. After much discussion, they prepared two reports which contained over 400 recommendations for action. With over 300 citizens in attendance these reports were formally presented and adopted by Council in January 1993.

LONG RANGE POLICY AND PLANNING DOCUMENTS

With the completion of the Task Force's mandate, a number of activities have been occurring to bring the decision making process in line with the desired vision. The first major action has been the revision or development of long range planning and policy documents. The Official Plan for Land-Use, Community Economic Strategy, Transport Review, and Comprehensive Pollution Prevention Plan are all used to guide decision making and are currently being revised to reflect the goals of the vision statement. This is one step towards ensuring that decisions made about the long term future of our community reflect the directions of Vision 2020. For example, the new Official Plan is named Towards a Sustainable Region and contains almost 100 recommendations made by the Task Force and was officially adopted by Regional Council on June 7, 1994.

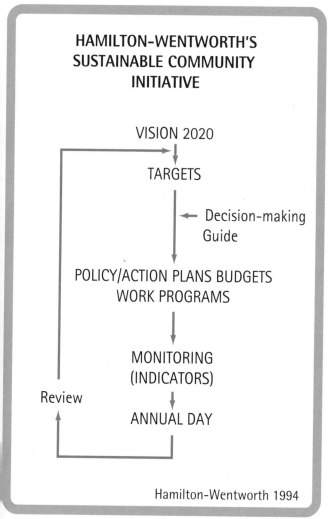

HAMILTON-WENTWORTH'S SUSTAINABLE COMMUNITY INITIATIVE

VISION 2020

TARGETS

← Decision-making Guide

POLICY/ACTION PLANS BUDGETS WORK PROGRAMS

MONITORING (INDICATORS)

Review

ANNUAL DAY

Hamilton-Wentworth 1994

Fig. 9

SPECIFIC SUSTAINABLE COMMUNITY INITIATIVES

The second major activity has been the actions of the Staff Working Group on Sustainable Development. This group comprised of senior staff from all departments and was mandated by Regional Council to develop mechanisms for formally integrating the principles of sustainable development and the vision statement into the process of developing of the capital budget. In response to this mandate the group prepared the Sustainable Community Decision Making Guide. Its purpose is to guide decision makers into considering the links between the economy, the environment and social issues and ensuring before a final decision is made that all possible implications are considered and dealt with. Currently we are in the process of revising the guide and preparing to conduct workshops for all Regional Staff on its use and purpose.

Another major activity centres on measuring and reporting on our progress in relation to the goals of Vision 2020. Although there will be a number of activities, the two major actions are the Indicators Project and the Annual Sustainable Community Day. The Indicators Project which is being done in partnership with McMaster University and with community dialogue will develop a set of indicators for measuring our progress in relation to Vision 2020. In addition to the indicators project we also have the annual sustainable community day program. At this day event the Region will report on what actions it has initiated to implement the vision and will ask community groups, individuals, and business to provide similar reports. It is a day for examining what is happening and deciding what should be the priorities in the coming year. The first day will be on June 11 and will involve over 125 organisations and businesses, and will be held at seven different sites in the Region. It is expected that between 500 to 1,000 citizens will attend the day.

The final major activity is the development of the Vision 2020 Implementation Guide. This report is being prepared by the Staff Working Group on Sustainable Development and presents detailed plans of action for implementing the 400 recommendations made by the Task Force. It also serves as a catalogue of action, as it summarises existing efforts which already fit with the directions of Vision 2020. It is expected that a final version of this report will be completed by September 1994.

The sustainable community initiative can be summarised in Fig. 9, Hamilton and Wentworth's Sustainable Community Initiative. Vision 2020 has provided us with a destination. Projects, like the Official Plan, and the Vision 2020 Implementation Strategy outline the specific mechanisms for moving towards that new destination while the Decision Making Guide ensures these strategies balance the three legs of sustainable development. The Indicators Project provides us with the tools for measuring whether ongoing activities are truly moving us towards the desired vision and the Annual Day creates an opportunity for the community to examine the progress and decide what should be the priorities for the coming year.

CONCLUSION

Through its sustainable community initiative our community has
started the process towards change in the operation and purpose
of Regional Government. The community vision process has
created a focus or goal against which we can measure all decisions
made by government, business, community groups, and individuals.
The community, as a whole, has been given the opportunity to
be part of the decision making process and consequently influence
the future of our community.

Although there is still a long way to go before we become the
sustainable community of Vision 2020, a solid foundation has
been created through the visioning process. From this foundation,
structural change and changes in decision making are occurring
and will continue to occur throughout Regional Government.
Within Regional Council we are increasingly seeing the debates
giving more consideration to the future and to whether decisions
truly fit the vision statement. The response by groups and
businesses to participating in the first annual sustainable
community day suggests an increasing number of people are
thinking and talking about sustainable development.

Whether Hamilton-Wentworth will move beyond the stage of
talking about sustainable development and into a phase involving
more serious commitment, will only be answered over time.
The process has created a lot of momentum and energy and
one thing's for sure, it won't end quickly.

2 - THE MUNICIPALITY OF CAJAMARCA

DEMOCRACY, CO-OPERATION AND THE SUSTAINABLE DEVELOPMENT PLAN

Luis S Guerrero Figueroa, Mayor Municipality of Cajamarca

This paper summarises the main points of the experience of the Provincial Municipality of Cajamarca (Peru): democratisation, co-operation and the sustainable development plan. It provides an example of the progress made by the local government with three initiatives which are currently being developed.

NATIONAL AND LOCAL CONTEXT

Since 1990, Peru has experienced a period of economic, political and institutional change, within a framework of a grave recession, growing poverty and persistent violence. To face this crisis, the national government is reorganising the State and applying a severe structural adjustment programme to the economy.

The crisis of legitimacy for national political and judicial institutions, prevalent in recent years, has not affected municipal institutions. All the new social participants (women's movements, country patrols, organisations for small businessmen, etc.) have identified with their municipalities and together are prepared to face the crisis.

This is the case of the province of Cajamarca. Situated in the Department of the same name in the northern sierra of Peru (between 1,600 and 4,188 metres above sea level), it has an urban population of almost 100,000 inhabitants and a rural population of 200,000. Cajamara city is an intermediate city where the rural activities of the province which are central to the functioning of the city are brought together in all of the city's operations, urban and rural.

Cajamarca's main economic activity is agriculture and the raising of livestock followed by commerce, mining and tourism.

Social indicators situate the population of the province among those least protected in the country. There is a shortage of both public and private services providing the necessary infrastructure and equipment for the main services (electricity, water and drainage) and of those supporting social health, education and housing services.

INITIATIVES

It is in this context, that the current municipal administration began a period of government in April 1993, its main aims are as follows: democratisation of political decisions, inter-institutional co-operation and the formulation of a provincial sustainable development plan.

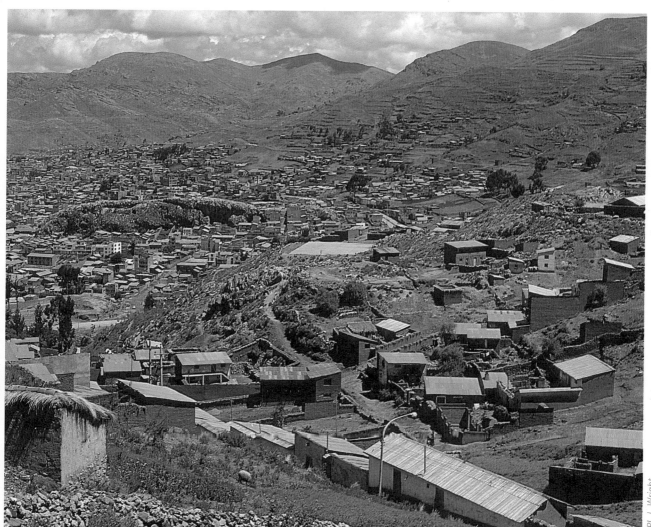

The highlands of Peru - rural activities are central to the functioning of the city (Cuezco, Peru)

EPL L. Wright

DEMOCRATISATION OF THE PROVINCIAL COUNCIL

On commencing our administration period, we proposed that the population of the city, the rural villages and the remote communities should participate in the decision-making of their local government. For this, we had to first deal with the limitations of our laws that had previously failed to define the duties at the different levels of government or the mechanisms for their election.

Far from constituting an obstacle to achieving our wish for democratisation, this legal vacuum became a catalyst. For example, this situation avoided potential problems of centralism within our Provincial Municipality, which could have basically focused on the problems of the city, which with 70% of the population living in rural areas, would be unacceptable.

The democratisation of the Provincial Council began by dividing the city into 12 districts and 64 less populated areas. In July 1993, general elections were held throughout the province, enabling local leaders to present their governmental plans and their prospectuses.

The quantitative and qualitative expansion of local leadership has provided an opportunity to strengthen the decision-making powers held by the basic organisations and to create a prior condition that the districts and their mayors should work in a co-ordinated manner.

We also set up the "Provincial Assembly of District Mayors" which is chaired by the Deputy Mayor and meets once a month in each district to discuss the respective problems of the host district and to draw up individual plans. We also set up the "Provincial Assembly for the Less Populated Areas and Local Mayors."

The local leaders are currently participating more by means of a Training Programme in which they present their initiatives and projects for the Provincial Sustainable Development Plan. The local mayors provide a direct channel for participation in setting priorities and identifying projects and investment. Their participation is demonstrated in the increase in the number of measures for the recovery and conservation of natural resources in the rural area and the improvement of the urban environment.

INTER-INSTITUTIONAL CO-OPERATION FOR SUSTAINABLE DEVELOPMENT.

A further initiative of the current administration is the co-operation of all social and political participants in Cajamarca in drawing up the Provincial Sustainable Development Plan. We are interested in developing a democratic culture for dialogue and participation for the execution of short, medium and long-term agreements. In this connection, we affirm that co-operation is a very necessary strategy, policy and methodology for bringing together all those who ought to be involved in the development of their nation and it is the most appropriate means of exercising local government.

The Council promoted the formation of the "Inter-Institutional Co-operation Board" which was set up in June 1993. It operates on the basis of the themes set out in the Provincial Sustainable Development Plan. There are six themes: urban environment, natural resources, agricultural and livestock production, production and employment, cultural and tourist, education and culture, and population, women and the family. The second meeting of the Co-operation Board was held on 19 January 1994 to discuss the main features of the Plan.

The theme boards provide technical mechanisms for drawing up policies and development proposals for the Provincial Sustainable Development Plan. One representative for each institution and municipal officials and councillors responsible for that area participate on each Theme Board.

The councillor chairing the Municipal Committee for Co-operation and Institutional Development is responsible for the general co-ordination of the various boards. The various Theme Boards also have their own chair who co-operates with the committee chair.

On the basis of the proposals submitted by the six Theme Boards, the Provincial Plan for Sustainable Development of the Province of Cajamarca has been defined as a means of *"generating well-being for the population within its own scope, by combining efforts made by the public and private institutions and the basic organisations, and combining resources and potential within an ecological, social and economic equilibrium. This is to be carried forward by the local government which is the institution promoting development and carrying out this process in an harmonic and self-sustained manner".*

The experts of the public and private institutions, NGOs , Government, basic organisations and local councils meet regularly to put forward policies, and to co-ordinate and agree on the execution of the projects they have in their portfolios. The Co-operation Board aims to arrive at common and central policies; it also seeks to optimise human, material, economic and professional resources in the province.

The 72 institutions comprising the Board have approved a preliminary version of the Plan. This Plan will be discussed again later in 1994 to approve a final version and submit it for the judgement of the citizens by referendum. Voting on the document will be preceded by a discussion and debate on all the societal responses and requests. The process that has begun is leading to a feeling that a firm "base of political will" has been created to work for the common good in the long term and that a feeling of political stability will exist in Cajamarca, which will endure to the year 2010.

MODEL OF ENVIRONMENTAL MUNICIPAL MANAGEMENT

We call ourselves the "First Ecological Municipality of Peru", because we believe that the theme of the environment is a central theme of the municipality. Just as no governor can fail to talk about the importance of peace, the theme of the environment is vital to humanity. In Cajamarca, the theme of the environment impinges upon the entire operation of the Co-operation Board. The strategies established to consolidate an environmental management and sustainable development model have included the following initiatives:

The Natural Resources and Agricultural and Livestock Production Co-operation Board has made progress in drawing up environmental development strategies and a programme for the development of a main drainage area in the province. Within this framework, the work of all the institutions has been facilitated to obtain more areas for land conservation, and municipal tree nurseries, as well as new funding mechanisms. The provision of machinery, other inputs and labour by the municipality facilitates these initiatives.

The Environment and Urban Development Board has drawn up a health package for Cajamarca, a refuse collection programme, and a parks and gardens improvement programme with a plan to sow more than 80,000 seedlings in the streets and parks. Projects have also been drawn up for a city ecological belt, urban expansion areas, rainwater drainage and plans for archeological and tourist areas.

The search for a healthy environment and the operation of the mining tax (tax on mining companies received by the province but deducted by the central Government) have also been topics upon which the residents of Cajamarca have had to seek agreements which overcome ideological and political differences.

In December 1993, the inhabitants and institutions demanded a tax and drew up a basic agreement with the mining companies operating in the province to avoid environmental contamination. A fair price for the farmers' land and protection for those areas supplying Cajamarca with water were agreed. Effective support for municipal works was also demanded on the part of the mining companies. The creation of an environmental authority at the provincial, district and drainage area level has required concerted action by civilian society and the State. At the same time, for this action to work, the populations needed to specify their requirements and their claims also needed to be assured a certain level of credibility in order that their more immediate requirements could be met.

AWARENESS AND ENVIRONMENTAL EDUCATION

Giving priority to the environment means establishing a long-term education policy directed mainly towards children and young people, together with a short-term policy intended for producers and institutions. A sustainable development programme needs people who have been educated on values of fairness, peace and a desire to conserve natural resources.

The provincial action plan for children is supported by UNICEF and was drawn up by the Committees for the Population, Women and the Family and Education and Culture, with support for the programmes by the Ministry for Education. It includes plans to improve educational infrastructures, provision of young people's homes, the reopening of libraries, student exchange programmes and for news programmes on the environment on all the broadcasting media.

Emphasis is being placed on training farmers and small businessmen to increase their capabilities and to involve them in the conservation of the natural resources. The local mayors, the council experts and the officials of the various institutions are also being trained in various areas.

PARTICIPATION OF INTERNATIONAL CO-OPERATION

International co-operation is a strategic component of environmental management. It is both necessary for identifying the necessary institutional and political aspects of the process and for increasing available resources (financial, human and material), which will facilitate the establishment of the programmes and projects.

CONCLUSIONS

Our proposals will be viable if there is institutional support and development. Our municipalities do not have clear and precise rules for directing their current organic style of administration and structure. They are over-directing and bureaucratic structures and lack rationalisation capabilities. The Council should be and is by nature able to promote development. For our aims to be achieveable a real process of decentralisation is necessary in three basic areas: a) strengthening and institutional development of local governments; b) democratic organisation of regional governments; and c) the political will of councillors to transfer power and resources to the issue.

It is in this context that an event of this nature is of vital importance in analysing the challenges of environmental development and the democratisation of local governments in developing countries.

3. CHIANG MAI, THAILAND

LOCAL AGENDA 21 AND
ENVIRONMENTAL PLANNING GUIDELINES
PHUKET AND CHIANG MAI, THAILAND
Ms. Maey-Ing Amarangkul, City Clerk, Phuket
Municipality and formerly of Chaing Mai Municipality

Thailand is a newly industrialised country. In developing our nation, we use many resources that cause imbalances in the natural environment. At present, Thailand faces an environmental crisis. Ecological threats such as air and water pollution have emerged as a result of an increasing population, rapid urbanisation, and advancements in technology. These problems are growing, and are affecting more humans and their well-being each day that they are ignored. The hazards are especially relevant to urban and surrounding areas. Thus, local organisations in Thailand, especially municipalities, must play an important role in managing the local environment.

Like many other countries, Thailand has generally neglected the environment in its plans for development. In the past, the main goals of development were economic growth and improvement in health and education. The environment, if it was considered at all, was a low priority issue.

Fortunately, the Thai government now realises the importance of the environment and of natural resource management, and has thus included an environment policy in its economic development plan. The present plan is the government's seventh and is effective from 1992 to 1996. It includes a clear policy for long-term environment preservation and natural resource management with an emphasis on the people's participation. Municipalities are one unit of the local administration which involve the people in management and administration in all areas. Their objectives include improving the quality of life and promoting the appropriate conditions for the areas. In 1992, seven Thai municipalities joined together in a project to develop and apply environmental planning guidelines for community priority-setting on environmental issues. Stakeholder groups were established with municipal support to engage residents and key sectors in the priority-setting process. Specific projects are now being funded to address the identified priorities. Fundamental strategies and guidelines have been set by government agencies in cooperation with active municipal leaders and NGOs.

URBAN ENVIRONMENTAL MANAGEMENT SYSTEM

The Urban Environmental Management System must include an environmental policy statement, an environmental action plan, and an administrative structure, personnel and budget.

ENVIRONMENTAL POLICY STATEMENT

The Environmental Policy Statement (Fig 10) is the guiding policy for the action plan.

- ✪ The Statement requires the **Stated Commitment of Local Decision-Makers**. Administrators of the municipality are responsible for forming an environmental policy.

- ✪ The Policy must be Supported by Municipal Council and Staff. In order to successfully implement the policy, the Municipal Council and Staff must agree to follow its guidelines.

- ✪ **Specifying development target groups.** The policy should identify target groups and specify objectives for developing them.

- ✪ **Information to related agencies and local people.** The municipality should inform local people and organisations about the policy and about its expectations from implementing the policy.

- ✪ **Need to be adjusted and evaluated.** The policy must be adjusted and evaluated when necessary.

ENVIRONMENTAL ACTION PLAN

The Environmental Action plan, (Fig. 11); includes:

- ✪ **Integration of Municipal and Provincial Plans.** The provincial and municipal plans should correspond. The municipality's action plan should be included as part of the provincial plan.

- ✪ **Raising consciousness.** In making this plan, we should emphasise the process of raising awareness among the people, and involving them in presentation and development.

- ✪ **Protection and cure.** The plan should seek to both prevent and solve problems.

- ✪ **Participatory.** In forming the plan, both the decision-makers and those individuals who are affected by the problems should be involved.

- ✪ **Rooted in local needs and problems.** The plan should serve the needs and problems of the local community.

THE BROWN AGENDA

The Brown Agenda addresses problems that urgently need to be solved, such as water pollution, drainage, solid and special waste, air pollution, and environmental health.

THE GREEN AGENDA

The Green Agenda addresses problems that, whilst not as serious as the Brown Agenda, still need to be solved. Most of it is concerned with prevention and management, including traffic and transportation, city greening, visual pollution, slums, land misuse and destruction of natural resources.

ACTORS IN URBAN ENVIRONMENTAL MANAGEMENT

Actors should form a local partnership, because the objective of Local Agenda 21 is to promote sustainable development in the local areas. Thus, we need a partnership of all the stakeholders in the community. (Fig. 12)

ENVIRONMENTAL POLICY STATEMENT

* Stated Commitment of Local Decision-makers.

* Supported by Municipal Council and Staff.

* Specifying development target groups.

* Publicly declared to related agencies and local people.

* Need to be adjusted and evaluated

UEGP, Bangkok, 1994

Fig. 10

STRUCTURE/PERSONNEL/BUDGET

* Workable mechanism responding to stated policies.

* Integrated into Municipal Development Committee and Municipal Development Plan.

* Strengthening internal and external coordination.

* Own budget, local support, central government fund.

UEGP, Bangkok, 1994

Fig. 13

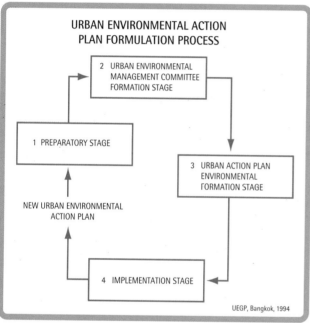

URBAN ENVIRONMENTAL ACTION PLAN FORMULATION PROCESS

UEGP, Bangkok, 1994

Fig. 11

GOOD MANAGEMENT SYSTEMS

* Understood and accepted by various partners.

* Taking protective measures rather than curative.

* Responding to stated policies.

* Dynamic and flexible.

UEGP, Bangkok, 1994

Fig. 14

THE STRUCTURE OF EACH GUIDELINE TOPIC

PROBLEMS

Characteristics and
Causes of Problems
* Physical
* Economic
* Social
* Management

1

ACTIONS

* General Strategies
* Alternatives for Actions
* Related Laws

2

USEFUL EXAMPLES 3

* Principles and Factors for Success
* Names and Addresses of Contacts

4 HELPS

Governmental Organizations
Academic Institutes
Non-Governmental
Organizations

* Planning and Research
* Training
* Finance

UEGP, Bangkok, 1994

Fig. 15

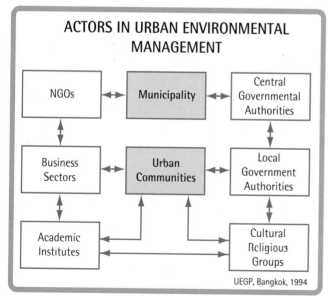

ACTORS IN URBAN ENVIRONMENTAL MANAGEMENT

UEGP, Bangkok, 1994

Fig. 12

Municipalities and urban communities, in the heart of management organisation, should cooperate with NGOs, business sectors and academic institutions. These groups should be supported by central governmental authorities, local governmental authorities, and cultural and religious groups. In conclusion, participation from every sector at every phase of the plan is necessary to best serve the needs of the people.

STRUCTURE/PERSONNEL/BUDGET

✪ **A workable mechanism responding to stated policies.** The structure of the plan serves as a tool to effectively implement the policy. It should coincide with the structure of the Municipality's Development Plan.

✪ **Integrating the Municipal Development Committee and Municipal Development Plan.** In forming committees, we should select interested persons who believe in the plan in order to work efficiently and ensure the plan's success.

✪ **Strengthening internal and external co-ordination.** Personnel should aim to strengthen internal and external co-ordination.

✪ **Own budget, local support, central government fund.** The municipality should have its own budget with funds provided by both local support and central government finance. (Fig.13)

A GOOD MANAGEMENT SYSTEM

✪ should be **Understood and accepted by various partners.**

✪ should **Take preventative measures rather than curative.**

✪ should **Respond to stated policies.**

✪ should be **Dynamic and flexible because of the present environment situation.**(Fig. 14)

Chiang Mai is a beautiful city in the northern part of Thailand and attracts tourists from every corner of the world. Chiang Mai is now rapidly changing because of economic growth. The beauty of nature has been obscured by high-rise buildings and increasing population, slums, and traffic jams. We might say that because urbanisation is causing so many environmental problems, Chiang Mai could become a second Bangkok.

Development in the past was plagued by weaknesses in technical management. Now, we have guidelines for managing the local environment.(Fig. 15) To solve Chiang Mai's environmental problems, we are focusing on the urgent problems, or on the Brown Agenda, and are planning solutions such as constructing a water treatment plant, a main drainage system, a garbage disposal area or sanitary landfill and an incinerator and composting scheme. On the other hand we are also looking forward and studying the environmental problems which require careful planning in order to successfully prevent them occurring in the future. Projects such as city greening, improving the built environment, slum upgrading, land use planning, and natural resource management are currently being developed.

Managing the local environment can be achieved by moving towards a participatory environmental action plan. By involving others, the plan will become more effective and more focused on sustainable development. In the case of Thailand, specifically Chiang Mai, plans for a GTZ Project coincides with projects from the Organisation of Urban Development and Municipal Staff. It also co-operates with NGOs.

Local Agenda 21 in Chiang Mai and the rest of Thailand needs local administrators to take much more interest in environmental problems in addition to a sincere will to solve these problems. In the end, we would like to be able to say that politics can go together with the environment.

In the year 1996, Chiang Mai will be 700 years old. At that time we will have many activities in celebration, including numerous activities on environmental management. We would like to welcome you to visit Chiang Mai.

A REPORT ON ENVIRONMENTAL ISSUES IN THE CITY OF CHIANG-MAI, THAILAND

I A. GENERAL INFORMATION

As population increases and economic activity accelerates, so advancing technology is leading to environmental problems. All over the world, decision-making in the nineties will focus upon the environment. The future of humankind is threatened by the deterioration of the global environment.

In a developing country, the fast expansion of communities leads to unbalanced development, resulting in environmental problems as well as social and cultural ones. Thailand is also affected by these, and Chiang Mai is an example of an urban community experiencing changes. Problems remain unsolved and may lead to environmental disasters at the local, national and even global level.

B. INTRODUCTION

Background Information – The Urban City of Chiang Mai.
Chiang Mai is situated in the north of Thailand, 750kms from Bangkok and 310 metres (1,027ft) above mean sea level. It covers a land area of 40 square kilometres and the population census in March 1994 was 163,568, with a total of 65,239 households. The average temperature is 26.280 celsius. Chiang Mai is the centre of the northern region for the economy, trade, some industries, education, tourism and others. The regional function of the city is resulting in a rapid growth of the city, both in population and in urban area.

II CRISIS AND ENVIRONMENTAL MANAGEMENT

A. These urban environmental problems need solutions
immediately, generally in the short term.

1) Water pollution control
2) Drainage
3) Solid waste management
4) Air pollution

B. These groups of environmental problems need planning
and prevention generally in the longer term.

5) Traffic and transport
6) The built environment
7) Slum improvements
8) Land use planning

III   CHIANG MAI AND ENVIRONMENTAL IMPROVEMENTS

A. Water pollution

The Mae Ping is a major river passing through the city, which is the main water source of Chiang Mai.

PROBLEM: It is polluted because of the many dwellings without proper sanitation established on both side of the river.

IMPROVEMENTS: A sewerage system is proposed beside the Mae Ping River with a sewage treatment plant located in the west of the city.

B. Drainage

PROBLEM: Floods occur almost once every two years as a result of heavy rain associated with the monsoon. (The average annual rainfall for the northern region is approximately 1240mm).

IMPROVEMENTS: Improvements plus extensions to the limited existing drainage system are proposed.

Muang Chiang Mai general plan 1997 - Dept. of Town and Country Planning.

C. Solid Waste Management

PROBLEMS: The collection system is one of the major problems in solid waste management in developing countries. Insufficient collection vehicles and lack of disposal facilities are some of the reasons.

IMPROVEMENTS: An incinerator and a new landfill site are proposed.

D. Air Pollution

PROBLEMS: Since the city is surrounded by mountains, affecting ventilation, still air is trapped and becomes heavily polluted, especially in areas of heavy traffic. (The number of vehicles, especially motorcycles, is exceptionally high at a multitude of about 100,000 registered vehicles).

Other causes of air pollution are: individual burning of garbage; construction activities; the dry season practice by farmers of burning dry rice straw and grass on rice-fields; the lighting of fire crackers during some festive seasons - this is especially the case in the annual floating celebration "Loy Krathong", when people usually use curved sheets of foam (a Fluorocarbon material) to make their individual floats resulting in accumulation of this

Exceptionally large volumes of traffic in all of Thailand's major cities cause heavy pollution (Bangkok, Thailand)

EPL J. Holmes

waste material which can only be disposed of by burning.

IMPROVEMENTS: The authorities have been very successful in their campaign for people to use alternative materials such as banana leaves and bark.

E. Traffic and Transport

PROBLEM: The traffic problem arises because of narrow roads, lack of parking space, and not enough road space. Illegal side-walk vendors are an additional cause of traffic jams, especially on narrow roads.

IMPROVEMENTS: Authorities are successfully eliminating illegal sidewalk vendors, especially in roads near markets resulting in wider pavements for pedestrians. It is proposed to improve mass transit. Computerised systems for traffic signals, the extension of some roads and widening of others are proposed.

F. Built environment

PROBLEM: Historically significant structures such as temples can still be seen everywhere in the old city. Part of the growth of the city involves constructing new buildings, and additional public facilities, sometimes immediately beside older buildings or ruins. Without proper consideration of the environment, the nature and culture of the community can be destroyed. Huge advertisement billboards are increasingly an eyesore to local people.

IMPROVEMENTS: In the conservation areas of the city, inside the moat, there are regulations requiring a particular architectural roof style; the Lanna-Thai roof style. Also no building should be higher than 12 metres.

G. Slum Improvements

With slum upgrading it should be possible to create living conditions that are at least healthy and safe.

H. Land Use Planning

PROBLEMS: The concentrated location of some schools, office buildings and department stores in certain areas has proven a disadvantage, especially by creating traffic jams.

IMPROVEMENTS: The Chiang Mai city planning by-law, effective since 1985, specifies the separation of areas for residential, commercial, light industrial, government, institutional, religious, recreational and open space. It also lays down the basis for the preservation and conservation of the area, for example no cinema or factory may be built in the area and near old temples and buildings should not be more than 12 metres high

4. GOTHENBURG, SWEDEN

LOCAL AGENDA 21 INITIATIVES; THE GOTHENBURG CASE
Ms Kerstin Svenson, City Commissioner for the Environment,
Authority of Gothenburg, Sweden

The Swedish people have a long tradition of close relationships with the environment. This has been an asset in recent decades as strong social impact on the environment has led to grave threats to our common future. Sweden has been in the forefront combatting the environmental problems, illustrated for example at the UN Environment Conference in Stockholm 1972.
But our initiatives have not been sufficient. We have only recently become fully aware of the impacts of our lifestyle and resource management. When these questions have been demonstrated, for example at the Rio Conference, we have been eager to address the problems. The Swedish government was the first in the world to have Agenda 21 translated, which was completed by October 1992, and there was a strong recommendation from the government to the local authorities to take action for a Local Agenda 21.

The response from the local authorities has been very strong! Today over 70 percent of the Swedish local authorities have decided to work out a Local Agenda 21 of their own! My city, Gothenburg, adopted a project plan in December 1993.

Gothenburg is the second largest city in Sweden with 435,000 inhabitants. The Gothenburg Region has 735,000 inhabitants. The city is located on the west coast of Sweden at the mouth of the Gota Rover. In many ways it is the Liverpool of Sweden with trade, shipping and industry as the main commercial activities. In recent years new technology, services and education have been the fastest growing employers.

Sweden has a geology which is very sensitive to acidification, and this is especially true on the west coast, where the soil layer is thin. The impact of West European emissions of sulphur and nitrogen has been severe. Gothenburg is located at the intersection of several valleys, giving a local climate which is sensitive to pollutant concentration from our own industry and traffic exhausts. We have therefore had obvious reasons to take action early for the protection of the environment.

Several of the environmental protection issues have been worked at for a couple of decades, often with success. Sulphur dioxide SO2 and particles in the air have been reduced by some 90% in twenty years, as has the content of heavy metals in the sludge from sewage treatment. An old Gothenburg tradition has been to find consensus and co-operation between the political parties and with business and industry. That tradition is also valid in our environmental work. A couple of the special projects which involve working together with business and industry are "Clean out" - a project working directly with industry to reduce hazardous waste and sewage - and "Chemical sweep" - exchanging environmentally hazardous chemicals for less dangerous substances in co-operation with wholesale and retail traders. In these projects the city acts as a catalyst - the local authority has marked out the targeted direction of the environment policy and offers the means for finding solutions that will eventually offer a pay-back to the company.

In recent years we have more and more turned to projects dealing with individuals' attitudes and consumption patterns. Right now we are publishing the third edition of the Eco Handbook. The main purpose of the Eco Handbook is to make people aware of the fact that we are all a powerful force in the work of improving the environment: "Green grass depends on the grassroots". By making conscious environmental demands on the goods we buy, we can for example speed up progress towards more environmentally safe products. The goal is to make people change their way of living to a more environmentally friendly way, based on eco-cycles and economising on resources. The handbook is supported by no less than 16 municipal departments and companies.

Projects dealing with consumption patterns -promoting environment-friendly products

The city has adopted a Waste Plan, addressing with the challenges for a sustainable society. The organic wastes from households should be treated so that the nutrient content is recycled. The means for this is composting, with emphasis on local handling, near the source, which is the household. Another eco-cycle related trend is to reclaim materials from waste. The system in Gothenburg is based on separation at source. So far, we have avoided big central sorting plants with hazardous working conditions.

The political decisions to take action against environmental problems have of course been important for the good-will of the city. But it is not enough to be open and truthful when it comes to changing attitudes and behaviour. The City Board has established an Environmental Policy Management Group with responsibility for the overall environment management of the local authority. It has developed an Environmental Policy, adopted by the City Council in 1992. The policy deals of course with the emissions from different activities of the city, but an important part of the policy is the question of the authority as a consumer. The city as a public consumer has a great effect on the market, and can, through environmental awareness push for the introduction of better management of natural resources. All municipal departments are supposed to develop environment management plans for their offices and to test them through environmental audits. The city has developed rules for environment-friendly purchasing, and through tough negotiations the costs have not increased, in spite of the lesser impacts on the environment!

We are also trying to introduce eco-balancing both in environmental protection/control and in physical planning. Matter and energy balances offer unique opportunities to describe and understand the management of natural resources. In our comprehensive plan for Gothenburg we have tried to pick out some parts of a matter balance and we have included a vision of the future Gothenburg, called "The competitive and sustainable city".

The question of developing and improving our policy-making is now being studied in a thorough discussion about our environment policy management in the broad sense. We have found business and industry are interested in aggressive environmental policy-making by the city. Our city district committees are deeply engaged in questions of sustainable development. Higher education is keen to co-operate in further development of the environmental work of the city. All in all we have the necessary prerequisites to go forward.

When we look back we can see that a broad view of environmental questions has had favourable results. We have not solved all the environmental problems, and we probably have the more difficult ones ahead of us. But we feel a strong backing from people and industry.

This gives us confidence when we approach the new challenge - Local Agenda 21! From the Rio Conference the urge for co-operation between business and the public was clear, we have interpreted it as a pre-requisite. It fits well with our tradition, and it has thus been natural to have representatives from business as well as from labour unions and NGOs in our steering group for Local Agenda 21.

Our idea is to have two platforms for the action plan. First we want to survey the present environmental situation and compare this with the needs of sustainability. This is already nearly done, as we have a long history of monitoring the environment. Secondly we want a broad discussion with all parties involved about the potential, appropriate and required actions to come closer to the sustainability. When we have all the suggestions we can draft an action plan which can be reviewed by all concerned before adoption by all parties in the steering group.

The formal action plan will not be enough to change attitudes and consumption patterns to the degree needed. But if we can combine the formal work with actions and campaigns that concern the grassroots in the city, and if we can encourage individual and group actions, then we can turn development towards a more sustainable direction. This means that Local Agenda 21 has to be a cultural project, not just an environmental and technical project.

Something has to be said about co-operation between local authorities! In Gothenburg we understood the importance of co-operation at an early point. We joined ICLEI from the beginning, and we have also had a long co-operation with twin cities like Tallin in Estonia and Crakow in Poland. Networks are developing fast in Sweden between different authorities. Gothenburg is also involved in a Regional Agenda for the Swedish west coast together with the county administration and the Gothenburg Region - so far the only example in Sweden of co-operation at the regional level. These networks and joint actions are important for sharing competence and experience. There might be a conflict in the fact that resources have to be taken from local work, but there are important gains to be harvested from national and international co-operation.

We are still only starting our work with Local Agenda 21. Our ambition and our hopes are high. And we don't intend to lower them!

Small scale recycling facilities near to households and separation of waste encouraged

Authority of Gothenburg

5. HARARE, ZIMBABWE

THE HARARE CITY COUNCIL : ZIMBABWE LOCAL AGENDA 21 INITIATIVE
Mayor Charles Tawengwa, Harare City Council

The Earth Summit which was held in Rio de Janeiro in Brazil in June 1992 was held against a background of declining air and water quality, and the deterioration of the earth's environment through industrial and agricultural pollution, toxic chemicals and nuclear waste disposal.

Thus, in order to improve the quality of life of our people in a sustainable manner, Local Authorities must translate the Rio agenda into a local programme of action to address their own environmental problems.

It is therefore pertinent at this juncture that I will review Agenda 21 and identify the link between the broad global issues from Rio and the many local issues surrounding sustainable development within the local authority of Harare City Council in Zimbabwe.

I will therefore address issues raised in Agenda 21 in sequence:-

COMBATING POVERTY

Local Authorities in developing countries are struggling against poverty, malnutrition, disease and declining economic growth as well as the same environmental problems faced by the industrialised local authorities.

The recent drought which crippled Zimbabwe propelled the high rural to urban migration resulting in high population pressure on the city's environmental quality and resources. Other socio-economic reasons for migration into cities are more or less universal and need not be over-emphasised.

To be objective the city's urban poverty can be divided into two types. The common urban poverty understood by all, is poverty, driven by high demographic growth, low productivity of house-holds, inadequate investment, health and education. The other type has been born of economic change, the need for Economic Structural Adjustment and even growth itself.

To combat urban poverty my Council has adopted the following policies:-

1. Building people's market structures with toilets, water and facilities for use by fruit and vegetable vendors.

2. Relocating people operating cottage industries from backyards into "home industries".

These are serviced areas which are subdivided to accommodate the various activities of manufacturers and traders. It is easy for the council to monitor air and water pollution from such areas. Refuse removal services are also provided for these specific ventures.

3. For people with special skills such as stone carving and doilie making, stands have also been provided from which they can operate and market their wares.

4. The council also has a department which assists groups of people who want to pursue business ventures on a co-operative basis. These beneficiaries are given advice, assistance and guidance.

However, to effectively address the problem of poverty, the provision of significant financial and technical resources, is a pre-requisite; a burden far too heavy for the Council to shoulder single-handed.

POPULATION AND SUSTAINABILITY

There are two factors of prime importance when considering population increases in urban areas:-

i)   The rural-urban migration which I have mentioned before.

ii)   The urban growth from natural population increases.

The social characteristics which determine population within urban areas are complex, but in general, fertility rates decline as socio-economic status and education increases. It has been demonstrated that decreased fertility is associated with longer residence in urban areas and that new migrants to cities tend to bring with them the high fertility rates of rural areas. Given the fluidity of population in the cities of developing countries, there is difficulty in devising appropriate concrete population reduction strategies.

To address this the council has clinics and two hospitals which all have family planning trained nurses. Men's workshops are held periodically in order to involve all players in the population control game.

Zimbabwean women are vital to the Local Agenda 21 effort in their country

Tony Stone Images/Ian Murphy

PROTECTING AND PROMOTING HUMAN HEALTH

As mentioned before, the drought accelerated rural to urban migration, resulting in more people seeking shelter, employment, food and health care in the city.

The city's health delivery and protection system, confronted by a stressful economic environment coupled with overcrowded living conditions and poor nutrition, was challenged by sexually transmitted diseases and the HIV epidemic.

For personal health services the city has twelve "polyclinics" and forty clinics which are classified into primary care clinics, family health services and satellite clinics, a medical examination centre and two infectious disease hospitals.

The services offered are primary care, maternity care, psychiatric services, chronic care, dental services and a nutrition service. These services are complemented by health education services, research and development and social work. The services are managed on a district health system which has the city divided into six districts. With this machinery the city is able to respond to the health needs of the residents. The focus is on:-

✪ equity

✪ accessibility

✪ emphasis on health promotion and prevention

✪ community involvement

✪ decentralisation of decision-making

✪ integration of health programmes and

✪ co-ordination of separate health activities.

DISEASE INTERVENTION PROGRAMMES

These are undertaken for the under-fives through the expanded immunisation programme which the city conducts. To encourage mothers to bring children for immunisation the city adopted a policy that all children under five children with an up-to-date immunisation card will be treated free of charge at our clinics and hospitals should they fall ill. Because of the cholera threat in the region the city also resolved that anyone in the city who is suffering from a diarrhoea disease should be treated free of charge.

The city has also engaged and trained carers known as health promoters who are selected by the communities in which they live. These carry out house to house inspections of their respective areas giving health education to the community.

ENVIRONMENTAL HEALTH SERVICES

For a holistic approach to the protection and promotion of human health the city offers environmental health services whose duties include:-

sampling of water and food stuffs, inspection of residential accommodation, the offer of consultancy services on waste management (domestic, human, industrial), licensing of business premises, inspection of licensed premises, pest control services, meat inspection services, air pollution control, occupational health services, control of public health nuisances, control of infectious diseases, health education, research and training and the administration of statutes and by-laws.

SUSTAINABLE HUMAN SETTLEMENTS

The shortage of housing is the most pressing social problem facing the council. This problem has resulted in overcrowding and the proliferation of illegal backyard structures which are used for human habitation under unhealthy conditions, and the mushrooming of peri-urban squatter settlements. This situation has contributed to the increase in tuberculosis and other infectious diseases.

The rapid increase in population has strained municipal services such as refuse removal, sewage drainage and water services. Unsightly heaps of refuse which provide habitats for flies to breed, and are conducive to rodents and vermin, while the frequent blockages to municipal sewers could be a reflection of Municipal Services approaching a critical position.

To alleviate the housing problem the Council has embarked on the following schemes:-

i) Site and Service Schemes

This is a scheme where private individuals with funds acquire a serviced plot of land to build their own accommodation. The scheme is also applicable to people who are acceptable for mortgage loans by building societies.

ii) Housing Co-operative Scheme

People in the city have grouped together to form housing cooperatives. They open a bank account and contribute money towards a housing co-operative scheme and when they have sufficient funds, the council gives them land to build houses for their members. Such schemes have been a great success in Harare.

iii) Employer Funded Schemes

These are schemes where an employer of a large labour force purchases land from the council and builds houses for his/her employees. The scheme is again doing well in Harare.

iv) Private Sector Participation Schemes

The scheme applies to private developers who purchase land from the council, service and develop it and sell houses to Harare residents.

v) Government Participation Schemes

This is a scheme which is undertaken by our Ministry of Public Construction and National Housing. The Ministry acquires land from the council to build either houses or flats. These are then allocated to people on the council's housing waiting list on a "rent to buy" basis.

vi) Council Funded Schemes

This is a council funded scheme where the council builds houses or flats and supplies this residential accommodation to people on the waiting list on a "rent to buy basis".

CONTROL OF SQUATTER SETTLEMENTS

An on-going policy of rounding up and screening squatters in the city is in place. The scheme is yielding positive results as the squatters are screened and classified into the following groups:-

a) Destitute cases which are referred to Government's Social Services Department.

b) Those in need of resettlement are provided with land by the relevant ministry.

c) Mentally ill persons are referred to the Ministry of Health.

d) Aliens or foreigners are repatriated accordingly.

e) Criminals are handled by the police.

However, despite a noticeable success I must say the problem of urban squatting is very difficult to contain, and some assistance in that direction is certainly most welcome.

PROTECTING THE ATMOSPHERE

The council's Health Department has a unit that monitors air pollution by :-

i) Monitoring air pollution of industrial firms which are required to reduce pollution.

Advice on the installation of pollution abatement equipment or training of boiler house attendants is also given.

ii) When a new industrial area is being developed, environment protection regulations are seriously considered.

iii) The daily quantity of sulphur dioxide in the atmosphere and suspended particulate matter is measured throughout the city's air pollution programme. The 1993 sulphur dioxide average for the city was 70.00 mg/m3 and that for suspended particulate matter was 40.64mg/m3.

The council intends to include oxides of nitrogen, carbon monoxide and ozone in its air pollution monitoring programme once funds become available for purchase of appropriate equipment.

COMBATING DEFORESTATION

Since the attainment of our independence in 1990, the 1st December of every year is designated as the National Tree Planting Day, where every person is encouraged to plant a tree. The city, in collaboration with the business community also manages "woodlots". The council merely provides a treeless piece of land and the business community donates tree seedlings to be planted on such woodlots. The council then protects and nurtures the seedlings to maturity. The council also encourages the use of alternative energy in the home.

CONSERVATION OF BIOLOGICAL DIVERSITY

The council encourages the conservation of biological diversity. Harare has two botanical gardens and a third one is being developed. The council has spearheaded the development of a wildlife sanctuary. Here a number of wild animals are kept and game viewing tours are conducted.

PROTECTING AND MANAGING FRESH WATER

Harare is primarily supplied with water from three dams, Lake Chivero, Harava and Seke dams for which it forms the catchment areas. Since rain falls in summer only, chemicals from various activities along the dam's catchment areas which find their way into the dams tend to accumulate because the dilution factor is low. However, eutrophication of the dams is fairly controlled since the quality of industrial effluents discharged into sewers are monitored in terms of the effluent's suspended solids, pH, heavy metals, permanganate and biological oxygen demand. The council has also invested a lot of money to protect fresh waters through the construction of a modern, multi-million dollar sewage treatment plant.

MANAGING HAZARDOUS AND SOLID WASTES AND SEWAGE

The city has two modern sewage treatments plants which allows re-use of the purified effluent. For solid wastes the city uses the controlled tipping method of disposal at two of its landfill sites.

Because of logistical problems in ferrying solid wastes from the point of generation to disposal site, the council also engages private contractors to move solid wastes from certain sections of the city to disposal sites.

The city manages the disposal of hazardous wastes at disposal sites. Certain wastes require pre-treatment before disposal, and accordingly the city has a toxic waste treatment site. Environmental Health Officers and the Industrial Toxic Waste Inspectors also monitor premises which produce hazardous wastes.

RADIOACTIVE MATERIAL

The City lacks expertise, human resources and equipment to monitor disposal of radioactive material which is quite minimal in our City.

WOMEN AND CHILDREN IN SUSTAINABLE DEVELOPMENT

The council, together with the private sector plays an important role in the involvement of women and children in sustainable development. There are several vocational centres where women are taught various trades.

A number of Women's Clubs exist where women meet and discuss issues of mutual concern. There are several organisations which have been offered land by the council for the construction of counselling "camps" for women facing domestic violence. The organisations even go further to give legal assistance to difficult cases (Musasa Project). Issues pertaining to women and health are dealt with at clinics- prenatal care, family planning, responsible parenthood and breastfeeding are taught. In fact one of our "polyclinics" was declared "Baby Friendly" by UNICEF.

The City has currently a total of 42 council-run nurseries and kindergartens where children are taught and looked after. Private individuals, churches and other organisations are also encouraged to provide nursery school and kindergarten services. As already mentioned immunisation for children is free of charge and those under five who have an up-to-date immunisation record are treated free at our clinics.

STRENGTHENING THE ROLE OF INDIGENOUS PEOPLE

The council encourages active participation of the indigenous people. To that end the council provides commercial and industrial sites to indigenous people and to other organisations which support them.

PARTNERSHIP WITH NON-GOVERNMENTAL ORGANISATIONS

There is liaison with Non-Governmental Organisations in addressing issues at a local level; for example, the women's organisations, street kids' organisations and squatters.

I am involved in raising funds for charity particularly towards Christmas, the 'Mayor's Christmas Cheer Fund'. Funds raised are distributed to over 32 charitable organisations. The council also supports some charitable organisations with grant in-aid funds.

WORKERS AND TRADE UNIONS

The council conducts dialogue with the Zimbabwe Congress of Trade Unions which is the main body that represents workers in Zimbabwe.

TECHNOLOGY TRANSFER

On technology transfer the city has entered into twinning relationships with cities in different parts of the world. Employees of the city have been seconded to cities in other countries to study various operations.

EDUCATION, TRAINING AND PUBLIC AWARENESS

The council has a Public Relations Division which facilitates flow of information from the council to the public and vice-versa. The Division also conducts various campaigns that require public awareness, for example anti-litter campaigns.

The council is actively involved in the improvement and development of education by building nursery schools, kindergartens and primary schools. For the under-privileged the council awards bursaries and scholarships which enable the pupils to complete secondary school education, university education and vocational and technical training courses.

6. HEIDELBERG, GERMANY

Ms B Weber, Mayor of Heidelberg

Information and comprehensive reports are really indispensable for effective local environmental policy-making and are the basis for mature and responsible citizenship. You can never expect your citizens to act properly, not only in elections but also in their own behaviour, if they are not really well informed and that is why the City of Heidelberg acted on the EC Directive on the Freedom of Access to Environmental Information. Following the example of Swedish, Dutch and the United States Freedom of Information Act, in a quite unusual step we transferred the Directive into local practice even before it became German law.

Secondly the City installed publicly visible computer screens into the centre of the city where citizens can always see the data, so that they can make proper judgements about environmental conditions. Normally if you hear about data in a special situation it can create chaos or misunderstanding, so if you train your people to steadily watch the data and see how it changes, they learn to make judgements for themselves without being constantly told that this is a bad sign and this is a good sign, it is now getting worse or it is now getting better. So we aim to inform rather than teach our citizens. This first public database was on Sulphur Dioxide, SO_2 and Carbon Dioxide, CO_2 emissions and we have just installed a new one on low level ozone with some advice for the public on how to react.

The third example I present to you refers to the OECD Project on environmental improvement through Urban Energy Management. There will be a conference in Heidelberg on this project.

Fourthly we had a Committee of Inquiry in the German Parliament, the Bundestat, on the protection of the atmosphere and this Committee of Inquiry decided with the Bundestat following this decision, to reduce carbon dioxide CO_2 emissions by 30% by the year 2005. We made the same decision in Heidelberg both for the City and the Council itself in June 1991. We then asked a famous Heidelberg research institute to elaborate on our Local Action Plan to produce a plan which would be "tailor made" for the City based on all the local data we had available. We decided one year later to approve this action plan. The plan is rather unique in Germany as it sets out very concrete, achievable steps based on specific information whereby we can reduce carbon dioxide emissions in the energy sector, for example by 200,000 tonnes per year. We have had to invest 1.7 million Marks per year to take all the steps outlined in the action plan. We now follow this action plan and there is a report given to the City Council every year to check how far we have progressed during the last year and what is still to be done.

It is very interesting to compare the energy field to the transport field. If we want to have an 8% reduction in carbon dioxide emissions from the transport sector we would have to make an investment of approximately 170 million Marks per year, which is an enormous amount of extra money.

Successful energy management is only possible with fruitful cooperation between all the important actors in the local area, this of course has been mentioned several times in this Conference. We have brought together the energy board, the transport services and local industry, even the electricity supply shops and department stores were included in a special action programme we initiated to promote the purchase of low energy light bulbs. The actions of other cities gave us the ideas and we followed their example. For instance, others have demonstrated that whilst promoting the sale and purchase of low energy bulbs reduces energy use in the City enormously, it can also give citizens the opportunity to talk with the personnel in the electricity supply shops who are trained to give advice on other ways of saving energy, and therefore facilitate the public's access to better information on these issues. This is especially important for those people who traditionally do not care for the environment. Many people still only take up the opportunity to talk to the people who can advise them on energy savings when they realise that they can save some money. We have to use all possible means of getting information to people even if at first sight they do not seem to be very interested.

Citizens in Heidelberg can now ask for their own personalised computer-generated carbon dioxide reduction balance sheet. The information on normal everyday families, based on so-called normal or average activities, is computerised so that it is now possible for individual families to discover what possibilities they may have to reduce their own carbon dioxide emissions. They are advised on what actions they will have to take to achieve these reductions and how much they will have to invest to do so. Experience of operating this system has shown that not every family will replace all their electrical installations immediately but when they are next in a position to purchase an electrical product they are more likely to consider buying an energy efficient device. Finally as a university town we have worked very closely and very intensively with academics and have used the expertise of our scientists for this project.

The fifth example - in May 1994 the City Council decided on our transport development plan. Transport is one of the most delicate political issues to date in Germany. I do not know how car drivers react in other cities but I suspect that they will react in the same way. The transport development plan is again the result of scientific data which has been collected since 1987 on car exhaust emissions and car usage. There was also a very broad citizens participation exercise called the "Transport Forum". We have tried to treat our citizens as welcomed experts, which is not the practice of many municipalities. We included interested groups from the Chamber of Commerce to trade unions, from parent groups to environmental organisations in the drafting of the concept. 116 groups met every three weeks for two years for several hours without being paid and helped enormously in the development of the plan. They helped the City Council to make proper decisions because they were the ones who really knew all about the different issues involved and had their own individual opinions. The City Council with their help tried to include everything in the plan and tried to make it all work together. As has already been mentioned on the subject of consensus building, normally if you put those organisations together there is confrontation because they are not used to talking together. They treat each other as enemies, although they live in the same City. However, after the first debates, and believe me some evenings were horrible and fighting almost erupted on a number of occasions, the participants suddenly realised that for many of the issues they could agree on common ground and common aims. Out of 100 or so different issues to be tackled they found that after intensive talking there were common aims upon which there could be no disagreement for 70-75 of the issues and there was a range of about 20 or so issues where compromise could be easily found. This was because they found that the interests and cases put forward by the other participants were convincing. It was only a very tiny part of the whole debate that remained controversial and this was eventually the only part that had to be voted on. The good thing about the exercise was that people talked to one another and they realised the value of debate and argument. This will have a valuable and sustainable effect on democratic debate within the City.

In a slightly different cooperation between the City and citizens we instigated a public roundtable debate with experts to work on guidelines for tourism. You probably know that Heidelberg is a tourist city, not only a university city but also a city with 3.5 million tourists per year. We needed guidelines on tourism that would lead our City towards tourism which is socially and environmentally sustainable. We now have an action plan on tourism which we can follow step-by-step.

The seventh point involves our decision in July 1991 to join the World Health Organisation's Network - Healthy Cities. I strongly think this belongs very much to all the environment debates. We engage in regular actions, discussions and decisions to try to improve living conditions. We are all aware that cities cannot change everything but we try to influence our future if only by trying to disseminate information. This year we are to deal with the issue of healthier children. Public forums together with practical action in schools and kindergartens will take place later this year. The campaign deals mainly with nutrition and the detrimental substances which affect children's health. However many other interesting issues will be tackled.

The eighth point - our waste management plans aim to reduce waste primarily by separating waste. We have encouraged this since 1992 by providing information and advice supplied by consultants who have talked to enterprises, private individuals and households about how to avoid, in the first instance, waste production and where this is not possible to separate waste. The results can be clearly see in 1989 to 1994 non-usable, non-separated waste has gone down by 50% in the City.

Ninth Point - we are now transforming an old train station into a social and cultural centre for different sorts of activities, including the "One World" issue. We hope that the centre will provide a base for public debate. By bringing the issues and local people together, basing actions on personal relations and seeing and feeling that someone is really behind the issues - all this enables people to really start believing in things. I believe this to be the really important factor. If we are not convinced that people who are acting in support of a cause are not acting with conviction then nothing will be achieved.

7. AALBORG, DENMARK

REPORT OF THE EUROPEAN CONFERENCE ON SUSTAINABLE CITIES AND TOWNS.

Mr Kaj Kjaer, Mayor of Aalborg

In this paper I will present the results of the European Conference on Sustainable Cities and Towns held in the City of Aalborg, Denmark, in May 1994. There were 670 participants from 27 countries and 150 cities - the Conference was seen as a great success. The purpose of the Aalborg conference was first to discuss the principles of sustainability, secondly to present the sustainable cities report of the European Commissions Urban Expert Group, thirdly to discuss and adopt the European Charter on Sustainable Cities and Towns and finally, to launch the European Campaign Network of Sustainable Cities and Towns. Eighty cities and a number of institutions and organisations signed the Charter. The Aalborg Charter was the most important result from the conference. To illustrate an abstract charter I will also highlight actions we have initiated in Aalborg and which are all part of a sustainable process.

Cities and towns have throughout history been the arena for our social, cultural and economic lives. The cities and towns have been the centre of industry, crafts, trades, education and government. We have learned that we cannot go on consuming nature's resources at the present level without destroying the natural capital. We are convinced that sustainable human life cannot be achieved without sustainable local communities. Cities and towns are key players in the process of changing lifestyle, consumption and spatial patterns. By understanding the notions and principles of sustainability we understand that our standard of living should be based on the caring capacity of nature. We seek to achieve social justice, sustainable economies and environmental sustainability. Environmental sustainability demands that we are not consuming more of the nature's capital than nature can renew, the rate at which we consume non-renewable resources does not exceed the rate at which sustainable renewable resources are replaced, and finally that we do not pollute more than the capacity of air, water and soil is able to absorb. We are convinced that the city is the largest unit able to address many of the urban architectural, social, economic, political, natural resource and environmental imbalances and the smallest scale to resolve the problems in an integrated, holistic and sustainable fashion. As each city is different we have to find our own way towards sustainability.

Sustainability is a creative local balance-seeking process. We recognise that sustainability is not a vision; it is a process extending into all areas of local decision making. For this process the city and its citizens may make informed choices. Sustainable decisions are not only representing the interests of current stakeholders but also future generations. It involves resolving problems by negotiating outwards. We recognise that the city cannot permit itself to export problems into larger environments or into the future, therefore, any problems of imbalance within the city are either brought to balance on their own level or absorbed by some larger society at a regional or national level. We understand that the limiting factor for economic development in our cities has become based on natural capital. We must therefore invest in this capital. This requires firstly the conservation of ground water stocks, soil and habitats of rare species, secondly the anchorage and the growth of natural capital by reducing our level of current exploitation of any non-renewable energy. We also need an expansion of cultivated natural capital, such as inner city parks and to increase the efficiency of products, the energy efficient buildings, and to promote environmentally friendly transport.

SOCIAL EQUITY FOR URBAN SUSTAINABILITY

We are aware that inequitable distribution of wealth creates unsustainable behaviour. We intend to integrate people's basic social needs as well as health care, employment and housing programmes with environmental protection. We wish to work for the improvement of the citizen's lifestyle. We will try to create jobs which can contribute to the sustainability of the community and therefore reduce unemployment. We will encourage any company to create sustainable production methods and products.

SUSTAINABLE LAND USE PATTERNS

We recognise that land use and development planning policies must be assessed for environmental effects at all levels in the local authority. In the urban renewal programme and in planning new suburbs we seek a mix so as to reduce the needs for mobility, to strengthen public transport and sustainable energy supply.

SUSTAINABLE URBAN MOBILITY PATTERNS

We shall strive to improve accessibility and sustain social welfare and urban lifestyle with less transport. A sustainable city must give priority to ecologically sound means of transport like walking, cycling and public transport.

RESPONSIBILITY FOR THE GLOBAL CLIMATE

We understand that we must try to protect the global climate by reducing emission of greenhouse gases into the atmosphere. This requires polices and initiatives based on an understanding of the urban environment as an energy system.

PREVENTION OF ECO-SYSTEM TOXIFICATION

We want to make every effort to see that further toxification of air, water, soil is stopped and prevented at source.

LOCAL SELF GOVERNMENTS AS A PRECONDITION

We hold the knowledge and take the responsibility for the task of developing sustainable ways of living and to design and manage our cities towards sustainability. The extent to which cities and towns are able to rise to this challenge depends upon their being given rights to local self government according to the principle of subsidiarity.

CITIZENS AND SECTORS AND THE INVOLVEMENT OF THE COMMUNITY

We pledge to work with all sectors of our communities - citizens, business and interest groups in developing our Local Agenda 21 plans. We shall ensure that all citizens and interest groups have access to information and are able to participate in local decision-making processes.

IMPLEMENTS AND TOOLS FOR URBAN MANAGEMENT TOWARDS SUSTAINABILITY

We pledge to use the political and technical instruments and tools available in urban management. We will collect and process environmental data, engage in environmental planning, use model economic and communication instruments.

MECHANISMS FOR AWARENESS-RAISING INCLUDING PUBLIC PARTICIPATION

We know that we must base our policy-making and controlling efforts on different types of urban indicators including those of urban environmental policy, urban flows, urban patterns and, most importantly, indicators of an urban systems sustainability.

We recognise that the whole range of policies and activities yielding positive ecological consequences have already been successfully applied in many cities throughout Europe. In the sustainability process we are called on to develop our own strategies, try them out and practice and share our experiences.

Finally, the campaign. We have an initiative - the European Sustainable Cities and Towns Campaign to encourage and support cities and towns working towards sustainability. The initial phase of the campaign will be for a two year period, after which progress will be assessed at a second conference to be held in 1996 in Lisbon. We invite every local European authority and any European network of local authorities to join the campaign. It is my hope that by studying the main lines of the Aalborg Charter and by seeing the main lines dressed up with examples from my city, you will be able to start your own sustainability process. A campaign network will be supported by a Secretariat managed by ICLEI and hosted by the City of Aalborg and will be situated in Brussels. It is also my hope that you will use this Secretariat and thereby will be a member of the campaign network.

LOCAL AGENDA 21 IMPLEMENTATION
DEBATE AND KEY ISSUES

There are many key issues involved in Local Agenda 21 which
are important topics in their own right and warrant a lot of
discussion and thought. All these topics come together to form
a whole when we look at the issue of sustainable development.

Debates on a number of these key issues are summarised here to
provide readers with some new perspectives, ideas and hopefully
answers which can be incorporated into any individual Local
Agenda 21 programme. The voices of the individual participants
in the conference are presented here as a means of capturing
the feeling of the conference and further disseminating the
experience of participants many of whom are actively involved
in a Local Agenda 21 process in their community.

IMPLEMENTING THE LOCAL AGENDA 21 MANDATE WHAT IS THE LOCAL GOVERNMENT RESPONSE TO LOCAL AGENDA 21?

Jeb Brugman, Secretary General, International Council For Local Environmental Initiatives.

Implementing the Local Agenda 21 Mandate

Sustainable Development - what are we talking about, what does this mean? In many ways this is nothing less than an ideology and we are in the complicated position of being local officials, local managers, local activists, who have to figure out how to take an ideology and do something with it. The ideology as I see it is the belief that if we make some adjustments to our current economic systems then they can continue to operate for many centuries to come. I am not going to give you my opinion as to whether this will work or not, but I want to just basically outline what I think this ideology is all about.

There are 3 processes of development that we are trying to integrate with one another. There is "economic development", I call it "capitalist" development here to make clear that we are not just dealing with a narrow definition of economic development. It is generally agreed that the development of capitalist economies have certain imperatives which are popularly understood as being good. Economic growth is something that is an imperative of capitalism and private profit is something which we generally believe is good or should be continued. Market expansion also involves the 'externalisation of costs', in capitalism in trying to reduce costs and to increase profit, we constantly externalise costs, these are often the social and environmental costs. The ideology of sustainable development recognises that problems are caused by proceeding with these kinds of imperatives and not addressing some other imperatives; the two further processes of development - the imperatives of the process of "community development" and "ecological development".

On the community development side we feel that people should have accountability in social terms and that people should be respectful to one another and should not be involved in acts of crime against one another. Participation is a belief that people should have a voice. Equity or local self-reliance or fulfiling basic needs, are issues discussed extensively in the sustainable development debate. Do these require other development processes at a local level?

There is also Ecological Development. Eco-systems are separate from human society and have their own imperatives of development. They have carrying capacity and limits. They develop so as to conserve resources, and operate highly efficient systems so in these respects they have the quality of "elegance". They continue to develop to try to get more and more bio-physical output from less and less input of energy.

Now in the overlapping areas between these types of development processes we have different schools of thought. There is "community economic development" and in that school of thought it is believed that we can continue to develop in line with our capitalist systems but that we have to take community development into consideration so that we can deal with equity issues.

On the other hand, between capitalist development and ecological development we have the 'conservationist' school of thought which is the basic philosophy of the environmental movement. It is the belief that we can have capitalist economies and that they can continue to grow, but what we need to do is protect natural areas from economic development.

Finally looking at the link between community and ecological development we have what people call these days "eco-ecology" or "utopianism" .

Where the three processes intersect we have this enigmatic thing we call sustainable development. There are many contradictions and challenges in trying to figure out the equation of how you make this intersection of ideologies work. I am going to present a definition of sustainable development that takes this ideological perspective and translates it into some useful terms.

Sustainable development is *'development that delivers basic environmental, social and economic services to all'* in other words, it addresses sustainable development and the community development imperatives without threatening the viability of the natural and social systems upon which these services depend and which also largely addresses the eco-systems imperatives.

What is the Local Government Response to Local Agenda 21?

Municipal officers are in the business of providing services to people, not just water services or energy services, but also a service to the constituent who calls you when you go home and says "I have a problem with my sidewalk", or "There are youths hanging out in our park who are vandalising the park facilities", the kind of services that address the most immediate of needs. At the same time you need to think about big and complex systems, which you do not really understand and often do not control. So the challenge is that on the one hand you have to satisfy service needs and demands there is an immediacy to your doing that, if you do not do it you are out of office, you have to prioritise resources, you do not have unlimited budgets and indeed you have shrinking budgets. On the other hand you have the new sustainability agenda, however you cannot deal with all of the issues on the sustainable agenda at once, you have to decide what you can do this year and what you can do next year. You have to deal with equity and affordability, for example there are people in constituencies who cannot afford services at current levels but need to get them provided nevertheless. Finally the outcome of your activities has to be an identifiable output. In other words there has to be a "deliverable".

In some ways in satisfying these services demands, you also have to respect system capacities. You cannot satisfy all service needs as the systems you depend upon have limits. While you deal with the immediate issues, Agenda 21 now requires that you also deal with long term issues -"intergenerational equity". You have got to think about 50 or 100 years ahead. Now you also have to address the whole global agenda. **In essence how do we take Agenda 21 - a giant plan and operationalise it all at the local level.** Normally you have to deal with affordability but now as part of sustainability you have to do full cost accounting - to charge the full cost of things, and that means that you may have to raise the price of your services. Normally you have to have action and outputs but at the same time you are told now that you should engage in a complicated long-term comprehensive planning process that diverts your municipal staff resources to develop a three or four year planning exercise. So, this is the extent of the challenge you face as municipal officers and council members. I want to put forward some additional key questions based upon my experiences of working with local authorities on Local Agenda 21.

1 **PARTNERSHIPS.** One of the main questions and challenges facing municipalities is how to include marginalised groups. Those of you who are involved in Local Agenda 21 process and have participatory efforts or environmental forums or stakeholder groups, should ask yourselves: are the unemployed involved? Are racial minorities involved? How are they going to participate on an equal basis with people in the community who have resources and power and how can they be equal parties of the planning process?

2. **CONSULTATION.** What is the relationship between the vision that the community develops and the strategic plans that you are required to develop by law by national or state governments? What is the relationship between a Local Agenda 21 vision document and statutory plans? How do you focus on local needs while addressing the whole breadth of Agenda 21? Time and again I hear this conflict arise when I work with local communities who are trying to develop a Local Agenda 21.

3. **AUDITING.** Some people are engaged in auditing, which is largely information-gathering. How do you know that the services that you are providing in your city are sustainable? You gather information on sewerage system capacity and estimates for the demand on that system, but how will you judge whether the whole system is sustainable? What are the implications of people increasing their consumption of water beyond the estimates and of the water supply running out, or of a new law that says you cannot continue to discharge the same kind of waste water as before? How do you deal with these questions?

4. **ACTION PLANS –** When you finally go through a public consultation and involvement process and you develop a plan of action, one of the things I commonly observe in the process is that there is a Local Agenda 21 plan in addition to the existing plans of the municipality, however the two do not relate to one another. So how do you get them to relate? Can you reform existing planning processes so that Local Agenda 21 recommendations get integrated into the municipal budget process? After building up community expectations how do they take the strategy you agreed with the community, and ensure that everything that is voted for in the budget of the city council is going to comply with that strategy.

5. **IMPLEMENTATION –** What are the institutional mechanisms that are needed to establish partnerships. We use the word partnership to also encompass a process which means that the private sector and NGO's or the community and the municipality will jointly implement programmes to provide the services that are identified in the Local Agenda 21, but do you need some new kind of institutional framework to achieve this?

6. **MONITORING AND EVALUATION –** How are you going to tell if your city or town or country is becoming more sustainable? Often when local government engages in these processes of consultation, planning and report preparation - producing programmes for recycling, CO_2 reduction strategies and cycle paths, the councils believe that they have achieved sustainability. But how do you really know if your community is becoming more sustainable? How do individual households, NGO's and businesses know what actions they will need to take on a regular basis to become more sustainable. For example what kind of information do they need so that when they hear CO_2 emissions are increasing, they immediately know how they should behave to address this increase?

7. **INDICATORS –** Indicators are the latest fad in this faddish area of sustainable development. Everyone feels they have to have indicators. Do we know why we are developing indicators, because often they are very academic and take years to develop? For example a municipality may determine that it is important to know whether CO_2 levels are increasing in their area and to publish this information, but what impact does this have? How does that allow people to know what kinds of behaviour they should engage in to reduce CO_2 pollution levels.

8. **PROCESS.** Finally the process itself, is it sustainable, or is it something you do for only two or three year? How will you sustain the process? Will you create a municipal department of sustainable development - or develop an institutional mechanism that you can put in place in your community that can continue to promote, and develop, revise and implement this plan in an ongoing way? However, both are unlikely.

So these are some of the questions that come to my mind as I listen to the case studies presented at this conference and as I think about the kinds of things that I know municipalities are tackling when developing a Local Agenda 21.

LOCAL AGENDA 21 IMPLEMENTATION DEBATE AND KEY ISSUES

CONTRADICTIONS IN LOCAL AGENDA 21

Q1 *PAUL DAVIES, BIRMINGHAM CITY COUNCIL, UK*

"Issues of social equity and systems development were emphasised when talking about sustainability which seemed to me to pertain more to some of the contradictions in trying to deal with business development and business regulation".

JB "I do not see any cities coming forward or towns saying we want to reduce economic growth, or that we want to reduce the profit of our businesses, so in many ways the whole notion of sustainable development can temper the negative economic development impacts. Local Agenda 21 is focusing on community development needs, equity and participation. On the other hand we are saying we need to have a more systemic idea of how our cities operate. We need to see our cities as ecosystems. All the infrastructure systems are interrelated and there is interdependency. So we are trying to bring these two forces to influence the way that the economic development happens in our community and to temper it a bit".

PRIVATISATION

Q2 *AYDAM ERIM - COUNCIL MEMBER. CANAKAYA, ANKARA, TURKEY*

"How do you think, especially in the developing world, we can make any meaningful national plans for Local Agenda 21 or for sustainable development, with increasing privatisation, can the two really be reconciled? The developed world can interpret new concepts more easily than developing countries because of their traditional institutions. The comprehensive planning concept is something that still has to be advocated for many in the developing world".

JB "The concept of sustainable development does not challenge in itself privatisation. Decision-making around privatisation or the choices of what you privatise and do not privatise would have to be done by different processes involving the public or taking into consideration the impacts upon the eco-system".

PUBLIC PARTICIPATION AND INVOLVING MARGINALISED GROUPS

Q3 *MR KATO, ICLEI JAPAN, GLOBAL ENVIRONMENT PROGRAM JAPAN*

"I would like to respond to questions relating to the relationship between the Local Agenda 21 and other conventional or traditional programmes by local government. In Japan we identified three items which should be incorporated when such a programme is to be called Local Agenda 21. The first element is sustainability of course. In other words we have to address both environment and development issues at the same time with a global scope in mind and with the 21st Century in mind. The second element is

that programmes should be action-oriented, in other words, we have to address the actions in concrete terms. It may be for instance, more intensive use of solar energy or the reduction of waste. The third element is the participation of citizens. For instance, in the case of Japan, in some cases the participation of citizens so far is not sufficient, we have decided that this process is very important. This is the criteria by which we can judge whether the programme is Local Agenda 21 or not"

Q4 *WAYNE WESCOTT, ST KILDA, AUSTRALIA*

"We have an inner city, highly urbanised Council and we have a fairly large group of local indigenous people who have been living in local parks around our shopping centres and this has caused an enormous amount of conflict. We involved them in working with the burgeoning eco-tourism work that is going along on the foreshore of our coast. They demonstrate the use of our indigenous plants and work on other forms of tourism in that area and we found that they actually began to change their relationship with local shops and local residents".

JB "From your experience what kind of advice would you give other municipalities that want to make sure they succeed in encouraging marginalised groups to take part in their Local Agenda 21 process?"

WW "The answer came from a very long process of involvement and communication. Our involvement came at the end of a community involvement process which had been going on for a couple of years. Things will not happen if you do not already have a strong ongoing community involvement programme, and if you are pragmatic enough to be able to grab an issue at the right time, that might be the catalyst to move you past simply communicating and sitting down talking to some kind of activity that will make a difference."

JB "Therefore it is important that you build on existing programmes or processes and that the Local Agenda 21 effort links itself with what might be more typical social programmes where community relationships are well established."

Q5 *PETER SMITH, FOUNDATION FOR GLOBAL COMMUNITY, USA*

"In every case the successful programmes were ones where we reached out to people, met them and found out what they were doing and got involved in their activities. One of the programmes I am aware of is the Piedmont Peace Project that registered thousands of low income people in North Carolina to vote. In other smaller efforts in the inner city in Boston we reached out to fairly young kids who were at risk of just dropping out of life. We found out what they wanted and we made resources available to them and worked with them".

WW "There are many groups within your communities that will want to be heard and quite ingenious ways need to be found to include all these voices and bring them together"

Q6 *MEXICAN POPULAR YOUTH REPRESENTATIVE*

"My name is Mauricio. I am from Mexico and am part of a youth group which used to be marginalized. I would like to tell you how we grouped together and how we linked up to form an organisation with a task. It is important to realise that, as individuals from the marginalized areas or from the ordinary people's areas, we have a lot to contribute. What happens is that, quite often,there isn't the chance for us to participate, or the programmes which governments carry out do not include the things we want and need. In other words, they, the governments, often give us things we do not need. Yes I do believe that, marginalized groups can be integrated in a positive way into the decision-making process, enabling them to gain wealth and lead a dignified life. What happens is that often people do not really know the true situation in which this kind of person is living. For example, I used to be a drug addict, an alcoholic and used to hang around in parks and in the street but that was because there was no-one who would listen to me or help me. When I realised that I was not alone but that there were a lot of others like me, then together we started to see that this was not a dignified or positive position to be in and, on occasions, in our frustration we even resorted to violence.

We started to join together and went to talk to government officials. What helped us was that many of those we talked to actually adapted their schemes to our situation, to our programmes and to our plans because, in one way or another, it was clear that we knew better what we wanted. I am trying to say here that it is important that, before doing something, you take into account the people actually affected and concerned by your proposals and you let them take part".

INTEGRATING LOCAL AGENDA 21 WITH TRADITIONAL MUNICIPAL PLANS AND EXISTING PROCESSES

JB "What is the relation between the Local Agenda 21 vision and your strategic planning processes at the municipal level. Or going down to action plans, how does the Local Agenda 21 plan get integrated in with your traditional plans, budget documents and procedures within the municipality? This is going to be one of the more challenging questions as we begin to evaluate whether Local Agenda 21 has really made any difference".

Q7 *JIM THOMS, HAMILTON AND WENTWORTH, REGIONAL MUNICIPALITY, CANADA*

"We are trying to integrate policy in a number of different ways. A Directive from the Chief Administrative Officer of the Region orders every report that goes to Council should include a statement on how the recommendation, action or programme will contribute to sustainable development. In many cases there will be no answer to that because it will not be something that applies, but it forces every report writer to think about that question every time a report is sent to Council. It also keeps the issue constantly in front of Council and that is good.

We are spending quite a bit of time on a formal and regular evaluation of budget proposals against a checklist of sustainable development objectives. We don't think we are anywhere near the end of that process because our expectation is that we will have to make many amendments as we do more work on indicators and more consultation through our "community days" on what the people actually want as indicators for a sustainable community.

We put as much of our Vision document (Local Agenda 21) as we could into the comprehensive planning document required by the Province . However, much of it does not fit very well because the legislation is based on physical land use planning and it is difficult to blend in some of the things. My best guess is that in fact we will start to look at a separate comprehensive planning document and Vision document, which we will not look to get approved under any larger process".

POLICY INTEGRATION – MUNICIPAL ENVIRONMENT EVALUATION PROCESS

Q8 *RASHEDA NAWAZ, CITY OF OTTAWA, CANADA*

"In our latest official plan which is the"Cities Comprehensive Plan," we have integrated the principles of sustainable development in plain words into the municipal planning process. Half of it or most of it will be implemented through the development approval process and that process gives it a legal basis. All programmes without a legal basis have almost no value, if any citizen or particular group or company challenges any of the actions taken by the local council it does not have a legal basis. MEEP which is the Municipal Environmental Evaluation Process was introduced at the local municipal level for development proposals as well as any of the reports written by any of the corporate departments. Each has to go through a checklist to see whether they are complying with the Municipal Environmental Evaluation Process or not. We do not ask for MEEP reports for housing extensions or little things but there is a checklist procedure if it is a larger project which for instance, is on a greenway system, on a contaminated site or on an unstable slope. This is very new and is working quite well in its first year".

Q9 *JAN IPLAND - CITY OF AALBORG, DENMARK*

"I can say that we have integrated environmental protection in our physical master plan. This has been done for the last few years. Yesterday the City Council decided on a master plan for traffic and environment which is an action plan that can lead to a car-free inner city. The City Council has decided that every decision made in the City Council should be evaluated on an environmental basis. We have been making annual environmental action plans for the last 5 years. For the local supply services system we have a local plan aimed at cutting down energy consumption by 30% and for connecting 95% of houses to the district heating system before the year 2000".

Q10 *UK DELEGATE*

"In the absence of a corporate approach and a plan, a very important element and something that we can all do, is to talk within our authorities to persuade and explain sustainability to the officers as well as the people in the district. Then the officers in the other service areas will also have ownership of the idea, they will not be doing things just because it says so in a Committee report".

Open microphone

POLICY INTEGRATION – PERFORMANCE MANAGEMENT

Q11 *FURTHER UK DELEGATE*

"We have made Local Agenda 21 one of the key aims for our Authority and we have made the development and the process of producing our strategy in partnership with people, the key aim of the Council for the next few years. As part of the process we specify tasks and objectives that we want to see being followed both within the Council and in partnership with people outside of the Council. We have a system called Performance Management operating within our Council whereby we do not just set ourselves, our Committees and our Departments, objectives which follow through into specific actions but we also set specific high level objectives for our Chief Officers. We monitor both these sets of objectives on an annual basis so that we can make sure that Agenda 21 is entirely integrated into the normal management systems of the Local Authority rather than being something that was bolted on afterwards".

JB "So in this case it is important that recommendation from the citizen-based stakeholder groups fit in with this Performance Management System. Therefore it is important that the stakeholder group itself should become educated and informed about the existing processes in the municipality".

Q12 *JIM THOMS, HAMILTON AND WENTWORTH, CANADA*

"It is dangerous to have a system which will become impenetrable to the other stakeholders and the onus is on both politicians and officials to make sure that it is a very transparent process. That is something which we are still working with. Hamilton and Wentworth have had sustainability paragraphs within reports for the last 7 years, but I have to be honest and say that we have found it to be the least effective tool for delivering such policies. Unless you embark upon the most vigorous of training programmes those who write these reports do not always take these paragraphs seriously".

POLICY INTEGRATION – AUDITING POLICY ASSESSMENTS

Q13 *BRETT WILLERS, CARDIFF CITY COUNCIL, UK*

"We have found in our authority that the auditing of policy assessments can be a very effective mechanism. Every so often we take aside the month's committee reports, analyse and assess them to see how effective the statements on sustainable development are and whether they are accurate".

NATIONAL POLICY

Q14 *BRETT WILLERS, CARDIFF CITY COUNCIL, UK*

"You talk about taking into account the sustainability dimension in the planning process i.e. within our local plans. There is a serious problem which we face in the UK and I am sure many of you face in your own countries, it is the relationship of these legislative documents to national documents and decision-making. For example, in Cardiff we opposed around five out-of-town shopping developments which had transport generation and serious environmental implications. They also were opposed by the local community. However despite being ruled out by our planning authority on the approval of the national government the projects went ahead".

AFFORDING THE LOCAL AGENDA 21 PROCESS ITSELF

Q15 *RASHEDA NAWAZ, CITY OF OTTAWA, CANADA*

"A dimension is missing here - we should have talked about budgeting in the beginning. In Ottawa it took 6 years, 10 full-time staff, many part time students, consultants, $3M and so forth to finish our sustainable plan for a city of 350,000. Most of our population today live in cities of 8-10M in the developing world, these cities do not have this kind of budget for sustainable planning. The northern countries, or national or international bodies have to consider where these cities are going to get the money for such an exercise? I think that this issue must be resolved and answered before we can go ahead".

JB "One way is to get the money to do this kind of process, the other way is to consider whether it makes sense for a city in the developing world to engage in a process that is so extensive. There might be other ways to develop sustainability issues that are much more incremental and less costly".

Q16 *DELEGATE FROM SUVA CITY, FIJI*

"Some have stated that it was their experience that they achieved their Local Agenda 21 through very diverse means and in some cases they actually had existing programmes which they integrated into Local Agenda 21. Others have explained that they actually just went out into "the deep" . This second approach seems to be quite meaningful for Fiji, where I come from. If you were to go through the steps of asking the questions related to the spirit of sustainability I think, because of the age of the city where I come from, people would understand the concept of sustainability. So it would appear that you don't have to go for funding through international agencies to make progress on Local Agenda 21. As Manchester's City Planner said earlier a lot of these things are felt through our senses - through smell, touch, taste - the environmental problems that we face are really things that we sense and in that respect, the problems are felt or sensed by the whole community which could therefore help in conveying the spirit of sustainability. The structure that has been outlined there could be implemented first through action and then eventually put in a proper framework through perhaps the assistance from local authorities from developed nations."

Q17 *LUIS B FIGUEROA, MUNICIPALITY OF CAJAMARCA, PERU*

"In Cajamarca, Peru we succeeded in formulating our plan of sustainable development for the province without access to international resources.

I do not have the same resources as Canada. We do not have $3 million, of for that matter, $30,000 for carrying out our plans.

What we have done is to optimise the resources of the borough - of other public sector agencies of the state, community organisations, a whole army of private institutions and other district and provincial institutions. In the past, each authority used to spend its resources in a different way and according to its own point of view. What we have done now is unify all these resources to draw up a plan for natural resources, agriculture, production, the urban environment and other main subjects. We have unified all these resources and we now have a draft plan ready for the public to be consulted. At the same time, we have arranged for these plans to go to the borough councils, councillors and mayors of districts, other population centres and small towns, so that they can look into the plan which has been drawn up.

On this basis it really is possible to draw up sustainable development plans. What is more important is that the social organisations and community should take a direct part in drawing up the plan. So, when we give the organisations the chance, they can take part directly and this way we can optimise resources. There are several kinds of resources. There are financial resources, but the other resources which we have and which are very valuable are human resources. We have to optimise and unify these human resources. I can very briefly give you details of one experience - when all these organisations worked separately they managed to plant a million trees a year, yet with all parties united they planted 8 million trees a year and did not need a single extra dollar. It is not that we needed more financial resources but that we just needed to unite in a single direction and a single objective. So I think that we, the local authorities, have a great responsibility to promote the unification of all sectors. For if we, the local authorities, manage to have the willingness to unify everyone, we could say - as I was indeed saying - that we could turn the resources of one into eight.

We also tackled our refuse disposal problems in the same way and organised for the first time ordered refuse collection. We organised all the 12 city districts through their respective acting mayors and they each in turn agreed to contact their neighbouring councils. Refuse collection times were specified and bags were prepared which could be put out to await the refuse collection lorry. We did not need any additional financial resources at all to organise ordered refuse collection in this way. We only needed some good manners, organisation and respect from society in general. We need financial resources, of course, but in a situation of poverty, we have to work with what we know".

Open microphone

INVOLVING YOUNG PEOPLE AND MARGINALISED GROUPS IN LOCAL AGENDA 21.

SPECIAL NOTE FROM THE CONFERENCE CHAIR:

"A group of 15 young people from Mexico travelled to Manchester especially for the Global Forum, finding the finance to do so themselves. They are part of an innovative project called the Mexican Popular Youth and they work with street children in Mexico city. They speak about young people and alternative ways of sustaining the local community. This is a welcome additional experience we can all share".

MEXICAN POPULAR YOUTH PRESENTATION

"We have a project in our country, Mexico, at the national level, which is called "Space for Students". It is a space for gang kids, which is what society calls us (and some people will know us by the name of "gangsters"). It is also a space for our native American brothers. We have worked on this project without resources, or with few resources which, fortunately, we obtained from our government and have tackled a range of problems. I would now also like to tell you that you should not think we have created paradise in our country. No. In our country, there are still needs, there is still marginalization and there is still repression. The proposal we have to make is for education, for the right to housing, for the right to health and for the right to work.

Our proposal is also psychological and cultural. We have a series of projects, one of these being employment. We have basic workshops for carpentry, silk screen printing and service work. These projects help us to support ourselves. One grievance which we have in common is that many of us young people, (and I am talking in particular about the gang kids, as they call us); many of us now do not have even the minimum right to demand, either legally or morally, that our parents keep feeding us, keep clothing us or keep sending us to school. We do not want to be independent but want to make enough money just for our school, our studies, for education.

The potential we have is cultural. They are training us now so that we can later train more people, more friends. With regard to culture, as I was saying, it is not just a matter of putting on a dance but implanting in the younger ones - in children - the idea of love; love of their culture.

I was saying to you that we saw it as something very urgent and very important that an opening should be given to all the young people in your country because, quite often, a lot more money is spent on patrols, prisons and other things and no resources are really invested in young people. We have shown that, without resources but with our own money, we have made this project work. The project exists in 22 states in our republic and, fortunately, has turned out well.

I would also like to tell you that we are not with any political party. We are not interested in political parties. Political parties often do nothing more than use us to make supporters of

theirs. We do not want any of that. We want real things. I mentioned our native friends earlier. I think there are native friends or native races all over the world. In our country, at least, this native race is totally neglected. 80% of our native race is neglected. There is always talk of supporting them but there is no such support. They carry on living in the same conditions, living by tilling the land and living in terrible conditions. We are concerned about them because it is urgent - and, what is more, we accept that it is more urgent - for them to have support as they have nothing at all. They live in conditions where they do not have lighting, water or drainage. They have nothing. If we are in the 20th century how can it be possible to talk of great advances and useful major projects when these marginalized people are so neglected?

We are young people who form part of the poverty belt; the ordinary people's urban settlements. It is not only in Mexico that they exist. They exist all over the world and there are special programmes with some resources, both institutional and under non-government organisations, to support these young people but they are not channelled to them. They do not reach us. This is why we feel the need to get organised. In our country, this is happening in the form of a youth manifesto. We exist, are qualified and have ability and, for this reason, we ask for institutional backing. Backing by the government is an obligation, it has to support and pay attention to these young people.

As my friend was saying, we are a non-party organisation. We receive very minimal support but now we are not looking for those who are to blame but are looking for solutions to the problems. This is another reason why we wanted people to listen to us, because the future depends on us. If they say we live on a planet where more than 50% are young people, why not take notice of us? We propose that, through self-productive workshops, general support, sources of income, sources of employment and also through training, optimizing cultural, sport and recreational activities, the high level of vandalism or gang culture will fall because the energy that these young people have is channelled towards a positive end. This is why we are here and we want our voice to be heard. We would ask young people to get organised as, through organisation a lot can be achieved and the government can be made to listen. We are part of the population, we are part of the planet and that is why we are here and we want to tell the authorities gathered here that they should give us opportunities.

As young people, we are looking for spaces, but spaces which are valid and real so that we do not keep being used because, to sociologists, we are a phenomenon and, to psychologists, we are an alternative or a proposed case which is found in a big fat book but goes no further than that. We are people, we are human beings and need to be heard.

Perhaps many of you are wondering how it was that these kids changed and what it was that made them decide to change their lives and do a 360 degree turn. It is nothing more than what you go through and it is what you have to do to get out of the rut. Many of us do not want people to

EPL, Rob Franklin

"Give young people an opening and listen to them. We want to participate" MPY

label us or feel pity for us but, in one way or another, the same system that has directed a country has at the same time given rise to poverty because people were not aware of these things.

When I was younger, when I started getting hold of drugs, it was because there was nothing, it was because I was always on the street corner or being hit and robbed and, whether you were a young person or a grown-up, you felt that there was no hope. We young people were thrown out on to the streets, intoxicated and, in those days, knew nothing but violence, violence and more violence, so that, when we were hit, you had to respond. Later on, when we saw how young people were dying, not just in our arms, or with us looking on - and, what is more, in many parts of the world - we started to be aware and we realised that if we did not get out, nobody at all was going to do it.

That was one of the things which made us decide to start getting organised and, to tell the truth. When I see all of you, people from many different countries, it is something incredible for me but I had to cross the seas to come and give you this message which has started in my country and is giving rise to good results. As my friends and I were saying, we are not solving all the problems but we are starting something off, as great ideas do start off.

Our proposal is very solid and definite. Give young people an opening and listen to them. Now that young people are trying to make their presence felt, they only need someone who will really listen to them and who will guide them. That way of dressing, that way of acting violently, those things that young people do all over the world is a way of saying to you "Here I am, I exist". Now we are saying to those in government "Here we are" in a positive way and, perhaps for this reason, they are listening to us. It is necessary for you to understand the way in which other young people are expressing themselves in other places, in that violent way. It is because, at a given time, young people want something.

In the past, we would meet up on street corners but it was because we did not have anywhere else to go. Now we have a home and we work. Now other friends in other states are making progress so that there is hope and so that we young people do not keep going to the wall. We feel that this is very important.

By our very nature, we young people have a lot of energy and that energy is moulded here, which is why we are here. You also have energy and also have that fundamental part which is important in a human being. You are also here , because, in one way or another, you are taking part. I have always said this and would like you to hear it:

"On the day when a child is truly a child, when a young person is truly a young person, when an adults truly meets his commitments and when officials fulfil the vocations they have; on that day the world can be reconciled."

Why are young children working? Why are young children, youths and adolescents being breadwinners for their families? Why? There is a lot of imbalance in this world and it is not just found in one country. I feel that this is happening all over the world. How can it be that you can ask for love if you have not been shown how to give it? This is one of the questions we often ask and I am going to ask you a favour: when you see a young person from the common people's districts, don't look down on him or her, don't criticise and don't try and call the police so they can come and give them a beating. That youngster has a lot of energy. We have done it, we have saved many people's lives and have even learned to love. We want to participate with our government, to try to pass on this information, because we love our country.

This is the message we have brought for you. We hope it is of some use to you".

CHAIR

"I think there is enough to think about in their words because if we talk about our Agenda 21 it is theirs - it is the young ones, it is the children of the 21st century we are working for and there is no use excluding them from the debate. If we do not feed, if we do not clothe, if we do not educate the children of this world properly there will not be sustainable development in the 21st Century".

(The speeches of the young people from the Mexican Popular Youth Group are presented in full and are a translation of the verbatim record of their contribution to the conference.)

SECTION SEVEN

INTERNATIONAL FRAMEWORKS FOR LOCAL AGENDA 21 IMPLEMENTATION

"Many of the problems and solutions listed in Agenda 21 have their roots in local authorities. As the level of government closest to the people, local councils play a vital role in educating and mobilising the public around sustainable development. During 1993 and 1994 local efforts should start to be linked at the international level, so people can share information and ideas and expertise from the community level". From "The Earth Summit's Agenda for Change: a Plain Language Version of Agenda 21" - Centre for our Common Future, 1992

Work to examine the framework for application and implementation of Local Agenda 21 is only just beginning to be done. This area of environmental policy-making as any other has to be continually put into a context. The International Council for Local Environmental Initiatives in its Local Agenda 21 Model Communities Programme and the "Group of Four"- The World Association of Major Metropolises, United Towns Organisation, International Union of Local Authorities, Summit Conference of the World's Major Cities present their proposals for implementation of a general framework and guidelines for local authorities on dealing with Local Agenda 21.

83

SECTION SEVEN

*INTERNATIONAL FRAMEWORKS FOR
LOCAL AGENDA 21 IMPLEMENTATION*

THE INTERNATIONAL FRAMEWORK
Jeb Brugman, Secretary General, ICLEI

THE ICLEI MODEL COMMUNITIES PROGRAMME
*Dr Mehta, Director,Local Agenda 21 Model Communities
Programme.*

PROPOSALS BY THE "GROUP OF FOUR" FOR
IMPLEMENTATION OF LOCAL AGENDA 21 –
"FROM RIO 92 TO ISTANBUL 96"
*Alain LE SAUX, Director Scientific, World Association of the
Major Metropolises Presentation for the "Group of Four" -
World Association of the Major Metropolises, International
Union of Local Authorities, United Towns Association, Summit
Conference of the World's Major Cities*

NETWORKING AND LOCAL AGENDA 21
*Marcello Nowersztern, Director of Programmes in Latin
America, United Towns Development.*

THE INTERNATIONAL FRAMEWORK
Jeb Bugman, Secretary General, ICLEI

As Director of ICLEI's Local Agenda 21 Programme I want to suggest some possible answers to questions which are being raised by local authorities working on Local Agenda 21. Namely how to balance the competing challenges of doing a Local Agenda 21, of addressing the immediate local service concerns on one hand and dealing with the global, more systematic issues, on the other hand. The Local Agenda 21 Model Communities Programme is an action research project that involves up to 20 municipalities from all of the different regions of the world. We will be working with these municipalities over a three year period to develop a planning framework which addresses these questions. The project will support the implementation of this framework in Model Cities, will address some specific issues in each community and will evaluate the framework. We hope to highlight what does and does not work and make comparisons between cities. Our hope is that out of this we can actually produce some general guidelines on how Local Authorities can deal with Local Agenda 21.

The general framework came out of a two year process of meetings with local government officials from all the different regions of the world. Work on the Local Agenda 21 project began in 1991, before the Earth Summit. In 1991 local authorities had two international meetings, each with about 30 local government representatives from about 25 different countries. We were trying to find out how municipalities were dealing with the environmental challenge. We looked at a variety of cases and we came to some general conclusions as a starting point for the Model Communities Programme.

The framework we present is not an answer in itself but a starting point. If you don't do every component of this framework it does not mean that you are not doing a Local Agenda 21. Whatever you can do to respond to this mandate is a positive step forward, something that should be celebrated and that you should be proud of locally. Obviously you can only do what your local resources permit, but there are some basics, some of which have been brought up during the debates at this conference. For instance in order to include the users of services in the planning process, there are some simple things that you can do that will make a big difference. We call the framework the Strategic Services Planning Framework (Fig. 16, 17 & 18).

What Local Agenda 21 at the local level involves is providing services with a longer term view. As it comes out of tradition of community-based strategic planning, which is now being used in many fields, it is therefore probably a framework which is familiar to many of you.

The process starts with partnerships. Once you have defined who your partners are, they should be involved in creating some kind of formal framework. The partners are the representatives of different sectors who are affected by municipal services, or who use municipal services. The second step is community priority setting. We feel that in most municipalities it would not be sensible to try to simultaneously address all of the challenges on the global agenda as local communities do not have the resources to do this effectively and in fact a municipality's main responsibility is to meet the most current community needs first. After deciding

who is to be involved in the planning process the next step is to decide what the focus of the process will be. We are urging municipalities to start with a community based process in which the community is not merely consulted but sets its own service priorities. Based on this priority-setting process, strategic services planning is applied to just one or two service areas. Progressing with one service area after another until eventually each service area has been addressed, it is essential not to tackle them all at once.

Having determined priorities and community preferences, the next step is to carry out a systems audit. Many local authorities involved in Local Agenda 21, are carrying out some kind of auditing. In some places they call it "state of the environment" reporting. In the UK it is called environmental auditing. Auditing is basically environmental information gathering. It is important from a municipality's point of view to use auditing to get a clear understanding of the conditions in each of the different system areas which are required to deliver the priority service. So for example, if the service priority is water, an understanding of the current conditions in the water supply and delivery system is needed - the drainage system, the waste water treatment system and the pricing system for water. After gathering the information then a strategic services plan for that service area should be created.

The plan should define the action and specify the programme but importantly, it also should do two other things, establish specific quantifiable targets that the municipality and its partners make a commitment to achieve within a specified time frame and refer to "triggers". In some cases, it will not be possible to achieve a consensus within the community on a specific target. It is too difficult from a technical point of view to say for instance that "a 20% reduction in private automobile use can be achieved by the year 2000". In those instances trends will need to be specified instead. For example the trend may be a regular annual reduction of private automobile use. However, one way or the other there has to be a specified goal.

We also suggest people consider using the concept of "triggers". level of activity and under certain conditions. The use of triggers permits the planning process to have a long term perspective. For example the City of Los Angeles has recently established a 100 year waste water management plan. It may seem ridiculous that a city with 6 or 7 million people is able to determine what kind of waste water management system they will need 50, 60 or 100 years from now. What they have done is to set a number of trigger levels so that when waste water levels reach certain volumes there is a commitment on the part of the municipality to begin planning for the next level of infrastructure.

Finally after completing the plan, the implementation and monitoring phases follow. Monitoring involves documenting what people are doing to implement the plan so that you can then actually evaluate the outcome. Information is then fed back into the system by a feedback loop. Establishing targets also allows you to create indicators which can be used to evaluate what is happening in the municipality or in the community. If the indicators tell you that things are not proceeding at the right level, then it can tell you that further action is needed. It either leads to further priority setting by the community, further auditing or further planning.

This is the general framework for Strategic Services Planning,
Figs. 19 to 22 provide diagrams and record sheets which have
been prepared by ICLEI to guide local authorities through the
Strategic Services Planning Process.

STRATEGIC SERVICES PLANNING
A Framework for Local Agenda 21
Stages and Processes

A   Partnerships

Establish an organisational structure and partnership
agreement for planning by service providers and
service users.

1   Identify partners.
2   Define partnership goals and objectives.
3   Determine the scope of planning.
4.   Establish terms of reference for the planning
     partnership
5   Create an organisational framework for
     partnership planning

B   Community Priority Setting

Perform community consultations to identify and prioritise
service needs and problems

1   Define "target" communities.
2   Select consultation methods.
3   Facilitate community issue identification.
4   Facilitate issues clarification: define the
     problems.
5   Facilitate community priority setting.
6   Document and evaluate the process.

C   System Audits

Perform audits of service systems related to prioritised
service needs and problems.

1   Establish terms of reference for the audit(s).
2   Characterise the service system to be audited
     using mapping techniques.
3   Prepare a service system map.
4   Identify data needs and sources.
5   Create norms for data processing and analysis.
6   Collect and process data.
7   Audit existing service system conditions and
     establish baseline data.
8   Determine the limits of current system capacity
     and performance.
9   Determine trends in system performance and
     capacity.
10   Produce an audit report

D   Strategic Services Plan

Define action objectives and identify options for action.
Set targets for service system improvement and create
partnerships and programmes to achieve targets. Establish
limits in system conditions which trigger further problem
analysis and planning.

1   Review community priorities and system audits.
2   Create a vision for a sustainable services system.
3   Define action objectives.
4   Identify action options.
5   Establish targets for system development and
     performance.
6   Specify partnerships and programmmes to
     achieve targets.
7   Establish triggers for future analysis and
     planning.
8   Produce an action plan report.

E   Implement and Monitor

Implement partnerships and programmes. Collect
information on activities and changes in services and
systems as plans are being implemented.

1   Identify resource needs and sources.
2   Establish an implementation timeline.
3   Create a "bridge" between the Action Plan and
     the Municipal Budget.
4   Establish implementation MOUs.
5   Implement programmes.
6   Document activities and achievements.
7   Identify and report on successes and problems.

F   Evaluate and Feedback

Perform regular progress and performance evaluations
using target-based indicators. Feed back results to service
providers and users. Repeat consultation, auditing and/or
action planning processes at specified trigger thresholds.

1   Create evaluation teams.
2   Create evaluation timetables.
3   Define indicators based upon targets.
4   Define and establish reporting framework.
5   Perform evaluations.
6   Report evaluation results to partners.
7   Initiate new problem analysis and/or planning at
     trigger thresholds

ICLEI, 1994

Fig. 16

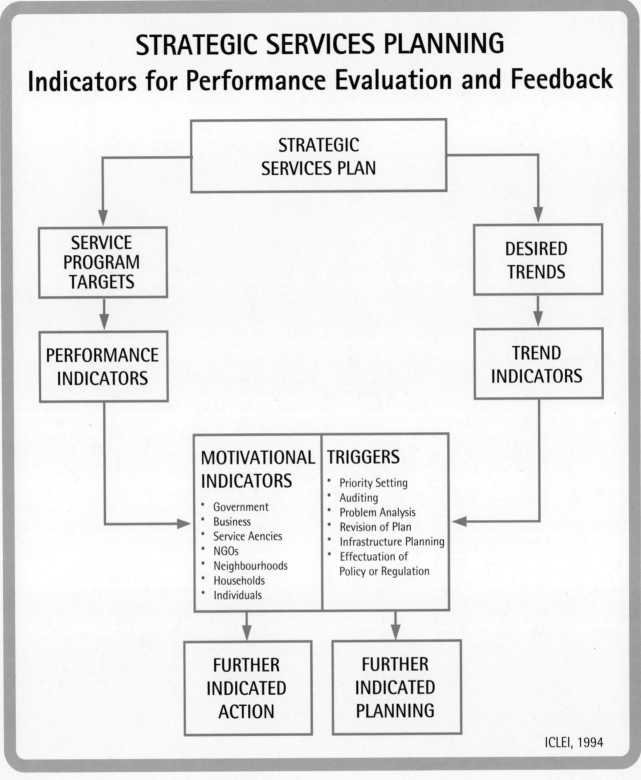

STRATEGIC SERVICES PLANNING
Indicators for Performance Evaluation and Feedback

STRATEGIC
SERVICES PLAN

SERVICE
PROGRAM
TARGETS

DESIRED
TRENDS

PERFORMANCE
INDICATORS

TREND
INDICATORS

MOTIVATIONAL
INDICATORS

* Government
* Business
* Service Aencies
* NGOs
* Neighbourhoods
* Households
* Individuals

TRIGGERS

* Priority Setting
* Auditing
* Problem Analysis
* Revision of Plan
* Infrastructure Planning
* Effectuation of
  Policy or Regulation

FURTHER
INDICATED
ACTION

FURTHER
INDICATED
PLANNING

ICLEI, 1994

Fig. 17

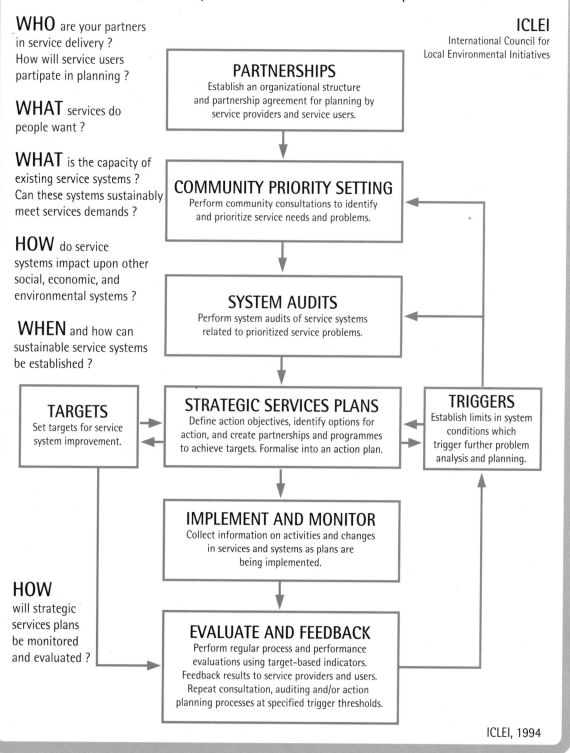

STRATEGIC SERVICES PLANNING
A Framework for Local Agenda 21

Sustainable development is development that delivers basic environmental, economic and social services to all without threatening the viability of the systems upon which these services depend.

WHO are your partners in service delivery ? How will service users partipate in planning ?

WHAT services do people want ?

WHAT is the capacity of existing service systems ? Can these systems sustainably meet services demands ?

HOW do service systems impact upon other social, economic, and environmental systems ?

WHEN and how can sustainable service systems be established ?

HOW will strategic services plans be monitored and evaluated ?

ICLEI
International Council for Local Environmental Initiatives

PARTNERSHIPS
Establish an organizational structure and partnership agreement for planning by service providers and service users.

COMMUNITY PRIORITY SETTING
Perform community consultations to identify and prioritize service needs and problems.

SYSTEM AUDITS
Perform system audits of service systems related to prioritized service problems.

TARGETS
Set targets for service system improvement.

STRATEGIC SERVICES PLANS
Define action objectives, identify options for action, and create partnerships and programmes to achieve targets. Formalise into an action plan.

TRIGGERS
Establish limits in system conditions which trigger further problem analysis and planning.

IMPLEMENT AND MONITOR
Collect information on activities and changes in services and systems as plans are being implemented.

EVALUATE AND FEEDBACK
Perform regular process and performance evaluations using target-based indicators. Feedback results to service providers and users. Repeat consultation, auditing and/or action planning processes at specified trigger thresholds.

ICLEI, 1994

Fig. 18

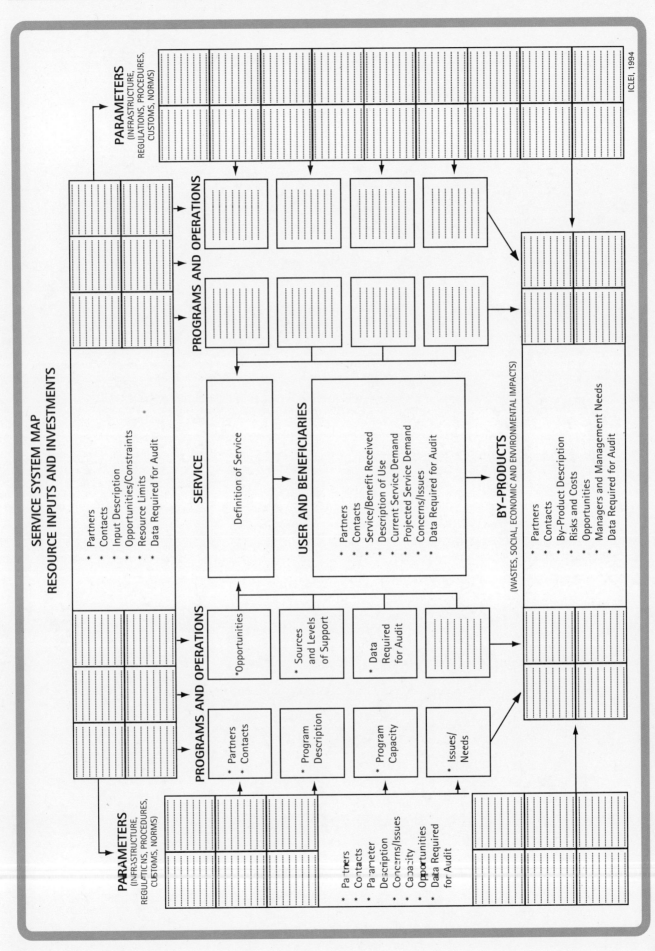

Fig. 19

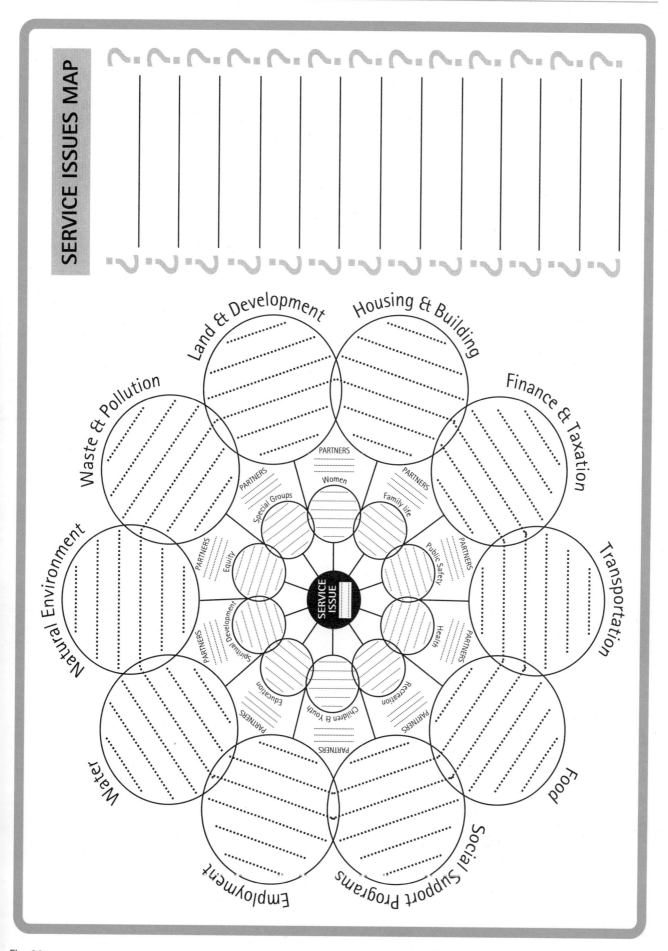

SERVICE ISSUES MAP

Fig. 20

LIVERPOOL HOPE UNIVERSITY COLLEGE

SERVICE SYSTEM AUDITING

Operational Steps

1   Establish terms of reference for the audit(s)

3   Identify data needs and sources. Create norms for data processing and analysis. Collect and process data.

5   Produce an audit report.

Analytical Steps

2   Use mapping technique with multi-sector group to identify service issues and partners.

Do preliminary analysis of key issues with related partners.

Identify service system elements (inputs, parameters, programs and operations, service outputs, and by-products).

Map the service system.

4   Audit existing conditions of service system elements. Establish baseline data.

Determine the limits of current system capacity and perfomance.

Determine trends in system performance and capacity using analysis and simple forecasting.

Fig. 21

SERVICE SYSTEM AUDIT RECORD SHEET

Resource Inputs and Investments
(Financial, Human and Natural Resources)

SERVICE SYSTEM   AUDIT DATE

Partner:

Contacts:

Input Description:

Opportunities/Constraints:

Resource Limits:

Data Required for Audit:

ICLEI, 1994

Fig. 22a

B

SERVICE SYSTEM AUDIT RECORD SHEET

Parameters
(Infrastructure, Regulations, Procedures, Customs, Norms)

SERVICE SYSTEM   AUDIT DATE

Partner:

Contacts:

Parameter Description:

Concerns/Issues:

Capacity:

Opportunities:

Data Required for Audit:

ICLEI, 1994

Fig. 22b

C

SERVICE SYSTEM AUDIT RECORD SHEET

Service Programs and Operations

SERVICE SYSTEM   AUDIT DATE

Partner:

Contacts:

Program Description:

Sources and Levels of Support:

Program Capacity:

Issues/Needs:

Opportunities:

Data Required for Audit:

ICLEI, 1994

Fig. 22c

D

SERVICE SYSTEM AUDIT RECORD SHEET

Service Users and Beneficiaries

SERVICE SYSTEM	AUDIT DATE

Partner:

Contacts:

Service/Benefit Received:

Description of Use:

Current Service Demand:

Projected Service Demand:

Concerns/Issues:

Data Required for Audit:

ICLEI, 1994

Fig. 22d

SERVICE SYSTEM AUDIT RECORD SHEET

Service By-Products
(Wastes, Social, Economic and Environmental Impacts)

SERVICE SYSTEM   AUDIT DATE

Partner:

Contacts:

By-Product Description:

Risks and Costs:

Opportunities:

Managers & Management Needs:

Data Required for Audit:

ICLEI, 1994

Fig. 22e

THE ICLEI MODEL COMMUNITIES PROGRAMME
Dr Pratibha Mehta, Director ICLEI Model Communities Programme

In this paper the framework and the details under each of the actions which have to be undertaken in a planning exercise will be outlined. Any planning undertaken under a participatory mode must include three fundamental principles- partnerships, consultation and transparency. The framework presented here reflects these three principles.

The first activity which has to be undertaken is to create partnerships, to bring people from various internal groups together to sit together and decide what the city must do, or what activities should be undertaken in cities. An organisational structure and partnership agreement for planning by service providers and service users needs to be established. A key question to ask is: "Who should the partners be and how should they be selected?" Next partnership goals and objectives must be established, the scope of planning exercise and the broad framework under which planning should be undertaken in the city also need to be agreed. Fourthly, terms of reference for the planning partnership should be set in place including reference to the type of organisation and the fundamental ethics behind the functioning of this partnership group. The final task would involve formally establishing an organisational framework for the partnership process. It is necessary to consider the "communities priority setting process" which follows the creation of this organisational structure. The objective of "community priority setting" is to consult the community about identifying and prioritising service needs and problems. This particular activity should begin by defining who the target communities are and what consultation tools are needed to engage them. A second set of key questions need to be asked: "How do we inform the communities about the planning effort?", " How do we facilitate community issues clarification and definition?", and finally, "How do we document the entire exercise?". Details of how to implement some of these broad elements follows below.

IDENTIFYING PARTNERS

WHO : PEOPLE WHO HAVE A STAKE IN THE CITY AND ITS QUALITY OF LIFE

Community sector : organisations/groups representing various constituencies in the community (i.e. neighbourhood organisations, women's groups, youth groups, the aged. Local research agencies, pressure groups, etc.)

Private sector : formal business, informal sector workers, unorganised workers, etc.

Public sector : local authority and its agencies and extension workers.

HOW : THROUGH AN OUTREACH AND CONSULTATIVE PROCESS INITIATED BY THE LOCAL AUTHORITY

ICLEI, 1994

Fig. 23

The first step is identifying the partners (Fig. 23). The partners have to be those who have a direct stake in the city in which they are living and its quality of life. Basically we can divide partners into three categories; the community sector, the private sector and the public sector. Under the community sector there should be representation from organisations and groups of different constituencies in the city. This means representation from neighbourhood organisations, women's groups, youth groups, the aged, local research agencies, and pressure groups, etc. has to be ensured. Within the private sector we should consider representation from the formal business sector, as well as from the informal sector, which is often overlooked yet very important. Within the public sector the partners must be from the local authorities, its agencies and workers.

Secondly, these partners are only from broad sectors within a community. How do we identify which individual organisations or groups should have representation on the committee?

The usual process is that the local authority or whoever is initiating this process, follows the information which they already have on the table, and at times that often overlooks constituencies and groups who have traditionally been excluded. As these groups continue to be overlooked in this process, one option is that before selecting partners an outreach programme and a consultative process at various levels and with various groups is initiated. In this way the representation could be made more "real" and "true".

How do we define the partnership goals and objectives? The sectors who are represented or should be represented will have diverse motivations so it is important that partners have a common vision of the future, which could be improving quality of life in their cities and a commitment to a sustained effort. Consensus building processes can be created to help to dilute the differences, bringing the partners together on a common platform to work for a common goal. However in the initial stage partnership goals must only be used as something which can guide the overall process of planning and they should not be taken as rules or as the fundamental principles for undertaking activities. As guides they serve to keep motivation high and to keep the effort in focus.

The next step, having identified the goals and objectives of the partnerships, is to determine the scope of planning process. In the initial stages again this serves merely to define the limits of planning exercise and not the content because the content of planning exercise has to come from the community itself (Fig. 24). Initially we are only putting together a broad framework and strategy within which the community based planning process can take place. The next step is to establish the terms of reference for the partnership group. "What are the goals of this partnership exercise?" and "What is the ethical code of conduct?" Quite often when people from diverse backgrounds come together, they have different ethical codes, different interests, different motivations and therefore they might have codes of conduct that may be very different from one another. What is necessary is that the group focuses on the main objective of the planning exercise, for instance to improve quality of life for everybody in the city. However issues such as access to information and everyone's right to participate must be appreciated by all the partners in the group. The relationship between the partners is important and they should be accountable not only to the city but to each other. It is essential to create transparency within the group.

COMMUNITY PRIORITY SETTING

Perform consultations to identify and prioritise service needs and problems

1   Define 'Target' Communities

2   Inform the Communities about the Planning Effort

3   Select Consultation Methods

4   Facilitate Clarification of Issues and Definition of Problems

5   Facilitate Community Priority Setting

6   Document and Evaluate the Process

ICLEI, 1994

Fig. 24

SELECTING CONSULTATION METHODS

*   Participatory

*   Provide a Framework of Options

*   Appropriate to the Target Groups and the Purpose of the Consultation

*   Provide Credible Data/Information/Insights.

Examples

Different Types of Community Mapping
Focus Group Discussions
Community Modelling
Questionnaires/Interviews

ICLEI, 1994

Fig. 25

Consideration of the organisational framework within which the group should function is important. The group must also have some kind of formal mandate so that the decisions taken by the group are accepted and have some importance. It is important that mechanisms for communication and consultation are created. These should be mechanisms which facilitate communication between the partners such as either a roundtable or a committee, or stakeholders group. The group should work at the policy level so that the policies framed by the group will be implemented. To make this happen another group can be set up which is operational in nature whose mandate is to turn the decisions into action.

Having these five steps in place is only part of the story. Depending on the context, the steps can be increased, however these are essential steps needed to create partnership groups. This entire process should be documented and evaluated to draw out the strengths and weaknesses of this whole process. "What facilitated and what hindered the whole process?" and "What interventions worked in overcoming bottlenecks?" It is important that it is not a once only activity, but that it is constantly revised and modified to suit objectives.

After creating a partnership a process of community consultation should be initiated (Fig. 25) involving a similar process of defining the target communities, informing the communities about the planning effort, selecting consultation methods, facilitating and clarifying the issues and defining the problems, facilitating community priority setting and finally documenting and evaluating the process. In the first step defining target communities (Fig. 26), a decision has to be made

on the selection of the target communities. The target communities are those who are most affected by the problems in a city, zone or area.

DEFINE TARGET COMMUNITIES

WHO AND WHERE :

Target Communities are those who are most affected by the problems in a City/Zone/Area.

The Inclusion of Gender, Age, Ethnicity, Special Needs Groups and Religion must be imperative in the Definition of a Target Group

ICLEI, 1994

Fig. 26

A planning exercise can be undertaken at city level, at a zone level, or in any particular area in which the city feels it is appropriate to initiate the action. The definition of the target communities must take into consideration gender, age, ethnicity, special needs groups and religion. Often, in the past, the planners decide who the community is on the basis of their own perceptions, which often excludes many marginalised groups, the poor, women, youth etc. So it's important that a conscious effort is made to include these groups when defining the target group. The second step is to inform the communities about the planning effort. A common experience is that cities initiate consultation processes without actually informing the community properly and as a result the community is often confused (Fig. 27). They don't know why they are being consulted and what the outcome of the consultation could be. It is not likely that everybody will want to participate or that everybody is interested in participating but if an open process is created it is likely more people will become involved in the approach and design of the planning effort. "How should this be done?" Mass media communications, announcements etc. all can be used. "How do you select the consultation methods?" The methods have to be participatory in nature and they have to be suited to the target groups. The purpose of the consultation process is to provide credible data and information. Examples of different types of consultation methods which have been used successfully include community mapping exercises, focus group discussions, community modelling, questionnaires and interviews.

They have to be ranked by the community itself. Finally one can select one or two problem areas for a detailed planning exercise. The last task involves again, documenting and evaluating the entire process itself to analyse what worked and what did not work, so that the processes and the methodologies can be refined for future exercises.

**INFORMING THE COMMUNITIES ABOUT
THE PLANNING EFFORT**

WHY :

* To make Communities Aware of the Effort

* To Create an interest

* To Allow Communities to Influence the Approach and Design of the Planning Effort

HOW :

* Mass Media (Both Modern and Traditional Methods of Communication).

* Group Communication : Plays, Meetings with Local Committees and Associations

* Announcements at Strategic Places.

ICLEI, 1994

Fig. 27

Having followed these steps and obtained clarification of what are the issues and problems which warrant consideration, but before progressing with implementation, it's important to build the capacity of those involved. It is not necessarily the case that everybody has the necessary skills and capacity to handle the consultation process and an understanding of the inter-linkages between problems and solutions and the limitations on implementation.

The list of needs may be long and many may be outside the limit and scope of the municipality, or the municipality may not have sufficient resources to do something about it. So there is a need to set priorities. Again, the community has to be informed about the scope of problems which have been identified and of the limitations to solving these problems.

American citizens show their concern - Agenda 21 will give them a chance to participate in decision-making

EPL James Perez

PROPOSALS BY "GROUP OF FOUR" FOR IMPLEMENTATION OF LOCAL AGENDA 21 - FROM RIO 92 TO ISTANBUL 96
Alain LE SAUX, Directeur Scientifique, World Association of Major Metropolises

By way of introduction to my subject, I would first of all like to thank the City of Manchester for having taken the initiative to hold this meeting. This meeting is indeed important as we are now half-way between Rio '92 and Istanbul '96, two international meetings which, to a large extent, condition the development of the small, medium and large cities of the world for the future.

To begin with, why and how did the 'Group 4' come to be set up, how does it act and what will its future actions be?

The Group of 4 was created out of the need for close co-operation between the associations of cities as part of the preparation of the United Nations Conference on the Environment and Development.

It is important to remember that, at the time of the preparatory meetings, whether they took place in New York, Geneva or elsewhere, it was absolutely out of the question for local authorities, cities or urban problems to be included in the texts drawn up in advance of the meetings by the United Nations. It was as if half the world's population no longer existed; as if the only environment problems which could beset the world were affecting Antarctica and its baby seals, Amazonia or the Gulf, which were, indeed, greatly threatened. Faced with this situation, it was necessary to react, and to react quickly and, as far as was possible, to react well. So the associations of cities decided to act together: The International Union of Local Authorities, IULA, the World Federation of Untied Cities, chaired by Mr Sampaio, who is Mayor of Lisbon and also Chairman of Euro-Cities, the Summit Conference of the World's Major Cities, chaired by the Governor of Tokyo and the Metropolis, the World Association of the Major Metropolises headed by the Chairman of the L'Isle de France Regional Council. With their combined resources they pressured the United Nations so that official recognition of local authorities should become a reality. It is clear that this work was not done in isolation. Several preparatory meetings took place in particular with the assistance of the City of Rio de Janeiro in January 1992, where the biggest international associations of cities met and decided to authorise the Group of 4 to take action officially with the United Nations.

The Group of 4 did the work and Chapter 28 of Agenda 21 was created and is a reality today. The World Cities Forum was organised in Curitiba, Brazil, to run in parallel with the United Nations Conference on the Environment and Development. We got a result; it is now for us to judge whether this result is totally satisfactory.

Speaking for myself, I do not think so; it is far from being satisfactory. We are still in the situation where local authorities and the associations which represent them are regarded as being like Non Governmental Organisations, NGOs. Now, I am not prejudiced against the NGOs, they are useful and necessary and they do some fantastic work, especially in the fields of the environment and development but I am afraid that the people in charge of the world's big cities are not heads of NGOs. So we now have to face a very great problem; that is the problem of the real status which local authorities must have with the United Nations with reference to all the discussions which affect the future development of cities.

It is quite clear that we cannot continue to accept that only countries, grouped together in the United Nations, should decide on the future of half the world's population. Today, we are just about at the point where 50% of the world's population live in cities; tomorrow, very probably 60% of the world's population will live in cites, in some continents, 80% of the population live in an urban environment.

We therefore have to consider that local government officials who control extremely large budgets and who, in a great many cases, work autonomously, must have the means of participating in all international meetings which condition the operation of the cities for which they are responsible.

So it will be necessary for us to find the methods for possible participation, bearing in mind that we would be fooling ouselves if, today, we believed that cities could have a role equal to that of the states within the United Nations.

At the level of the Group of 4, we decided to take action on this subject and it is International Union of Authorities, IULA who are giving us guidance on the legal framework which could be put forward to the UN. At the forthcoming meetings and particularly in Habitat II in Istanbul in 1992, local authorities need to be heard - not on a consultative basis any more but as a prime participant on all matters of urban development.

The four chairmen of the associations have written to the UN and have had meetings with them and have raised this matter and to date although the replies received have shown quite an interest and are quite polite, they are not **really** responding to our request. However let us not loose heart, local authorities should be aware of this reality and should try to act so that, in each country, pressure is brought to bear on the national governments. Local Authorities will also have to apply pressure so that, in the national delegations to the UN, there are increasing numbers of local government officials taking part in the meetings. Cities' problems again need to emerge and should not be distorted by diverging interests.

Secondly a few words should be said on the problems involved in implementing Action 21 as we say in French, or the Agenda 21 programme.

In my opinion, Agenda 21 raises more questions than it resolves. Clearly the essence of pollution problems, environmental matters and social exclusion due to poverty are being experienced most acutely in cities today and it is obvious that the city is the preferred place for finding solutions to these problems. However, I do not think you can produce checklists or guidelines of easy or less easy ways of implementing Agenda 21 without raising the issue of resources.

In the developing world, one in three people lacks safe drinking water and sanitation

EPL Rob Hadley

Representatives from a number of European cities had a meeting in Aalborg, Denmark in April 1994 and it is clear that, between the north and the south of Europe, we can already detect fairly large differences. These may be the result of historical background, culture, climate variations and different economic situations but it is obvious that all the cities in the north of Europe are a long way ahead of the cities in the south of Europe in environmental matters. You can imagine the disparities which can exist there when we compare northern Europe and the south of the world. The African countries, some Latin American and Asian countries do not necessarily have the implementation of Agenda 21 as their prime or only preoccupation.

True, it has been agreed that sustainable development has to become the world's priority. This is all very well but the issue for a large number of local decision-makers, before thinking of sustainable development, is in fact what to do with the thousands of migrants who swarm into the cities every day for whom there is no housing infrastructure and no mains drinking water. It is absolutely out of the question to talk of sanitation and household refuse collection. When you are up against this kind of situation, what becomes of Agenda 21 and what becomes of the literature on the implementation of Agenda 21? If there were representatives from Calcutta for example here I would like to ask them this:

"What is the Agenda 21 implementation programme for Calcutta?"

This is not intended to be provocation but applies equally to dozens and dozens of large cities.

The Group of 4 are aware that there are problems but we are also aware that we will have to make compromises as it is our role to help local authorities as much as possible so that, in line with their resources and individual timetables which are set in accordance with the everyday reality of their respective cities, they can attempt to gain some positive elements from this programme.

It was therefore out of the question in the Local Agenda 21 guide that we have recently produced to advocate methods that can be applied across the globe. In my opinion, there are no methods which could be applied equally to a city with a population of 20 million and to a village of 2,500 people. I think we will each really need to have the capability of developing methods which are specifically tailored to our own requirements.

What we have tried to do simply with our document on Local Agenda 21 - which is available in French, English and Spanish, from the four associations of the Group of 4 - is to draw out broad guidelines from Agenda 21 that seem to us to constitute the most fundamental points which need to be handled as a top priority by local authorities.

Of these points, I will cover only two here. The first point is the fight against poverty. I think that poverty today, in a considerable number of cities around the world and more especially in a number of cities in developing countries, is a solid barrier to implementing Agenda 21. As a result, the first problem which has to be raised is how can local authorities - knowing that they do not have any particular competence or resources for this enable underprivileged populations to become active participants in local development? In this we have a major problem. Several

times at this conference the subject of water has been raised and we must realise that water is becoming a factor of social exclusion - water is not free any more. Constructing a water supply system right to the users is very expensive and is becoming more expensive. No water; no hygiene. No hygiene; no health. The consequences could go on growing like that. So the issue of poverty really is, for a great many of the world's cities, one of the most fundamental problems to be tackled with regard to implementing Agenda 21.

There are other such problems however, and one important matter which has to be tackled is the administrative organisation of cities. Indeed, when a local authority is fully autonomous and fully demarcated, with it's own budget, quite a few difficulties arise. However, if you are a metropolitan area, which is a metropolitan area only in name, but not administratively formed as such, how can you co-ordinate the actions of the various different component authorities and how can you define priorities? Who will define the priorities if there are no coherent administrative structures for doing this? Who will determine the budget allocations if there are no authorities with the power to do so? Quite often in these circumstances it is the state which then takes the problem into its own hands but it does not handle it in the same way as local authorities would, after all, the states' interests are different from those of local authorities. So, for a considerable number of cites, before dealing with Agenda 21, it will be necessary to consider administrative reorganisation.

Agenda 21 also signifies the need to change our habits. Here, too, we could spend hours and days debating this subject. The consumer society we live in, is a society of wastage rather than a society of economy, and, a society which has a tendency to pollute rather than anything else.

It would perhaps, be necessary for cities to begin by changing habits at the level of their own operation, being the first level of government close to the population, it should set a good example. In many cases, they control their budgets very strictly but, at other times, the "pomp" and "ceremony" in which they indulge, does not set a good example. Changes in their acquisitions i.e. car fleets and equipment, could by example prompt the population itself to change.

Finally it is essential for cities to use the opportunity of Agenda 21 to develop bilateral co-operation. These days, many cities are truly exemplary in terms of their provision of quality techniques and are therefore in quite a good position to allow other cities to take advantage of their experience. When I talk of bilateral co-operation, this does not necessarily mean co-operation being provided by the North to the South. A number of cities in the South have also developed techniques which may become advantageous to cities in the North. So I think it is necessary for local authorities, on their own initiative, if they can, but also through their representative associations, to give priority to thinking about exchanges of knowledge and technologies by means of decentralised co-operation. I believe that this is one of the most effective means by which cities can push Agenda 21 forward.

But above all, we must show nation states that we are willing to act even if our nation states do not give us the resources to do so.

NETWORKING AND LOCAL AGENDA 21

Marcello Nowersztern, Director of Programmes in Latin America, United Town Development

This paper is about decentralised co-operation and Alain LE SAUX of Metropolis has provided me, to some extent, with an introduction to the subject.

We are faced with a situation in which the municipalities, for various different reasons, whether political, economic or to do with institutional organisation have increasing responsibilities not only to provide services for the people resident in their areas but also to develop a framework of life for their residents. The principle of decentralised co-operation which we in our organisation and others are trying to develop is that municipalities should be capable also in the field of co-operation and in the field of the international work . That is that municipalities as political entities, as service-providing units, as technical units and as work units can, by themselves, develop ties of work and co-operation at international level.

At the risk of producing a caricature, it can be said that, in the last 20 or 30 years, we have known two basic procedures for co-operation: firstly there is the co-operation between States, which has been developed particularly by European countries, the United States and Canada, and which is, in general, extremely closely linked with interests of a political, geo-political, economic and even military nature. This form of co-operation is of course very structured and has in the main been developed by the large bureaucracies of the States concerned and, contrasts with the co-operation which is traditionally between non-governmental organisations and which tries to develop on the principle of solidarity between basic organisations. In my view, this dichotomy can, to a certain extent, be overcome by the work of decentralised co-operation between municipalities.

Decentralised co-operation between municipalities brings in a procedure for international co-operation in which a level of effectiveness in transferring technical and financial resources can be achieved without imposing interests which are of a global nature which often form a real barrier to co-operation. This is why we maintain that a basic principle of this decentralised co-operation or co-operation between municipalities is that the decisions on co-operation, the methods of co-operation and the staff who carry out the co-operation have to come from the municipalities themselves. Municipalities have to know, and this is gradually being brought into their working practices, that they are also called upon to make decisions on the international activity of their cities and towns . In view of this, to take up what Alain LE SAUX said, we would ask you as municipal repre-sentatives to try and achieve a situation whereby, in Agenda 21, there is a maximisation of the work which is undertaken by the municipalities themselves based on their own experience, their own staff and involving their own objectives.

Secondly decentralised co-operation between municipalities involves a great problem which is that, in general, it is of an isolated nature. Municipalities are often small and isolated, territorial unit and developing relations between two municipalities of two different countries cannot really tackle this problem of isolation. This is why we have brought into the decentralised co-operation work the concept of networks, in other words, the grouping of municipalities in the North and in the South. This prevents the experience from being an extremely isolating one and from having any deleterious effects on the overall scope of the general policy of a country or continent.

Agenda 21 offers the possibility of forming and developing these networks and therefore linking the activity of individual municipalities to a general framework. This increases its effectiveness and improves upon the possible consequences of developing relationships between the populations of different continents.

USA

UK

Canada

Japan

New Zealand

Brazil

Africa

Australia

Austria

Sweden

India

The West Indies

Turkey

THE WAY FORWARD
WORKSHOPS AND FINAL REPORTS

"Case studies which have come from so many different countries around the world have demonstrated the scope of Local Agenda 21 and the wide range of issues involved.

I hope the conference has promoted better understanding of what Local Agenda 21 can achieve and its different contexts and has reinforced the importance of international co-operation, particularly in the North/South dimension"

Cllr Louise Ellman, Leader Lancashire County Council

Final reports from the workshops and conference provide the reader with ideas for future work on Local Agenda 21 including calls to strengthen the local authority and Local Agenda 21 input to the Habitat II Conference on "Human Settlements" in Istanbul in 1996.

THE WAY FORWARD
WORKSHOPS AND FINAL REPORTS

WORKSHOP REPORTS

1. Bernie Cotter, Project Manager,
Australian Local Agenda 21 Programme.

2. John Craddock, Director,
Muncie Water Quality Bureau, USA.

3. Sneha Palnitkar, Director,
All India Institute for Local Self-Government, India.

4. Bret Willers, Environment Strategy Co-ordinator,
Cardiff City Council, UK.

5. Aydam Erim, Council Member, Cankaya,
Ankara, Turkey.

6. Roger Levett, Environment Team Leader,
CAG Consultant, UK.

THE WAY FORWARD
FINAL REPORTS

WHERE DO WE GO FROM HERE?

Margarita Pachenco. Environmental Studies Institute,
National University. Columbia.

PRIORITIES FOR ACTION

Councillor Louise Ellman, Leader, Lancashire County Council, UK.

POSTER PRESENTATION
WORKSHOP ONE

*CREATING A COMMUNITY BASE FOR PLANNING LOCAL
AGENDA 21 PUBLIC AWARENESS
AND CONSENSUS BUILDING*

KEY POINTS:

COMMUNITY MAPPING

ENJOYABLE

INFORMATIVE

SIMPLE

FUN

PRO-ACTIVE

APPROPRIATE

DEDICATED COUNCIL OFFICERS

INVOLVE CHILDREN

CONSULT ALL INTERESTS

LINK TO NEIGHBOUR MUNICIPALITIES

OPEN

LONG-TERM

LEGITIMISE

NO JARGON

NO PRESUMPTIONS

DO NOT EXCLUDE GROUPS

ISSUES:

LINKS POLICY TO GRASSROOTS

RESOURCES - NUMBERS OF STAFF TO PEOPLE

THE COMMUNITY IS PEOPLE!

WHICH GROUPS ARE INVOLVED?

LOCATION - GO TO THE PEOPLE

IDENTIFY HOW THE COMMUNITY WORKS

THE FRAMEWORK IS IMPORTANT

DEVELOP THE CONCEPT OF "KIN"

POSTER PRESENTATION
WORKSHOP ONE

*CREATING A COMMUNITY BASE FOR PLANNING LOCAL
AGENDA 21 PUBLIC AWARENESS
AND CONSENSUS BUILDING
ROUNDTABLES*

KEY POINTS:

OPEN

STRICT RULES NEEDED

CREATE ON-GOING PROCESS

IDENTIFY SPECIFIC ACTIONS

ROUNDTABLES ONLY ADVISORY

BE DEMOCRATIC

BE CREDIBLE

EQUAL VETO POWERS FOR ALL

AVOID LOBBYING

NOT LEGISLATIVE

DO NOT MAKE POLITICAL DEALS

DO NOT SPECIFY VAGUE OR BROAD

ACTIONS

ISSUES:

MEET WHERE PEOPLE FEEL COMFORTABLE

MAKE GRANTS AVAILABLE TO ASSIST PARTICIPATION

*LIMIT SIZE TO TWENTY AND
MAKE SMALLER OVER TIME*

APPOINT A FACILITATOR AND A CHAIR PERSON

CONFLICT IS PART OF THE PROCESS

TRY TO BALANCE COMPETING NEEDS

*LOCAL, REGIONAL, STATE, INTERGOVERNMENTAL
LEVEL ROUNDTABLES*

*EACH PARTICIPANT TELLS THE OTHERS:
"WHY YOU SHOULD AGREE WITH ME"*

POSTER PRESENTATION
WORKSHOP TWO

*HOW TO SET UP AN ENVIRONMENTAL ACTION
PROGRAMME, PRIORITISE TASKS AND SET TARGETS*

STEP ONE

STATEMENT OF ENVIRONMENTAL INTENT

*INCLUDE DISCUSSION OF ENVIRONMENTAL ETHICS
STATUTORY NEEDS AND NON-STATUTORY NEED
FREE AND CREATIVE PROCESS*

STEP TWO

SUSTAINABLE MANAGEMENT OF RESOURCES

REMOVAL OF RULES THAT INHIBIT SUSTAINABILITY

THINK OF CITIES AS ECOSYSTEMS

STEP THREE

COMMUNITY INVOLVEMENT

OFFICIAL MEETINGS

FESTIVALS

INTERNATIONAL CONFERENCES

STEP FOUR

CHANGING CITIZENS' LIFESTYLES

NEED TO CHANGE: HOW PEOPLE LIVE

HOW OPERATE IN BUILT AND NATURAL ENVIRONMENT

*RELATIONSHIP BETWEEN ECONOMIC AND SOCIAL
FACTORS*

STEP FIVE

FACILITATING CITIZENS' INPUT

IMPORTANT TO INVOLVE INDIGENOUS PEOPLE

*NVOLVE MORE THAN NON- GOVERNMENTAL
ORGANISATION*

BUSINESS AND INDUSTRY IMPORTANT

POSTER PRESENTATION
WORKSHOP THREE

*ENVIRONMENTAL INFORMATION GATHERING AND
INTERPRETATION*

KEY POINTS:

ACCURATE, AUTHENTIC AND RELEVANT

INTERDISCIPLINARY-ECONOMIC,

DEMOGRAPHIC, SOCIAL, GEOGRAPHICAL,

DATABASE FIRST THEN POLICIES

IMPROVE INFORMATION COMPILING

*USE VARIETY OF INFORMATION SYSTEMS LOCAL,
CITY. NEIGHBOURHOOD, COMMUNITY*

INCREASE TRANSPARENCY

FREE FLOW OF INFORMATION

CREATE CHANNELS FOR INFORMATION EXCHANGE

STATUTORY BASIS FOR INFORMATION GATHERING

POLITICAL SUPPORT AND BACKING

*USE COMMUNITIES TO COLLECT AND
PROCESS DATA FOR THEMSELVES*

COORDINATION PRIOR TO APPLICATION

ISSUES:

DATABASES ESSENTIAL TO LOCAL AGENDA 21

*FINANCIAL IMPLICATIONS OF DATA
GATHERING IMPORTANT*

*INFORMATION SOURCES SPREAD
OUT AND IN MANY FORMS*

POSTER PRESENTATION
WORKSHOP FOUR

*LOCAL ECONOMIC STRATEGIES FOR SUSTAINABLE
DEVELOPMENT*

KEY POINTS:

INVOLVE ALL TYPES OF COMPANIES

WORK WITH ALL EMPLOYEES

LINK WITH RESEARCHERS IN UNIVERSITIES

PARTNERSHIPS VITAL

ELIMINATE THE CONCEPT OF WASTE

*TRY A VARIETY OF APPROACHES
TO GET THE MESSAGE ACROSS*

EMPLOYEES ARE GOOD SELLERS OF IDEAS

WORD OF MOUTH COMMUNICATION IMPORTANT

*DISTINGUISH BETWEEN
ENVIRONMENTAL ISSUES AND REGULATION*

ISSUES :

*CONFLICT BETWEEN ECONOMIC
DEVELOPMENT AND ENVIRONMENT*

*RESEARCH SHOWS MONEY AND JOBS
SAVED IN GREEN INDUSTRY*

JOBS MAY BE LOST IF SOMETHING IS NOT DONE

*SUPPORT OF NATIONAL GOVERNMENT E.G. WASTE
AND RECYCLING REGULATIONS*

POSTER PRESENTATION
WORKSHOP FIVE
INDICATORS OF SUSTAINABILITY

KEY POINTS:

CONSENSUS MAINTAINS ENTHUSIASM

INVOLVE PEOPLE IN IDENTIFYING INDICATORS

*CHILDREN AND STUDENTS
INVOLVEMENT IN DATA GATHERING*

*CITIZENS AS GOOD AS EXPERTS
AT IDENTIFYING PROBLEMS*

MUST BE APPROPRIATE

*"CARRYING CAPACITY" IDEA -
GET THIS ACROSS TO PEOPLE*

GET PEOPLE INVOLVED AND KEEP THEM INVOLVED

*DEVELOP BASIC UNDERSTANDING
OF CONCEPT OF SUSTAINABILITY*

*INVOLVE THE MEDIA -
PRESENT THE RESULTS IN AN ACCESSIBLE WAY*

*CONTROVERSIAL INDICATORS USEFUL -
STIMULATE MEDIA INTEREST*

COMPILE DIRECTORY OF GROUPS INVOLVED

USE DIVERSE INFORMATION SOURCES

MAKE COMPARISONS BETWEEN CITIES

EXTRACT RELEVANT LOCAL INFORMATION

NEED SOME (AT LEAST ONE) GLOBAL TARGETS

DO NOT GET BOGGED DOWN IN THEORY

AVOID OVERSIMPLIFYING

NOT JUST FOR EXPERTS

ISSUES:

*INDICATORS PAINT A PICTURE
THERE IS A DIFFERENCE BETWEEN AN INDICATOR
- SIGN OF DIRECTION
AND A BENCHMARK
- GOAL/TARGET*

*INFORMATION OFTEN ALREADY EXISTS BUT NEED TO
IMPROVE ACCESS AND DISSEMINATION*

POSTER PRESENTATION
WORKSHOP SIX

ECOSYSTEMS APPROACH TO URBAN ENVIRONMENTAL MANAGEMENT

ISSUES:

CONTRADICTIONS –
SUSTAINABILITY VERSUS POVERTY
ECONOMIC GROWTH VERSUS ENVIRONMENT
EQUITY VERSUS SERVICE

NEW WAYS OF THINKING AND NEW CRITERIA NEEDED

PERSONAL LIFESTYLES ARE A
CRUCIAL PART OF PROBLEMS

THINK IN BROADER TERMS

HAVE SCIENTIFIC KNOWLEDGE AT PRESENT
BUT IS IT THE RIGHT SCIENTIFIC KNOWLEDGE?

NEED TO WORK TOGETHER LOCALLY

NEED TO HELP PEOPLE UNDERSTAND THE ISSUES

MUNICIPAL SERVICES UNDER-PRICED

IMPORTANT TO TACKLE ACTION WHICH
MIGHT BE TAKING US BACKWARDS

NOT THINKING GLOBAL ENOUGH AT PRESENT

USE OF "FOCUSED ANALYSIS" TO ASK
SIMPLE QUESTIONS ABOUT IMPACT OF ACTIONS

ECOSYSTEMS APPROACH USED TO
BRAINSTORM AND SHARE IDEAS

COMBINE REGULATION WITH
EDUCATION AND UNDERSTANDING

PUTTING A VALUE ON ENVIRONMENTAL QUALITY

THERE IS A LOT TO LEARN FROM DEVELOPING NATIONS

THE WAY FORWARD
WORKSHOP REPORTS

WORKSHOP 1 -
CREATING A COMMUNITY BASE FOR PLANNING LOCAL
AGENDA 21 - PUBLIC AWARENESS AND CONSENSUS
BUILDING.
*Bernie Cotter, Project Manager, Australian Local Agenda 21
Programme.*

A few key concepts came out of the discussion at the workshop.

Firstly, when talking about community involvement and
community participation there is a need to look at how people
effectively hear, how they get messages and how we inform
them - this has to be done in a whole number of ways. It cannot
be done simply by speaking to people, we have to consider who
we are talking to, who is the community - how to go about
developing a community profile. There is a need to look at doing
this in a fun way too, it cannot be done in a way that is going
to be onerous and tedious, we have to use music, we have to use
song, we have to use rituals even. It is important to go to places
where it is comfortable for people to be involved in the process
and to move away from informing people or consulting people
in a passive to a very active way, so it is an open partnership.
The best successes come when there is a real commitment to an
open process. There has to be effective leadership - the process
cannot be driven by an environmental activist who is rather
powerless within Council. This has to be something that is core
to functioning of local government, involving the Chief Executive,
the Mayor and the Councillors. If we do it in a marginal way we
cannot really start to address some of the true issues of sustainability
because it needs to be considered across the whole Council's
operations. As someone said in the workshop!

*"It is necessary to take really bold steps to make it a simple
process, to keep it simple, especially the language used and to
use methods that are comfortable for people to understand."*

There was some discussion about community - the word community
is used to mean a cluster of people in any one location, we can
say the participants at a conference are a community , and we
also use it in terms of a global community, so there are different
ways of using the term. There is a need to use good adjectives
to describe who we mean. Perhaps we are talking about kin, tribe
or neighbourhood precincts but whatever or whoever we are
talking about, we have to operate at all levels simultaneously. It
is not appropriate to just involve a small group. Other levels of
government, local authorities within the same region, central
government, business and industry all have to be incorporated in
partnership, which brings the debate back to the notion of an
open process again.

The workshop talked about who, how and where it has to be
done. It has to be an open process, it has to involve effective
communication - simple ways of communicating in a very real
way that is meaningful, (not talk about chloroforms and what
they do, but put it into a message that means people might get
sick). For this it is necessary to develop new skills. People within
local authorities need to be able to consult and to be able to
work effectively with the community. Generally it is no good

getting people from the outside in, only when it is facilitated and
it is part of the core business of the local authority will it work.

In the workshop methods of involving people in India were
presented. Their participation was made realistic and purposeful
by focusing on issues such as health. Local people and groups
got involved in projects in which they mapped their environment.
We then had a report from a local authority in the UK, Mendip
District Council, who are operating in a very positive way with
every group within their local authority and then reports on
inter-governmental and partnership arrangements ie. roundtables,
as an effective way of getting everyone around the table in an
attempt to reach consensus and then taking examples from Japan
to show how a Council takes sustainability on as a corporate
responsibility. **It was agreed that corporate responsibility has
to be the basis for all processes.**

WORKSHOP 2 -
HOW TO SET UP AN ENVIRONMENTAL ACTION
PROGRAMME, PRIORITISE TASKS AND SET TARGETS
John Craddock - Director, Muncie Water Quality Bureau,
Indiana, USA & Member of ICLEI Strategic Planning Committee.

Three case studies were presented, one from Japan, one from
Brazil and one from New Zealand. After the case studies a list
was compiled which it was felt should be included as basic
concepts for a Local Agenda 21. The first is the Statement of
Environmental Intent and this should include a discussion of
environmental ethics, the efficient use of resources and the
reduction of pollution and citizens' actions. The general plan
should have statutory needs instituted along with non-statutory.
The idea behind the inclusion of non-statutory needs is to give
freedom and creativity to the process so that we are not stuck
within a structured plan that we have to live by, but with one
that can change. The second concept - the sustainable
management of resources and the removal of rules that inhibit
sustainability were discussed. Thinking of the cities as an
ecosystem within themselves and part of a total ecosystem,
along with concepts of vision and principles of the sustainable
development were considered. Thirdly, the variety of forms to
facilitate community involvement - from official meetings to
festivals to promote interest on a local level were all discussed.
Fourthly - changing citizens' lifestyles was seen as probably one
of the most difficult subject areas. The need to change how
they live, how they operate in the built and the natural
environments and the relationships between these and social
and economic considerations became a very large proportion of
our discussion. Finally the importance of facilitating the input
by citizens, especially indigenous people, not just the
governmental organisations, in the implementation of plans and
action programmes, as well as ideas for business and industry
and creating environmental partnership were discussed.

WORKSHOP 3 -
ENVIRONMENTAL INFORMATION GATHERING
AND INTERPRETATION

Sneha Palnitkar - Director, All India Institute of Local Self-Government, India.

The workshop included three presentations. The first was the use of environmental information to create a Local Agenda 21 programme for Lancashire City Council and the second was about the role of environmental information exchange and reporting within and between local authorities in Australia, and the third presentation concentrated upon the different facets of the Urban Management Programme and its implementation in Africa.

The discussions during most of the workshops centred around several factors related to environmental information, its interpretation and application and the importance of databases for an environmental programme and particularly for the Local Agenda 21 process. Some of the key points emerging from both workshops were

(1) the successful protection and improvement of urban environments is dependent upon accurate and comprehensive data on environmental conditions and their impacts.

(2) urban issues are interlinked and interdisciplinary urban policy makers are required to make links to central economic, demographic, geographical, social and environmental data.

(3) it is essential to have a sound database on several urban environmental issues before policies are formulated.

Local authorities should establish an urban information system at a local, city, neighbourhood and community level. Governments at various levels should undertake steps to increase transfer and encourage the free flow of relevant information not only among government and local government departments, but also among communities, community-based organisations and non-governmental organisations. A channel should be developed for exchange of information related to environmental issues among various cities. Several partnerships are required to be developed for information exchange, interpretation and implementation. Information gathering and interpretation requires political support and backing. In urban planning the process of collection of data by concerned communities is an important facet which requires to be more focused into the actual environmental planning process. Accuracy and authenticity are the main aspects in environmental information collection and interpretation and hence these factors should be considered and taken into consideration while formulating environmental programmes at various city levels.

Information exists at different levels from international to national government to local and is collected by para-government, non-government, academic and private sectors. The information is in different forms and is gathered for different reasons, some organisations have knowledge solely based upon their experience, others are involved solely in monitoring and recording information for databases - all these factors need to be coordinated prior to application. For the implementation of Local Agenda 21, it is essential to have database development and for the community to participate in this task. In environmental auditing the financial implications require adequate attention. Social aspects also require consideration. **Finally and importantly, information gathering needs to have some kind of statutory basis and provision.**

WORKSHOP 4 -
LOCAL ECONOMIC STRATEGIES FOR SUSTAINABLE
DEVELOPMENT
Bret Willers - Environmental Strategy Coordinator,
Cardiff City Council, UK.

One of the things highlighted is that cleaner production definitely
pays. Not dealing with cleaner production and the waste produced,
will result in high levels of unemployment. This is a very important
message that really does need to get across to industry. An
example was quoted in the workshop - "waste and emissions
are bought for money but are not converted into products that
can be sold for money" - there is a need to sell that message to
industry. It is long overdue. Also, there is a need to move away
from focusing solely on the enforcement role. In the main, local
authorities and municipalities are enforcers involved in regulating
and stamping on industry. There is need for a change of role to
become more enabling, to actually provide advice and support for
industry, to show them a new way forward, to show them that
there is an alternative way and that not only can cleaner production
be achieved, but it is actually going to be for their benefit. In
order to do that, we need to establish partnerships between
industry, local authorities and particularly with the community.

Another aspect that is needed is to concentrate and focus on
demand management. It is much cheaper for example to conserve
energy in the home than to build a new power station. An
example was given from the US where 6 jobs are created in
building one power station per unit of electricity produced but
that energy efficiency measures could result in the creation of
10 jobs per unit of electricity. In fact it pays more in terms of
employment opportunities to deal with the low-technology
approaches and actually reducing production and consumption.
It is advocated that moving away from something that is more
capital high-technology intensive to things which are more
labour intensive, but also more in tune with the communities'
needs and things which actually provide opportunities within
the community themselves, will reap benefits. So therefore the
high-technology approach is not seen as the sole option,
admittedly we still have to use it, but it is not the only answer.

There is a need to invest and create incentives for businesses in
the local area. Far too often we have been focusing on companies
and large corporations from outside and ignoring the needs of
companies within our areas. It is also important to recognise that
industry is not necessarily a bad thing and that industry needs to
be offered protection, particularly when we see that many of our
workforces are people who are, what we call 'blue collar' workers
who actually desperately need employment opportunities. If the
service industry is developed at the expense of industries then
we are not going to meet the needs of many who are disadvantaged
within our communities. So, in other words, by supporting the
development of industry and actively promoting it, but industry
which respects the environment, we are more likely to create
job employment opportunities for those on lowest incomes.

There is also a need to evaluate the true costs of our activities.
Whenever we buy goods in the shops we do not pay the true
price, which includes the effects of vehicle emissions etc. and
look at the social costs because, without this we are merely
passing our problems onto others.

The ultimate question is when to say no to industry or any
form of related activity at the expense of jobs? There is a
time when we will need to say for certain activities that we
should not go for jobs at any cost.

WORKSHOP 5 - SUSTAINABILITY INDICATORS
Aydam Erim - Council Member Canakaya, Ankara, Turkey.

This workshop was closely related to the workshop on environmental information because you start with urban databases and you do something to the data, usually combining it with other data and so ultimately it becomes an indicator. We had three presentations, one was the European project which compared about 15 European cities on a very large set of criteria of urban quality, the other one was the UK experience with the model sustainability indicators project which offers a menu to municipalities and the third one was an example of a completely different approach where the community decides the criteria, or what indicators they wanted - this was a unique approach. In the first case, in the comparative European study, the expert- designed approach leads to my favourite question, which is still largely unanswered - "So what?" Do we know what this comparative data will be used for other than by the narrow world of experts in urban affairs? The second approach explained, the UK experience, is again expert-designed, but very highly sensitive to users so it has a flexibility and the means of interpretation, making it a very useful tool. The third example from Seattle in the US, is unique in the sense that it was born out of a community with very specific characteristics, because it is so specific and culture-based, it is a very exciting model but how applicable it is, how much can we have similar experiences in other places? It is not a model that the World Bank can just impose on all developing countries, for instance, it is very specific and local. However as an approach and as a process, I think it is very valuable.

No one said "why do we need them?". There was also no open or aggressive opposition to indicators, but nobody took them as gospel either. After all we have been living with GNP which is the "indicator of the indicators" for decades and now it makes people wary of many other indicators. The conflicts between global, national and local community level indicators was taken by some as a problem and by others as a possibility and potential for development. However, one thing we did not touch much upon was the concept of values and of value judgements, because after all whether an indicator is going in the positive or a negative direction, is relative to a static point or line or axis. The decision on the axis or point involves a value judgement. We did not have much chance to consider cross-cultural evaluation of indicators. We left a lot of ground uncovered but our general conclusion was that the process of creating indicators was, using the analogy of a big United Nations meeting, even more valuable than the meeting itself. It was said at the workshop, *"this is a new thing because people actually now have to solidify this concept of sustainability which is still very controversial, it can be something very meaningless if you translate it into other languages."* For example, the Turkish Government interpretation has put everyone off the concept. It is a very difficult concept and one that is not such an easy word to transfer culturally. The international community have now put out this concept of Agenda 21 and they want to see how it goes. They want some solid concrete criteria to justify the work and justify themselves, so we as the practitioners have to live with the task of creating indicators. However, there will be a lot of people brought into this in order to develop it and I think the best thing will be, because of the tremendous number of people brought in, that it has a value in information dissemination and consciousness-

raising. To touch upon the Habitat II conference; the first Habitat conference in Nairobi came out with proposals for a draft paper for urban indicators - they already had a set of housing indicators and now they want a set of urban indicators. These have been developed after a meeting of experts by the United Nations secretariat, and they will be asking the national governments to develop their national urban indicators along these lines. In 99% of the cases, the national governments will delegate this task to their appropriate ministry with or without the involvement of the appropriate department in charge of the necessary and vital statistics. The process will be solely of benefit to the experts but today our workshop showed that like everything else, experts are necessary but not enough in dealing with environmental or sustainability matters. They have to be made aware of our efforts. If the Habitat conference insists on this approach our efforts need be opened up to governments, to local governments and to citizens in general. Somehow the details of this conference should be fed into the Habitat II preparations by whatever mechanism is available. **Indicators are too important to be left in the hands of the expert!**

WORKSHOP 6 –
AN ECOSYSTEMS APPROACH TO
URBAN ENVIRONMENTAL MANAGEMENT
Roger Levett- Environmental Team Leader,
CAG Consultants, UK

The first key message which came from all the speakers was that the idea of looking at an urban system as if it was an ecological system, modelling it in terms of flows and processes, is useful. It is useful for two things: the first thing is modelling physical resource flows and the second, and this is more difficult and complex, is the interrelations of different social processes, different institutions, different activities, different economic constraints and pressures.

First of all with regard to the physical ecosystems, the point was made that modelling a city in literal terms, understanding it as an ecosystem, finding out everything that is going on is very complex, it requires an immense amount of information. People who have tried it said, they could not do it completely. So there is a warning signal about complexity. However, there are some positive points too. The basic idea is clear and the concept can help people understand and crystallise what is going on. Also, although not everything is known there is enough to be very clear about the sort of directions of change that are needed in cities. The point was also made, this overlaps with indicators' work, that the hope is that once a proper ecosystem's analysis is carried out in some places, developing sufficiently strong physical sustainability indicators, that those indicators can then be used as proxies elsewhere. This would avoid having to go into the full ecosystems approach everywhere. Again there was a call for further indicators development work.

So much for the purely physical issues, a very important part of the discussion involved saying that we cannot deduce our goals from science. Aims, goals and values - the sort of things being sought, can only be found and determined through social processes, through consultation and through the partnership process. A question which was posed very forcefully was - *"What counts as development? Why do we say the northern countries are more developed than the southern countries? On what index are we more developed, is it that we use more fuel, is it that we throw away more rubbish, what is it?"* This can be seen as another northern analytical model and it must not be imposed on the south as another bit of cultural imperialism. It may be something which is helpful but it has to be reinterpreted. It has to be used by southern countries in their own terms and not used if they don't want it.

Looking at social, economic and institutional systems, a model which has been tried in Toronto was presented which has been used to look at the way that one specialist policy issue affects lots of other issues. The example that was given was child care. Childcare in Toronto raises all sorts of unexpected problems, it is more subsidised in the suburbs than it is in central Toronto, so some people move to the suburbs in order to afford child care, which has implications for housing and obviously for transport as people have to travel to work who didn't have to before. There are also questions of the standards required for kindergartens. Apparently this analysis revealed that the standards set were so high, that it precluded cheap childcare being available to many people in inner Toronto who needed it.

This doesn't give you any answers but it raises questions about the way that specialists in one area need to look at the implications of what they are doing in other areas. So the key message about the institutional side of this is that the ecosystems approach, looking at things in the round, is a necessary tool for making sure that technical specialists, experts and people with one departmental interest, see the bigger picture and see the broader implications of what they can do. This helps deal with one of the questions which is raised both here and very forcibly at the Aalborg Conference on European Sustainable Cities and Towns, which is how to assess whether all the individual projects or things we believe in actually move us towards sustainability, how to judge for example that more recycling is sustainable? This kind of analysis can be used to see the connections and make sure that our sectoral or individual initiatives do actually add up to moving towards sustainability.

The point was made that there are a number of barriers to this, this isn't all magic, it will not solve all problems, there are economic barriers, there are limits to how far companies can afford to push the sustainability arguments, limits as to how far they can change their actions without becoming uncompetitive, there are also limits as to how much power local authorities have to make decisions. In the UK there are some notorious examples where many decisions are under central government control, which is not currently driven by sustainability criteria. Again there is a positive point as well as a negative point. The negative point is that it cannot be expected that a proper ecosystems analysis will solve our problems instantly. The positive point is that this makes the partnership approach even more important. If different stakeholders can get together and work on people's expectations, people's assumptions and the way that institutions work then progress can be made. So finally and perhaps this is a suitable ending for all of the workshop reports, **the partnership approach is essential to make this work.**

THE WAY FORWARD - FINAL REPORTS
WHERE DO WE GO FROM HERE?
Margarita Pachenco, Environmental Studies Institute, National University of Colombia

"I had the chance to be at the Global Forum Conference . I think it is very important to relate Global Forum to this Forum. I want to highlight firstly the fact that both the North and South are building simultaneously a culture for sustainability. We are all involved in this process and I think it is the first time that we are more or less on the same level. We have to exchange expertise between the North and the South and vice versa and in an even way. We can see this at the academic level, or in the work of NGO's or local authorities. If we listen to the work that is being done in the UK or Australia or Colombia, what we can see is that we are developing together at the same time new methods, and new scientific knowledge and that gives us a chance to establish new ways of co-operating internationally. I mean co-operation on different levels among cities, within cities and between cities and international agencies. In that sense, the Urban Forum held in Curitiba in 1992 gave us an example of the ways in which local authorities were able to negotiate with international agencies. In most of our countries, national governments have been the filter for that kind of contact, funding or investments, and now I think we are acquiring that capacity for ourselves. So much so that by the end of the twentieth century we will have acquired an increased capacity for negotiation and I would say that the South is making real advances, in that sense, and in particularly in Latin America.

Another point is the political aspect of Global Forum and the Local Authorities Programme. I would say that it is very important to consider how are we going to be organised for Habitat II at the local and national level. What we have to think about is a model of organisation for how as local authorities, you are going to be really represented at Habitat II. It should not be as it was in Rio. Of course, Rio had its own importance, the heads of nations were there and they signed agreements, in some instances they created ministries of the environment for the first time. However, the positions presented by the different countries were not really representative of the different local actors. Now for Habitat II we have to create something very different and I think that Global Forum's lesson of gathering together people who have never gathered together previously - the trade unions, business and industry, academics, local authorities and NGO's should be followed. It was a very interesting human experience and I think that we should try to strengthen it for Habitat II and try in our own countries to set up really representative commissions.

Another very interesting point, one that the workshops underlined, is the way we are proceeding with the development of indicators, using cultural and educational processes with a new input and new passion and having fun with what we are doing. I think if we are having fun ourselves talking about this, we should transmit this fun and joy to the people who are going to be involved in the process. So let us keep this in mind and be joyful about it.

Now finally, I think it is very important that we introduce the issues of gender and of equal participation into this exciting process. In our countries, women from different social sectors are becoming more involved in the participatory processes. What is important is that we have decision-making that increasingly helps more and more women to get involved, for example, services to look after children while women can do other things are important. There are many people in society who would like to participate but cannot because either they do not have the time or resources, or because they have to think primarily in terms of their survival. It is essential that we think about how to help them to also become part of the process".

THE WAY FORWARD - FINAL REPORTS
PRIORITIES FOR ACTION
Councillor Louise Ellman - Leader Lancashire County Council , UK

"This international Local Agenda 21 conference has focused attention on the significance of sustainable development in both the community and global context. That is what has made this conference unique and I hope that it will be the experiences that have come from that intermingling of people from throughout the world, looking at this important issue locally as well as globally, that will enable us to find new mechanisms to develop this valuable networking that has taken place here in this conference. I would like to thank, and indeed congratulate, those who have done so much work to allow this conference to take place, the UK local authorities, the UK Local Agenda 21 Committee, IULA, CEMR, ICLEI, the United Towns Organisation, the British Council and of course our host, Manchester City Council and perhaps it demonstrates the increasing importance attached to the issue of sustainable development in an international context, that we see such a wide range of organisations who have been prepared to work together and to come together to give all of us the opportunity to discuss important issues and to exchange experience. It is very clear from the discussions, and the workshops, that have taken place over the past couple of days that the concept of Local Agenda 21 has captured the imagination of increasing numbers of local authorities. Local Agenda 21 puts local authorities in a pivotal position, in a position where local authorities take up the responsibility of developing local strategies for sustainable development but do that in a community and in a partnership context. It is very apparent when we enter into discussions about how Local Agenda 21 programmes are progressing, that we must recognise the significance of local involvement and local initiative, because without that I believe we will not make any progress. We must also recognise that the issues involved in sustainable development cannot be separated from their economic and political context whether that be local, whether it be national or whether it be international, and while we must hold strongly to the importance of the role of local authorities in starting, developing and sustaining important environmental and other issues, we must never forget the significance of the context in which that takes place - local and international.

I am pleased that the experiences that we have had in my own authority, the County of Lancashire, have been of some assistance in forwarding discussion. Since we started to develop our Local Agenda 21 going back to 1989, we have found that we have become increasingly involved in a process that has allowed us to look in a much more comprehensive way at what is happening in the county, a process that has led us to form the county's environmental forum bringing 85 different organisations and groups together, not just to discuss somebody else's ideas but to form working groups which then develop programmes and new policies. Our green audit has developed into our environmental action programme with timetabled policies for improvements, but that process, while it has brought about greater understanding of some of the complexities involved and led to some new and welcome developments and policy changes, has also highlighted the limitations of geographical boundaries in promoting sustainable development. So while we all work and must continue to work

Lancashire's environmental forum brings together over 85 different organisations - discussing, pressurising and lobbying for change

within our own areas, we must also recognise the importance of a lobbying and pressurising role on others who may have the power which regrettably some of us at local level do not have.

The case studies which have come from so many different countries around the world have demonstrated the scope of Local Agenda 21 and the wide range of the issues that are involved. Some of the key issues discussed in the workshops have centred around economic development, public awareness, setting of targets, the information and distribution of environmental information, indicators and the whole concept of accounting. All of those topics are important in their own right and all of those topics warrant a lot of discussion and a lot of thought, but perhaps what is most important is for all of us to recognise that all of those topics come together to form a whole when we look at the issue of sustainable development, what it means, how we move it forward, how we measure progress and how we ensure that the whole of our communities are involved. One of the invaluable parts of this conference is the way in which it has reinforced the global significance of Agenda 21 initiatives. We have all had a powerful reminder that the processes involved must extend worldwide. The young people who came here on their own initiative from Mexico spoke eloquently on behalf of the youth of the world. If sustainable development is to be meaningful it must be meaningful in terms of different generations, in terms of the world as a whole.

I draw two main types of conclusions:

✪ First we can see clearly how the two years since Rio have led to exciting and innovative Local Agenda 21 work, stressing the importance of local authorities and allowing us to see that increasing awareness of the complexity of some of the issues involved can only assist in helping to resolve them. It is increasingly evident that action from national government is required to match local initiatives and indeed the inter-relationships between different aspects of sustainable development only reinforce the importance of the interrelationship that is required at local, regional, national and the international levels. This also means it becomes increasingly important that the profile of the efforts of everyone involved here at this conference is raised. It should be raised at the Commission

Lancashire County Council

Improved bathing water quality - a concern and aspiration for many Lancastrians (Blackpool, UK)

for Sustainable Development, at the Habitat II conference on "Human Settlements" in Istanbul in 1996 and constantly within our own countries and within our own continents. And when we raise the profile of effort, at every opportunity, as indeed we must - it is essential that we raise the profile of all the aspects involved in promoting sustainable development and that means making economic development a key part of our discussions. If we allow the apparent divide to develop between economic development and peoples' legitimate desire for prosperity and economic progress and the whole concept of sustainable development, I think, in an international context we are doomed to failure. So we must continue to promote what we are doing, promote it at all levels and in all contexts, but to do that in a holistic way, resolving ourselves to the different issues involved.

✪ Secondly, it is also clear that we must maintain and develop the global perspective of what we are doing, particularly in relation to the North/South perspectives and I go back to a point I made at the beginning of my contribution, and that is the significance of remembering the economic and political context of the work in which we are all engaged. I suspect that the different development of Local Agenda 21 work between North and South reflects an unequal distribution of economic resources and political power and that is a basic issue which all of us have a responsibility to address. This also is a key reason why the international programmes promoted by ICLEI and IULA are so very, very important and I hope that all of us together will continue to participate in the international programmes because all of us have a great deal to learn from one another from whichever part of the

world we come from. I hope that when delegates leave this conference they will not leave behind the ideas, the exchange of experience and the networking that has been developed successfully here.

Lancashire County Council

Councils can have a pivotal role in promoting environmentally -friendly goods

I hope we have promoted a better understanding of what Local Agenda 21 can achieve and its different contexts, and have reinforced the importance of international cooperation, particularly in the North South dimension. This international conference can have a lasting impact if we all learn from what we have heard, analyse what we have listened to, share our experiences and above all, cooperate".

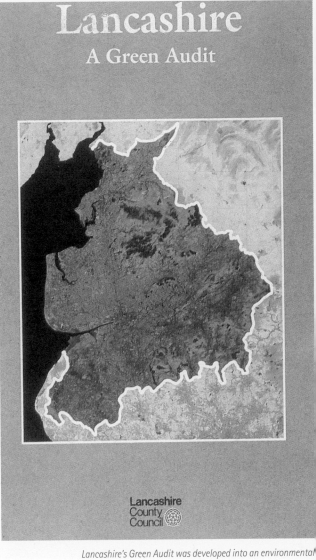

Lancashire's Green Audit was developed into an environmental action programme for the country

WORKSHOP PAPERS AND CASE STUDIES

CREATING A COMMUNITY BASE FOR PLANNING LOCAL AGENDA 21 – PUBLIC AWARENESS & CONSENSUS BUILDING.

Rio's Agenda 21 calls upon municipalities to enter into a dialogue with the citizens, organisations and private enterprises in their areas to create locally-based action plans. All sectors of the local community need to meet together at the local as well as national level to push forward the sustainability debate. Co-operation at the local level offers the chance to make the process more democratic and to increase community acceptance of sustainability goals. The participation of people representing different backgrounds is important though not always easy. In this workshop, mechanisms for raising awareness and involving the public in the decision-making of local authorities were explored. Various aspects of community involvement from citizens' initiatives to conflict minimising tools were considered.

CREATING A COMMUNITY BASE FOR PLANNING LOCAL AGENDA 21 - PUBLIC AWARENESS & CONSENSUS BUILDING.

COMMUNITY BASED ENVIRONMENTAL BENEFIT PROGRAMMES IN NEW YORK CITY

Yves B Mikol, Deputy Director Community Environmental Development, New York, USA

POLICIES AND GRASSROOT ACTION - A VITAL MIX

Ruth Allen, Environmental Initiatives Officer, Mendip District Council, UK

PUBLIC AWARENESS AND CONSENSUS BUILDING LOCAL ROUNDTABLES - HOW THEY WORK IN BRITISH COLUMBIA

Cathy Alplaugh, Consultant, Vancouver, Canada

ECO FEEDBACK PROJECT - THE FIRST STEP FOR FORMING AN ENVIRONMENTAL MANAGEMENT PLAN FOR MUNICIPALITIES

Mitswro Tanaka, City of Kawasaki and Representative of All Japan Municipal Workers Union, Japan

COMMUNITY-BASED ENVIRONMENTAL BENEFIT PROGRAMS IN NEW YORK CITY

Yves Mikol New York City Department of Environmental Protection New York, USA

Environmental Benefits Programs (EBPs) are partnerships between the local government and communities to develop action projects and informational "power tools". EBP's goals are to ensure that communities have access to resources for community-based planning to protect the environment, and can implement the projects they have selected. As a result, community-based organisations can influence environmental policy and foster equitable land use decisions.

The New York City Department of Environmental Protection (DEP) developed EBPs with communities in Greenpoint/Williamsburg (Brooklyn) and West Harlem (Manhattan). EBP's funds were established by Consent Orders between the City of New York and the State of New York to settle violations at city-owned sewage treatment plants. The Greenpoint/Williamsburg EBP received $850,000 in 1992 and the West Harlem EBP received $1,000,000 in 1994. Funds are managed by DEP which is responsible for the procurement of all services selected by the communities.

While the communities are distinct and certain activities may be more specific to one neighbourhood than another, the following projects have been selected by the citizens advisory committees.

Health studies followed by community health education and requests for additional funding to support occupational/environmental health clinics.

Pollution prevention initiatives and enhanced enforcement of environmental laws.

Watchperson office to provide environmental educational services and monitor proposed new developments.

Geographic Information Systems to provide power tools to the Watchperson and to support a baseline aggregate environmental assessment.

Job training and economic development geared to non-polluting activities.

New York City

Community Based Planning - a tool for decision-making on derelict industrial land use in New York.

POLICY AND GRASSROOTS ACTION - A Vital Mix
Ruth Allen, Environmental Initiatives Officer, Mendip District Council, UK

The concept of environmental sustainability is now beginning to underlie some UK Government policies. Practical implementation of these national and international policies, however, has not kept up with their development.

The growing movement of local authorities prepararing Local Agenda 21 strategies is now beginning to bridge this gap. If these strategies are to stimulate practical action that halts environmental decline and protects our natural resources, people at all levels will have to work together, setting tangible goals, based on a thorough understanding of their environment.

Community-based environmental action in the UK has until recently been largely reactive, responding to local environmental quality issues. Grassroots action, stimulated by people caring for their own neighbourhoods, however, is essential if sustainability is not to remain a hollow and academic concept.

Public involvement in the development of the Mendip Local Agenda 21 programme is therefore based on two fundamental principles:

✪ dissemination of information about Mendip's natural resources, the people and their activities to residents in the district.

✪ preparation of core aims, objectives and action plans with the involvement of relevant local interest groups, alternated with the development of these core elements by other groups and organisations.

People are often inhibited from caring for their local environments by the difficulty of obtaining the 'publicly available' information which is held in different forms by a variety of agencies.

Mendip District Council's "Health of the Environment" community project gives people map-based information about their local environment, using computerised Geographic Information Systems, and enables them to undertake their own local environmental audit.

Relevant local knowledge gathered through the project will eventually feed back to the council's environmental database and will assist in developing Local Agenda 21 policies. It will also help to stimulate effective community action leading towards environmental sustainability.

Production of the council's initial Local Agenda 21 Strategy is being developed through a structured programme involving the public at key stages (Fig. 28). Core aims, objectives and action plans are being developed through environmental auditing processes, with the involvement of the Mendip Environmental Forum and town and parish councils.

This process does not reach the whole community. At each stage, therefore, the core elements of the strategy will be devel-

oped further by other organisations (eg businesses, parent and youth groups, arts organisations) and the general public, after being agreed by elected members of the Council. Eventually, the draft strategy will be disseminated for consultation with the community.

Development of local action leading to environmental sustainability will be a gradual process, often stimulated by specific local concerns. Local Agenda 21 strategies should therefore be seen as constantly evolving processes which will continue to develop far beyond the target date of 1996.

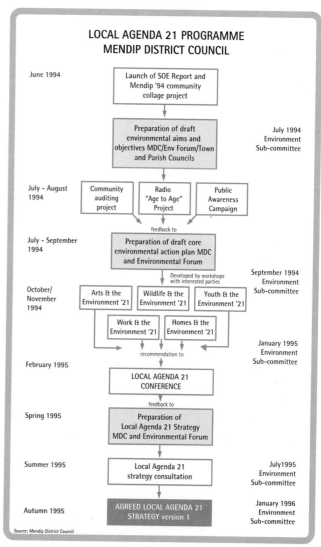

Fig. 28

Source: *Mendip District Council, 1994*

PUBLIC AWARENESS AND CONSENSUS BUILDING: LOCAL ROUNDTABLES AND HOW THEY WORK IN BRITISH COLUMBIA
Cathy Alpaugh, Environmental Consultant, Vancouver, Canada

Local Roundtables in British Columbia

A roundtable on the economy and the environment is an open forum at which all relevant parties are represented, which addresses issues of sustainability within a community, and arrives at decisions by consensus. The typical local British Columbia roundtable adopts as its raison d'etre land and resource use planning for a specific geographic region and has been established in the last three years. It is based on a small urban centre, or encompasses a few small towns, and more than likely one or two First Nations communities, and considers within its purview wilderness areas and waterways.

British Columbia's economy is resource-based. Discussions over bio-diversity, clear-cutting, building of logging roads, pulp and paper production, overfishing, strip mining and hiking trails are prominent in debates about economic and environmental issues. These issues involve preservation of the natural environment, water and air quality. Still, the Pacific Northwest is the fastest growing region in North America, both in terms of population and of economic activity, creating pressures of development even in less populated Northern regions. Sixty percent of the provincial population is urban, and transportation, housing, sewage treatment and so on are therefore concerns. Overall, the general issues of how roundtables work are not substantially different from place to place.

This presentation focuses on the creation of roundtables, and on assessing their success. Arguably their success depends upon enhancing and capitalizing upon public awareness and upon building community consensus. It is at the local level that the impact of economic transition, and environmental change matters most. It is also at this level that the knowledge of what can be done, and the commitment to make changes, lies. Governments, environmentalists, social activists and anyone wishing to move toward a sustainable future, cannot empower roundtables, but in providing the means to generate support, they enable communities to empower themselves.

The major areas of concern are: legitimacy, membership, terms of reference, implementation and monitoring.

Legitimacy:
The creation of roundtables is largely a response to the failure of the present political-economic system to respond to environmental conflicts and crises. The objective is sustainability, which denies that economic well-being is dependent upon environmental destruction and so a roundtable begins with an assumption of the possibility of a win-win outcome. Given that, success depends upon the "influence" which flows from obtaining a consensus among interested parties. If the relevant sectors can agree, then it becomes politically expedient to act on that agreement. "Influence" then depends upon the perceived quality of membership, the issues with which the roundtable is concerned, and the outcomes it produces. These all involve a commitment on the part of the community, and more

specifically of governments, to provide the support and resources necessary to make roundtables effective.

Membership:
In British Colombia's local planning processes, membership issues are being addressed by allowing membership to be open and fluid, but ensuring that all identified community values are reflected. The participants are encourage to see themselves both as educators and as reporters of their constituency. Facilitators endeavour to maintain individual contacts and community outreach. Roundtable information is distributed through existing community activities and through the media. Contact with "everyday" people and organisations gives them a presence at the table, and ensures sensitivity to the conditions of the community. This raises expectations, and ensures the accountability of the roundtable on the one hand, and of the government which is responding to it on the other.

Terms of reference
(or what do roundtables do?): Facilitators and participants in roundtables stress the need for an articulated "purpose", both to attract members and to focus debate. A balance must be struck, though, between action and process. Because the process is usually an unfamiliar one, and because there will be conflicts to be resolved, taking the "time" to define what is to be discussed, how it will be discussed and decided upon, and what sort of follow up will be taken on, is essential to the success of a roundtable.

Roundtables can be temporary or permanent. They may address the creation of processes and policies, they may draw up plans and they may co-ordinate communication between agencies. They are most successful when they co-ordinate their efforts with others within the community and outside it, and when they do not limit, but clarify, their mandate.

Implementation and Monitoring:
Roundtables rely heavily on government "buy-in" at all levels. The most successful to date contain a manifest high degree of community involvement and the evident support of local government. Responsiveness and support from regional, provincial and national agencies is essential. In order for the roundtable and, indeed, the movement towards sustainable communities to be credible, tangible results such as the implementation of recommendations and commitments to monitor the progress of that implementation must be apparent.

ECO FEEDBACK PROJECT - THE FIRST STEP FOR FORMING AN ENVIRONMENTAL MANAGEMENT PLAN FOR MUNICIPALITIES.

Mitswro Tanaka, City of Kawasaki, and
All Japan Municipal Workers Union, Japan

INTRODUCTION OF JICHIRO

"Jichiro" is a shortened form of "Zen Nihon Jichi Dantai Rodo Kumiai" - the all Japan Prefectural & Municipal Workers' Union. It is Japan's largest single labour union, representing over one million workers employed in local government at prefectural, municipal, town and village levels, along with employees of public corporations related to local governments.

Jichiro plays a leading role in the activities of Rengo - Japan's Trade Union Congress. Jichiro executives have often served in leading posts within that comprehensive umbrella group, indeed the current Vice-President of Rengo is the current President of Jichiro.

Thus more than 2,800 local unions affiliated under Jichiro, combine to develop a unified struggle against the governments anti-labour policies. Jichiro bases its own activities on the following three fundamental principles:

1. We shall strengthen our organisation and oppose all reactionary forces, in order to improve living standards and working conditions for our membership;

2. We shall accept responsibility for class-conscious workers employed at local government level by fighting for the establishment of full local autonomy.

3. We shall co-operate closely with all democratic forces in fighting for the peace, freedom and independence of Japan, thus contributing to a lasting world peace.

Jichiro contributes to the welfare of its membership by establishing activities such as its mutual aid association and its self-help division; these organise co-operative businesses such as group life and automobile insurance for the members.

FIGHTING TO IMPROVE LOCAL LIVELIHOODS

The so-called "administrative reform" now being strongly promoted by Japan's government has taken the form of cuts in welfare and services while military spending has increased.

This has caused considerable concern among the people of Japan, who have seen their public services dwindle to finance such expenditures. Under these circumstances, Jichiro feels an urgent need to promote joint action to protect the livelihoods of residents at the community level. Jichiro has learned from its experience that workers' livelihoods can no longer be fully protected just by negotiating terms with management; Jichiro is extending into joint struggles together with residents at the community level.

Such activity links Jichiro and local people in opposition to the false "administrative reform" advocated and led by business; instead, Jichiro advocates a public administration so as to genuinely contribute to peoples' livelihood and has further developed its own activity on behalf of health and welfare improvements. Concretely, it is vital that each worker reviews his own job performance and duties, and works to change the present administrative and fiscal system that sets the existing administrative framework. We believe that this activity contributes to political reform and to the establishment of a new local autonomy with the active participation of residents in a community.

Recently Jichiro has been working hard on environmental problems, forwarding the "Earth Day Movement" all over Japan and trying to extend this movement to all Asian regions.

Details of Eco-Check 25 and Municipal Environmental Management Principles developed by Jichiro are included in the following sections.

ECO-CHECK 25
DIAGNOSIS OF A CITY'S ENVIRONMENT

Steps toward Kankyo Jichitai (an environmentally oriented municipality).

Various procedures and activities must be considered in order to create a Kankyo Jichitai and we have tried to devise procedural steps that are necessary. (Fig 29) Needless to say, the most important requirement for the creation of Kankyo Jichitai is the decision by and support from the heads of municipalities and authorities. However, citizens' will and involvement are needed to promote and support the movement. It is also necessary to have co-operation from, and good ties with, municipal workers who have special knowledge about the environment. This means that the main participants for the creation of a Kankyo Jichitai should be individual residents and municipal workers. So we designed "the Municipal Environmental Diagnosis" to create the opportunity for clarifying issues in the hope that this will encourage activities to protect the environment.

There are some points that need to be changed in the present municipalities to turn them into Kankyo Jichitai. First, we must assess the environmental needs of our communities. Second, we must investigate whether environmental policies are carried out properly in our municipalities. Therefore, we have to diagnose the problems of our own communities and make a chart to help plan solutions to those problems before the birth of a Kankyo Jichitai is possible. Eco-check 25 can be used as the instrument to diagnose the environment of a municipality.

THE PURPOSE OF ECO-CHECK

The environmental diagnosis undertaken by a municipality should hopefully be as broad as possible, ranging from citizens' security and health to the global environment. In Eco-check 25 we itemised resources, waste, trees, air, energy, poisons, town restoration, environmental study and the environment in general. Then we listed 25 questions concerning these issues (refer to Eco-check list), aimed at understanding three main points:

(1) An environmental diagnosis of present conditions which assesses the realities of the environment such as water, trees and air quality in a municipality;

(2) The Town Hall provides a service for citizens and undertakes public business, so it is important to examine the activities of that office and its workers from the environmental point of view. Therefore, we are carrying out an "Eco Office Diagnosis" to assess the environmental impacts of the offices of a municipality;

(3) Municipalities have been undertaking various policies concerned with parks, roads and environmental restrictions for business. We therefore conduct an "Environmental Policy Diagnosis" to examine the real situation of environment policies in municipalities.

The process of an Eco-check is as follows:-

(1) Establish who is interested in being involved. If possible, the participation of experts and municipal workers is desirable. Municipal workers are of great value because they know where the information about an office is available.

(2) Hold an eco-check meeting at least once a month. The municipal workers and experts can explain the meaning of each item, provide background information and analyse the data.

(3) Collect statistical data and public information available from municipalities. Offices can be contacted by telephone or letter, or can be directly visited by a group or an individual. This allows a survey of what is going on in the office.

(4) Complete the eco-check form using the collected data. The meaning and background of the questions asked and information collected should be considered to highlight and explore weaknesses in municipal environmental policy, and recommend improvements.

(5) The points on the chart can be totalled, and the results compared with those of other municipalities.

Fig. 29

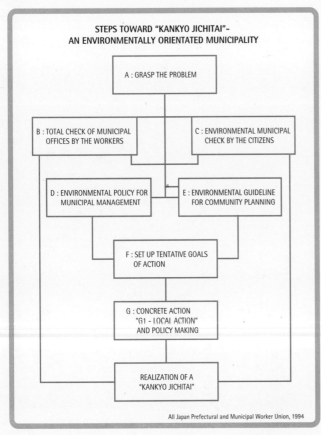

STEPS TOWARD "KANKYO JICHITAI"-
AN ENVIRONMENTALLY ORIENTATED MUNICIPALITY

A : GRASP THE PROBLEM

B : TOTAL CHECK OF MUNICIPAL OFFICES BY THE WORKERS

C : ENVIRONMENTAL MUNICIPAL CHECK BY THE CITIZENS

D : ENVIRONMENTAL POLICY FOR MUNICIPAL MANAGEMENT

E : ENVIRONMENTAL GUIDELINE FOR COMMUNITY PLANNING

F : SET UP TENTATIVE GOALS OF ACTION

G : CONCRETE ACTION "G1 - LOCAL ACTION" AND POLICY MAKING

REALIZATION OF A "KANKYO JICHITAI"

All Japan Prefectural and Municipal Worker Union, 1994

RESULTS OF ECO-CHECK

We anticipate various results from the Eco-check surveys. First of all, we can objectively determine the state of the environment and of related policies in our municipalities, although, the importance of accurate information must be emphasised. Information should be given to the citizens and municipal institutions, and we will insist on this happening. Secondly, we can identify what is lacking in environmental policies and institutions. We will demand better institutions and policies based on the results which we can use to initiate activities. Thirdly, the results collected from all around Japan will be collected in the Earth Day Office and in Jichiro just like medical records. In co-operation with Jichiro, which is a labour union of municipal workers, we are planning to undertake Eco-check environmental diagnosis throughout Japan. From the results we can make comparisons and figure out the averages, which will show what is lacking in each municipality and how each one is ranked. The results will encourage competition and lead to a demand for better environmental policies and institutions. Eco-check is thus the first step towards forming a Kankyo Jichitai or an environmental municipality.

ECO-CHECK LIST

Q1. How much waste is generated per citizen?

Q2. Are recyclable wastes separated?

Q3. Is there a system to monitor industrial wastes and provide guidance on their safe transportation and disposal?

Q4. Are initiatives taken to reduce the use of tropical timber in public construction?

Water

Q5. How much is used per citizen?

Q6. Is there a statute to conserve water resources, including ground water?

Q7. Is there wildlife such as dragonflies, frogs, crabs, fish, water birds and plants in local water ways?

Land

Q8. How much have forests, agricultural areas and parks changed during this decade?

Q9. How much food is produced daily in your area?

Q10. What systems exist to protect trees and forests in your town?

Air

Q11. Are there any plans or policies to reduce emissions of the global warming gas CO_2?

Q12. Are there any measures to stabilise or reduce energy consumption in your town?

Q13. Does your town have an air pollution problem? What are the concentrations of NO_2?

Q14. Are current measures to protect against car pollution adequate?

Harmful Wastes

Q15. Does your town have a problem with environmental pollution due to chemical and harmful substances?

Q16. Are there adequate pollution prevention measures for harmful chemical substances and wastes?

Q17. Is food safety ensured?

Community Planning

Q18. Is there a system for assessing the environmental impacts of proposed developments and road schemes?

Q19. Is there any system whereby citizens' voices can directly input into the measurement process?

Q20. Are there systems to promote integrated community planning? Does the administration structure to realise such planning exist?

Consciousness

Q21. Is a local environmental policy officer employed to initiate environment planning? Is adequate training provided?

Q22. Is there a system of training to promote environmental awareness among municipal workers?

Q23. Is environmental information collected and presented properly?

Q24. Has an administration system been formulated to promote the protection of the environment?

Q25. Has your municipality agreed any environmental principles or policies to be applied to all its business and activities?

10 PRINCIPLES OF MUNICIPAL ENVIRONMENTAL MANAGEMENT
(MUNICIPAL GOVERNMENT VERSION OF THE VALDEZ PRINCIPLES)

The Valdez Principles were devised by a civil organisation in the US to call for environmental responsibility on the part of enterprises. This movement has become popular in Japan and has led to the establishment of an "Earth Charter" by the Federation of Economic Organisation in Japan. The following 10 principles were initiated in co-operation with Jichiro (the All Japan Prefectural and Municipal Workers' Union with one million members), experts and individual environmentalists in order to work towards the common goal of G1-local action to establish "Kankyo Jichitai" and to take action from next year to make these principles into the guidelines for municipality management.

1. Basic Concept –

(the environment as a fundamental principle): for municipalities to declare their intention to become good models of environmentally sound business bodies and to take the following ideas into account in their business activities and policies;

A) To establish environmentally sound urban policies and infrastructure.

B) To preserve and restore the natural environment.

C) To acknowledge the finite nature of natural resources and the global environment.

D) To establish a society founded on environmental principles.

2. Basic Principles –

(municipalities as business bodies should develop environmentally sound policies) To establish basic principles which can apply to all municipal government management.

A) to establish environmentalism - make "environment" the basis of all management policies.

B) to strive for integrity regarding the environment.

C) to promote business and policies based on scientifically sound environmental principles.

3. Action Guidelines

A) Establishment of a System of Environmental Auditing/Assessment. (To develop a municipal system to ensure environmentally sound business and policies in all sections);

(A-1) To appoint an Environment Deputy Mayor,

(A-2) To create an Environment Committee in each section which will be chaired by a mayor,

(A-3) To create an independent "Environmental Committee" to audit and advise on environmental policies.

B) Establishment of Individual Environmental Standards:

(B-1) A Kankyo Jichitai should establish stricter environmental regulations on its own initiative rather than just follow existing standards, so as to continually develop environmental policies.

(B-2) Municipalities should publish these more rigid regulations and standards and apply them to all activities and businesses.

(B-3) Standards should be established relating to wastes, harmful materials, energy, air, water, forests and ecology.

C) Establishment of a System of Environmental Assessment:

(C-1) To establish a set of indicators to clarify when the activities of a large scale municipality (such as construction of public facilities, roads and rivers) require environmental assessment.

(C-2) To conduct environmental assessment of these municipal activities and to carry out necessary remedial measures.

4) Grasp of Environmental Resources and Publication of Annual Report:

(A) To collect data regarding the state of the municipal environment for example regarding plants, animals and soil, and the social, historical and cultural environment, and take measures to protect them.

(B) To quantify the consumption and creation of natural resources and wastes between municipalities, and with other nations.

(C) To publish the results, as an annual report and to highlight changes from the previous year.

5) Environmental Auditing:

To undertake and publish an audit of how environmental regulations are functioning in municipalities at least once a year. An independent organisation, such as the environmental committee mentioned in 3A above should undertake this audit.

6) Remediation and Compensation for Environmental Damage Caused by Municipal Governments' Activities:

Where environmental damage and related claim occur as a result of a municipal government's activities and business, that government must be responsible for the remediation. In case of damage to human health, that government must compensate regardless of obligation.

7) Selection of Environmentally Sound Contractors:

When municipalities employ contractors, the selection process should include environmental criteria.

8) Public Disclosure of Information:

All data from environmental research, and on wastes from public facilities, e.g. incinerators must on principle be published. All minutes of any council meetings should also be published.

9) Environmental Awareness for Municipal Government Workers:

To undertake training programs to encourage the environmental awareness of employees.

10) International and Inter-municipal co-operation:

International communication on environmental issues; to develop and share technology, knowledge and information regarding pollution prevention, conservation, recycling, and energy and resource efficiency, and to accept overseas trainees or employees as the Japanese contribution to international environmental solutions. Inter-municipality communication; to promote similar exchanges in order to encourage co-operation between municipalities.

WORKSHOP PAPERS AND CASE STUDIES

HOW TO SET UP AN ENVIRONMENTAL ACTION PROGRAMME, PRIORITISE TASKS AND SET TARGETS.

Rio's Agenda 21 argues that sustainable development will not be achieved by accident but that there must be a conscious plan which is worked on at all levels. Two thirds of the actions in Agenda 21 require the active involvement of local authorities and Chapter 28 invites local authorities to initiate a Local Agenda 21. The Local Agenda 21 process has to start from a commitment to sustainability and work through a participatory and comprehensive process to address the Agenda 21 mandate in the context of local needs and concerns. There is no single right way to implement this mandate which has been presented to local authorities. This workshop looks at the many and varied experience of local authorities from around the globe engaged in the process of establishing a Local Agenda 21. Many of the components of a Local Agenda 21 may already be in place in a municipality; the key is to recognise these as part of the sustainable development agenda.

HOW TO SET UP AN ENVIRONMENTAL ACTION PROGRAMME, PRIORITISE TASKS AND SET TARGETS

HOW TO SET UP AN ENVIRONMENTAL ACTION PLAN.
Dr. Werner Eugenio Zulauf, (Secretary of) Green and the Environment, City of Sao Paulo, Brazil.

THE EXPERIENCE OF WELLINGTON, NEW ZEALAND
Neville Lewthwaite, Manager, Environmental Resource Management Services, Wellington City Council, New Zealand

PROMOTING COMPREHENSIVE ENVIRONMENTAL ADMINISTRATION IN KAWASAKI CITY.
Takashi Yamashiro, Director, Environment Policy Section, Kanagawa Prefecture.

HOW TO SET UP AN ENVIRONMENTAL ACTION PLAN
Dr. Werner Eugenio Zulauf, Secretariat for the Green and the Environment, City of Sao Paulo, Brazil

It is acknowledged that poverty and environmental degradation are closely inter-related and have been the result of unsustainable patterns of certain kinds of consumption and production processes, especially in industrialised countries.

This global imbalance in production and consumption has to be taken into account in the setting up of an Environmental Action Programme.

To this end a wholly new relationship is called for between government and all key sectors of society, as well as the public at large, in order to involve them in an overall strategy for global transition.

Our City - Sao Paulo - is a 440 year old metropolis, with grievous problems and conflicts, and is also the capital of the State of Sao Paulo, with 900 kms^2 of its 1509 kms^2 densely urbanised and only 17% green coverage. It is one of the 38 municipalities that make up the Greater Sao Paulo Metropolitan Area and houses 10 million of the 17 million inhabitants of the greater Sao Paulo area.

The metropolis has a varied and rich economy, with diversified activities, including many industries. There are also universities and research institutes. Despite all this it has a very deficient environmental infrastructure because:

- ✪ 90% of its sewage remains untreated

- ✪ 45% of its sewage is not even drained

- ✪ 12,000 tons of solid waste are generated daily

- ✪ There are 468 points of flooding

- ✪ 4 million motor vehicles emit 4,000 tons of carbon dioxide every day

- ✪ more than one million persons live in reservoir protection areas that are devoid of any kind of infrastructure.

To be able to solve such complex problems and organise, co-ordinate and plan environmental protection strategies it is necessary to act at the institutional level. To this end, in October 1993 the Secretariat for the Green and the Environment (SVMA) was instituted and will work in close partnership with other governmental and non-governmental sectors as well as with research institutes and society as a whole.

To establish formal channels of communication with all sectors of government and society the SVMA has in its structure CADES - the Municipal Council for Sustainable Development with equal representation of governmental and non-governmental institutions.

At the present moment SVMA is involved in the formulation of its Environmental Action Programme.

To this end we are prioritising our tasks in order to:

1. Establish the necessary legal basis for our actions (the City's Environmental Code);

2. Establish and prioritise plans, programs and projects in response to demands and needs (first, perceive the problems and needs, then research possible solutions and prevent recurrences of the problems);

3. Plan for the future and involve key sectors of society as well as the public at large, in the promotion of environmentally sound and sustainable development.

HOW TO SET UP AN ENVIRONMENTAL ACTION PROGRAMME
THE EXPERIENCE OF WELLINGTON, NEW ZEALAND
Dr N.B. Lewthwaite, Manager, Environmental Resource Management Services, Wellington City Council, New Zealand

Wellington was built on a site of intermittent settlement over about 1000 years before European settlement which began in 1839. It is now the central local authority (population 150,000). This region has a rugged physical form, which has determined the shape of settlement as a series of beads along two transport corridors running north from the city centre. The city has a wild and beautiful coastline, and a windy maritime climate. It has a great diversity of peoples and forms of development, it is a cultural, intellectual and political capital, and its citizens are well informed and involved in community affairs.

Wellington is highly centralised and has a relatively well developed and well used public transport system compared to other New Zealand cities. Its compactness is the feature most frequently identified by residents as what they like most about the city. Public transport usage for the journey to work is two to three times higher than in other New Zealand cities and appears to be growing after a long period of decline. However, residential densities are low. They are typically under 20 persons per hectare in the outer suburbs and about 70 persons per hectare in some inner suburbs. In the past, densities have been kept low by regulation, by hidden subsidies for new development on the rural margins of the city and by low land and energy prices. Town planning practice has been based on the idea that segregation of land uses is necessary to control effects on the environment. Regulations preventing commercial activities in residential areas and rigid separation of different classes of commercial activity are a long-standing tradition. This has led to a greater need to travel, more social isolation, and less vitality in those parts of the city built in the last fifty years.

This is a city with many opportunities for more sustainable living, and these opportunities are beginning to be taken. In developing a new strategic plan for the city a commitment was made to seven "operating principles". These include 'striving to ensure an environmentally sustainable outcome in all areas of operation', and commitments to financial responsibility, to equity, and to honour obligations under treaty to the indigenous people of the city.

THE LOCAL GOVERNMENT FRAMEWORK
Major reform of local government was introduced in 1989. This was one part of a programme of major reform which has swept the country since the election of the fourth Labour Government in 1984. The reforms were influenced by the theories of public choice that had affected much central government reform over the previous five years. Local government had been accused of resource duplication, meaningless boundaries, inadequate service, paternalism and perpetuation of oases of privilege. The number of units of local Government was reduced from 625 with multiple tiers and many ad hoc units, to a two tier system involving 94 units. Principles of accountability, transparency and separation of trading and regulatory from other functions were built into the law.

The whole reform was frantic and heroic. A confluence of ideas about government and reforming zeal, together with a politically inspired choice of the person to chair the Local Government Commission (Sir Brian Elwood, a lawyer and former mayor), was critical to success. While the reform was centrally directed, and rights of appeal against reform were curtailed, there was no pre-prepared master plan. The Commission's approach was consultative and emphasised locally agreed solutions.

At the same time, three streams of thinking were beginning to gel in the reform of the nation's resource management law. Ideas derived from ecology, ethics and economics were being brought together into what is now the Resource Management Act 1991. This involved a massive reform of over 70 other acts driven by Geoffrey Palmer as Minister for the Environment. An intensive effort involving a series of discussion papers, background reports and extensive public consultation was involved. It was finally passed without fundamental change by a government which was in opposition during most of its preparation. According to its chief political author, it was only made possible by the prior abolition of a major state department (the Ministry of Works) which had captured environmental policy but had important conflicting interests.

The purpose of the Resource Management Act 1991 is 'the sustainable management of natural and physical resources'. It brings together principles of ecological integrity, ethical obligations to future generations, and a community-based consultative approach, with an emphasis on market processes and deregulation. It invites the use of economic instruments, persuasion, service provision and information, in preference to regulation, to promote sustainability.

In the resulting structure, the national government has reserve powers and a monitoring role. It can issue national policy statements which are binding (eg. the recent Coastal Policy Statement). Regional councils have a primarily resource management role particularly in relation to water, air and the coast and an important function in co-ordinating transport. District councils are less confined, but in resource management their attention is directed toward land use. Financially, local government is fairly independent of central government (except in transport funding) and is therefore free to develop and implement its own policy within the framework of the law.

WELLINGTON – The Vision of a Sustainable City
Wellington is developing its own vision of a more sustainable Wellington City. In our context, sustainability is seen as being primarily about natural resource use, but it involves other issues. The focus is on;

- ✪ Managing the adverse effects of human activities on the environment,
- ✪ Taking account of natural environment values,
- ✪ Enabling people to meet their needs,
- ✪ Respecting future and past generations.

A sustainable Wellington would be efficient in its use of resources, be compact and have a strong commercial centre. It would be a competitive market place without unnecessary regulation. It would have a quality environment where people feel safe, can gain access to its various parts easily, and can orient themselves to familiar public spaces and to the city as a whole. Elements that give identity and vibrancy to the city would be enhanced through the promotion of urban design principles. The city would be diverse and the needs of all would be met without the alienation of any group. It would welcome change and innovation whilst retaining character and connections with the past. People would experience healthy, functioning natural ecosystems, and both enjoy and respect recreational, educational and intrinsic values in nature.

This vision is being pursued in the context of Agenda 21, and of national legislation aimed at promoting sustainability as a policy objective.

The political context and public support have been crucial. Although local politics does not follow national party structures, the elected members of the council include four Green Party councillors. They have gained important support on key issues from other councillors whose commitments are quite different. The mayor was a cabinet minister in the government that conceived the Resource Management Act and is an enthusiast for positive action. Public values surveys have indicated a strong desire for improved local action on the environment and on heritage.

A meeting of minds between the politicians and professional officers has developed. Sustainability has become a vehicle for synergy to arise from sometimes uneasy alliances. These alliances have involved those concerned for the natural environment, those who seek improved action on heritage and design, those who promote revitalisation of the inner city, those who seek improved relationships with the indigenous people of the city, and those who promote reduced government regulation.

INITIATIVES

There are several existing and prospective initiatives in Wellington. The development of priorities and targets has been evolutionary.

THE DRAFT STATEMENT OF ENVIRONMENTAL INTENT 1993

This document was a first move toward a Local Agenda 21. It grew out of the appointment of a staff member whose first full time duty is to advocate for the environment. About 1991, several councils and major private corporations produced statements of corporate environmental policy. Wellington City Council participated in this trend by producing the Statement which records the council's position on several environmental issues. It highlights concerns to influence internal decisions, and provides an inventory of actions. It identifies four goals:

○ Developing an environmental ethic in its operations and decision making,
○ Using resources efficiently,
○ Pollution reduction, and
○ Maintaining ecological integrity.

For each goal there is a set of objectives and an action list specifying what division of council is responsible and setting a target date for completion.

The Statement was prepared with the active support of an Environmental Liaison Sub Committee, which involved many community environmental organisations in directly contributing to council decisions. It was issued for community debate and submissions, but has been overtaken by the growing breadth of the vision of sustainability within the council.

THE DISTRICT PLAN

The council's primary action and statement of strategic intent on sustainability has been the preparation of a new 'District Plan'. This is a statutory plan prepared under the Resource Management Act. Its concern is to promote the sustainable management of resources by influencing patterns of land use. It challenges traditional approaches to city planning by focusing on the effects of activities rather than on the activities themselves. The idea that segregation of activities (zoning) is desirable has been rejected. The plan emphasises promotion of a more sustainable urban form, a centralised structure and denser residential development within existing urban boundaries. It removes many regulations that previously constrained development of a more sustainable urban form, and it removes property rights and subsidies that have encouraged dispersal of low density development in the past. Whether this is sufficient to outweigh past trends based on low real land and energy costs is yet to be seen.

The plan is respectful of the city's built, cultural and natural heritage. It links development of a comprehensive inventory of heritage and conservation sites with regulations and financial incentives for their protection. It will encourage market mechanisms by using a system of development impact fees based on the estimated marginal costs of servicing in different parts of the city, and by introducing environmental compensation payments to internalise environmental costs.

The plan also removes many of the previous rules which sought to direct where development should occur, so that there will no longer be restraint on what activities can be undertaken in the central or commercial parts of the city. Residential areas have not been liberalised in this way. A vigorous urban design approach has been adopted using design guides within a precinct framework to influence private development backed up by regulation. An Urban Design Strategy for the city is in preparation to guide the development of its public spaces and will be completed this year.

The Plan was prepared in an intensively interactive way involving several rounds of public submission on issues, concepts and drafts, consultation with community stakeholders, workshops with councillors facilitated or addressed by leading political and professional people, workshops with key interest groups, debates and meetings. In this process roles were sometimes reversed with former critics becoming allies, and unexpected alliances emerging. It is this vitality of process that has refined our priorities and defined our targets. Its robustness will be tested over the next few months as we move into a phase of formal submission and hearing. Any person can participate in that process.

THE SUSTAINABLE CITY STRATEGY – our Local Agenda 21

Having completed the District Plan to the stage of formal submissions, we are looking at ways to broaden our approach to sustainability. The 'Sustainable City Strategy' (SCS) initiative is now being commenced. It will draw on the several existing policies or strategies of council which are relevant for community involvement and generate a future program of projects. It will provide guidelines, principles and indicators for sustainability, and build on the vision described above, with emphasis on the natural and built environments.

It is expected that the SCS process will comprise five development steps.

1. A conceptual framework: This would be based on a vision and principles relating to the achievement of a sustainable city, building on work undertaken for the District Plan. Guideline criteria for future council policy and projects will be developed and implemented through a central vetting process.

2. A model of the city's processes: This will be based on the idea of the city as an ecosystem. Such a model would recognise the inter-relatedness of economic, social, natural and physical processes and enable tracing of patterns of resource use. Our objective is to be able to identify and prioritise areas or processes that may be altered to better meet sustainability criteria. An example would be energy efficiency expressed in areas such as waste production, transport, and building design and use.

3. A programme of project and policy initiatives: The SCS will provide a strategic framework for a series of projects and policy initiatives along the following lines (those marked have been commenced, others are planned or prospective):

   ✪ The Statement of Environmental Intent (see above)

   ✪ The District Plan (see above)

   ✪ The development of a partnership with the indigenous people of the city in its management of resources. Council has established a Maori standing committee and a Maori Unit in the office of the Chief Executive. A specialist appointment is about to be made in the Resource Management section of my department. The

District Plan envisages joint development of management plans for natural resources, and extensive consultation and involvement.

✪ Establishment of community forums on the natural and built environment, as a vehicle for real work contributions to sustainable city projects. A first meeting of these forums will take place shortly to develop terms of reference and ideas and priorities for the SCS. The forums are not intended as a talkfest, but as community involvement by undertaking real work.

✪ The South Coast Management Plan. This is a joint initiative with other government, private and community organisations aimed at 'Healing the South Coast' of the city through the development of management guidelines. The south coast is an exposed and rugged area with a unique blend of natural historical, cultural, spiritual and recreational values. It contains unique geology, rare species, good fishing and popular areas for walking, off road driving and trail cycling.

✪ Further development of a Heritage Strategy. This involves an inventory of over 700 buildings and sites, a financial incentives programme and regulatory support.

✪ Further development of a waste minimisation and recycling programme using kerbside sorting of recyclable materials.

✪ The development of an area of indigenous forest as a sanctuary within the city for endangered species (Karori Reservoir). This is an initiative of local environmental groups relying on support from central and local government agencies.

✪ A transport strategy which builds on sustainability as a key principle. An inner city transport strategy which gave emphasis to accessibility was prepared in 1992. A current extension and review is giving more explicit recognition for sustainability as a policy objective.

✪ A conservation strategy aimed at the further identification and protection of sites of special natural value. The District Plan specifically lists, and gives regulatory protection to sites of ecological importance following a field based study in 1992. The strategy will promote other positive moves such as conservation covenants.

✪ Environmental monitoring programmes including state of the local environment reporting, the development of indicators of sustainability and systematic review of the effectiveness of policy, and the costs of implementation and compliance are planned

✪ Development of an energy in building programme aimed at energy efficiency in building design, construction, use and adaptive re-use.

4. A process for community involvement: An emphasis on community consultation and involvement is a theme of Agenda 21. Two on-going forums are planned, one on the natural and one on the built environment. This will become a means of joint work involving the council and community, and will be supplementary to our normal consultation processes in the development and implementation of the City's Strategic Plan.

5. Priorities and council planning links: Formal procedures are being developed to ensure appropriate co-ordination between the sustainability objectives of the SCS and the other objectives which drive many of the council's operational activities. The intention is to make sustainability criteria relevant to all of the council's activities through its strategic planning processes, and to influence the development of private initiatives. To some degree, this is achieved through the regulatory aspects of the District Plan which are binding on the council, but this is not seen as sufficient, nor as sufficiently flexible.

CONCLUSION

Wellington city is fortunate in the development of a local response to Agenda 21. The city's form and structure present opportunities for credible early action, there is political commitment, a willing and diverse community, and a sound legal framework in the Resource Management Act.

Our experience to date has convinced me of the power of ideas in the setting up of local action. The process of local government reform in New Zealand, the development of the Resource Management Act and the response of Council outlined in this paper, indicate this power. Sustainability is beginning to be seen as a unifying influence for apparently diverse ideas and apparently conflicting values that can all contribute to a positive urban future.

I think that the key elements in a successful action programme include political will, the development of community values, the power of an idea whose time has come, a willingness of the bureaucracy to plan with an open ear, and the courage to take opportunities.

PROMOTING COMPREHENSIVE ENVIRONMENTAL ADMINISTRATION IN KAWASAKI CITY

Takashi Yamashiro, Director, Environmental Policy Section, Kanagawa Prefecture and Mitswo Tanaka, Environmental Planning Department, City of Kawasaki, Japan.

Kawasaki City, against a background of geographical factors, industrial build-up and rapid population growth, is confronted by various environmental problems, including serious industrial pollution. Consequently, we are promoting active environmental management.

Based on our previous history of environmental administration in Kawasaki and on new environmental issues, we are aiming to develop a comprehensive environmental administration for the new perspective of the 21st century. This paper lays out those goals and issues.

1. ENVIRONMENTAL CONTAMINATION FROM INDUSTRIAL ACTIVITY

Environmental contamination in the Kawasaki city area was first recognised as full-blown "pollution" after the period of rapid economic growth in the 1960's. In particular, air pollution from an increased use of petroleum fuels rose, and the reduction of industrial pollution became an urgent and serious environmental issue for Kawasaki City.

In order to promote anti-pollution measures, Kawasaki enacted the "Kawasaki City Pollution Prevention Ordinance" in March 1972, which introduced a regulatory system that limits the gross volume of pollutant exhaust amounts at individual workplaces (an original system developed by Kawasaki City).

Meanwhile, vital green areas rapidly diminished due to the extensive residential development that accompanied fast economic growth. In October 1973 we enacted the "Kawasaki City Natural Environment Protection and Restoration Ordinance" and are working to restore natural greenery. Also, because the new city environment that appeared lacked harmony with its surroundings, owing to wide spread development, we established the "Kawasaki Environmental Impact Assessment Ordinance" in 1976. Applying to pre-implementation stages, this ordinance is aimed at incorporating environmental policy into development activities.

2. ENVIRONMENTAL ISSUES IN KAWASAKI TODAY

Through the development of these ordinances, results have been achieved in combatting industrial pollution. However, despite qualitative and quantitative changes in social and economic activities in recent years, many environmental problems still remain and new problems have emerged. As well as the serious problem of roadside pollution from automobile exhausts, sewage pollution has appeared due to organic chlorine solvents. Environmental pollution also accompanies the increasing unregulated use of hazardous chemical substances.

In addition to the problem of cleaning up and disposing of rapidly increasing quantities of waste, environmental problems such as noise pollution are resulting from citizens' lifestyles. At the same time, the desire for a pleasant city environment is increasing. In addition to these problems in our city environment, world environmental problems have recently come into focus.

In order to solve these many problems, it is necessary to recognise that human activities are having a major effect on the environment and to develop a desire to take care of the environment. While the administration must take the lead in environmental activities, it must also encourage the environmental education of its citizens.

3. THE CONSTRUCTION AND PROMOTION OF A NEW ENVIRONMENTAL ADMINISTRATION SYSTEM

These environmental issues have many complex connections with societal and economic activities and with citizens' lifestyles. Because solutions were difficult to achieve under the previous vertically imposed system of laws and administration, we felt it necessary to construct our environmental policies from a broadly synthesised, long-term point of view, in order for citizens, business and public administration to co-operate and take action together. Therefore, we enacted the "Kawasaki Fundamental Environmental Ordinance" in December of 1991 and put it into effect in July 1992. (Fig. 30) It acts as an "all-agency horizontal ordinance" with the important function of integrating city policy on environmental issues under the keyword of "synthesis".

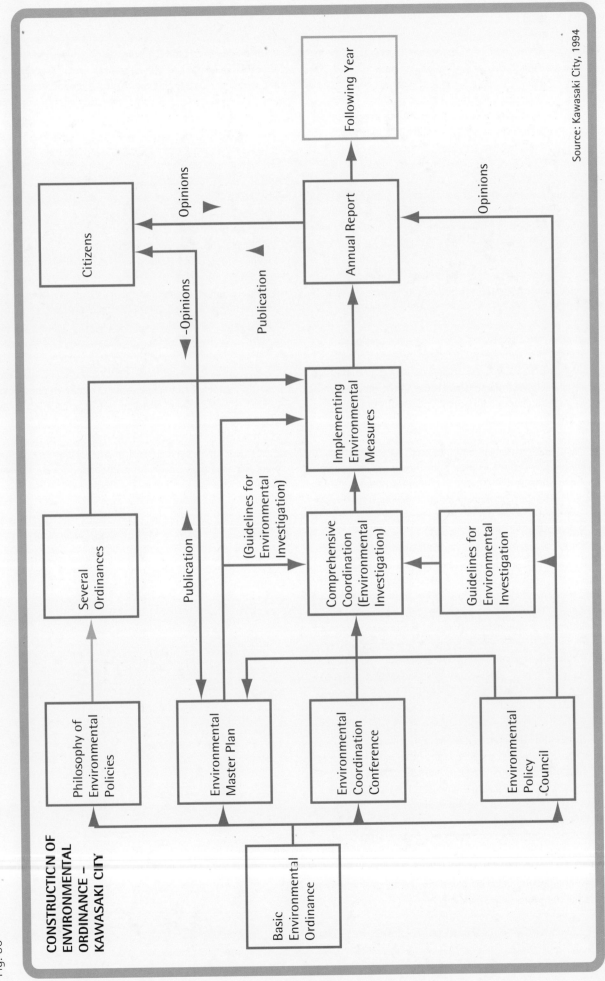

Fig. 30

CONSTRUCTION OF ENVIRONMENTAL ORDINANCE – KAWASAKI CITY

Source: Kawasaki City, 1994

Under this ordinance, our new conceptual future environmental policies will aim at:

1) Environmental rights: in other words, striving to realise the right to attain a healthy and pleasant environment, while bequeathing a good environment to the next generation.

2) Improving the quality of citizens' life by the proper management of environmental resources, and

3) Creating the basis for sound environmental city policies.

Other stipulations are-

1) Drafting a "Fundamental Environmental Plan" (Fig 32 and 33), which will guide environmental administration,

2) Introduction of an "Environmental Research" system which will provide an accurate environmental check of the city's main policies and guidelines on the environment;

3) Establishment of an "Environmental Regulation Conference" to synthesise environmental policy;

4) Establishment of an "Environmental Policy Deliberation Council" as an external institution to monitor environmental policy;

5) Publication of an "Annual Report" which will accurately monitor environmental developments.

6) A new system of public participation which will enable the expression of public opinion on environmental planning and the Annual Report.

4. FUTURE ENVIRONMENTAL ADMINISTRATION IN KAWASAKI

Future environmental administration in Kawasaki will incorporate every type of environmental measure into fundamental environmental planning, in line with this ordinance. We will also strive to build environmental considerations into all city policies and undertakings through an environmental research system.

The fundamental environmental plan will be drawn up by the Policy Deliberation Council in consultation with public opinion. Its principle content will be 1) environmental aims and objectives, and 2) measures to achieve those objectives and to improve resource management.

Environmental research, at the planning stages of city policies and business, will consider whether choices are acceptable from an environmental standpoint. It will attempt to ensure the consistency and comprehensiveness of the city's environmental policies. Procedures and documentation will be decided along environmental research guidelines.

The Environmental Policy Deliberation Council will be composed of officials approved by Council members, and in addition to its capacity as a consulting organisation, it will observe the city's

environmental administration and take an ombudsman role by offering advice or recommendations on crucial points.

Co-operation between citizens and businesses is indispensable to future environmental administration. Therefore, we have stated that one principle of our environmental policy is "public participation and co-operation". Public involvement is built into the process of drafting the fundamental environmental plan, and encouraged by the Annual Report, which lists environmental policies and the results of economic research carried out by the City.

SUMMARY

In Kawasaki City, based on previous environmental administration, which focused on counteracting industrial pollution and on new environmental issues, we have created the "Fundamental Environmental Ordinance" to develop broad comprehensive environmental policies aimed at the 21st century. However, under the present legal system and administrative structure, many issues need to be solved in order to begin a new administrative challenge. Institutionally, in order for local government to be able to deal with local problems autonomously, a reform of the present legal system and of the rights of local government, a guarantee of principles of sovereignty, and a strengthening of co-operation between local governments are necessary.

Also, to achieve changes in lifestyle, the city, citizens and business need to jointly increase their understanding of the environment, and undertake constant activities to protect the environment.

This new environmental administration system will lead towards sustainable development, and we believe that we can make a real contribution to the protection of the global environment and the creation of a beautiful city environment.

Fig. 31

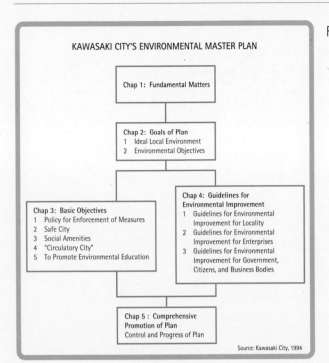

KAWASAKI CITY'S ENVIRONMENTAL MASTER PLAN

Chap 1: Fundamental Matters

Chap 2: Goals of Plan
1   Ideal Local Environment
2   Environmental Objectives

Chap 3: Basic Objectives
1   Policy for Enforcement of Measures
2   Safe City
3   Social Amenities
4   "Circulatory City"
5   To Promote Environmental Education

Chap 4: Guidelines for Environmental Improvement
1   Guidelines for Environmental Improvement for Locality
2   Guidelines for Environmental Improvement for Enterprises
3   Guidelines for Environmental Improvement for Government, Citizens, and Business Bodies

Chap 5 : Comprehensive Promotion of Plan
Control and Progress of Plan

Source: Kawasaki City, 1994

Fig. 32

ENVIRONMENTAL ELEMENTS OF KAWASAKI CITY ENVIRONMENTAL MASTER PLAN

ELEMENTS	ISSUES
1 Atmosphere	Air quality, Greenhouse effect, Destruction of the Ozone Layer
2 Water	Water Quality, Water Quantity, Waterfront, Water Cycle
3 Ground	Topography, Soil Quality, Ocean Bed, Building Foundations
4 Living Things	Plants, Animals
5 Green Space	Forests, Farmland, Parks, Tree-Planting
6 Noise	Noise, Vibration
7 City Climate	Energy Consumption, Heat Pollution
8 Chemical Substances	Harmful Chemicals, Drinking Water, Foodstuffs
9 Resources and Wastes	Resources, Wastes
10 Impacts of Construction	Electrical Fields, Wind Tunnels, Loss of Sunlight, Light Pollution
11 Social Amenity	Town Landscape, Open Space, Historical and Cultural Heritage, Recreational Facilities, User-Friendly Public Facilities

Source: Kawasaki City, 1994

CONTENTS OF SPECIFIC INDICATORS OF THE OBJECTIVES – KAWASAKI CITY ENVIRONMENTAL MASTER PLAN

ENVIRONMENTAL ELEMENTS	ITEMS
Atmosphere	NO_2 : Nitrogen Dioxide The target is to reduce the total amount of NO_2, from motor vehicle exhausts by 40% and factory emissions by 20%, compared with the level of 1990, by the year 2000. CO_2 : Carbon Dioxide The target is to stabilise domestic and industrial CO2 emissions by the year 2000. CFC-11,12,113,114,115 : The aim is to restrict the domestic use of CFCs in the city and to abolish its use in major public facilities by the end of 1995. Also, to establish a recovery system for CFCs from large waste products (disused cars, refrigerators etc) by the year 2000.
Water	Water Quality : The aim is to achieve environmental and ecological goals of water quality objectives for city rivers by the year 2000. Water Circulation : The aim is to preserve the water cycle in the city, and to restore rainwater replenishment of groundwater to 1990 levels by the year 2000.
Green Space	Green Space : The target is to conserve and create green space so that more than 30% of the city area is a green area (forests, farmland, parks, tree-planting) by the year 2000.
Resources and Wastes	Water Resources : The aim is to control and maintain domestic water use at 1990 levels, by the year 2000. Tropical Rain Forests Timber (TRFT) : The target is to reduce the volume of TRFT used in public works by 70% compared with that used in 1990, and to restrain the use of TRFT as much as possible in domestic use, by 1995. Wastes : The aim is to stabilise and maintain control of the volume of household waste at 1990 levels, by the year 2000 and 2010.

Source: Kawasaki City, 1994

Fig. 33

KAWASAKI CITY BASIC ENVIRONMENTAL ORDINANCE
(Established on December 25, 1991)
(Kawasaki City Ordinance No. 28)

Table of Contents

Chapter 1 General Provisions (Article 1 to Article 7)
Chapter 2 Environmental Master Plan (Article 8 and Article 9)
Chapter 3 Comprehensive Coordination of Environmental Administration
(Article 10 to Article 12)
Chapter 4 Environmental Policy Council (Article 13)
Chapter 5 Annual Report (Article 14 to Article 16)
Chapter 6 Additional Provisions (Article 17 to Article 19)
Supplementary Provision

Chapter 1

General Provisions

Purpose
Article 1.

The purpose of this Ordinance is to conserve and create a sound urban environment in order to contribute to the welfare of citizens by recognizing the limited capacity of environmental resources, making efforts to properly conserve and utilize them, and establishing the philosophy and basic principles of environmental policies of Kawasaki City (hereafter referred to as the "City"), as well as basic matters concerning environmental measures and procedures to establish such measures.

Philosophy of Environmental Policies
Article 2.

1.The environmental policies of the City shall be developed in order to realize citizens' right to enjoy a safe, healthy and comfortable environment, and pass a sound environment onto future generations.

2.In cooperation with citizens and business, the City shall improve the quality of life for present and future citizens through appropriate management of environmental resources and creation of a sound environment in a comprehensive and sustainable way.

3.All measures of the City shall be based on and respect environmental policies to the greatest extent possible.

Basic Principles of Environmental Policies
Article 3.

The environmental policies of the City are subject to the following principles:

(1) comprehensiveness of measures;
(2) scientific predictability;
(3) consideration of ecosystems;
(4) consideration of the global environment; and
(5) participation of and collaboration with citizens.

Responsibilities of the City
Article 4.

When implementing measures of the City, the City must endeavour to conserve and create a sound environment, taking into account the impact on the environment and respecting citizens' opinions.

Responsibilities of Citizens
Article 5.

Citizens must address themselves to conserving and creating a sound environment, make efforts to prevent possible damage to the environment through their daily activities and positively participate and cooperate in promotion of the environmental measures of the City.

Responsibilities of Businesses
Article 6.

Businesses must recognise that their activities affect the environment, endeavour to prevent environmental pollution and to conserve and create a sound environment, comply with regulations and administrative guidance of the City, and positively cooperate in the environmental measures of the City.

Basic Measures
Article 7.

To realise the philosophy of the environmental policies described in Article 2 of this Ordinance, the City shall endeavour to continue and enhance measures related to pollution prevention, conservation of the natural environment, etc. in accordance with the procedures described in this Ordinance and give priority to implementing the following measures:

(1) Promotion of new anti-pollution measures such as prevention of environmental pollution caused by newly developed industries, appropriate disposal of industrial wastes, etc;

(2) Mitigation of urban/life type pollution through prevention of car pollution, prevention of deterioration of water quality due to household effluent, appropriate disposal of general wastes, development of urban infrastructure, etc.;

(3) Promotion of urban amenities through construction of public facilities, etc. which are more accessible and useful to users, construction of urban facilities introducing water and greeenery, creation of good urban scenery, conservation and utilization of historic and cultural heritages, etc. in order to create a more liveable environment;

(4) Conservation and utilization of environmental resources in the City In accordance with natural cycles through conservation of water cycle structure, efficient use of energy, promotion of the use of recycled resources, etc.;

(5) Promotion of local measures for conserving the global environment such as prevention of a global warming, ozone layer protection, international exchange of pollution prevention technologies, etc.; and

(6) Promotion of systematic environmental education, etc. so that citizens can further their understanding and recognition of the relationship between human beings and the environment and become more responsible for their activities.

(7) When the City puts into practice the measures described in the preceding paragraph, the City shall endeavour to consider comprehensive measures including reforms of urban structures, economic activities, citizens' lifestyles, etc. and to introduce appropriate ways in which citizens can participate.

(8) The City shall actively consult with the nation, neighbouring municipalities, etc. on those measures described in the first paragraph of this Article which require regional solution, and endeavour to promote such consultation.

Chapter 2
Environmental Master Plan

Environmental Master Plan
Article 8.

1. The Mayor shall establish an Environmental Master Plan for Kawasaki City (hereafter referred to as the "Master Plan") which serves as a basic guideline for environmental administration in accordance with the basic ideas described in Article 2 (5) of the Law of Local Governments (Law No. 67, 1947), in order to comprehensively and systematically promote environmental administration.

2. The Master Plan shall decide the following matters:
(1) Goals of the environmental policies: identifying the ideal local environment towards which the Master Plan will aim and indicating specific objectives in respective of environmental elements needed to achieve the goals;

(2) Basic measures: indicating concrete environmental measures to which the City should give priority in order to achieve the goals of the environmental policies described in the preceding paragraphs.

(3) Guidelines for environmental improvement: indicating each matters that the City, citizens and businesses should each consider for conserving and creating a sound environment when they utilize environmental resources; and

(4) Other important matters related to the conservation and creation of a sound environment.

3. The Master Plan will apply to the whole of Kawasaki City and be decided from this broad viewpoint.

4. Deadlines targeted in the Master Plan shall be decided upon consideration of such factors as the progress of science and technology and changes in social conditions.

5. Environmental elements included in the Master Plan shall apply to citizens' lives in many ways.

Establishing the Master Plan

Article 9.

1. When the Mayor establishes the Master Plan described in the preceding Article, he must first devise measures necessary to reflect citizens' opinions and ask the Kawasaki City Environmental Policy Council (hereafter referred to as the "Council") for its opinions.

2. When the Mayor establishes the Master Plan, he must publish it as soon as possible.

3. The provisions of the preceding two (2) paragraphs shall apply to any amendments to the Master Plan.

Chapter 3
Comprehensive Coordination of Environmental Administration

Comprehensive Coordination
Article 10.

Concerning the following matters, the City will undertake the necessary measures to ensure comprehensive action and decision-making in accordance with the provisions of this Chapter:

(1) matters concerning establishment and amendment of the Master Plan;
(2) matters concerning environmental measures; and
(3) other matters concerning the overall promotion of environmental administration.

Environmental Coordination Conference
Article 11.

1.A Kawasaki City Environmental Coordination Conference (hereafter referred to as the "Coordination Conference") will be established to implement the comprehensive coordination measures described in the preceding Article.

2.The Coordination Conference will consist of the deputy mayor and managers of City bureaus involved with environmental measures.

3.In addition to the provision described in the preceeding paragraph, the Mayor shall decide other necessary matters of concern to the Coordination Conference.

Environmental Investigation
Article 12.

1.When implementing comprehensive coordination with respect to matters described in Article 10 (2) and (3), the City shall investigate whether enough environmental consideration has been carried out on the impact of the decision, and whether a decision is desirable in terms of the environment, etc. (hereafter referred to as "environmental investigation").

2.A Mayor shall establish necessary guidelines for environmental investigation in consultation with the Kawasaki City Environmental Policy Council.

Chapter 4
Environmental Policy Council

Environmental Policy Council
Article 13.

1. A Kawasaki City Environmental Policy Council (hereafter referred to as the "Council") shall be established to investigate and deliberate on whether environmental administration is being promoted comprehensively and systematically.

2. The Council shall investigate and deliberate the following matters :

(1) matters concerning establishment and amendment of the Master Plan;
(2) matters concerning guidelines described in Article 12 (2);
(3) matters concerning the annual report; and
(4) other important matters related to the overall promotion of environmental administration.

3. When investigating and deliberating the matters described in the preceding paragraph, the Council may request the Mayor and other related institutions to submit environmental information and other necessary materials whenever the council deems necessary.

4. The Council may give advice or make recommendations to a Mayor and other related institutions to submit environmental information and other necessary materials whenever the Council deems necessary.

5. The number of members of the Council shall be not more than five (5).

6. Members of the Council are appointed by the Mayor, from among persons having extensive knowledge of the environment and with the consent of the City assembly.

7. The term of office of a member of the Council shall be 2 years, and the term of office of a member appointed to fill any vacancy shall be the balance of the predecessor's term of office. However, members of the Council may be reappointed.

8. Members of the Council must not disclose any confidential information that they learn during their term of office. The same shall apply after they depart from office.

9. In addition to the provision described in each of the preceding paragraphs, the Mayor shall decide other necessary matters related to the Council.

Chapter 5
Annual Report

Annual Report
Article 14.

In order to provide appropriate management structures for progressing the Master Plan, the Mayor must prepare and publish an annual report which describes the current environmental conditions of the City, measures taken to conserve and create the environment etc.

Opinions of Citizens
Article 15.

Citizens may submit their opinion on the annual report to the Mayor during a specified consultation period established by the Mayor.

Opinions of the Council, etc.
Article 16.

1. The Mayor must ask the Council for its opinions with respect to the annual report during the consultation period in accordance with the preceding Article.

2. The Mayor shall submit citizens' opinion described in the preceding Article to the Council in accordance with the provision in the preceding paragraph.

3. When the Council expresses its opinions on the annual report, the mayor shall respect their intentions and take the necessary measures.

Chapter 6
Additional Provisions

Improvement of Survey and Research System, etc.
Article 17.

The City must endeavour to improve the survey and research systems on the environment, the collection and analysis of environmental information, the exchange between research institutions, the education and training of technologists, etc. in order to promote an environmental administration based on scientific knowledge and expertise.

Support of Citizens' Activities
Article 18.

The City must endeavour to provide environmental information and make technology, etc. available to citizens and to take measures necessary to support citizens' voluntary activities for conserving and creating a sound environment.

Entrustment
Article 19.

The Mayor shall decide necessary matters related to the enforcement of this Ordinance.

Supplementary Provision

The Mayor shall decide the effective date of this Ordinance.

WORKSHOP PAPERS AND CASE STUDIES

ENVIRONMENTAL INFORMATION GATHERING AND INTERPRETATION.

A thorough understanding of the state of the local environment is essential to any environmental programme and to the Local Agenda 21 process. Environmental monitoring systems provide an insight into the quality and development of the local environment and sound environmental information is needed to monitor goals and targets and ultimately the effects of environmental policy. It is often not the lack of will that hinders the process but rather the lack of knowledge about the tools and instruments that are needed to accomplish the practical work. A wealth of experience already exists on methods for collecting and analysing environmental information on a local area or an organisation as a basis for formulating environmental policy. Experience in environmental auditing and urban management programmes are presented in this workshop.

ENVIRONMENTAL INFORMATION GATHERING AND INTERPRETATION.

USING ENVIRONMENTAL INFORMATION TO CREATE A LOCAL AGENDA 21 PROGRAMME FOR LANCASHIRE COUNTY.
Derek Taylor, Head of Policy, Lancashire County Council, UK.

RAPID URBAN ENVIRONMENTAL ASSESSMENT: A TOOL FOR URBAN ENVIRONMENTAL URBAN MANAGEMENT IN AFRICA
Alione Badiane, Regional Coordinator for Africa, United Nations Development Programme.

THE ROLE OF ENVIRONMENTAL INFORMATION EXCHANGE AND REPORTING WITHIN AUSTRALIA & BETWEEN LOCAL AUTHORITIES.
Wayne Westcott, President, Municipal Conservation Association of Australia & Director Waste Management Services, St Kilda City Council, Victoria, Australia

USING ENVIRONMENTAL INFORMATION TO CREATE A LOCAL AGENDA 21 PROGRAMME FOR LANCASHIRE COUNTY

Derek Taylor, Head of Policy, Lancashire County Council, UK.

PROLOGUE

Local Agenda 21 is a process for communities to agree and implement actions for sustainable development in their own back yards. The process is a continuous one based on round-tabling and dialogue. Setting targets for reaching sustainable development goals is a key step and the success, or otherwise, in meeting these goals has to be measured. From the outset, a thorough understanding of the health and status of local conditions is essential to inform dialogue about the programme and to help identify detailed measures. Sound environmental information is also needed to monitor goals and targets. This paper outlines the steps taken by Lancashire County Council, in the UK to collect, organise and analyse such information and to present it to local stakeholder groups. It also explains how the data have been used to create a Local Agenda 21 Programme.

GETTING STARTED – ASSEMBLING THE INFORMATION

The story begins in 1989. In March the County Council decided it had to up-rate its performance on the environment. There were four principal reasons:

✪ Environmental concerns reached the top of the UK agenda towards the end of the 1980s. The Council shared these concerns and had a responsibility to respond to public opinion.

✪ As a major provider and purchaser of services, materials, etc., the Council, itself, was having a considerable environmental impact. We had to put our own house in order, and be seen to be doing so.

✪ The environmental ethic had to be built into all parts of the Council's organisation and management operations.

✪ The same principles applied outside County Hall. Different agencies were looking after their own interests. Nobody was saying "here is a total environment for which we are all responsible. Somebody needs to assume overall stewardship of it".

It was decided to proceed on three fronts:

✪ An appraisal of the state of the environment of the Council's area, known as the Lancashire Green Audit.(Fig. 34)

✪ An internal review of the environmental impacts of the Council's policies and practices.

✪ An appraisal of the Council's management arrangements for delivering environmental responsibilities and involving the community.

The first, and last, of these have been the basis for the Lancashire version of Local Agenda 21. The Green Audit is a comprehensive analysis of the condition of environmental resources throughout the geographical county. It has two aims:

✪ To give Lancastrians the first ever complete picture of the state of health of their own surroundings.

✪ To supply data for generating an action programme for sustaining the County environment. (Fig. 35)

The Audit covers a wide range of conditions. (Fig. 36 and 37) It identifies the assets and quality of natural and man-made resources and considers how human activies and natural processes are influencing them. (Fig. 38) Data came from exist-

Fig. 34

STATE OF THE ENVIRONMENT AUDIT :
WHAT IS IT ?

A comprehensive analysis of the health and status of environmental resources throughout the County of Lancashire

SOE AUDIT : WHAT IS IT FOR ?

* Public Information ➔

* Environmental Action Programme

Lancashire County Council, 1994

Fig. 35

WHY DID WE AUDIT ?

* Public concerns

* Own Impacts

* Corporate Overview

* Stewardship/Leadership

Lancashire County Council, 1994

WHAT DID WE AUDIT ?

* The State of Lancashire's Environment

* Ourselves

  - Policies/Practices

  - Structure/Responsibilities

Lancashire County Council, 1994

Fig. 36

SOE AUDIT : WHAT DOES IT COVER ?

* Resources/Conditions
  Air : Water : Land
* Stresses/Agents of Change
  Natural : Human

..... AND HOW ?

* Indicators
* Data Collection/Analysis
* Issues
* State of the Environment Presentation

Lancashire County Council, 1994

Fig. 37

ing, publicly-available sources. In addition to collation in written form, the information has been placed on a computerised Geographical Information System. Steps in hand will open this system to public access.

For ease of understanding, the environment was broken down into broad components: structure (geology, topography, soils, climate, population), air and water quality, waste generation and disposal, noise pollution, energy use and sources, land and agricultural pollution, resources of wildlife, landscape, townscape and open spaces (and their integrity) and transport impacts. (Fig. 39 and 40) Indicators of environmental quality, or status, were identified for all components. (Fig. 41) Information from the data base helped measure each indicator. In combination, the results give a detailed profile of the stresses, pressures and threats we are experiencing. A final section draws out the issues arising from the analysis, the bridge to the Action Programme.

The Green Audit was launched in May 1991, in three versions:

✪ A technical report aimed at the informed reader, decision-makers, colleges and secondary schools.

✪ A summary in accessible style for the public and primary schools.

✪ A simple, illustrated leaflet flagging-up key findings for the wider community.

GETTING STARTED - PARTNERSHIP AND COMMUNITY DIALOGUE

Consensus through partnership had to be an underlying principle. The exercise concerns the environment of Lancashire in which the whole population, and the organisations which

represent them, are stakeholders. To facilitate this from the outset, the Lancashire Environmental Forum was created (Fig. 42). Now comprizing 85 organisations drawn from the public, private and NGO sectors, the Forum has guided the whole initiative. It agreed how the Green Audit should be carried out, what it should contain and supplied the data. It converted the findings into the Action Programme explained below.

Data collection and analysis was the first stage in which the public were involved. The second followed the launch of the results. This is when citizens in the wider community were involved for the first time by:

✪ Circulation of reports and leaflets to libraries, information centres, voluntary and local groups, Council offices and Forum partner networks.

✪ Free copies to every school, college and university.

✪ A Green Audit roadshow.

✪ A media campaign highlighting Green Audit findings relevant to each part of the County.

A major purpose of this dialogue was to gather opinion to inform the Action Programme. A reply-paid questionnaire invited people to tell the Forum about the issues which concerned them most. Responses helped prioritize issues. In this way, a manageable agenda was produced for the Action Programme. An agenda reflecting the concerns and aspirations of Lancastrians.

ENVIRONMENTAL DATA

SUBJECT	Drinking Water Quality	Dominant Agricultural type
DATA SOURCE	NRA Public Register	MAFF Agricultural Census
DATA FORMAT	OS Maps and Computer Print-out	Parish Returns and Book
DATA TRANSFER	GIS	Manual
DATA OUTPUT	Maps, Diagrams and Statistics	Maps and Description

Lancashire County Council, 1994

Fig. 38

USING THE INFORMATION FOR A LOCAL AGENDA 21

The Forum's Programme depends for implementation on the goodwill and co-operation of its members and the general public. From the beginning, Forum membership has brought with it the responsibility for individual members to act in accordance with consensus. Thus, the Forum had to prepare its Programme in a way that maximized the potential for consensus. This was achieved by giving responsibility direct to the Forum. Four Specialist Working Groups were created from the membership with a brief to produce proposals for topic areas based on Green Audit headings:
- Air, Energy, Transport, Noise;
- Water, Waste, Land and Agriculture;
- Wildlife, Landscape, Townscape, Openspace;
- Education and Public Awareness.

This worked extremely well. It allowed the full range of expertise held by Forum organisations to be made available at no cost to the initiative. Giving all members a direct role increased ownership of the product, enhancing the prospects for implementation.

Working Group activity was co-ordinated by a small Steering Group. Towards the end, all four Groups spent the day together to discuss, challenge and defend each other's draft proposals. University and sixth-form students brought an inter-generational input to the debate. The outcome was converted into the Lancashire Environmental Action Programme (LEAP). (Fig. 43 and 44)

Environmental Components
AIR

ENVIRONMENTAL COMPONENT	AIR	
INDICATOR	SO$_2$	Emissions from Register Works
STANDARD	EC Guide & Limit Values	Depends on Gas
DATA SOURCE	Warren Spring Laboratory	HMIP
TREND	10 years	Specific Incidents
COMMENTS	Environmental Quality Indicator	Agent of Environmental Change

Lancashire County Council, 1994

Fig. 39

LEAP contains over 200 strategic measures which have been embraced by the bodies on the Forum. Each identifies the organisation(s) who must carry them out. Each sets a timescale or incorporates other targets. Green Audit updates will give an independent measure of the LEAP's success.

For the wider community a "personal action programme" is targeted at Lancashire families, schools and businesses. Sponsorship packages helped with finance, endorsement and assistance in kind. At its core, is a ten-point personal plan which each Lancastrian has been asked to pledge themselves to. Each point echoes key measures that have been endorsed by Forum organisations in their own Programme.

EPILOGUE

It is too early to gauge the overall impact of Lancashire's efforts. The first annual review of the Programme is in progress as this is being written. Some measures will succeed better than others. Action depends on the community itself, and the bodies on the Forum. But a start has been made, and it is a focused one. It mirrors Local Agenda 21, and translates it into practice. (Fig. 45) A sound basis of environmental information has been the cornerstone of the operation and will continue to be. Green Audit II is now commencing - indicators are being refined and they will more closely reflect the requirements of moving Lancashire further down the road towards a more sustainable future.

Editor's note:
Environmental, economic and social information on Lancashire County, UK was supplied and can be obtained from Lancashire County Council on request.

Fig. 40

ENVIRONMENTAL CHANGE AND CONDITIONS

AGENTS OF ENVIRONMENTAL CHANGE

ENVIRONMENTAL CONDITIONS

HUMAN

* Waste
* Development
* Depletion of non-renewables
* Harvesting
* Pollution etc

NATURAL

* Climate
* Erosion
* Flooding
* Landslip
* Vulcanism etc

ASSETS/ QUANTITY

* Rivers
* Aquifers
* Fisheries
* Habitats
* Minerals
* Forests
* Soil etc

RESOURCE QUALITY

* Air
* Water
* Soil
* Human Health
* Species Pops.
* Landscape etc

Lancashire County Council, 1994

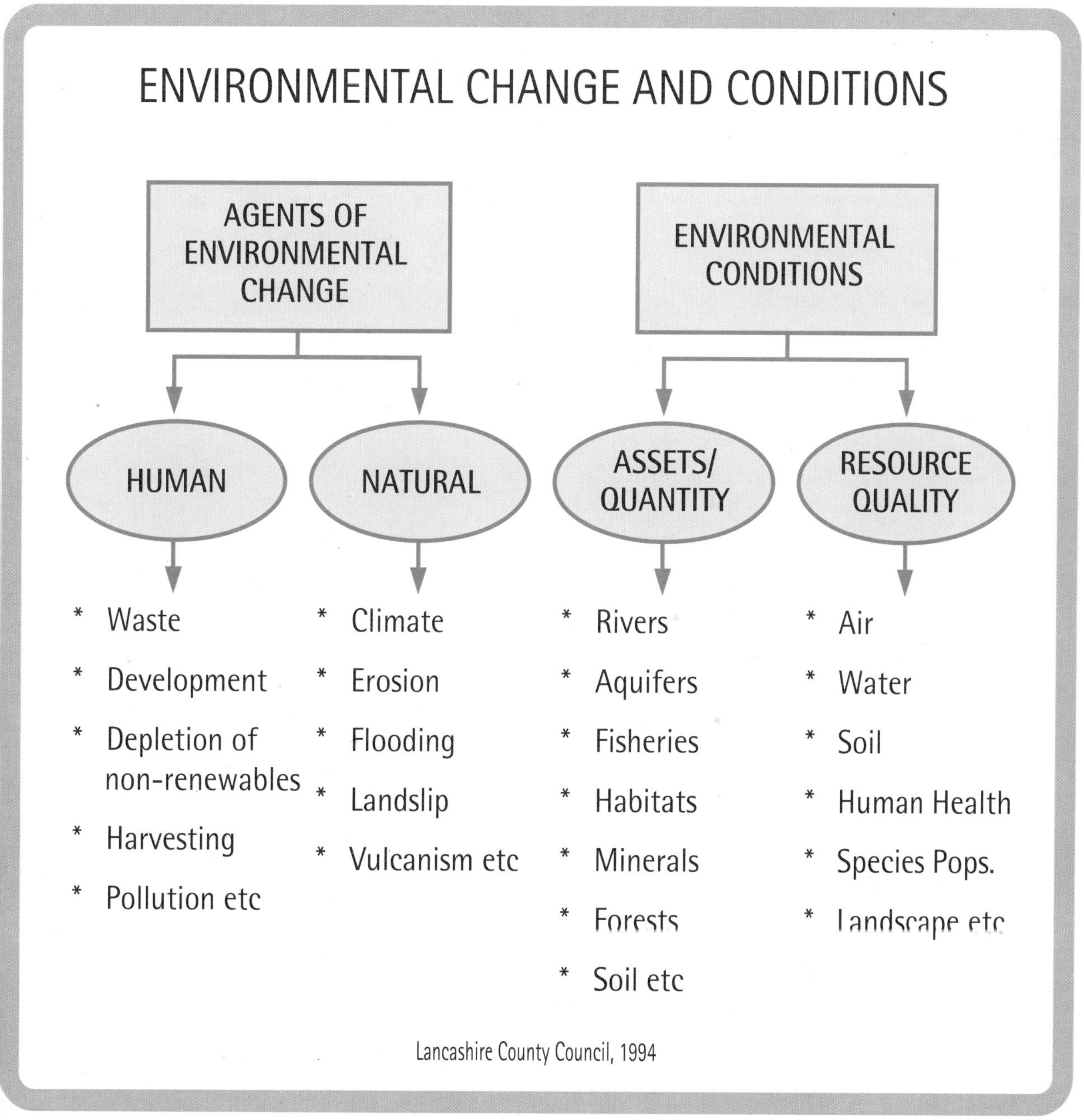

Fig. 41

ENVIRONMENTAL INDICATORS

ENVIRONMENTAL
INDICATOR

"An environmental parameter or aggregation
of data that provides a surrogate representation
of environmental quality or conditions"

ENVIRONMENTAL
**QUALITY
PROFILE**

"A number of indicators presented at the same time
to give a representation of environmental conditions"

Lancashire County Council, 1994

Fig. 42

LANCASHIRE ENVIRONMENTAL FORUM

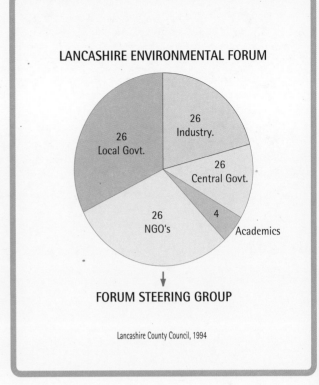

FORUM STEERING GROUP

Lancashire County Council, 1994

Fig. 43

WHAT DOES LEAP DO ?

* Charts Path → Sustainability

* Involves/Commits Key Actors

* Energizes Community

* Sets Co-ordinating Framework
  for :
    Information
    Implementation
    Monitoring/Review

* Delivers Local Agenda 21

Lancashire County Council, 1994

Fig. 44

HOW DO WE PRODUCE LEAP ?

* SOE Audit/Issues

* Dialogue with Community

* Round-Tables

* Consensus Building

* Proposals

* LEAP

Lancashire County Council, 1994

Fig. 45

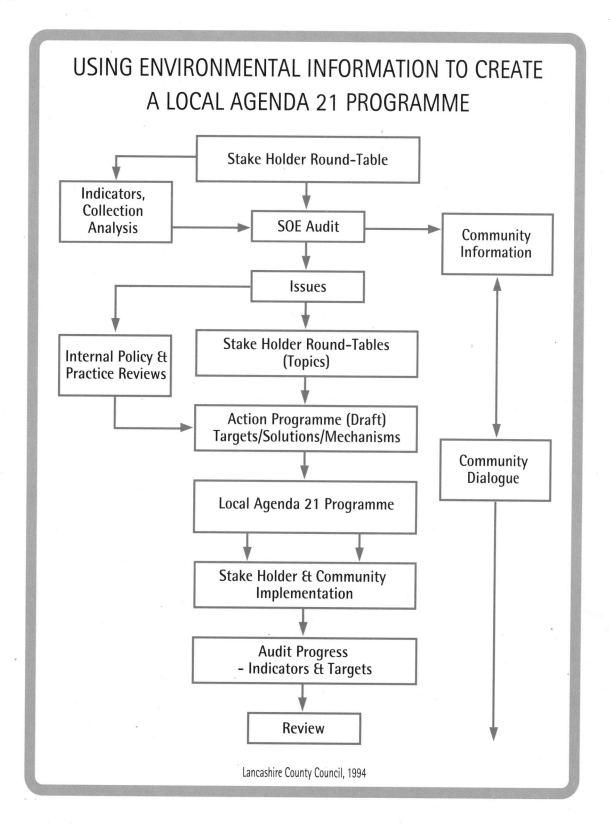

USING ENVIRONMENTAL INFORMATION TO CREATE A LOCAL AGENDA 21 PROGRAMME

Lancashire County Council, 1994

RAPID URBAN ENVIRONMENTAL ASSESSMENT (RUEA):
A TOOL FOR URBAN ENVIRONMENTAL MANAGEMENT IN
AFRICA. CASE STUDIES OF COTE D'IVOIRE AND SENEGAL
*Alioune Badiane Urban Management Programme, Regional
Co-ordinator for Africa*

Introduction:

The poorer you are, the greater the threat. In human settlements, especially in large cities, the poor, undoubtedly, are
disproportionately threatened by hazards and health risks posed
by air and ground pollution, inadequate housing, poor sanitation, polluted water and lack of other basic services. Many of
these already deprived people also live in the most ecologically
vulnerable areas and on marginal lands characterised by high
susceptibility to environmental degradation - in urban slums
and squatter settlements, on steep slopes and flood plains.
One of the greatest threats to sustainable human and economic
development comes from the downward, mutually reinforcing
spiral of poverty and environmental degradation which is
endangering current and future generations in developing
countries, and more precisely in Africa.

The 1992 UNCED Earth summit in Rio concluded that the
environmental problems of the world's growing urban population need attention; however, the 1993 Ford Foundation supported evaluation of urban research in developing countries but
noted that scant data are available on the urban environment,
as little research has been done on this topic. Thus, there is a
need for environmental action at the local level, but there is
little solid information available for building public commitment, planning and decision making.

One of the solutions identified by the Urban Management
Programme (UMP), for resolving this contradiction is to apply
the methodology for Rapid Urban Environmental Assessment
(RUEA). The methodology has been explicitly designed to be
low cost, rapid, locally managed and participatory; it is also a
possible starting point for Environmental Planning and
management.

The Urban Management Programme (UMP) funded by the UNDP
and a number of bilateral agencies and executed by UNCHS
(habitat) and the World Bank, concentrates on capacity building
in the areas of urban land management, urban infrastructure,
municipal finance and administration, urban environmental
management and poverty alleviation. The Programme catalyses
national and municipal dialogue on policy and programme
options in these critical areas.

The UMP has regional offices for Africa. the Arab States, Asia
and the Pacific and Latin America and the Caribbean that draw
upon the strength of developing country experts and disseminate that expertise at the local, national, regional and global
levels. An important focus of the UMP activities is to devote
considerable attention to the cross-cutting issues in urban
management, e.g. the relationship between urban transport and
environmental degradation and the impact of urban land management on urban environmental improvement and urban
poverty alleviation strategies.

The RUEA approach was developed by the Environment component of the UMP. This activity had two objectives: to address
gaps in knowledge and to test a process that can support
efforts to manage the urban environment. Very little information is readily available on environmental conditions, the inter-
action between urban development and ecosystems, or the
managerial setting that exists to respond to environmental
problems in the cities of the developing world. Recent attempts
to develop such information have been incomplete. Thus, there
appears to be a need for urban environmental research that is
comprehensive, multi-sectoral, relatively short term and consistent between cities. Similarly, there is need for an informed
action-orientated process that can support better environmental
planning and management at the city level.

Any methodology that meets these objectives must face a more
important test: relevance and utility in a diversity of cities.

METHODOLOGY:

In the same spirit as rapid and participatory rural appraisal, a
three step process was developed by the UMP Regional Office
for Africa (ROA) to rapidly assess the state of the urban environment in Cote d'Ivoire (Abidjan + 7 secondary towns) and in
Senegal (focused on the Dakar Metropolitan Area).

✪ An urban Environmental data questionnaire was designed to
   measure a consistent set of data that are cross sectoral and
   cross-media in nature.

✪ An urban environmental profile was outlined to analyse the
   nature trends and factors that influence environmental quality in cities in both countries.

✪ The framework of a consultation process was developed
   and implemented to initiate a public dialogue on environmental priorities and options as well as to partially validate
   the results of the questionnaire and profile through public
   discussion at the city/municipal level.

CASE STUDIES : SENEGAL AND COTE D'IVOIRE

**Environmental Action Planning and Management in Dakar,
Senegal.**

In order to improve the quality of the environmental conditions
in the Dakar Metropolitan Area, technical support was provided
to the city by the UMP. The Rapid Urban Environmental
Assessment methodology was utilised with the close collaboration of the African Institute of Urban Management (IAGU), a
regional NGO supported by Swiss-SIDA. The Rapid assessment
process started in March 1993 with a launching workshop during which the methodology of the assessment was presented
and discussed with the partners. Following the consultation, a
local consultant was contracted and a team set up to prepare
the Dakar Environmental Profile.

In October 1993, an Environmental Town Meeting was organised during which a) the Environmental Profile was discussed
and reviewed, b) environmental issues were prioritised, c) on-

going and planned environmental activities in the city were discussed, and d) follow-up was agreed upon.

Among the priorities set up, two of them will be addressed by follow-up activities. The two major environmental issues identified were:

Industrial risk management:

In the recent past several accidents have put the issue at the top of the agenda of the central government and the municipality as well as the population.

Citizen groups and Neighbourhood Associations.

The environmental degradation of the Bay of Hann: the importance of the Bay for the overall socio-economic development of the city is critical.

These two issues were selected because:
- a) they will at the same time allow other issues identified during the rapid assessment to be addressed.
- b) they will allow demonstration of a process which could be replicated for issues of a similar nature.

The activity will promote:
- a) mobilisation of local resources (human as well as financial),
- b) involvement of all actors,
- c) use of the full range of implementation instruments.

The activity will address the issues at three levels:
- a) technical / operational (mobilisation of information and expertise, co-ordination and decision-making, implementation), b) managerial (setting up of appropriate institutional arrangements) and political (securing required political support).

Abidjan Environmental City Consultation.

After the RUEA questionnaire was prepared and executed, a city profile for Abidjan and seven other secondary cities was elaborated by two local consultancy firms for discussion and as input in the environmental planning and management process. On June 2-4 1994, the Environmental Town Meeting for the City of Abidjan was hosted by the Municipality of the Greater Abidjan. High level representation from the Government attended the meeting including the Ministry of Local Government and the Ministry of Environment and Tourism. One hundred and thirty (130) participants from Central Government, Municipalities, private sector and business community NGOs, Academic and Citizen groups attended the three day event. The meeting discussed key environmental issues that the city is confronting. Among them: the natural resources pollution case of the EBRIE Lagoon which is the heart of Abidjan, air pollution, solid waste management, the sprawling squatter settlements etc... At the close, a strong statement called "Declaration of Abidjan on Urban Environment" was made along with the draft action plan and a list of recommendations for the attention of the City and the Government. UMP and the major bilaterals and multilateral present at the meeting will be called upon to support the follow up phase.

Lessons Learned from the Process

RUEA can be the first step in a strategic approach to urban environmental planning and management. The technique helps to clarify issues, involves key actors, identifies priorities and builds political commitment in a setting where some or all of these elements are lacking. Subsequent steps in the strategic approach are:
- a) the formulation of an integrated Urban Environmental Strategy that embodies issue-specific strategies, long term environmental goals and phased targets for meeting the goals;
- b) agreement on issues-orientated action plans for achieving the targets, including identification of least-cost project options, policy reform and institutional actions; and
- c) a Consolidation phase where agreed programmes and projects are initiated, policy reforms and institutional arrangements are solidified, the overall process is made routine and monitoring and evaluation procedures are put in place.

✪ At the beginning, the case study approach was selected by the Core Team based in the World Bank in Washington to test the methodology because it is a valid research tool in the absence of theoretical guidance in the field. The following criteria were used to select the case studies:

- a) the cities should be chosen from different continents, cultures and political systems;
- b) they should reflect different levels of per-capita income with varying degrees of poverty;
- c) they should be characterised by different stages and types of industrialisation;
- d) both large and small cities should be included in the sample;
- e) baseline data should be available from on-going activities so that primary research can be minimised. These criteria were combined with a resource constraint to select six cities and one urbanising areas: Accra (Ghana), Jakarta (Indonesia), Kotowice (Poland), Sao Paulo (Brazil), Tianjin (China), Tunis (Tunisia) and the Singraul Region (India).

✪ After applying the technique in these cities, several lessons were learned about its strengths and limitations as well as areas for further inquiry.

The advantages of the RUEA are that it:

- a) is indeed rapid;
- b) cost-effective;
- c) centralises diverse information;
- d) benefits from local knowledge, access to, and discussion of information.

Taken in isolation from the other phases in the strategic approach to environmental management, the technique suffers from three limitations:

a) it provides guidance as to what might be a priority problem but gives little indication as to what might constitute the range of possible solutions;

    b) by using secondary data, it is confined by the range and quality of work that has already been done;

    c) results cannot always be compared between cities because data apply to different time periods, were derived in different ways or are based on different samples.

✪ Some topics that would constitute fruitful areas for future research include: gathering data on low income communities; linking health effects with environmental conditions; valuing the economic costs and benefits of urban environmental activities using alternative methods to assess public priorities; matching jurisdiction with ecological boundaries; and comparing policy instruments for environmental management. New researches are already being initiated on some of these topics by the UMP and partners. Four cities in South Africa will be studied using RUEA methodology. As new knowledge is developed from this research and from increasing use of the RUEA methodology, the approach will be refined and modified to better serve as an initial instrument for managing environmental quality in our cities.

Tentative Conclusions for Urban Environmental Planning and Management

Initial results from the RUEA have yielded three sets of preliminary findings:

✪ In the areas of urban poverty and economic structure, it appears that:

    a) Urban environmental degradation has a disproportionately negative impact on the poor. The poor suffer disproportionately from urban environmental insults; environmentally sensitive and hazardous urban areas are often inhabited by the poor; the poor may pay more for basic environmental services and infrastructure; income is not always the best measure of poor quality of life; and targeted interventions can improve the environmental conditions of low-income groups.

    b) Economic structure shapes environmental problems. The structure and location of economic activities in and around cities affects the prevalence and severity of particular environmental problems. The important economic variables that appear to influence environmental problems are: spatial pattern of industrial location and impacts on health; the effectiveness of industrial pollution control and risk management, energy use and industrial structure; and the size and nature of the informal sector.

    c) The level of urban wealth is linked to certain environmental problems. Basic sanitation is a problem of low income cities. Hazardous wastes, ambient air pollution and lack of green space are priority problems of higher income cities. Surface water pollution and inadequate solid waste management are problems that plague developing urban areas regardless of their level of wealth.

2. In the area of urban institutions and management, the following is suggested from the RUEA.

    a) Environmental management is complex. Managing urban environmental problems is complicated because of the following: the large number of actors per problem area; cross-jurisdictional conflicts; central-local conflicts and tensions between forces for centralisation and devolution of authority to local government bodies.

    b) Institutions, policies and problems are not synchronised. Part of the managerial complexity stems from the fact that there is often little relationship between the spatial scale or nature of urban environmental problems, which are often sectoral, and the design of sectoral institutions and policies;

    c) Municipal capacity affects environmental quality. If solutions to particular environmental problems are within the purview of municipal institutions, they must have appropriate financial and human resources. When resources are inadequate, the maintenance and/or expansion of environmental services and infrastructure will be constrained.

3. In the areas of problem analysis and prioritisation preliminary conclusions indicate that:

    a) Public opinion and professional/scientific priorities may differ. Neither public opinion nor scientific analysis provides the optimal means of ranking urban environmental problems: both the public and the analytical processes have their biases; and only a combined approach can offer the potential for improving each process;

    b) Cities have significant extra urban environmental impacts. Urban demand for resources and the disposal of city wastes that result from resource transformation can harm environmental systems outside the city proper.

Conclusion

These findings offer potentially useful advice for those seeking to improve the environmental management of cities in the developing world, The following general conclusions flow from these tentative results of the assessment exercise:

a) urban environmental strategies should be guided by the configuration of key economic variables;

b) solutions that are not heavily dependent on institutional performance may be necessary in the short run because of the organisational problems of complexity and synchronisation;

c) enhanced public awareness, consultation and participation can improve environmental management; and

d) careful attention must be paid to the selection of problem areas, their scale and institutional capacity when designing interventions.

THE AUSTRALIA CASE

Wayne Wescott Director of Waste Management and Environmental Services for the City of St Kilda, in Victoria, Australia and President of the Municipal Conservation Association.

The MCA is a national group that assists local communities to develop better sustainable development practices. The MCA is the primary group developing Local Agenda 21 in Australia.

The role of information in Agenda 21

Information exchange is one of the key elements of the national strategy for the development of Local Agenda 21 programs in Australia. This is achieved through some national mechanisms, such as the Environmental Information System, EIS, which is based at the Australian National University and the Municipal Conservation Society. The most innovative of these mechanisms is "Councilnet", an electronic communications system facilitated by the MCA.

Many forms of information gathering and exchange are also becoming part of the normal way that Councils are doing business. These include State of the Environment reporting, sophisticated environment impact assessment and Integrated Local Area Planning Programs.

Community Monitoring and Interpretation

Across the country there has been a specific drive to involve - rather than just consult - the community. In St Kilda, Victoria, the gathering of information by local community groups has been a way for groups to directly involve themselves in the long term planning of the heavily forested foreshore area in the municipality. The information gathered is on litter counts on the beach, penguin colony movements around the breakwater, possum numbers in the Catani Gardens and other habitat related information.

The Council has resourced these efforts through the purchasing of electronic equipment for the penguin monitoring and technical and other assistance for the litter counts.

Through a program called Community Recycling Co-ordinators, community members also give direct feedback to the councils on the recycling rates across the city, the participation by residents, new opportunities, range of products that are successful and so on.

Both of these programs (as well as others) are integrated into mainstream community and Council priorities for action because of the consequences to the local economy of reduced litter, increased habitat protection and improved waste management. This ensures that the data collected has a definable and identifiable outcome.

Council Monitoring and Interpretation

The community efforts supplement the various Council systems. They are usually co-ordinated with specific programs as part of an overall process to ensure accountability.

These cover a range of issues across the community including recycling and waste minimisation, energy management, transportation systems, ecotourism development and so on.

Integration of Data Collection, Planning, Action and Evaluation

The processes of data collection, planning, taking action and evaluation are in the end about changing behaviour. If Agenda 21 changes nothing then it has failed.

The process of collecting data is in itself an educational and motivational activity. Following the process through to a change in current behaviour reinforces the original educational message.

It is crucial therefore that the data collection processes do not become an end in themselves. Integrated into the total process, they are a critical element in a Local Agenda 21.

Strengthening the role of Indigenous People, 2% of Australia's population, a key element of Local Agenda 21

WORKSHOP PAPERS AND CASE STUDIES

LOCAL ECONOMIC STRATEGIES FOR SUSTAINABLE DEVELOPMENT

Rio's Agenda 21 calls upon municipalities to enter into a dialogue with all sectors to create local environmental action plans. Partnerships and consultation with private enterprise is to be encouraged. Models of public-private partnerships for the environment are presented based on innovative projects which aim to encourage and support local businesses to develop sustainable environmental policies in all their business and workplace activities. Many local authorities are showing they have an important role to play in reconciling environmental and economic aims by promoting existing good practice, demonstration models, training and information dissemination. This workshop also seeks to clarify what the concept of a sustainable or green local economy can mean in practice.

LOCAL ECONOMIC STRATEGIES FOR SUSTAINABLE DEVELOPMENT

BERKELEY'S ECONOMIC DEVELOPMENT STRATEGY PROTECTING JOBS AND THE ENVIRONMENT
Nancy Skinner, Member of Berkley Environment Commission and Executive Director, Local Solutions to Global Pollutions, California, USA.

ECOPROFIT GRAZ–CLEANER PRODUCTION IN A CITY-BASED PROJECT.
Karl Neiderl, Head of the Department of Environment Protection, City of Graz, Austria.

COVENTRY–GREENING INDUSTRY.
Penny Duggan, Head of Environmental Development, City of Coventry, UK.

BERKELEY'S ECONOMIC DEVELOPMENT STRATEGY - PROTECTING JOBS AND THE ENVIRONMENT
Nancy Skinner, Member, City of Berkeley Environment Commission

Berkeley's economic development program has two parallel and equally important goals: protecting and increasing jobs and protecting the environment.

The initial thinking to make environmental protection the theme for Berkeley's economic development strategy began in the early 1980's. Just as California's Silicon Valley was the centre for computer and information technology, the desire was to make Berkeley the centre for alternative energy and appropriate technology research, development and businesses. But there were major obstacles: the city had no entrepreneurial history and no office of economic development. There was no staff base to drive the program forward. Also, the governmental programs that make this kind of innovative business development favourable, eg; special tax credits, Federal Research & Development funds and small business development loans were by and large eliminated with the election of Ronald Reagan to the White House and a change of Governors in California. So much of Berkeley's plans had to be put on the back burner.

Though initially haphazard because the City did not have economic development staff to drive the effort, by 1987 Berkeley had begun a coordinated and comprehensive effort to make protection of the environment and retaining and increasing jobs the focus of the city's economic development activities. The first issue we faced was: what is the definition of an "environmental" or "green" business?. To answer that concern the following criteria was evolved:

Targeted businesses had to either:

✪ provide environmental services, eg. energy conservation services, recycling collection, company or hazardous materials remediation service,

✪ produce environmental related goods and products, eg. a manufacturer of goods made from recycled or secondary materials, manufacturer of non-toxic household cleaners, etc.

✪ be any business that in its management, production, and/or operations applied state of the art environmental practice, eg, pollution prevention, hazardous and toxic material use reduction, and waste minimisation.

Berkeley's interest in becoming the centre for "green businesses" was motivated not only by our desire to protect the environment and, of course, increase the city's revenue base, but also to promote community development. Maintaining the ethnic, cultural and economic diversity of Berkeley's population has been an explicit goal underlying many of the city's policies. Job retention and job growth, especially in good entry level jobs for Berkeley's unemployed and underemployed residents, is an important component in preserving the community's diversity. So our environmental economic development strategy could not just be based on attracting established businesses from outside areas bringing their employees with them and relocating to Berkeley,

we had to design a strategy that would retain existing industry and business and help maintain and create additional well-paying entry level jobs for a "blue collar" work force - not an easy accomplishment for a built up West Coast city with high land costs and strict environmental standards. We knew that we had to be daring, innovative and offer unusual incentives.

Early on we realised that the city government could not accomplish this challenge alone. Success could only be achieved by tapping into and expanding resources from our community, every level of government eg. coordinating efforts between existing city departments, working with the Chamber of Commerce and other business groups, utilizing our community college and other job training programs and drawing on county, state and federal funding. The process has taken a number of years and, of course, is still in progress. I will describe now the steps we took, in more or less chronological order:

1.   **Established an Office of Economic Development.**

Activities of the office include:

✪ creating a database which identified existing businesses, and described Berkeley's labour pool, and labour/job training resources;

✪ maintaining a database of available commercial properties and rentals;

✪ working with the local community college district, Berkeley's adult school and other job training organizations to develop programs and curriculum focusing on environmental service related fields and in skill areas that were identified as lacking within Berkeley's labour pool;

✪ developing promotional brochures and business attraction materials focused on the city's environmental protection and "green business" theme;

✪ promoting the concept of job and economic development through environmental protection and then enlisting the cooperation and support from labour groups and trade unions, the County Economic Development Task Force, the Private Industry Council and other groups;

✪ drawing on the resources of the City's Environmental Health Staff, the County Waste Management Authority, State Public Health and Environmental Services and other offices to provide technical assistance to help new and existing businesses practice pollution prevention and other state of the art environmental practices;

✪ applying the concept of mitigations to fund environmental programs and improvements. In negotiating permits with new housing or business developers, the Office of Economic Development has established a set of mitigations for environmental detriment which then funds environmental benefits, eg; a recent new development was required as part of their permit to fund the construction of bike paths as a mitigation for increased traffic resulting from their development.

2. Assisting Existing Community-Based Environmental Businesses

Because one of our main interests was to retain and increase our job base, we focused first on the businesses and environmental services that already existed in the community. Berkeley was fortunate to have a number of small community based businesses that grew out of the informal sector which had been providing environmental services like residential kerbside and commercial collection of recyclable materials and compost processing for many years. But the business skills of these community organization based efforts, and their access to capital, was limited. It was in the City's interest for these businesses to succeed. We began providing technical assistance and setting up arrangements for the use of city equipment, city owned property or facilities, providing the businesses rent free space, low cost leases, low interest to no interest loans, contracts for material collection, etc. The result is that these businesses remain an economically vital force which has preserved existing jobs, kept revenue and expenditures within the Berkeley economy and freed the City from having to establish and operate these services ourselves.

3. Providing Technical Assistance

To help business and industry adopt the environmental practices, like pollution prevention and waste minimization, that the city was advocating, we reorganized the Environmental Health Department to include a technical assistance component. Last year the Department initiated an environmental business awards program. Businesses that have made the greatest progress in pollution prevention or environmental protection are given awards by the Mayor and honoured at a citywide reception. The Department has also made stickers which announce "We recycle with the City of Berkeley" or "Pollution Prevention Award Winner" and are given to appropriate businesses to display on their doors or windows .

4. New Business Development Through Private/Public Partnerships

We established a Community Energy Services Corporation (CESC), a private public partnership providing energy audits, lighting retrofits and other energy conservation services to Berkeley businesses and city owned facilities and operations. The CESC works with the local utility company to leverage financing to help the businesses pay for energy conservation improvements. To date over 75% of the City owned buildings have been retrofitted and more than 100 private businesses have used the company's services. The retrofitting of the city owned buildings has saved the City government over $75,000 a year in utility costs. CESC: the City's office created in the weatherization insulation services 10 jobs and multiplier effects result in approximately 50-75 additional jobs.

5. Incorporating Job Training

To keep with Berkeley's goal of increasing jobs to our under-employed residents, the City worked with existing job training programs and established new programs to provide training in environmental related fields like energy conservation and hazardous materials management. Many of the staff the Community Energy Services Corporation uses for commercial building audits and lighting retrofits are young adults trained by the city's youth employment training program. This same training program also trains youth in how to conduct residential energy audits and install weatherization insulation and other residential energy conservation improvements.

6. Use of Zoning and Other Land Use Tools

Working with our citizen member planning commission, we began a series of area specific plans to review land uses, policies and regulations to make them consistent with the goals of economic development through the protection of both jobs and the environment. The focus of this effort was the creation of the West Berkeley Area plan. West Berkeley is our community's industrial and manufacturing area. The plan aims to preserve manufacturing and light industry while implementing strict environmental controls and standards. Currently the City's general plan is being revised to incorporate "creating a sustainable urban environment" as its central theme .

7. Designation as a Recycling Market Development Zone

Berkeley applied to the State of California and was one of the first 4 cities in the State of California to receive designation as a "Recycling Market Development Zone". The intent of this program is to "close the loop in recycling" so that the city is not only collecting materials to be recycled but also ensuring that those materials are used again. The Development Zone's purpose is to encourage the expansion of existing businesses and the development of new business which utilize recycled materials, eg; manufacturers that use recycled materials as their feedstock for product manufacturing, building materials salvage operations and other re-use businesses, etc. Through the program the State is offering low interest business development and expansion loans technical assistance, some tax credits and other incentives. Berkeley received the designation less than 9 months ago and already we've secured attractive loan packages for two existing businesses and one new business.

A Case Study: The West Berkeley Area Plan

One key component of Berkeley's Environment and Economic Development Plan is the preservation of manufacturing and light industry in the West Berkeley industrial area. This may seem like an oxymoron since when we think of industry we most often think of environmental degradation. One of the major challenges facing environmentalists and cities committed to restoring and maintaining environmental quality is the development of environmentally sound production and manufacturing capabilities.

The well-being of an urban area is dependent on both a healthy environment and a vibrant economy. Unemployment and related social problems detract from a community's ability to focus on environmental restoration and management. Plant closures and the loss of industrial and manufacturing jobs have not been an environmental benefit. Encouraging sustainable industry by assisting in the implementation of pollution prevention and environmentally sound practices is one of the most sound and forward thinking urban environmental strategies.

In undertaking the planning process for West Berkeley, historically the city's industrial and manufacturing area, the challenge was to preserve the area's uses and prevent the area's success from pricing out manufacturing and industry. Successful mixed use areas often become attractive to developers promoting retail and office complexes which can afford higher square foot leases and land costs, forcing out industry and manufacturing. To prevent the eroding of Berkeley's industrial base the West Berkeley plan designates specific areas for light manufacturing and industrial uses and excludes from those areas any conflicting uses.

A central, driving premise of the plan is to ensure that maintaining and expanding West Berkeley's manufacturing and industrial base is fully consistent with maintaining and improving West Berkeley's environment. The plan relies on strict environmental quality regulations so that industrial and other development will not mean environmental degradation. But the city doesn't only act as enforcer, to assist the businesses in complying with environmental regulations, city staff provide technical assistance and help package attractive loans and other financing mechanisms.

The plan also includes a job training and development component for Berkeley residents. A major environmental benefit of West Berkeley jobs going to Berkeley residents is the potential reduction in automobile commuting traffic. The plan includes employer based automobile trip reduction strategies and improved pedestrian access and bikeways to make it easier to move around West Berkeley without driving.

West Berkeley Plan Highlights:

✪ Creates districts designed to retain light industry and manufacturing.

✪ Focuses comprehensive environmental enforcement and technical assistance to achieve environmental goals.

✪ Supports the creation of a central, accessible location where the businesses and the community can obtain environmental information.

✪ Establishes reductions in the production, transport, and handling of toxic and hazardous materials.

✪ Incorporates the concept of self enforcing "good neighbour" agreements between existing industries, institutions and adjacent residents/businesses.

✪ Seeks to focus economic development efforts on retaining and attracting appropriate industries.

✪ Proposes a variety of measures to reduce the use of single-occupant automobiles.

✪ Supports the achievement of these goals and activities through City staff provided with environmental and economic development technical assistance.

CONCLUSION

Recent census tract data and information compiled by Berkeley's Office of Economic Development would indicate that so far Berkeley's strategy has been successful. The steady decrease in minority residents, particularly Berkeley's African American population, that was evident in the 70's and early 80's has stabilized. Unemployment figures for the last two years have improved and best of all, 1992 showed the first increase in both manufacturing jobs and new industrial businesses in over a decade.

ECOPROFIT GRAZ

Cleaner Production in a City-Based Project: Profiting From
Pollution Prevention
Karl Niederl, Head of City of Graz
Department of Environmental Protection

Many businesses use hazardous chemicals and other substances in
their production processes. The cumulative loading of pollution
and wastes to the urban environment from these companies is
significant. Furthermore, because of the relatively small
amounts of wastes and pollution that small and medium sized
firms generate individually, they are often not subject to regulatory
measures, or they may simply escape detection due to a lack of
municipal resources to enforce pollution regulations. Corrective
and regulatory approaches to pollution problems in this case are
proving to be ineffective and unworkable for local governments.

Preventing pollution is a superior approach to "end of pipe"
waste management techniques as the benefits include both a
reduction in wastes and emissions as well as in resource consumption. Moreover, changing production processes to prevent pollution may be the only viable option for many smaller businesses.
Cleaner production is a pollution prevention approach which
avoids wastes and emissions and also increases industrial
production efficiency and can ultimately lower overall costs.

Although many small and medium sized enterprises may have
neither the technical expertise nor the financial resources to
change from a corrective to a preventative approach for handling
their wastes, municipal governments have compelling reasons to
promote pollution prevention through cleaner production. The
municipal mandate to manage wastes and to deliver clean
water means that local governments have a vested interest in
pollution prevention in order to avoid the steadily increasing
costs of water treatment facilities, waste management and
other remediation measures. Municipalities also have a pecu-
niary interest in helping local companies to increase efficiency
and profitability in order to support the municipal tax base.

Local governments can facilitate a preventative approach to
pollution and waste problems by mobilising the technical expertise
and entrepreneurial skills of the academic, business and industrial
sectors within their communities. In this way local government
can play a role in demonstrating to industries and businesses
how they can profit from pollution prevention.

Goals

The primary goal of ECOPROFIT was to introduce companies to
new low and non-waste technologies and to demonstrate how
these technologies could increase efficiency and profits while
preventing pollution. The goal was to produce successful private
sector examples of economic and ecological waste minimisation
and to market these successes in order to attract wider acceptance
of the preventative approach within the business community.

ECOPROFIT Graz is an on-going project which attempts to put
into practice the concept of profit from pollution prevention.
The program works within the existing legislative framework to
introduce the local industrial and business communities to the
financial benefits of cleaner production technologies and

processes. The program recruits companies on a voluntary basis
and facilitates access to technical assistance to help companies
identify and implement cleaner production technologies and
process changes. The program succeeds in convincing companies
to implement these changes by demonstrating that these improved
management techniques will result in increased efficiency and
profits. (Fig. 46)

The project uses an innovative approach which couples information and technical assistance with marketing support. The
Municipality facilitates the transfer of technology from a local
academic institution to the local industrial/business community
through a three-way partnership. Companies are assisted to
put in place cleaner production processes which reduce wastes
and pollution and increase efficiency and profits. Successful
companies are promoted as "ecological market leaders" and are
awarded ECOPROFIT "mark of quality" product labels.
Rewarding participating companies through promotional activities motivates other companies to adopt similar pollution
prevention measures and leads to the wider application of
pollution prevention approaches.

GRAZ AND THE PROFIT PROJECT

Graz, Austria is a city of 240,000. The main economic activities
are automobile and machine production, shoe manufacturing
and brewing. The City is surrounded by mountains to the north
resulting in poor air circulation, especially in winter, when temperature inversions occur. Water and air pollution from industrial
emissions are the main environmental problems in Graz.

Due to the limits of the corrective approach to pollution and
waste problems and the enormously complex problem associated
with the existence of many small polluters in Graz, the
Municipality wanted to introduce local industries and businesses
to the benefits of a preventative approach which would operate
within the existing legislative and economic context.

The Municipality of Graz felt that it was essential to highlight
improved management techniques and production processes
which are based on the closed-cycle concept. The closed-cycle
production scheme used in ECOPROFIT is based on the concept
of a circular, non-linear flow of materials similar to the recycling of materials in natural ecosystems. Although there are
always some losses of materials from the production process,
the idea is to maximise the recycling of materials, either back
into the original production process, or to use the materials lost
from one production process as inputs into another production
process. The application of closed-cycle pollution prevention
measures integrates economic and ecological considerations by
increasing efficiency and profits while reducing wastes and
pollution.

The Municipality's Department of Environmental Protection, in
co-operation with the Graz University of Technology, initiated
ECOPROFIT - ECOlogical PROject For Integrated environmental
Technologies. This city based project was begun in 1991 and is
headed by the Waste Minimisation Research Group of the
Institute for Chemical Engineering at the Graz University of
Technology. This group is investigating strategies for closed-
cycle production and has investigated related international

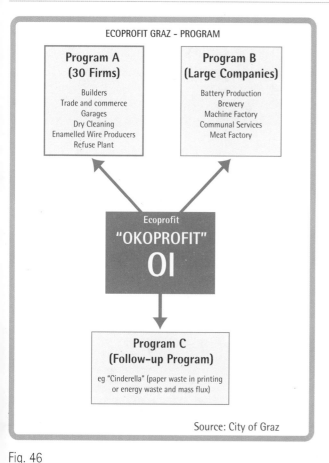

ECOPROFIT GRAZ - PROGRAM

Program A
(30 Firms)

Builders
Trade and commerce
Garages
Dry Cleaning
Enamelled Wire Producers
Refuse Plant

Program B
(Large Companies)

Battery Production
Brewery
Machine Factory
Communal Services
Meat Factory

Ecoprofit
"OKOPROFIT"
OI

Program C
(Follow-up Program)

eg "Cinderella" (paper waste in printing
or energy waste and mass flux)

Source: City of Graz

Fig. 46

research activities on waste minimisation and ecologically -
conscious design.

Information about the ECOPROFIT project was widely disseminated
to the public and to local companies in order to recruit interested
participants. Five companies were chosen for the initial phase of
the program according to criteria based on their potential to
represent examples for a wider application of the project results.
Each company had to be a "typical" size for the City, had to
employ commonly used technology, and had to be willing to
play a role in the public relations activities associated with the
project. Following selection, company personnel were trained in
the concept of closed-cycle production. A tool kit was made
available to interested companies which included manuals, data
sheets, videos and other training materials.

The initial companies in the ECOPROFIT project included three
printing companies of different sizes (from 6 employees to 500
employees), a large vehicle repair garage with 230 employees,
and a wholesale coffee roaster and chain-store company with
342 employees. Each produced emissions into the air and water,
as well as solid wastes, of varying toxicity. An introductory workshop was held to train the concerned representatives of these
companies in ECOPROFIT methods and data collection methodologies. Program managers felt that it was necessary to establish a
basis for trust and the company representatives were assured that
the internal data of the companies would be confidential and
would not be released to regulatory authorities.

The following principles were used as guidelines which the
participating companies were encouraged to adopt:

✪ anything that leaves the production process should be
considered as a product or raw material that can be used
directly, or after processing, as an input for another production
process;

✪ every product is optimised regarding reparability and recycla-
bility;

✪ production is based on renewable sources of energy and
substances as far as possible or is based on recycled
(secondary) materials;

✪ the producer is responsible for the whole life cycle of his
product, including energy consumption and emissions during
the use of the product, its reparability and ability to be recycled
or disposed of;

✪ the producer chooses materials from renewable resources and
releases wastes in a way that does not diminish nature;

✪ the producer minimises the energy demand to a level that
can be covered from renewable energy sources.

Project managers recognise that these guidelines are general
and that they can be transferred from one company to another
in their principle ideas and strategies, but not in their details.
According to the project, it is extremely important that the
solutions be worked out within each company by the employees
of that company as part of their own particular internal structure. The support from external experts was limited to training
in implementation of the approach.

In order to integrate waste minimisation into the production
process the companies were required to:

✪ avoid all substances that cannot be kept in closed cycles;

✪ reduce all substances outside of closed cycles to an amount
which can be borne by ecosystems;

✪ reduce the demand for non-renewable resources to a level
that does not compromise future generations.

ECOPROFIT uses emissions standards contained in legislation
enacted as part of the Austrian National Clean Air and Clean
Water Acts. These emissions standards are relatively stringent
compared to those in many other countries.

Each company was required to form a project team made up of
members of different disciplines. Business, technical, legal and
maintenance personnel were all considered equally important.
The basis for a cleaner production program is the fostering of an
understanding of flows from inputs to outputs. Therefore, the
first phase of the project concentrated on the awareness of
personnel of flows of mass - materials and energy - to wastes.
Company operations and maintenance procedures were assessed
with regard to the flows of materials and energy. For each
company, an input/output analysis was carried out and was
displayed in flowsheets. These analyses examined manufacturing
techniques and processes, organisational structures, and the raw
and process materials used.

Companies were classified according to the characteristics of their waste stream. There were three classifications: dangerous or hazardous waste streams (requiring some form of security); waste streams that entail high costs; and waste streams that could be minimised or prevented. Waste minimisation measures that could be carried out without investment were introduced during this phase of the project. In the next phase of the project, the company's existing internal materials and energy flows were compared with those attainable with the application of state-of-the-art low and non-waste technologies. The possibilities for incorporating low and non-waste technologies into each company's production processes were assessed. A list of proposed measures that could improve the situation of the company was compiled. This list included actions aimed at all levels of the organisation.

For example, it included:

✪ the organisation of responsibilities regarding the environment, material handling and waste treatment;

✪ the reorganisation of the accounting system in order to improve knowledge about the costs of generation and treatment of wastes;

✪ training and education of personnel at all levels (from top management to cleaning personnel) to increase levels of awareness about waste issues;

✪ changes in product design in order to minimise wastes during production, use and disposal;

✪ technological changes in production to minimise consumption of materials and energy while at the same time reducing the generation of wastes and emissions;

✪ changes in raw materials acquisition in order to reduce the amount of toxicity of wastes and to increase the utilisation of renewable resources;

✪ improvement of waste management processes in order to maximise the reuse and recycling of materials.

The overall goal of the identified measures was the minimisation of wastes and emissions through increased efficiency. Emphasis was placed on measures that could be carried out with little or no investment. The options were graded according to their technical and economic feasibility. In particular, identified measures were classified according to their pay-back (or amortisation) period. For example, it was determined that the printers' garages had 54 technically feasible management options for waste minimisation and pollution prevention and that 24% of the suggested measures would be profitable within one year, 30% would be profitable within 2 years, and 15% would have no impact on profit or loss. Company personnel chose the low and non-waste technologies which they felt would benefit them the most.

In all, thirty of the originally identified measures were classified as "possible in the short term" meaning that they made sense from both a technical and an economic perspective, and were implemented immediately. Company personnel were trained in the new procedures and equipment and results were monitored.

Project managers concluded that it is more costly to generate emissions and wastes than it is to prevent them in the first place - usually by a factor of ten or more. It was felt that reductions in waste generation could reach up to 60% or 90% for materials that are not part of the product, and that toxic substances (heavy metals, halogenated carbons) could be eliminated or replaced. Overall, it was anticipated that cleaner production measures could lead to a reduction in the total amount of wastes and emission by a factor of ten. The overriding issue for the project was to determine how much of the existing wastes and emissions could be prevented within the existing legislative and economic context with an economic benefit for the company.

In addition to the efficiency and productivity gains resulting from this program, the Municipality provides a further incentive for companies to participate. Successful companies will be promoted as ecological market leaders to the local community.

THE ECOPROFIT LABEL

Companies which achieve a significant reduction in wastes and emissions as defined by the project are awarded an "ECOPROFIT label" by the Municipality and are authorised to use the label for marketing purposes for one year. Successful companies to date include: several vehicle repair garages, several printers, the public transit authority, a brewery, a car production plant, several home construction companies, a coffee roaster/chain store enterprise, a machine fabricator, one hospital, one health services company, one home construction supply store, and one company which restores antiques.

After one year, companies will have to continue to participate in the on-going activities of the program and will have to implement further waste minimisation and pollution prevention measures in order to gain re-authorisation to continue to use the label.

The criteria for earning the label include implementing management options as well as achieving quantifiable improvements. The criteria are derived from the European Union environmental auditing scheme - Eco-Audit - modified for small and medium sized enterprises. The standards that must be achieved in order to receive the ECOPROFIT mark of quality label include: 30% solid waste reduction; 50% hazardous waste and air emissions reductions; environmental capability in production and handling; transparent internal and external information; and compliance with all legal regulations. The goal of the label is to promote participating companies and to provide an incentive to other companies to join the project and incorporate improved environmental management techniques into their operations. The 1st European Round Table on Cleaner Production (held in Graz in October of 1994) was chosen as the occasion to hand out the first ECOPROFIT awards to local companies.

In order to accommodate as many companies as possible, a continuous training program called ECOPROFIT II has been established. For a period of ten months, leading employees from about 20 companies of varying sizes attend workshops where they are educated and trained in closed-cycle production processes. Companies are required to form eco-teams of employees who are encouraged to formulate theoretical programs and modifications specific to their companies. These are reported to the training program groups as well as to the public. An ECOPROFIT III project will soon be established which involves an auditing process based on the European Eco-Audit standard.

New targets will be defined after each phase. Approximately 40 projects with firms of different sizes have been carried out or are on-going. The participating companies vary in size from very small companies having no more than 6 employees, to those with 1,000 employees, and include printers, breweries, vehicle repair garages, dry cleaners, hospitals, building contractors, mechanical engineering firms, a battery production and a wire coating company, a food (sausage) production company and the municipal public transport.

RESULTS

Project follow-up indicates that there has been an overall reduction of more then 50% in the generation of toxic and solid wastes from participating companies. In some garages the reductions are as high as 82%. Halogenated and oil containing materials have been completely eliminated from the participating garages (100% reduction) and solvents have been reduced by 50% or more. The material efficiency of enamelling (spray painting) has increased by 91% in some cases. Overall costs have been reduced by as much as 60%.

Specific improvements were achieved through better environmental management including improved housekeeping, changes in material selections, and the implementation of new technologies and process modifications. For example, in the vehicle repair garages, a high volume / low pressure spraying technique reduced the overspray by 25%. In printing enterprises, mixing inks in gravure printing cut down on hazardous wastes. Chemical inputs

in reproduction processes were reduced by as much as 70%. (Figs. 47 and 48) Changing material selection was also effective. Toxic halogenated degreasing agents were replaced with waterbased cold dip degreasers in garages to reduce solvent emissions. Water-based paints were selected wherever possible for printing enterprises and resulted in a reduction of 80% to 90% in solvent emissions. Oil-based offset cleaners were replaced with less volatile vegetable oil cleaners and in-bulk purchasing of inks reduced the generation of empty containers by 50%.

The results of the program, including evidence of reduced production inputs, wastes, emissions and costs attributable to the new low and non-waste processes, were tabulated and distributed through a public information campaign.

The municipal administration feels that these measures are proving to be more effective than regulations, and that there is now better co-operation with companies. In addition, the program is producing useful environmental data. The companies report financial savings, higher productivity, improved relations with the municipal administration, and an improved public image. The Technical University of Graz benefits from the practical nature of the research project, improved education through the case study approach, and better job prospects for graduating students.

The project does not aim to financially support the efforts of specific companies. Rather, it places an emphasis on successful results that are of general applicability. ECOPROFIT is a continuing effort by the City of Graz to generate local examples of waste minimisation projects which are successful both in terms of economy and ecology. Through this on-going project the City of Graz is proving that pollution prevention pays.

(This paper has been reproduced with the premission of ICLEI and has been extracted from ICLEI Case Study 24)

Fig. 47

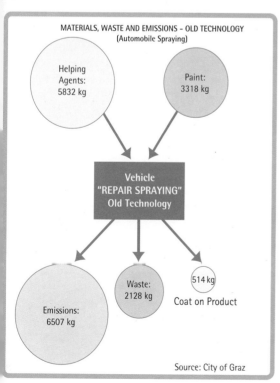

Fig. 48

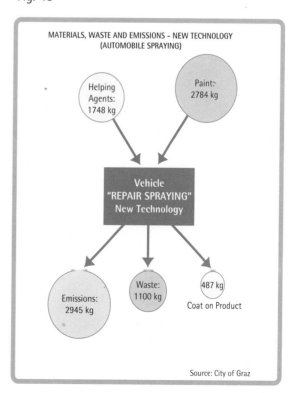

"COVENTRY - GREENING INDUSTRY"
Penny Duggan Head of Environmental Development,
Coventry City Council

INTRODUCTION

Coventry is a major West Midlands City with an international reputation for engineering excellence. Despite a decline in its traditional manufacturing industries over recent years, 33% of employment is still within the manufacturing sector. The environmental and economic impact of this, in conjunction with the engineering and metal processing industries, is significant.

Coventry has a long history of collaboration between the Council and the business community, since the formation of the Coventry Pollution Prevention Panel established some twenty three years ago. This forum established a body of experience, expertise and advice on pollution prevention and was renamed in 1992 as the Coventry Regional Environmental Management Panel, in response to the changing needs of industry. This new approach was the result of a major piece of research undertaken in the region which examined the impact of environmental pressures on key industries.

The research identified twenty-four possible actions that could assist industry in responding to the opportunities and threats presented by environmental pressures and directly led to the development of Coventry's Greening Industry Policy, one of 8 key policies of the Council's overall Environmental Strategy. The Greening Industry policy aim is to:

"improve the environmental performance of industry, thereby reducing pollution and assisting sustainable economic growth"

TURNING POLICY INTO PRACTICE

A Corporate Working Group was established to ensure the continued development of the Greening Industry Policy and the progression of its annual action plans. All of the projects within these action plans can trace their origins to one or more of the twenty-four recommendations in the research study, and are implemented through a variety of partnerships including:-

The Radcliffe Group - a joint venture between Rover Group, Warwick University and seven Local Authorities to develop, test, monitor and evaluate practical projects designed to improve the relationship of Rover Group's activities with the local environment, incorporating:- improving the environmental performance of Rover Group's suppliers, environmental training, recycling and traffic management.

Coventry Regional Environmental Management Panel - a forum for industry, the regulatory authorities and other business organisations to address environmental issues. Representatives from these organisations are elected on to a Management Board to steer the panel's activities which are:- seminars; workshops; award schemes; newsletters; networking; consultation and research.

Environmental Advice Service - a free service to small and medium sized businesses on environmental management involving:- awareness raising; advisory visits; topic audits; environmental assessments; environmental reviews; seminars; breakfast briefings, newsletters and an information centre.

CONCLUSIONS

Since the development of the Greening Industry Policy two years ago, local industry in Coventry has undergone a steady transformation. Recent market research has shown that following an initial visit, companies are three times more likely to want individual assistance, and five times more likely to want an environmental audit. Over 550 advisory visits have been undertaken, resulting in direct savings of over £2,000,000 to those companies together with reduced waste, lower energy consumption, raw materials savings and less pollution.

The approach taken by Coventry to help its local industries respond to environmental pressures could be adopted by other municipalities, bearing in mind the following issues:-

✪ Political Support

✪ Historically Good Links

✪ A Strategic Overview

✪ Partnership

✪ Practical Advice

✪ Funding

The overriding key to success in Coventry has undoubtedly been the strategic overview, clearly linking the environment and business into one key policy:- *"Greening Industry".*

WORKSHOP PAPERS AND CASE STUDIES

SUSTAINABILITY INDICATORS

In order to ensure that a town or city is moving towards sustainability there is a need to be able to measure performance against a set of targets. Environmental or sustainability indicators serve as a basic means of monitoring, reporting and target-setting. Even if the problems facing an area are relatively well known, information concerning the environment when it exists is scattered. The creation of indicators contributes to the process of analysing data on the environment. Indicators can also provide a means for citizens and businesses to understand the environmental situation in their area as complex data can be depicted in a simple and direct form which is understandable to the general public. Although the use of indicators of sustainability is relatively new there is a wealth of experience in some countries. Sustainable Seattle have been at the forefront of developing and using indicators and their experience and expertise is presented along with the EC's Indicators Project and the UK's Indicators Pilot Project

SUSTAINABILITY INDICATORS.

THE EUROPEAN COMMISSION'S INDICATORS PROJECT
Marina Alberti, European Commission DGX1, Belguim.

THE SUSTAINABLE SEATTLE PROJECT
Nea Carroll, Trustee and Coordinator for Sustainable Seattle,USA.

SUSTAINABILITY INDICATORS – THE MENU APPROACH
Perry Walker, Chair, New Economics Foundation, UK.

THE EUROPEAN COMMISSION'S INDICATORS PROJECT
Marina Alberti, European Commission DGXI

This is the first report on the state of the environment in
Europe. This was requested by ministers and will be a pioneer
programme for Europe.

The study has been undertaken in 17 cities. Urban areas require
specific assessment. The study is currently in draft and will be
available in the summer.

INDICATORS FOR URBAN SUSTAINABILITY - STATE OF THE ENVIRONMENT

Focus on the quality of the urban environment.

Selected:

Indicators which describe pressure.
Indicators which describe response.
Indicators which describe state.

Urban areas have impact not only on the immediate vicinity but
internationally. Indicators are needed to measure the flow of
resources in cities and the spatial impact of cities.

Urban quality, urban processes and urban structure are all
examined via indicators such as air pollution, each is broken
down into symptoms and causes.

A list of 55 indicators for the environment are used in the
report . This is only a limited set. However the aim is to get
standards which are applicable across Europe.

In selecting cities - geography etc. is taken into account.

We have produced classification tables with ranges which will
identify trends- 'Urban Flows Indicators'.

Energy data is normally available for cities but the use of energy
statistics does not necessarily indicate pressure on the urban
environment. There are also problems with accuracy, disaggregation and reliability. This is an urban emphasis but it is easier
to do this analysis at the city level. Environmental quality is
only part of sustainable development so the project also looks
at equity and distributional aspects.

THE SUSTAINABLE SEATTLE PROJECT
Nea Carroll, Trustee and Coordinator for Sustainable Seattle

In 1993, after two years of work involving over 200 citizens and local leaders, Sustainable Seattle published the first INDICATORS OF SUSTAINABLE COMMUNITY: A REPORT TO CITIZENS ON LONG-TERM TRENDS IN OUR COMMUNITY.

Author Donella Meadows, writing about this project, said,
"The indicators a society chooses to report to itself about itself are surprisingly powerful. They reflect collective values and inform collective decisions. A nation that keeps a watchful eye on its salmon runs or on the safety of its streets makes different choices than does a nation that is only paying attention to its Gross National Product. The idea of citizens choosing their own indicators is something new under the sun - something intensely democratic."

Nea Carroll, a founder and coordinator of Sustainable Seattle, a civic forum currently led by 75 active volunteers, presented the 20 indicators that compose this report and described the
participatory civic process used to develop them for the Seattle urban area. She described how topics were selected, groups were formed and criteria established for selecting indicators; and how the data was collected and researched by a citizen team. The Seattle report has received high praise from local officials and other cities and has been presented to Present Clinton's Council on Sustainable Development. Seattle is one of the first USA cities to develop indicators of sustainability.

Sustainable Seattle is a voluntary network and civic forum that brings together citizens from all sectors of the community - government, business and industry, neighbourhoods and civic organisations, labour, education and religion - to work together on issues related to sustainability, which they define as "long term cultural, environmental and economic health and vitality."

The Sustainable Seattle 1993
"Indicators of Sustainable Community"

A Report to Citizens
on Long-Term Trends in Our Community

Presented By Sustainable Seattle

"What legacy will we leave to future generations?"

"A sustainable world can never come into being if it cannot be envisioned. The vision must be built up from the contributions of many people before it is complete and compelling."

Donella H. Meadows, Dennis Meadows, and Jorgen Randers from Beyond the Limits: Confronting Global Collapse, Envisioning a Sustainable Future, 1992

Thank You

Sustainable Seattle wishes to acknowledge the invaluable contribution of time, knowledge, wisdom, and sustained effort provided by the more than 50 volunteers who have served on our Task Teams and Board of Trustees; the 150 volunteer participants in the 1992 Civic Panel; student interns from the University of Washington and University of Oregon; and many other individuals. A list of participants appears at the end of this document.

We also wish to acknowledge those organisations who have made financial or in-kind contributions to Sustainable Seattle as we've developed this project, especially Metrocentre YMCA, which has provided us with our administrative home during the past year. Contributions have included Atkisson & Associates, Boeing Company, Bullitt Foundation, Context Institute, Environmental Toxicology International, Metrocentre YMCA, New Road Map Foundation, The Stanford Club, and Triangle Associates. Special thanks go to the Global Tomorrow Coalition and Kay Bullitt, who sponsored the one-day meeting in November 1990 that gave birth to this effort.

SUMMARY

As a city, a nation, and a world, we are facing crucial decisions. Population growth, the advance of technology and industry, and growing urban centers have put enormous pressures on both the human and natural world. Increasing concerns about our social, economic, and environmental welfare require that we face the future with clearer eyes and a more integrated, longer-term perspective.

These "Indicators of Sustainable Community" are designed to help us in this task. The concept of "sustainability" first emerged during the 1980s and rose to international prominence during the 1992 Earth Summit in Rio de Janeiro. The term is increasingly being used by the United Nations, the United States government, states, cities, communities and individuals to help us think about the major challenges that confront us — and what we can do about them.

"Sustainability" refers to something specific and critically important, albeit complex: our long-term cultural, economic, and environmental health and vitality. It links these issues together rather than thinking of them as separate. It is often defined as "meeting the needs of the present without compromising the ability of future generations to meet their own needs." A society that is sustainable will endure for generations and improve over time; one that is not will experience a decline in quality, equity and prosperity.

Indicators are measurements, the vital signs of any society. Over the past two years, forty different "Indicators of Sustainable Community" were developed for the Seattle area by more than two hundred volunteers. The citizens saw the need to gather information on the overall health of our society here on the shores of Puget Sound. Twenty indicators have now been researched and analysed. The trends they reveal are at times encouraging, more often disturbing.

Recent years have seen improvements in such key indicators as overall air quality, water consumption, and the diversity of the local economy. There has been little measurable change in adult literacy rates or the number of hours one has to work at the average wage to support a family's basic needs. But many other trends are carrying us away from sustainability and toward an uncertain — and potentially very unpleasant — future.

Increasing numbers of children are being born with low birth-weights, or being raised in poverty, or turning to violent crime. Fewer people are voting. Wild salmon are disappearing. More of us are driving more miles, consuming more energy, and producing more garbage per person every year.

Overall, the Seattle area is not moving toward the goal of long-term sustainability. Instead, it is moving in the wrong direction.

Our goal in presenting these indicators is to alert the people of Seattle to the significant challenges we face, and to ask them to get involved in finding solutions to our problems. We hope to inspire a renewed sense of citizenship and participation. These problems are only insurmountable if we fail to respond to them with courage, creativity, and compassion. With all of us working together — committed to a better future for our children, and our children's children — we can create a truly sustainable Seattle.

"The gross national product includes air pollution and advertising for cigarettes, and ambulances to clear our highways of carnage. It counts special locks for our doors, and jails for the people who break them.

The gross national product includes all this, there is much that it does not comprehend. It does not allow for the health of our families, the quality of their education, or the joy of their play. It is indifferent to the decency of our factories and the safety of our streets alike. It does not include the beauty of our poetry or the strength of our marriages, the intelligence of our public debate or the integrity of our public officials ....

The gross national product measures neither our wit nor our courage, neither our wisdom nor our learning, neither our compassion nor our devotion to country. It measures everything, in short, except that which makes life worthwhile; and it can tell us everything about America — except whether we are proud to be Americans."

Robert F. Kennedy

THE SUSTAINABLE SEATTLE
Indicators of Sustainable Community
Master List – June, 1993

These 40 indicators – selected from a broader list of 100 developed through a community participation process – were chosen for data development because they meet the criteria for good indicators as described later in this report. The first 20 indicators (✪) have been researched in detail; data for the second set of 20 indicators will be researched over the next year.

ENVIRONMENT

- ✪ Wild salmon runs through local streams
  Biodiversity in the region (specific indicator species to be identified and indicator to be developed)
- ✪ Number of good air quality days per year, as reported by the Pollutant Standards Index
  Amount of topsoil lost in King County.
  Acres of wetlands remaining in King County
- ✪ Percentage of Seattle streets meeting "Pedestrian-Friendly" criteria

POPULATION AND RESOURCES

- ✪ Total population of King County (with annual growth rate)
- ✪ Gallons of water consumed per capita
- ✪ Tons of solid waste generated and recycled per capita
- ✪ Vehicle miles travelled per capita and gasoline consumption per capita
- ✪ Renewable and nonrenewable energy (in BTUs) consumed per capita
  Acres of land per capita for a range of land uses (residential, commercial, open space, transportation, wilderness)
  Amount of food grown in Washington, food exports, and food imports
  Emergency room use for non-emergency purposes.

ECONOMY

- ✪ Percentage of employment concentrated in the top ten employers
- ✪ Hours of paid employment at the average wage required to support basic needs
  Real unemployment, including discouraged workers, with differentiation by ethnicity and gender
  Average savings rate per household
  Reliance on renewable or local resources in the economy (specific indicator to be developed)
- ✪ Percentage of children living in poverty
- ✪ Housing affordability gap
- ✪ Health care expenditures per capita

CULTURE AND SOCIETY

- ✪ Percentage of infants born with low birthweight (including disaggregation by ethnicity)
  Ethnic diversity of teaching staff in elementary and secondary schools
  Number of hours per week devoted to instruction in the arts for elementary and secondary schools.   Percent of parent/guardian population that is involved in school activities
- ✪ Juvenile crime rate
- ✪ Percent of youth participating in some form of community service
  Percent of enrolled 9th grades who graduate from high school (by ethnicity, gender, and income level)
- ✪ Percent of population voting in odd-year (local) primary-elections
- ✪ Adult literacy rate
  Average number of neighbours the average citizen reports knowing by name
  Equitable treatment in the justice system (specific indicator to be developed)
  Ratio of money spent on drug and alcohol prevention and treatment to money spent on incarceration for drug and alcohol related crimes
  Percentage of population that gardens
- ✪ Usage rates for libraries and community centres
- ✪ Public participation in the arts
  Percent of adult population donating time to community service
  Individual sense of well-being.

- ✪ *Indicators researched for this project*

Fig. 49

186

The Sustainable Seattle 1993
Indicators of Sustainable Community

ENVIRONMENT

q   Wild salmon runs through local streams

  e   Number of good air quality days per year

k   Percentage of Seattle streets meeting
        "Pedestrian-Friendly" criteria

POPULATION AND RESOURCES

q   Total population of King County

  e   Gallons of water consumed per capita in King
        County

q   Tons of solid waste generated and recycled
        per year in King County

q   Vehicle miles travelled per capita and gasoline
        consumption per capita

q   Renewable and non-renewable energy (in
        BTUs) consumed per capita

ECONOMY

  e   Percentage of employment concentrated in
        the top ten employees

k   Hours of paid work at the average wage
        required to support basic needs

q   Percentage of children living in poverty

q   Housing affordability for median-and low-
        income households

q   Per capita health expenditures

CULTURE AND SOCIETY

q   Percentage of infants born with low birth
        weight

q   Juvenile crime rate

k   Percent of youth participating in some form of
        community service

q   Percent of population voting in odd-year
        (local) primary elections

k   Adult literacy rate

  e   Library and community centre usage rates

k   Participation in the arts

q Moving away e Toward Sustainability k No movement

Fig. 50

INTRODUCTION

*"The indicators a society chooses to report to itself about
itself are surprisingly powerful. They reflect collective values
and inform collective decisions. A nation that keeps a watchful
eye on its salmon runs or the safety of its streets makes
different choices than does a nation that is only paying
attention to its GNP. The idea of citizens choosing their own
indicators is something new under the sun — something
intensely democratic."*

Donella Meadows,
writing about
Sustainable Seattle.

OVERVIEW!

These proposed "Indicators of Sustainable Community" are the
product of a creative community dialogue about our common
future.

As a community, now and in the future, we face many difficult
decisions. How do we protect our environment, meet everyone's
basic needs, keep our economy healthy, create justice and well-
being? How do we make hard trade-offs and balanced decisions
that take all of our interests into account? What do we need to
change, personally and collectively? How do we keep track of
our progress?

Over the past two years, hundreds of volunteers have worked
with such questions over thousands of hours in order to improve
our community's capacity to assess its present well-being, and
to make well-informed decisions about its future.

This document is a product of their work. This array of indicators
is intended to provide a snapshot of the concept of sustainability.
It is intended to stimulate vision, trigger insight, provoke
discussion, draw criticism, challenge assumptions, and inspire
action. As George Bernard Shaw once said, "The sign of a truly
educated man is to be deeply moved by statistics." We hope you
will be moved by the reality behind the numbers and trends
described here, and we invite you to participate in a continuing
dialogue.

A Vision of Hope! Hope is a choice and a vision. It takes
imagination to hope: to see beyond our immediate reality to a
place we might go, and to muster the will to get there. We
need vision to inspire us and to help us move through hard
times. We need vision to help us face the inevitable tensions
and conflicts that occur as we begin to make changes.

Visions, like people, are complex, multi-dimensional, and full of
potential. A vision is a community looking forward together
and saying, "Yes, this is where we will go, what we will be".
Visions may be fuzzy in the details, but clear and compelling in
their central images.

The central image in our vision is a person — your child, grand-
child, great-grandchild, or the descendant of someone you've
loved in your life. The details about how this person will live
and work are unknowable. But the vision of your descendant
being well, happy, fulfilled in life, and living in a healthy world

is central to our work. The well-being of our descendants, one,
two, or even seven generations from now depends on our
decisions today. And making good decisions today requires the
best understanding possible about where we've been — and
where we might be going.

WHAT ARE INDICATORS?

Indicators are bits of information that reflect the status of large
systems. They are a way of seeing the "big picture" by looking
at a smaller piece of it. They tell us which direction a system is
going: up or down, forward or backward, getting better or worse
or staying the same.

For example, the Dow Jones Industrial Average is an indicator of
the health of the stock market. It doesn't measure every stock,
but it does measure a representative sample. Trends in that
sample closely match trends in the stock market as a whole.
Similarly, the Northern Spotted Owl is an indicator of the health
of old growth forest habitat in the Pacific Northwest: knowing
the owl's status tells us the likely status of many other plants
and animals, without having to measure each one individually.

Indicators are like the gauges and dials of an aircraft's instrument
panel. By designing them carefully, watching them closely, and
interpreting them wisely, we know the status of our flight and can
make good decisions about where to go. Without indicators,
we're just "flying by the seat of our pants."

*"The concept of sustainability does not really refer to some
equilibrium state, not even the stationary state of classical
economists, but to a sustainable evolutionary process of
continuous change. We certainly don't want the existing world
structure to be sustainable. We want to improve it".*
- Kenneth Boulding

WHAT IS "SUSTAINABILITY"?

We in Sustainable Seattle define the term "sustainability" as
"long-term cultural, economic, and environmental health and
vitality." We emphasize the "long-term" part of that definition,
together with the importance of linking our social, financial,
and environmental well-being.

While our definition is unique to us, it is one of many similar
definitions that have been produced world-wide since the concept was first introduced. During the late 1970's and early
1980's, a number of independent scientists, activists, and poli-
cy-makers were working on responses to the linked problems
concerning issues of environment and development. They began
to use the term "sustainability" to describe the goal of integrating environment and development concerns.

It was not, however, until the 1987 United Nations' "World
Commission on Environment and Development" released its
report Our Common Future that the terms "sustainability" and
"sustainable development" came into wide-spread use. Our
Common Future (or the "Brundtland Report," after the
Commission's Chair, Norwegian Prime Minister Gro Harlem
Brundtland) defined sustainable development as "development

which meets the needs of the present without endangering the ability of future generations to meet their own needs."

The Commission established several key principles of sustainability:

✪ that the needs of the future must not be sacrificed to the demands of the present;

✪ that humanity's economic future is linked to the integrity of natural systems;

✪ and that protecting the environment is impossible unless we improve the economic prospects of the Earth's poorest peoples.

At the June 1992 United Nations' Conference on Environment and Development (the "Earth Summit"), representatives from nearly every nation on Earth adopted these principles in the form of international treaties and agreements designed to begin protecting natural systems while meeting the needs of the world's poor. At the same time, a "Global Forum" of citizens' groups from around the world developed grass-roots initiatives designed to monitor governments and push sustainability efforts beyond what governmental processes were able to do.

The Sustainable Seattle Indicators Project is in part a local response to these very global efforts. It is a first step in the long process of assessing our progress toward (or away from) long-term sustainability; identifying key steps we can take to improve our progress; and making those changes real.

WHAT IS SUSTAINABLE SEATTLE?

Since its first meeting in November of 1990, Sustainable Seattle has operated as a voluntary network and civic forum, bringing together citizens from many different sectors of our community to promote the concept and practice of sustainability. Business, environmental groups, city and county government, labour, the religious community, educators and social activists have all been represented. While our name connotes our original focus on the Seattle area, we recognise that sustainability concerns always cross borders, and we consider our focus to extend to the Puget Sound region. We have welcomed the participation of people from communities throughout this larger area.

Sustainable Seattle has hosted many different events and round table discussions, but our primary project during the past two years has been the development of these Indicators of Sustainable Community. We see them as a first step in an ambitious, multi-year effort to create positive change in our area.

Sustainable Seattle is administered by Metrocentre YMCA, a non-profit community service organisation, and governed by an independent board of trustees. Monetary support has come in the form of small grants and donations from foundations, corporations, and individuals. The bulk of our work has been done by volunteers.

THE INDICATORS PROJECT

"History has thrust upon our generation an indescribably important destiny — to complete a process of democratisation which our nation has too long developed too slowly...

How we deal with this crucial situation will determine our moral health as individuals, our cultural health as a region, our political health as a nation, and our prestige as a leader of the free world."

Martin Luther King, Jr.

The work on this project was begun by a volunteer Task Team of some fifteen people in the fall of 1991. That group developed the indicators concept and took a draft list through four iterations, producing a document that then became the focus for a much larger review process.

In the Spring of 1992, Sustainable Seattle convened a Civic Panel of more than 150 distinguished citizens from many different sectors of Seattle society, with the goal of expanding the Task Team's work. The process consisted of four plenary meetings in addition to individual and committee work.

At its final meeting in December 1992, the Civic Panel proposed 99 indicators grouped into ten topic areas. In early 1993 the Task Team began a technical review process, with the goal of refining the Panel's suggestions and winnowing the list down to a manageable size. Data collection began shortly thereafter, and data availability further modified our selection.

WHAT MAKES A GOOD INDICATOR?

These Indicators of Sustainable Community have been selected because they meet the following criteria, which were developed by the Task Team:

Good indicators..

✪ **are bellwether tests of sustainability** and reflect something basic and fundamental to the long term economic, social, or environmental health of a community over generations.

✪ **can be understood and accepted by the community** as a valid sign of sustainability or symptom of distress.

✪ **have interest and appeal for use by local media** in monitoring, reporting and analysing general trends toward or away from sustainable community practices.

✪ **are statistically measurable** in our geographic area, and preferably comparable to other cities/communities; a practical form of data collection or measurement exists or can be created.

The geographic scope of an indicator depends on the context and accessibility of the data, with some indicators referring to Seattle city limits, others to King County (our first choice, when available), and still others placing Seattle in a statewide context.

A WORK IN PROGRESS!

The first 20 indicators were chosen for data development because they provide a good overview of key trends, they demonstrate how the indicators can be used and interpreted, and there was some degree of confidence in the available data.

A second set of 20 indicators, still to be developed, include some that will require new designs and data-gathering. Some will involve testing public opinions and attitudes.

Each indicator measures an important dimension of sustainability. But this collection is not intended to be a comprehensive measurement of all its dimensions; indeed, no scientifically-tested and refined model of sustainability exists. However, neither are the indicators arbitrary, having evolved through long deliberations with people of knowledge and insight. We do not present them as perfect nor even complete. Instead, we expect the dialogue on what constitutes a sustainable society, what makes a good indicator, and what the indicators mean to continue into the indefinite future.

We also feel confident that this first version of the indicators tells us something important: while some aspects of life in the Seattle/King County area are improving, others are rapidly moving away from the direction of sustainability and demand urgent attention from as many of us as possible.

"If we're going to create a sustainable and liveable society.... we cannot talk about the economics of competition without also talking about the ethics of co-operation. This means recognising our capacity to make common cause... to create a political culture that nurtures obligation and honors trust."

Bill Moyers

FINDING LINKAGES!

Indicators are not a new idea. They have long been useful in science, economics, public policy, health, and many other areas as a feedback mechanism to tell us how we are doing.

What is different about these indicators is that they attempt to bring into focus a "whole system" view of how we are doing as a society, here on the shores of Puget Sound.

These first twenty indicators provide more than just glimpses of our activities. They compel us to seek understanding of linkages within and among human and natural systems. They suggest different criteria for making decisions and measuring our progress.

For example, can we say our economy is sustainable if we have a growing number of children living in poverty, or a dwindling supply of natural resources? Can we make decisions about the future shape and character of our neighbourhoods and schools without thinking about trends in the juvenile crime rate or the use of the automobile? How do choices in our personal lives - such as the amount of money we save — affect our society's long-term viability?

Looking at the indicators as a whole raises many such questions, so we have briefly noted key linkages on the individual indicator reports. We do not presume to have rigorously identified and measured these linkages, but we believe that understanding them is critical to building a sustainable society. By keeping the whole picture before us, we can begin to shift our priorities, address problems at their roots, and act with greater clarity and wisdom over time.

"There is an uncanny resemblance between our behaviour toward each other and our behaviour towards the earth. By some connection we do not recognise, the willingness to exploit one becomes the willingness to exploit the other. It is impossible to care for each other more or differently than we care for the earth."
Wendell Berry

HOW TO USE THE INDICATORS!

In general, we see these Indicators being used in the following ways:

The Media — We encourage local media to publish and broad-cast the indicators regularly, so that the community as a whole can begin to see and understand the status of the indicators and the linkages between them.

Growth Management and Public Policy — The indicators can be a powerful tool for clarifying values and informing decisions with regard to growth and development planning.

Business and Economic Development — The indicators can help economic decision-makers analyse market trends and think more systematically about how their decisions impact on issues that are not reflected in the bottom line.

Personal Lifestyle — Indicators can challenge individuals to explore how the way we live affects the world and moves the indicators in one direction or another, demonstrating how each individual makes a difference.

Education — Indicators can be educative tools about important trends in our environment, economy, and social well-being that may indicate broader trends and shifts towards or away from sustainability.

At work — Indicators can be used to assess the policies and activities of an agency, business, organisation, or institution in terms of how they affect these trends.

Future Plans — Our plans include data collection and analysis of additional indicators; creation of programs to promote the development of sustainable homes, businesses, and communities; possible development of a "Sustainability Impact Assessment," an instrument to help people think through the broader impacts of major policy or development decisions; continuing forums for dialogue and networking; and publishing a directory of organisations involved.

DESCRIPTION!

Salmon and humans have a long history in Puget Sound. Native

Americans have always revered the salmon as a link to the earth and as a source of food. Salmon have astonished and nourished visitors and immigrants since the first Europeans arrived, and they continue to be an important economic resource as well as an environmental indicator to Northwesterners of many different origins. (Fig. 51)

Hatchery-raised salmon spend much of their lives in a controlled,

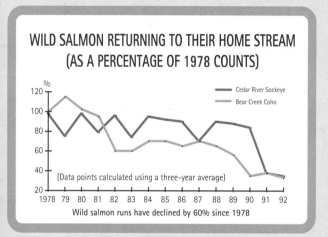

Fig. 51

human-made environment, so they do not adequately reflect the health of watersheds and ecosystems. Wild salmon, however, are totally dependent on the health of the freshwater environment for reproduction. They need clean water and a passable stream. Native salmon have evolved to meet the specific natural characteristics of their local environment: their eggs, for example, are adapted to specific gravel size and water chemistry. Changes in bottom conditions, local plants and animals, and water chemistry — such as those that accompany urban or suburban development — usually result in a reduced number of fish surviving. Decreased genetic diversity caused by the loss of a salmon stock in one stream can affect the viability of stocks in adjacent habitats. The health of wild salmon populations is thus an indicator of overall environmental health in a watershed.

DEFINITION!

Salmon from the Cedar River and Bear Creek were chosen as representative examples for surviving King County salmon runs. Data were collected by the Washington State Department of Fisheries and reported in the Washington State 1992 Salmon and Steelhead Stock Inventory (SASSI), conducted by the Departments of Fisheries and Wildlife in conjunction with the Western Washington Treaty Indian Tribes. Estimates based on counts of wild salmon returning to their home stream are smoothed out using a three-year rolling average. No attempt has been made to estimate past extinctions.

INTERPRETATION!

There is a clear trend toward reduced wild salmon survival, reflecting a state-wide pattern. Of the seventy-one salmon runs in the North Puget Sound area, twelve have been classified as "depressed," the Cedar River Sockeye and Lake Washington Coho salmon among them. Four are "critical" — heading toward the threshold below which a salmon stock can no longer sustain itself. And even healthy stocks are also trending toward lower returns.

EVALUATION!

The sharp downward trend in the health of local salmon runs marks a significant trend away from sustainability. Many local salmon runs have been extinct for decades, and we are in danger of losing many more if we do not take swift and effective action to preserve the integrity of freshwater habitat.

LINKAGES!

The health of salmon runs is linked to the economy as well as the environment: tourism, recreation, and food production are all affected. The 1992 SASSI notes that".. . activities impacting on wild salmon habitat and survival (e.g. urban and industrial growth, forest practices, agricultural practices, municipal, industrial and hydropower) have reduced Washington's salmon .. and continue to do so."

This information is not new: for over a century we have been aware of these problems. Runoff from streets carries oil-based pollutants. Drainage from lawns and farms carry pesticides, toxins, fertiliser, and silt. Construction diverts streams. Poor forestry practices increase silt loading, disrupt food chains, and change water temperature and runoff patterns. Dams, supplying us with water and electricity, make it difficult or impossible for salmon to return upstream, and often lethal to make the first journey out to sea. Salmon are sensitive to a very broad range of human practices.

We have created a social and economic system that does not yet give the health of streams and salmon sufficiently high priority. Our careless stewardship of the salmon — perhaps the most symbolically and economically important creature to share Puget Sound with us — is reflective of our attitude toward a variety of living systems, from neighbourhoods to ecosystems. Restoration of salmon runs will require not only immediate work to repair damage, but also rethinking our concepts of development and our understanding of what causes negative effects. Only such a change in our understanding will enable us to incorporate concerns for sustainability in our policies and practices.

This report has been reproduced with the kind permission of 'Sustainable Seattle'. To order copies of the original document, please contact Sustainable Seattle c/o Metrocentre YMCA, 909 Fourth Avenue, Seattle, WA 98104, Tel: 206/382-5013. Individual copies are $10 postpaid. To order in bulk, please call for pricing information. The update of this report is also available and will contain completed research on a total of 40 indicators of sustainable community. To order, please contact Richard Conlin at the above address.

SUSTAINABILITY INDICATORS THE MENU APPROACH
THE UK LOCAL AGENDA 21 PROJECT
Perry Walker, Chair, New Economics Foundation, UK.

Introduction

This is a project to produce a menu of indicators of sustainable development for use by local authorities and their communities. It has been commissioned by the Local Government Management Board and undertaken by the New Economics Foundation, United Nations Association and Touche Ross.

A framework for indicators

The indicators are set into a framework to provide context. The starting point for the framework is the definition of sustainable development in UNEP's 'Caring for the Earth' as 'improving the quality of life while living within the carrying capacity of supporting ecosystems'. This was adapted to provide a local definition:

> 'A sustainable community lives in harmony with its local environment and does not cause damage to distant environments or other communities - now or in the future. Quality of life and the interests of future generations are valued above immediate material consumption and economic growth.'

The next stage of the framework is to break down the two main elements of the definition into their components. For quality of life this is done on the basis of human needs. Carrying capacity is divided according to the various functions of the environment. These needs and functions provide thirteen themes. These were developed into 'key sustainability factors'.

The indicators

Each theme has several potential indicators. There are a hundred indicators in all.

In order that the indicators stimulate progress towards sustainable development, rather than simply to measure it, the different information needs of policymakers and citizens have been analysed. Crudely, the differences are as follows.

Policy-makers	Citizens
✪ Aggregated	✪ Detailed
✪ Impact of and on their area	✪ Impact on their area
✪ Prospective	✪ Retrospective
✪ Objective	✪ Subjective

Seattle draws a similar distinction between primary and secondary indicators, on the one hand, and provocative indicators on the other.

Piloting the indicators

The indicators are being piloted in six local authorities over the next six months. Local Agenda 21 places great weight on participation, so local communities will be involved in both choosing and using the indicators. In order to do this, local authorities are currently identifying and approaching 'stakeholders' - groups that have a stake in the community such as voluntary groups, business and young people.

The indicators will be chosen from the menu to suit local circumstances. Each pilot will as a minimum choose one indicator for each theme. Some indicators will be easy to measure. Others may need work on the definition and be hard to measure. Indicators requiring surveys, which will probably best reflect people's perception of their quality of life, will certainly take a lot of effort.

Conclusion

At the end of the six month pilot, the indicators will be revised and improved in the light of experience. They will then be made available to all UK local authorities. We believe the UK to be the first country to provide such support, so the next few months will be extremely exciting. Nonetheless, the success of the project can only be seen in the longer term, when decisions and behaviour change as a result of the indicators.

WORKSHOP PAPERS AND CASE STUDIES

THE ECOSYSTEM APPROACH TO
URBAN ENVIRONMENTAL MANAGEMENT

Cities and communities in many ways are like natural ecosystems. Analysing them as if they were ecosystems can help us recognise their environmental impacts, understand the complex relationships that exist between the physical, economic and social processes in cities - and especially to integrate environmental action. This workshop presents this new approach to urban environmental management as an approach that can be used by municipalities in formulating their Local Agenda 21 Campaign.

THE ECOSYSTEM APPROACH TO URBAN ENVIRONMENTAL MANAGEMENT

TWENTY YEARS OF ACTIVITIES WITHIN UNESCO'S MAN AND THE BIOSPHERE (MAB) PROGRAMME

John Celecia, Senior Programme Specialist Division Ecological Sciences UNESCO, Paris, France.

ECO BALANCING – A GOTHENBURG EXAMPLE

Lars Berggrund, Senior Comprehensive Planner, Authority of Gothenburg, Sweden.

APPLYING THE ECOSYSTEMS APPROACH : THE UK NATIONAL OVERVIEW AND CASE STUDY FOR OECD ECOLOGICAL CITY PROJECT

Roger Levett, Environmental Team Leader, CAG Consultants, UK

FOCUSED ANALYSIS

Eva Grundelius, Swedish Association of Local Authorities

TWENTY YEARS OF ACTIVITIES WITHIN UNESCO'S MAN AND THE BIOSPHERE (MAB) PROGRAMME

JOHN CELECIA , Division of Ecological Sciences,
UNESCO, Paris

Towards the Resourceful City:

MAB Research in Urban, Peri-urban and Industrial Systems

Since the early 1970's, the MAB Programme is the first international venture to consider cities - the places where already half of the world's population lives and works - as ecological systems. In fact, upon developing a progressive and evolving research agenda in cities and other human settlements, MAB has contributed both to establishing the basis for the formulation of an ecological paradigm for urban systems and to testing interdisciplinary, integrative conceptual and methodological approaches for problem-oriented research that aims at enhancing knowledge and understanding of these complex human systems. Such research should contribute to improved planning, management and policy-making and more specifically, to make cities impose and impact less on the near and far hinterlands upon which they depend to fulfil their needs for energy, materials, food, labour and land. Most importantly, MAB research aims to make cities more liveable and human, and to harmonise development planning with conservation, with sustainable and equitable use of natural resources, and with full involvement of local populations. The notion of the sustainable city thus becomes synonymous with that of the resourceful, liveable, ecological city, for the people and by the people.

MAB Studies on Urban and Peri-urban Areas considered as Ecological Systems.

Background: The main lines of MAB work on urban and peri-urban systems were outlined by an Expert Panel which met at Bad Neuheim, Germany, in 1973 in consideration of the urgent need to develop sound ecologically orientated conceptual and methodological approaches to improving knowledge and understanding of these complex human systems and which would provide the basis for planning, management and decision-making. A number of pioneering projects were initiated (Hong Kong, Frankfurt, Gotland, Rome, Toronto, Tokyo, Barcelona, Vienna, Dayton), which took into consideration different points of entry (eg. energy and materials flows, perception , urban/rural interfaces) into their conceptual frameworks and recognised the need to adopt regional and subregional strategies in view of the great diversity of biogeographical, social, cultural and political situations in what are obviously the most human of systems. At the same time, they acknowledged the need to provide inter-regional exchanges and harmonisation of approaches to foster comparability.

In 1975, UNESCO, MAB and UNEP established the basis for a co-operative programme of integrated ecological studies of human settlements as a basis for decision-making in different regions of the world. This co-operation resulted in a most productive series of actions which carried over into the 1980s and which included a "second generation" of case studies (Lae, PNG; Bangkok; Mexico City; Xalapa, Mexico; Ciudad Guyana,

Venezuela; Alexandria, Egypt; Chipata, Zambia) several of which remain exemplary to date.

The above was followed by a series of planning meetings in both industrialised countries (Amsterdam, 1976; Poznan, 1977; Warsaw and Bad Homburg, 1979) and in developing regions (Khartoum, 1981, Mexico City, 1983; Montevideo, 1987), which became the starting point of new projects and the reinforcement of earlier projects. In the 1980s important interregional conferences and symposia around MAB Projects Area on urban systems permitted the review and analysis of results, exchange of experiences and recommendations for future work (Suzdal, USSR, 1984; Beijing, 1987; Amsterdam, 1989). More recently, national and regional seminars and workshops have been organised in France, Germany, UK, Sweden, Spain, Poland, and the Ukraine, among others.

Since the mid-1980s four areas of focus for research themes were approved by the MAB Council and constitute a scientific basis for action which is still prevalent today:

a) The development of models on the relationship between urbanisation and environmental transformation, taking into account the rural areas around cities.

b) Empirical studies on demographic changes induced by urbanisation, in particular migratory movements between rural and urban areas and their environmental consequences.

c) Studies including pilot demonstration field projects, on biological productivity in urban zones and on the improved utilisation and/or recycling of energy and other resources (particularly water), in order to reduce the pressure and impact exerted by cities on their hinterlands.

d) Studies on the management (use, planning and handling) of green urban spaces, including need for open spaces and of the impact exerted on the natural environment of such spaces.

An examination of trends shows clearly that the major concern of cities in industrialised countries is for maintaining or restoring "quality of life" while in Third World megalopolises the major concern is for the minimum conditions for adequate life which for large numbers of marginalised populations represents sheer survival. In either case, we are facing crisis situations which require new approaches and concerted efforts.

The current "third generation projects" are more interdisciplinary as well as more problem and planning orientated and include Buenos Aires and Cordoba, Argentina; Xalapa, Mexico; Seoul, Republic.of Korea; Barcelona, Madrid and Valencia, Spain; Rome, Italy; Bangkok, Thailand; and Bauru, Brazil, among others.

Trends and Perspectives: The "resourcefulness" of cities has been and continues to be a major research concern in which special emphasis is laid on measures aimed at reducing waste, pollution and risks, and at promoting proper use of energy, materials, water and food (efficiency), while improving both tangible and less tangible and unquantifiable issues related to life conditions (human satisfaction). This corresponds with current global concerns to increase recycling, re-use, and source reduction of materials when considering how the exigencies of consumerism and waste production in industrialised urban areas can affect remote areas in the world. The inter-relationships between urban/industrial systems and their near and far natural/rural hinterlands has thus become a major focus of research. This is an important research topic in the case of biosphere reserves and is now suggested as a part of future strategies.

Another concern for MAB research is that of perception, and public awareness and participation. The "liveability" and experiential value of an urban area depends upon the enhancement of emotional, behavioural and cognitive growth of citizens and on their access to and engagement in urban life and the total environment with the corresponding development of value systems and environmental ethics. European countries have placed considerable emphasis on the planning, management, use and manipulation of green and other open spaces. In Third World cities the emphasis is more on alternative, practical, scientifically-based issues such as subsistence agroforestry, intensive food gardening and fruit-tree planting, composting of city wastes, fuelwood, charcoal and biogas production, which would enhance local development with the active leadership and participation of local communities.

Optimally these would be part of an overall intersectoral effort involving housing, water provision and quality, literacy and different dimensions in education with special attention to women and youth. There are good indications that some MAB National Committees in industrialised countries are disposed to continue their efforts at national and regional levels and to co-operate and assist developing countries along such lines. Efforts have begun to launch an inter-sectorial and inter-regional programme to be developed in the period, to seek extra-budgetary financial support to allow fieldwork in Third World cities on the theme of the Resourceful, Liveable City.

Co-operation has already begun between MAB National Committees and the MAB Secretariat to undertake a comprehensive compilation, analysis and synthesis of the abundant volume of work (comprising over one thousand references), resulting from the last 17 years of MAB and related activities in urban systems as well as booklets for different audiences. In fact, the MAB Urban and Human Ecology Digest was the first of its kind published in English and in Spanish in the late 1980s. Specialised journals, magazines, bulletins and newsletters regularly introduce a section on MAB urban activities (eg. Urban Wildlife News and Urban Ecologist, United Kingdom; Ambiente Magazine, Argentina; Dialogo Magazine, Venezuela, among many others).

ECO-BALANCING, A GOTHENBURG EXAMPLE
Mr Lars Berggrund, Senior Comprehensive Planner
City Planning Authority of Gothenburg, Sweden

Matter and energy balances offer unique opportunities to describe and understand management of natural resources. In Gothenburg we are trying to introduce eco-balancing both in environmental protection control and in physical planning.

A model for physical planning within the limits of long-term sustainability could be the following:

1. Description of the present situation
    How do we manage natural resources today? What are the problems and possibilities? A physical description has to be added to the traditional monetary description. This can be done with a matter balance and an energy balance. An energy analysis (an analysis of energy quality) adds information about weak points in conversion.

2. Long-term environmental goals
    We have to formulate the vision of a society that meets with long-term sustainability. Partly that is a question of facts - resources, capacities and consumption. But the more important part is political discussion about the qualities of this sustainable society.

    In general a lot of the apparent political disagreements on environmental questions are due to different opinions on how fast we have to or are able to solve problems. The fact that we have a problem is undisputed.

3. Step-by-step change
    Given an understanding of the present situation and a vision of future goals we can compare each small decision with the direction needed. If this can be done in a convincing way it will have a great impact on present political decisions. Economical and other factors will sometimes force us to make decisions in the wrong direction, but then we know we have done so, and we also know that we have to balance it sooner or later.

In our comprehensive plan for Gothenburg we have tried to pick out some parts of a matter balance: the circulation of water, of nitrogen and an energy analysis. We have also completed an analysis of carbon circulation. Of course a complete matter balance is complicated to establish - this is our first step. The first main goal is to increase the understanding of resource management. Our experience is that these matter balances carry important knowledge, necessary to induce changes in attitudes and behaviour for both decision-makers and the public.

One interesting future development will be to use resource management indicators - research on this is in progress right now at the Chalmers University of Technology in Gothenburg. We are looking for indicators that are relevant, easy to understand and sensitive.

In the plan we have included a vision about the future Gothenburg, called "The competitive and sustainable city". In the study we investigate the possibility of combining competitiveness and longterm sustainability: the competitive vision as the goal, the sustainable vision giving the conditions. The idea is to try to find a common area between the competitive and the sustainable visions. Not to find the ideal future, nor to settle for the easiest market force vision, but to find land use decisions acceptable to competitiveness and still not wrong from the sustainable point of view. This would also be the only vision that could reach political legitimacy.

This idea to seek the common area between the visions has been shown to be successful. One of the questions we asked in the public consultation for the plan was "Do you believe that it is possible to combine competitiveness and sustainability, that the vision is possible?" The question was answered with a very strong "Yes" - 2/3 of the replies stated this. The response was unexpectedly strong.

Some questions have to be further investigated. The balance between public and private transport, or you might even say the conflict between them, is a problem both from the planning and the political point of view. Transport is the major environmental problem and also a gigantic problem when it comes to management of natural resources. At the same time it is a symbol of personal freedom and a dominating factor for business and industry location. Here is one of our major challenges for future planning and policy making.

Another problem is the regional question. Neither transport nor environment problems can be solved if we cannot find regional solutions. Today Gothenburg has 60% of the regional population, but only a small part of the urban area. We have to find common solutions together with about 10 other local authorities, suburbs of Gothenburg. Besides, they belong to three different Counties, the local administration of the national government. Between the suburbs and Gothenburg there is a big brother-small brother relationship that makes rational planning and policy-making difficult. This most certainly is one of the major challenges.

We have added a couple of scenarios to the plan - sketches of possible futures of different areas in Gothenburg. These are not parts of the concrete land use plan, but of a discussion about the future. Visions and scenarios might be important tools for mental identification with possible futures. What we have to discuss today is what we find acceptable and unacceptable in these visions, to be able to find out what we have to decide today to make the future possible.

Many people find it difficult to accept that land use policies should reflect ideas of resource management and personal life styles. And that is the great question for physical planning: should we integrate land use planning and strategic planning for the environment, the economy and the socio-cultural sector. Talking about sustainable development the answer seems to be yes, but we have not had the full political reactions yet.

We are also working on a project on Green budgeting. The main idea of this is closely linked to ideas of eco-balancing. If the project is successful, we are aiming to put the question of sustainable development down in tables and figures in our city council decisions!

So far we have found eco-balancing an interesting tool to develop for a sustainable future, including a great potential to give understanding to the public on environmental matters. We will go on to develop this tool, and we do it with strong backing from both politicians, scientists and the NGOs. Eco-balancing has come to stay!

APPLYING THE ECOSYSTEMS APPROACH:
THE UK NATIONAL OVERVIEW AND CASE STUDY FOR THE OECD ECOLOGICAL CITY PROJECT
Roger Levett, Environment Team Leader, CAG Consultants, UK.

INTRODUCTION

Jeb Brugman in "Managing Human Ecosystems: Principles for Ecological Municipal Management (ICLEI, 1992) and others have pointed out that cities are in many ways like natural ecosystems. Analysing them as if they were ecosystems can help us recognise their environmental impacts, understand the complex relationships between physical, economic and social processes in cities, and design policy tools to improve environmental performance - and especially to integrate action across what have traditionally been seen as different areas of activity.

C.A.G. Consultants are leading a project for the British government to produce the UK Overview and Case Study for the OECD project group on the ecological city. Land Use Consultants, the New Economic Foundation and expert individuals are contributing to the project. We are developing an ecosystems - based approach to provide a tool for appraising how far British cities are 'ecological', and how far current policies and activities help them become more so.

This paper summarises this approach. It is very much a presentation of 'work in progress'.

DIFFERENT SENSES OF 'ECOLOGICAL CITY'

Physical ecological impact of cities

Cities as major influencers of the physical environment:

(1) Global impacts: energy and resource use, wastes
(2) Regional impacts: river catchments and flows, land use, regional stresses from pollution, development, access recreation
(3) The city as habitat for plants, animals etc.

Human ecology of cities

Cities as habitats for humans in all their variety:

(4) Providers of choice and opportunity - or constraint and frustrations?
(5) Liveability: are cities pleasant, welcoming, convenient, supportive, easy to live in.
(6) Equity: how benefits of urban life are shared, whether particular ethnic, cultural, age, income, gender, occupational or other groups are disadvantaged.

Ecology as metaphor or model

(7) Categories for describing urban features without sectoral parochialism: abundance, dominance, trophic flows, growth form, diversity.
(8) 'Systems' concepts to analyse how cities as complex systems develop, regulate themselves and respond to change: posi

tive or negative feedback, emergence of more complex levels of structure.

USE OF THE DIFFERENT SENSES

The first six senses provide criteria against which we can measure cities and policies: a city is more ecological (less unecological) if it:

(1)   Minimises global sustainability impacts
(2)   Does not breach regional carrying capacities
(3)   Provides maximum choice and opportunity
(5)   Is liveable
(6)   Is equitable

Policies are more ecological if they help cities to become more ecological - on all these criteria, not some at the expense of others. There is an integration question: how can we design and choose policies which make cities more ecological on all these criteria?

The seventh sense provides categories for describing key features of cities without jumping straight to sectors / activities and thus losing integration. The Table of Issues, Fig. 52A, is the starting point for our analysis. It maps ecological criteria (senses 1 to 6) along the top, and urban characteristics (sense 7) down the side. These are the ways that ecosystem characteristics manifest themselves in cities:

TABLE OF ISSUES

The full tables appear below (Figs 52B and C). The boxes contain issues, either positive (bold) or negative (ordinary type). There is nothing magic about this. It is simply a convenient way of breaking down a complex problem. It has a family resemblance to the OECD's pressure - state -response model.

ACCESS, MOBILITY AND TRANSPORT TABLES

USES OF THE ISSUES TABLE

The table clarifies relationships for example: the table indicates that cities are generally good for global ecology but bad for regional ecology. Why is this?

Density:

✪ allows satisfaction of many human wants with lower energy use and more efficient resource use per inhabitant
✪ means high energy and resource loadings per area.

So a key physical integrative aim is to achieve high density without excessive concentration of ecosystem loading.

Density also:

✪ makes cities good for choice, but also
✪ threatens quality of life, especially for the poor.

So a key *social* integrative aim is to reduce the frustrations and hardships of urban life without sacrificing density.

The analysis helps us define 'functional subsystems'

✪ Groups of cells in the table i.e. impacts and characteristics which can be managed together.

✪ Integrative policies and actions are ones which positively affect the greatest number of cells.

✪ Existing policies can be appraised according to how they affect the different cells in a subsystem.

✪ New policies can be designed and refined by considering potential effects on different cells.

USE OF ECOLOGICAL SYSTEMS CONCEPTS

The eighth sense of 'the ecological city' will help us consider the interrelation of disparate elements - the physical environment, the economy and welfare. Some of the most significant concepts, and examples of their application are:

✪ Negative feedback, or 'damping', where the system reacts to change in such a way as to limit or contain it. Example: a local authority's development plan can respond to increasing development pressures on urban greenspace by strengthening its protection and encouraging development to follow a different pattern.

✪ Positive feedback, or 'snowballing', where the system reacts to change in such a way as to stoke it up further. Example: the choice by some individuals to shift from bus to car will (at the margin) make the bus service slower and less reliable, and encourage amenities to move from bus-accessible to car-accessible sites, thus encouraging more people to shift from bus to car and amplifying the original change.

✪ Homeostasis, or change within stability, where negative feedback loops keep the overall system much the same while elements within it alter considerably. Example: a city which accommodates a complete change in its main industries without disintegrating or indeed changing its overall character much.

✪ State transition, or 'step' change, where the way the components of a system mesh together alters fundamentally and irreversibly. Example: the change in many British cities between 1950 and 1970, from homeostasis in travel patterns to positive feedback encouraging car use.

✪ Closure versus openness: the degree to which a system is insulated from, or vulnerable to, external changes. Example: the single market and restrictions on 'anticompetitive' practices have in recent years opened local economies to world markets to the extent that 'the local economy' often means little more than the enterprises which happen to be located in a particular area.

A benefit of the systems approach is to illuminate the relationship between individual behaviour choices and the contexts in which they occur. For example, rather than having to interpret car use as an issue of personal freedom versus environmental imperatives we can ask what it is about our current circumstances which makes so many people choose to use cars, how those circumstances could be altered to encourage different choices, and whether (and in what ways) those changes would make people better or worse off.

Fig.52A

Ecosystem Approach
ACCESS, MOBILITY AND TRANSPORT – ISSUES TABLE (Master)

		STATES					
PRESSURES		Global impact	Regional impact	City as ecosystem	Choice / opportunity	Liveability	Equity
Ecosystem characteristic	Manifestation in cities						
ABUNDANCE	High density of human population						
DOMINANCE	Buildings and other human - built 'hard' land uses predominate						
	Industrial, commercial and service activities predominate						
TROPHIC STRUCTURE	Large flows of energy and materials through human processes and activities						
	Large daily movements of people (commuting)						
GROWTH FORM & STRUCTURE DIVERSITY	Zoned / Specialised / controlled land use patterns						
	Random / uncontrolled land use patterns						
DIVERSITY	Racial, cultural, social						
	Of occupations, livelihoods and 'lifestyle' options						

Source: CAG, 1994

Fig.52B

Ecosystem Approach
ACCESS, MOBILITY AND TRANSPORT – ISSUES TABLE Physical Ecology

PRESSURES	Ecosystem characteristic / Manifestation in cities	STATES (physical ecology)		
		Global ecological impact	Regional ecological impact	City as ecosystem
ABUNDANCE	High density of human population	**Reduces land needed directly to support populations**	City depends on wider hinterland for many resource requirements	Pressure of human presence discourages some species
	Buildings and other human-built 'hard' land uses predominate	High embodied energy and resources	Resources sucked in from ever-increasing distance	**Built environment can provide extra habitats** Or can impoverish them!
DOMINANCE	Industrial, commercial and service activities predominate	Cities contain high proportion of potentially damaging activities	Concentration of 'value-adding' activities in cities pushes rural areas into 'primary producer' role	Pressure of commercial development reduces space for wildlife
TROPHIC STRUCTURE	Large flows of energy and materials through human processes and activities	**Potential for integrated, circular flows (eg materials reuse / recycling, waste heat use).** Commercial constraints to realising potential.	Urban resource / waste flows can integrate with rural waste / resource flows Concentration threatens carrying capacities	Local higher temperatures and air / water loadings
	Large daily movements of people (commuting)	**Short distances allow walking and cycling ; high densities allow public transport.** But cars increasingly dominate, increasing CO_2	Ease of movement spreads cities and urban pressures into surrounding areas	Road Sterilise land, sever wildlife corridors, accelerate water runoff. Traffic kills wildlife
GROWTH FORM & STRUCTURE DIVERSITY	Zoned / Specialised / controlled land use patterns	**Synergies and economies of scale in providing specialist infrastructure (eg for heat reuse)** Transport intensity increased		Larger individual habitats Isolated from each other
	Random / uncontrolled land use patterns	Synergies lost Randomised travel patterns cannot be served by mass transit	Point sources of pollution spread out Sprawl	**Diversity at "street block" scale** Risk of fragmentation at larger scales
DIVERSITY	Racial, cultural, social	**Variety of human resources facilitates variety of resource management practices**		
	Of occupations, livelihoods and 'lifestyle' options	**Efficient exploitation of resources and different urban 'niches'**		Diversity and richness in city habitats

Source: CAG, 1994

Fig.52C

Ecosystem Approach
ACCESS, MOBILITY AND TRANSPORT – ISSUES TABLE _ Human Ecology

PRESSURES		STATES (human ecology)		
Ecosystem characteristic	Manifestation in cities	Choice / opportunity	Liveability	Equity
ABUNDANCE	High density of human population	**Choice of social, cultural amenities increased by density**	**Facilitates range of social groupings and community structures** 'Density stress': inability to 'escape', loss of peace	Density stress worst for the poor
	Buildings and other human-built 'hard' land uses predominate		**Richness of experience of townscape, architectural, heritage** Lack of access to nature	
DOMINANCE	Industrial, commercial and service activities predominate	**Choice of employment, occupation, services increased by density** Simple lifestyles elusive	**All traded services** and amenities available Non-traded amenities elusive	People outside the trading economy disadvantaged
TROPHIC STRUCTURE	Large flows of energy and materials through human processes and activities	Choice of materials, resources increased by density	**Ready access to services, facilities** Overload of noise, activity, mechanical processes	Poor least able to insulate themselves from resource stresses
	Large daily movements of people (commuting)	Many patterns of life impossible without heavy commuting	Time, energy, stress and loss of community caused by commuting	Poor face worst journeys and/or greater restrictions on life patterns
GROWTH FORM & STRUCTURE	Zoned / Specialised / controlled land use patterns	Zoning restricts locational choice, or forces movement	**Improves health and perceived environmental quality** High travel requirements built in to many patterns of life	The less mobile (for whatever reason) are unable to access certain amenities
DIVERSITY	Random / uncontrolled land use patterns	**Freedom to do whatever you want where you want** Inability to avoid uncongenial activities	Inability to avoid noise, pollution, other nuisances	Amenity value rationed solely by price
DIVERSITY	Racial, cultural, social	**City can accommodate widest range of people** Risk of anomie	**Cultural tolerance**	Minorities blamed / scapegoated when majorities under pressure (eg unemployment) Social unrest
	Of occupations, livelihoods and 'lifestyle' options	**City offers wide range of opportunities Maximum choice at 'consumerist' level** Simple, not-consumerist options less available	**Most people can find congenial lifestyle**	Wide wealth disparities encourage exploitation of disadvantaged Underclass relatively disadvantaged

Source: CAG, 1994

FOCUSED ANALYSIS - ASKING THE RIGHT QUESTIONS

Eva Grundelius, Head of Section for Housing, Urban and Regional Planning & Environment Swedish Association of Local Authorities

Abstract

The FOCUSED ANALYSIS is a pedagogical instrument and a guidance for sustainable political decisions which is approved by the board of the Swedish Association of Local Authorities and used by various Swedish Local Authorities. The FOCUSED ANALYSIS is based on the concept of ecological cycles and the aim is to restore the balance between resource-generating and degrading processes. The FOCUSED ANALYSIS consists of six questions that can be asked before every type of decision is made that in one way or another affects our physical environment. If all six questions can be answered "yes", from a holistic point of view, we know that the planned project or measure will lead towards sustainable development.

Demanding Environmental Impact Assessments before decisions, will not solve problems alone. An Environmental Impact Assessment just provides facts and figures. When a decision is made, whether by a single person, a local organisation, a private enterprise or a national government, environmental issues will be weighed in the balance against other issues, including social and economic ones. If we are to move towards sustainable development, we must have greater insight into the consequences of being nonchalant about the environment, and we must have the will to change.

But once we have decided that we want sustainable development - which is a political decision - how can we know if a measure, an investment or an urban development project will result in increased or decreased environmental problems in the long run? What are the most important questions to ask and answer before a decisions is made? We can find these things out by making a FOCUSED ANALYSIS - that means asking a number of basic questions about potential effects.

The FOCUSED ANALYSIS is based on the concept of ecocycles. Take a natural ecological cycle where a fox eats a field mouse which, in turn, has eaten various plants. The plants live on photosynthesis - carbon dioxide, water and nutrients under the influence of sunlight. Examining this ecocycle in physical terms, we can see plant photosynthesis as a resource-generating process. It allows plants to grow, with sunlight as its fuel.

This resource-generating process is balanced by various degrading processes. The field mouse consumes and digests plants, and the fox consumes and digests the field mouse. The urine and excrement of both animals and dead vegetation are all degraded, as are the animals themselves when they eventually die. Processes of degradation give rise to solid, liquid and gaseous wastes.

Resource-generating processes are characterised by being sun-fuelled, and by the very important fact that they generate no material waste but only surplus heat which radiates out into the universe. Degrading processes are on-going spontaneously

in nature and to a larger extent in the human society. As a matter of fact all processes created and carried out by humans are degrading processes.

Only nature and nature-based processes can generate resources and in an evolutionary perspective the resource-generating processes have been predominant. Resources are characterised by having a higher degree of order and structure than the products and waste, which result from degrading processes, have together. It is true that the products themselves often represent a good portion of order and structure, but in an evolutionary perspective there is a very short time before the products are also turned into waste.

Our society today is not a sustainable one. As people use increasing amounts of material and energy, degrading processes are becoming more and more extensive while, at the same time, the space and capacity of the resource-generating processes of nature decrease. Therefore, in physical terms, the aim of a sustainable development must be to restore the balance between resource-generating and degrading processes. That is also the purpose of the FOCUSED ANALYSIS.

The FOCUSED ANALYSIS consists of six questions. If all six questions can be answered "yes", we know that the planned project or measure will lead towards sustainable development. If the answer to any of the questions is negative, there is good reason to modify the project. If the answer to most of the questions is "no", however, there is every probability that the project in question will require costly supplementary measures and investments in the foreseeable future. There might even be a great risk that the project will have to be phased out before completion, owing to excessive environmental costs. Financially, it will be a loss-making project.

A FOCUSED ANALYSIS can be carried out as a part of most decision-making processes and as a complement to Environmental Impact Assessments. It does not matter if it is a big project or plan with a budget of billions or a small decision concerning our personal finances. The findings in the FOCUSED ANALYSIS can be displayed simply and on a single page.

Now to the questions. The first one reads: "Does the project reduce energy consumption and move us towards greater use of renewable sources of energy?". The aim is to reduce the degrading processes in the ecological cycle. The more energy we use the more waste is generated. Furthermore it is of great importance which type of energy we use. For instance, fossil fuels and nuclear energy will always make a negative net contribution to the environment. The more and the longer we exploit these sources of energy, the greater the problems will be. Solar-powered sources of energy however, such as wind power, hydropower, solar energy and biofuels can make a positive net contribution to the environment. Municipalities can direct development sustainability by concentrating their efforts on advisory services for energy conservation, energy economisation and social planning.

Consistently, the aim of the second question is to strengthen the generation of resources. It is formulated: "Does the project increase biodiversity and the resource-generating capacity of nature?" Many species are threatened with extinction. As much as 40% of the photosynthesis which takes place on the earth's continents is used to satisfy the needs and desires of the global human population. Using large amounts of fossil fuels for mechanical labour, fertilisers and pesticides in industrialised agriculture consumes more resources than it delivers, from a holistic point of view. On the other hand, municipal land and parks can fill an important function as sanctuaries for certain threatened species and as a place for resource-generating processes in general, provided that the management of such areas is purposefully formed.

The degrading and resource-generating processes must be able to somehow meet in physical and chemical aspects. That leads us to the third question: "Does the project bring ecological cycles full course"? Whatever waste we leave to nature must be biodegradable and free from poisons. It also has to be delivered at the right place. For example the waste from our toilets should be brought back to the farmland where new food products can be grown. Environmentally conscious municipal procurement can be one important way of turning the market in this direction.

We must also recognise the limits of nature. The atmosphere and the oceans are not infinite and no matter is ever destroyed. Question four reads: "Does the project keep us within the limits of what mankind and nature can withstand?" For example, when land is exploited, is there tolerance for increased emissions or do we need the land to maintain nature's own functions?

Whenever nature uses material and energy it serves several purposes. We must try to do the same and this leads us to question no.5 : "Does the project solve more problems than it creates?" Most things that are done in society are done because they will be advantageous to someone. However, the disadvantages must also be taken into consideration. Measures which solve several problems at the same time without creating new ones are called solution multipliers. I will take up one example of a solution multiplier later in this paper.

The sixth question finally is: "Does the project observe the precautionary principle?" This question arises from the fact that nature's systems are too complicated to be fully understood. When we are uncertain as to whether a certain measure is harmful or not to the environment and the life-sustaining systems we should refrain from taking that measure.

The board of the Swedish Association of Local Authorities has approved the guidelines of the FOCUSED ANALYSIS and FOCUSED ANALYSIS is today used by Swedish Local Authorities as a pedagogical instrument and as a guidance for sustainable political decision-making. Various educational institutions and environmental organisations are also using the FOCUSED ANALYSIS. It may seem to be a difficult task to arrive at six "yes" answers in the FOCUSED ANALYSIS. I will conclude by showing that this does not always have to be the case.

Taking the example of what used to be a very ordinary Swedish apartment house in Gothenburg with ordinary people living there. In 1987 the house was renovated. A solar panel was

installed on the roof and coupled to a circulating air heating system. At the same time a greenhouse was built at the southern facade and the tenants were offered the opportunity of raising vegetables there. The interest in gardening grew and a year later the lawn adjacent to the building was converted into allotments. The need for fertilisers and soil improvement materials, arose and the apartment dwellers began composting their organic household waste.

Asking the six questions in the FOCUSED ANALYSIS we firstly see that energy is not only saved through solar heating but less food has to be transported to the building and about half the waste (that is the organic part) is circulated back into the system at the place. We can also assume that the time people spend gardening means savings in transportation to and from other recreational activities. Maybe this type of lifestyle also reduces the interest in material consumption as a whole.

The gardening, on the other hand, is a resource-generating process. It reduces the demand for industrial agricultural products which also, on a larger scale, would be beneficial to biological diversity. Thirdly, the gardening and composting give rise to a complete on-site ecocycle. And the fact that about 40 percent of the heating for the building is supplied by the sun instead of combustion of fossil fuels, improves the balance between resource -generating and degrading processes.

All the described reductions in resource and energy use, make it easier to cope within the limits of nature. For example, the per capita emissions of carbon dioxide decreases substantially.

The renovation of this building in Gothenburg is a solution multiplier. It may be of special interest to highlight the conceivable social, cultural and pedagogical benefits. The people living in the building have definitely gained a strengthened sense of community, they derive pleasure from gardening and seeing things grow, and they gain concrete insight into what it means to bring ecological cycles full course. Finally, this kind of small-scale cultivation may be done with minimum use of chemical pesticides and artificial fertilisers, which is beneficial to the environment. It is thus possible to apply the precautionary principle.

LOCAL ENVIRONMENTAL MANAGEMENT SEMINAR REPORTS AND INDIVIDUAL CASE STUDIES

INTEGRATED ECONOMIC AND ENVIRONMENTAL DEVELOPMENT AT THE LOCAL LEVEL
Jane Stevens, Environment Coordinator, East Sussex County Council

DESIGNING FOR SUSTAINABLE CITIES – ACCESS, MOBILITY AND PUBLIC TRANSPORT
Dr John Whitelegg, Ecologica, UK

INTERNATIONAL LINKS AND SUSTAINABLE DEVELOPMENT
Vernon Smith, Local Government International Bureau

INTEGRATED SUSTAINABLE ENERGY STRATEGIES FOR URBAN AREAS
Trevor Houghton, Centre for Sustainable Energy, Bristol, UK

INTEGRATED ECONOMIC AND ENVIRONMENTAL DEVELOPMENT AT THE LOCAL LEVEL - SEMINAR REPORT
Jane Stevens, Environment Coordinator, East Sussex County Council

A variety of speakers throughout the day were keen to get across the message that it was not about choosing between economic development and the environment - but that it was necessary to support both.

This echoed a conclusion from an opinion poll carried out for the European Commission (Eurobarometer 37.0, 1992), which found that 69% of Europeans considered that economic development must be ensured, but that the environment should be protected at the same time (with 22% supporting environmental protection before the economy, and 4% giving priority to economic development).

Case Study : East Sussex County Council & Upper Normandy Environmental Management of SMEs (Small and medium sized enterprises)

The session was introduced by considering the integration of economic development with enhancing and conserving the environment - two strands of local authority policy, which are often viewed as being in conflict. In particular, East Sussex County Council has come to view environmental and economic well-being as symbiotic: the high quality of the local environment is one of the County's greatest economic strengths and thus needs to be protected if the economy is to prosper, while a successful economy is more likely to ensure sound environmental performance.

By way of illustration, a number of examples were given of initiatives and current achievements in East Sussex :
* incorporation of the principles of sustainability into plans and strategies;
* investigation of seawater quality and its impact on the tourism industry;
* creation of a partnership venture to attract private investment to a country park;
* support for the marketing of timber from sustainably managed woodlands;
* promotion of environmental management within other organisations in the County.

This last example was considered in more detail to demonstrate the collaborative work on environmental management being carried out by East Sussex County Council and the Conseil Regional de Haute-Normandie. Both Councils aim to help businesses benefit from a greater awareness of their environmental impact, but have adopted quite different approaches.

The former uses its own wide range of environmental specialists to offer a free environmental advisory service to businesses within targeted areas. Whereas the latter uses private sector consultants, offering participation in its environmental programme to all businesses across the whole region, but usually demanding a financial contribution from them.

(i)   'Newhaven Green Business Initiative'

At the end of 1993 a pilot project was started, aimed at developing the environmental advisory service already offered to businesses, by focusing attention on a specific industrial estate in East Sussex - the 'Newhaven Green Business Initiative'. The prime objective was to stimulate the interest of small businesses and encourage them to improve their environmental performance. The original intention was to take a number of the businesses through a full 'environmental review' as the first stage of introducing them to the European Community Eco-Management and Audit Scheme. In practice, the project has concentrated on three main areas, namely energy and water conservation, waste management and improving the external environment of the industrial estate.

Achievements to date have included a complete waste survey of the estate, improvements in waste management and waste minimisation, setting up of co-ordinated waste collection schemes. Energy audits have identified ways of conserving both energy and water, with some of the early recommendations now being adopted. Draft proposals for improvements to the external environment (including landscaping, better signing, litter clearing and drainage improvements), are now awaiting final approval before adoption.

(ii) 'Environmental Advantage in Upper-Normandy'

Environmental action in the Haute-Normandie Region has concentrated on the promotion and introduction of clean technology to reduce local pollution within mainly large industrial sites, and developing ways of re-using and recycling industrial waste products.

At the end of 1993, the 'Environment Advantage in Haute-Normandie' operation was launched. This aimed to encourage businesses to become more interested in strategic undertakings to improve their environmental performance. It emphasised the competitive advantage to be gained through qualification under a recognised 'ecolabelling' scheme (which in itself demands improvement in production techniques, waste minimisation, energy and water conservation, pollution control etc.) and offered financial assistance, publicity and specialist advice to businesses to participate in the scheme.

Conclusions:

The next phase of both projects aims to help individual businesses set systems in place to prepare them for the European Community Eco-Management and Audit Scheme.

Both projects acknowledged the difficulties in stimulating interest from businesses in the first instance. It was also agreed that whatever the approach (whether by geographical location, type or size of business), emphasis on the economic benefits of the environment, as opposed to the regulatory constraints, produced greater interest and participation.

Later discussion acknowledged that an effective form of marketing was by example - through promotion and publicity of examples of environmental best practice, and case studies in which individual businesses had gained proven financial benefits from improved environmental performance. It was also agreed that the provision of financial incentives, whether in the form of free specialist advice, grants, environmental awards or publicity also ensure greater participation and involvement.

DESIGNING SUSTAINABLE CITIES: ACCESS, MOBILITY AND PUBLIC TRANSPORT- SEMINAR REPORT

OVERVIEW: PROBLEMS, CHALLENGES AND POTENTIAL
Dr John Whitelegg Eco-Logica Ltd

A remarkable feature of our current transport policies in Britain both nationally and locally is that they do not work even within the very narrow confines of their own terms of reference. Traffic congestion is now not only part of urban life but extends to many sections of motorway that were designed and built as long-distance economic arteries. Roads like the M25 in London, designed as major national highways for longer distance journeys have become incorporated into trips of less than five miles in length to supermarkets, schools and work. The countryside is plagued by traffic volumes and the carving up effects of new roads to such an extent that it is increasingly difficult to find areas to walk and cycle in peace and quiet and it is impossible to use rural roads unless also in a car. These unpleasant consequences of our degree of dependence on motorised transport are not the result of natural laws. They are the result of many years of heavily subsidised private transport, neglect of public transport and road construction on a scale that has created the demand it claims to satisfy.

Our transport systems are very expensive to build and maintain and are normally justified on the grounds that they stimulate economic activity and reduce road traffic accidents. Both justifications are seriously flawed. The changes in economic activity over the last twenty years have all been in the direction of significant losses in manufacturing employment and major reductions in the number of firms operating in any particular industry. The increase in accessibility by high quality roads has permitted a smaller number of firms to service a larger market area depriving many local economies of employment. This has been documented in some detail in studies of industrial location and of warehousing and distribution. Roads may have an effect on stimulating economic activity but a much more important effect is to reduce the number of places that share the jobs. Roads are just as likely to export jobs as to import them.

In road safety terms a dependence on motorised transport simply reduces the total amount of walking and cycling and reduces accidents by frightening people out of public space. Children in particular have been deprived of independent mobility and freedom to accentuate the dominance of the private car.

Our transport system is dirty, dangerous, expensive and bad value for money. It makes people ill and it does not create varied employment in local communities. It destroys the countryside, threatens global environmental stability and in the main serves well only that part of the population well off enough and fit enough to own a car and commandeer it for most of the time. The young, the elderly, the handicapped and the poor all lose out.

It is quite clear that we cannot support a situation where every individual aged 17-70 who is fit owns a car. We dare not even think about the consequences if the populations of China and India own and use cars at the rate we do. We can't build enough road space and car parking space to cope with this number of vehicles, and life in cities and the countryside would become intolerable. Globally our physical systems cannot absorb the carbon dioxide and other greenhouse gases emitted without tripping critical thresholds that signal rising sea levels, increasingly severe weather conditions and major problems for the plant life on which our food chains depend. Interestingly all our planning is rooted in a "business as usual" way of thinking which assumes we can continue to expand car ownership and use and the space allocated to vehicles.

There is no doubt whatsoever that we are on a thoroughly non-sustainable course which has not been altered by the UK government statements on sustainability in January 1994. The irony of all this is that we can move rapidly towards sustainability in transport and in other sectors of the economy simply by reducing our dependence on fossil fuels for transport, reducing the amount of travel by car and lorry and by encouraging forms of land use and transport that maximise accessibility, minimise mobility, maximise health and urban quality of life and restore peace and tranquillity to the countryside. None of this is pie in the sky. It is all achievable and it will cost less than the disastrous transport and environment policies we now have in place.

TRANSPORT FOR NEIGHBOURHOODS
KEY ISSUES

- ✪ Minimise the use of the private car.

- ✪ Reducing the need to travel and linking land use transport planning is very important.

- ✪ Increase liveability and participation.

- ✪ Evaluate transport and job arguments and take into account gender.

- ✪ Re-allocate space to pedestrians and cyclists away from cars.

- ✪ Improve public transport and bicycle technology and ensure gender and age responsiveness.

- ✪ Transport planning should be people centred.

- ✪ Wider public debate/awareness of issues and choices.

- ✪ Plan for neighbourhood schools to minimise travel.

- ✪ Encourage informal sector/public transport (middle-class, not just poor people) for high socio-economic class.

- ✪ Encourage worker participation/representation in organising transportation in developing countries.

- ✪ Question privatisation - Does it Work? Does it improve total quality. Privatisation is not the same as de-regulation.

- ✪ Pay attention to gender issues/safety/security.

- ✪ Pay attention to the needs of disabled/elderly.

- ✪ Push for non-motorised transport (NMT).

- ✪ Increase the attention given to pedestrians - increase respect.

- ✪ Special attention is needed for cities in Eastern Europe which are seeing the run-down of public transport and a large increase in private transport.

- ✪ "Clean Technology" is not the answer. Encourage modal diversity, NMT and reduced demand for transport.

- ✪ Private car substitution strategies.

CASE STUDY ONE
EUROPEAN EXPERIENCE OF PUBLIC TRANSPORT AND
SUSTAINABLE CITIES.
*Mr Gijs Kuneman, Co-ordinator of the European Federation for
Transport and Environment (T&E).*

If we are serious in aiming for sustainability, we need to give
priority to sustainable modes of transport: cycling, walking and
public transport. This prioritisation needs to be accompanied by
a restriction of car and lorry use in cities, otherwise there will
be no effect. For instance: improving public transport alone will
attract more users, but only a few former car users.

Transport prioritisation must be broad: in investment, in traffic
management and sometimes literally, on the streets. In this
order:

1   Pedestrian
2   Cyclists
3   Public Transport
4   Commercial/business vehicles requiring access;
     Residents
5   Car borne shopper
6   Car borne commuters

There are ample examples of successful sustainable urban transport policies. I will describe some European examples.

GRONINGEN

Groningen is the capital of the province of Groningen (NL),
170,000 inhabitants. The city centre dates from 1047. The
objectives of transport policy are to: preserve and improve
accessibility, and to improve viability and safety.

There are three mainline measures:
- town planning: a short distance between areas of living,
  working and facilities.
- infrastructure and facilities for public transport and
  cycling.
- traffic management: further curtailing of car use.

In 1977 Groningen established the city circulation plan. The
central city was divided into 4 cells. Cars have access to these
cells, but cannot go from one to another, while public transport
(PT) and cyclists can. (The same policy has proven effective in
Italian historic cities, and also in Gothenburg (S), where it has
proven to be very effective. There the system was extended to
areas outside the central business district). Further policy elements in Groningen in 1977 were: one way streets, except for
cyclists; no access except cyclists and PT; creation of pedestrian
zone. Ten years later, a comprehensive cycling policy was
implemented, followed by plans for regional transportation and
a parking policy.

Important aspects of these policies are: good connection by
regional and urban buses, car-pool areas, improvement of
rolling stock (including tests on buses with different fuels), park
and ride buses, concentration in railway station areas, and for
cycling policy: network creation, signposting, anti-theft programmes, and priority for cyclists: short cuts to avoid traffic
lights, no one-way streets for bikes.

Furthermore two nationally instituted features of public transport helped developments in Groningen. Firstly a standardised
national ticket, for sale and use in all buses, trams, metros and
urban trains in the Netherlands. Secondly, the 'train taxi' , a
(subsidised) taxi service to and from railway stations. One buys
a ticket for these taxis in the stations, and shares it with several
others. The system has proved very successful.

It is hard to evaluate the effect of this long-term comprehensive policy, as it is more or less ongoing. The 1977 circulation
plan was evaluated:
-    improvement of quality of life and shopping environment
     in the inner city.
-    increase in number of visitors.
-    increased use of PT and bike, 47% decrease in use of car.
-    initially, a decreased spending in the city, with improve-
     ment later on.

Currently, Groningen has one of the highest shares of cycling in
Europe: more than 50% of all commuting traffic occurs on bicycle. It must be said, however, that the PT share is low at 5%,
while walking accounts for 15%.

COPENHAGEN

When looking at Copenhagen, we see a lower share for cycling,
but a higher share for public transport.

The agglomeration of Copenhagen, capital of Denmark, has 1.7
million inhabitants. Congestion is not a great problem yet, due
to low car ownership: 200/1000 persons. (Incidentally, the
whole of Denmark has low car ownership: 400 per 1,000 persons which is most likely linked to a high tax on cars). Denmark
has a tradition of cycling, for commuting as well as other purposes. Copenhagen has an extensive network of cycle tracks,
currently, the share of cycling, cars and PT are more or less
equal: each 1/3. Even in winter, 20% of the working population uses the bike to go to work. Since 1970, cycling increased
by 60%, while car use was reduced by 10%. And in the summer
of 1990, more people went to work on bikes than any other
mode (which is a rare feat in Europe).

Even so, the city and more importantly, the inhabitants are not
satisfied: as a member of the WHO Programme, 'Healthy Cities'.
Copenhagen has worked out a City Health Plan, which includes
quantitative aims and concrete actions to be taken to reach the
objectives. Strikingly, the citizens, when asked to propose initiatives, pointed out traffic as a sector where most improvements could be made.

Therefore, the City will take more measures to improve cycle
facilities, including free city bikes, measures to further improve
public transport, and measures to restrict car traffic in residential areas and the city centre. The City says that the envisaged
result of these measures is a share of 50% for cycling.
Not only does this example show that cycling policy can also be
put to work in larger cities, but also that it is important to
include the citizens in the process.

ZURICH

Cycling is just one of three sustainable modes. And even if public transport has a high share in Copenhagen, it has been given full priority in the often quoted example of Zurich (Switzerland). Zurich is a conurbation of around one million inhabitants. The aim of the urban transport policy is to improve the living environment and reduce pollution.

The public transport measures include:
✪ a speed-up programme for public transport (separate bus lanes, maximum priority at traffic lights directly operated by trams and buses)
✪ introduction of a regional metro system
✪ increase in seat-capacity in the morning peak hours by 20%
✪ new connections and diametrical lines
✪ basic interval timetable and tariff agreement
✪ construction of new, and extension of existing stations
✪ incorporation of all transport authorities within the Zurich Transport Authority
✪ a major marketing strategy

In addition, Zurich has a very restrictive policy on private cars, without actually banning them: reduction of highway and parking capacity, parking control, diversion of through traffic etc. But probably the most important feature of the policy is the coherence of all measures.

The result is a staggering 75-80% share for public transport in the city centre and 50% in the outskirts (it should be noted that car use is low in the whole of Switzerland). On average, inhabitants make 470 trips by public transport annually, which is probably the highest in the world.

Other examples of good practice in public transport can be found throughout Europe. The French city of La Rochelle has a full range of transport services in addition to regular buses. There are: the 'Sea Bus', both running on regular schedules and on demand, public bicycles, taxis with a fixed low price and several 'Van pools'. It was already mentioned that in the Netherlands, most medium and smaller cities have 'train taxis' at a fixed low price. In the German city of Karlsruhe, regular trains and urban trains run on the same tracks enabling a well-connected service.

AMSTERDAM

As is demonstrated in the examples, the three sustainable modes of transport need to be given priority, but to be effective, policy should include restricting car use.

In Amsterdam, the reduction of car use is not an end in itself, but a means to improve urban quality of life. In 1992, the city held a referendum about restricting car use in the inner city. Although the turnout was very low and the 'yes' vote came through only by a margin, the decision was made to put the plan into operation. Between 1994 and 2000, car traffic will be reduced, while inner city facilities for cyclists, pedestrians and public transport will be improved.

The plan will result in a reduction in number of car trips by 31% compared to the projected trips in 2003, and a reduction of 25% compared to 1993 figures. The city administration has realised that reducing car use by 50% will most probably "impede the proper functioning of the city". This means that a reduction of 25-30% is very well possible without impending the city's proper functioning!

Furthermore, outside Western Europe there are many cities that do not yet have a high share of car traffic. These will experience no negative effect from restricting car use. In other words: such a city may still be in time to stop the growing flow of private cars. This is mainly the case with Eastern European cities.

ECONOMY

A major question is: what are the effects of car restrictions on the city's economy?

First, I would like to mention the theory of internalisation of external costs, which has been accepted as an element of European transport policy. There are costs in transport which are not paid for by the users, but by society at large. According to the polluter pays principle, these costs should be included ("internalised") into the price of transport. In principle it means that we put a value on silence, clean air and road safety. However, important as it is, two years ago, a broad European opinion poll was carried out, commissioned by the UITP and the EC. European citizens and elected officials were asked their opinion on urban transport. There were some striking results.

Some key findings are:

✪ Both the citizens and the politicians agree, that the car is the biggest traffic problem. Furthermore, one third of the citizens and politicians think car traffic is difficult to tolerate, while 25% think it is no longer tolerable.

✪ The majority of European citizens, on average as well as in absolute terms in each country, feel that in conflict situations, public transport, cyclists and pedestrians should be given priority over the car.

While elected officials fully agree, they underestimate the public support for this.

✪ In general elected officials overestimate the public love affair with the car, or in other words, they underestimate the public support for restriction measures.

The conclusion is: at least in Europe, you do not have to be reluctant to tackle the car.

LESSONS LEARNED

✪ There are many policy measures available to make urban transport more sustainable. In general, they comprise the reduction of car use, combined with the often forgotten element in transport policy, land use planning. To be effective, these policies should go hand in hand.

The three sustainable models of transport - walking, cycling and public ransport have priority in Amsterdam, The Netherlands

EPL

✪ It is good to include the residents and companies in decision-making. Restricting car use is probably more politically accepted than is thought. Information and goodwill
campaigns are a necessary and important accompanying
policy measure.

FINALLY

It is clear that these European examples may not be applicable
to cities on other continents. The USA is in general much more
car dependent and has a completely different approach to land
use. Furthermore, cities in developing countries will have completely different mobility patterns. However, there is also the
very often quoted example of Curibita in Brazil, which has
implemented a very effective policy.

But one thing is sure: the problems and solutions are universal.
Cars and lorries are the cause of the larger part of pollution and
noise in cities, and the sustainable modes are sustainable everywhere. To the administrators of cities in developing countries
and Eastern Europe, where the large growth of car use is only
beginning, I would like to say, "please do not copy our outdated
blueprint", and to administrators of cities in the West I say:
"show the world that we are serious about sustainability, or we
have no right to speak at all."

CASE STUDY TWO
URBAN PUBLIC TRANSPORT PROVISION, PATTERNS AND
SUSTAINABILITY: AN EXAMPLE FROM ZIMBABWE
Charles Kunaka, Centre for Transport Studies

The transport problems of developing countries and in particular, cities in developing countries have been well recounted and documented over the years. These problems are often to do with various permutations of different types of congestion, states of disrepair of infrastructure and poor management. In most cases it has been argued that the main cure for these problems would be an injection of capital. While it is accepted that this is part of the solution to transport problems in these countries, the aim of this paper is to outline and discuss some of the processes occurring which should be an important indicator of the transport systems which can thrive in such cities. These processes are identified using the example of Harare, the capital city of Zimbabwe.

The presentation is in three parts: an essential outline of the evolution of public transport provision in the city, a discussion of the forces behind some of the changes taking place and finally an assessment of these changes and their implications on future transport patterns.

The roots of public transport provision in Harare as it presently exists go back to the 1950s. The post second world war expansion in industry gave rise to rapid urbanisation and the need for a wider transport service. Both the current two main suppliers of public transport, the bus company and the informal operators, started during this period. The two operations have co-existed since then, but with no official acknowledgement of the latter until the 1980s. Even since then, the major part of the resource commitments to transport and policy formulations for the sector have been targeted at the bus company. Increasing problems arising from an unacceptable level of service provided by the bus company have however led to more recent policy changes to broaden the role of the informal sector.

The current changes have to be seen in the broader context of contemporary global economic trends which emphasise deregulation and increased competition as the watchwords for economic activity. In developing countries this has meant the adoption and implementation of various types of economic reform programmes. As part of these programmes governments have had to consider privatisation of state companies and allowing increased competition in most sectors of the economy. In the transport sector there has been a noticeable movement towards deregulation by removing quantity controls in the industry thereby permitting more vehicles and in most cases more operators to provide competing services. It is generally argued that such changes would result in improved service levels. In Zimbabwe the government virtually scrapped the monopoly which was enjoyed by the bus company and allowed other operators to run vehicles of any size which they were previously barred from doing. Harare has since seen the introduction and use of a variety of vehicles covering most parts of the city.

The above developments have two important implications: they are an acknowledgement that big bus companies may not necessarily provide adequate transport services; and, the informal sector can play an important role in public transport provision and that contrary to widespread views held in the sixties and seventies, informal transport services are not a temporary phenomenon which will disappear with time. As a result of this, other issues also have to be considered including the increasing tendency towards more smaller vehicle models and their energy implications, the rising cost of travel and its relationship to the increasing levels of trips made on foot, and impact on employment and wealth creation of these changes.

Generally, there is a need to understand the way formal and informal operators can work together and there is evidence that considerable benefits can arise by trying to incorporate them both in policy making but that this has to be done without altering to a large extent those aspects that make them different.

INTERNATIONAL LINKS AND SUSTAINABLE DEVELOPMENT SEMINAR REPORT

NORTH/SOUTH PARTNERSHIPS
FOR SUSTAINABLE DEVELOPMENT
Vernon Smith, Local Government International Bureau

The two-part seminar on International Links and Sustainable Development reminded all participants that LOCAL AGENDA 21 issues and processes cannot be seen in isolation. Information was presented about relevant initiatives overseas, about international links and programmes of co-operation and about different perspectives and priorities in Northern Industrialised countries and in the developing countries of the South. The first session was organised and sponsored by Leicester City Council and chaired by Mayor Adelina Auguste, President of the Caribbean Association of Local Government Authorities. The second session, sponsored by the Local Government International Bureau, was chaired by Councillor Ken Bodfish of East Sussex County Council, Chairman of the International Committee of the UK Association of County Councils. In both, opportunities for participation in international networks and in North/South partnerships with a focus on sustainable development and environmental action were highlighted.

Leicester City Council gave three presentations on its involvement in joint environmental initiatives. In using its twinning link with Strasbourg, Leicester had developed an accord to help obtain European Union, EU funding for joint initiatives, encourage staff exchanges and find ways of contributing to environmental improvements in the Third World. Leicester was part of an international energy network of more than 20 cities in the EU and Eastern Europe, as well as part of the ICLEI Urban CO2 Reduction Programme. With Barcelona, Leicester had developed an urban energy planning project. In the Third World, Leicester described how it had developed twinning links through MASINFA, a community-based organisation, to help provide North/South partnership for local projects in Masaya, Nicaragua. The Friends of Vrindavan was a further project involving Leicester schools and community groups in reviving the forest and improving the environment in Vrindavan, India, a Hindu place of pilgrimage.

Focusing more on practical examples of North/South linking produced some stimulating debate. Participants heard a description from Professor Sneha Palnitkar, of the newly formed Commonwealth Local Government Forum, on the mobilisation of networks supporting sustainable development. Councillor Abdul Choundray of Rochdale gave a practical demonstration of how his town had been mobilised to assist Sahiwal in Pakistan, with funds raised voluntarily, workers recruited from local organisations on a voluntary basis and participation from all sectors of the community (including exchanges of teachers and health workers). Twinning, he said, gives access to ordinary people, rather than to governments and officials.

Marcello Nowersztern of the United Town Development Agency described development co-operation between cities in Europe and those in Latin America, particularly now that many countries were returning to democracy and governments were decentralising their powers. An account of the new situation in

South Africa, given by Lolo Ditshego of Towns and Development also brought another dimension to the proceedings. He stressed that it was important that the North did not monopolise all the project facilities in any linking but that links should work on a mutual basis.

Finally information, projects and networks offering assistance to local authorities wishing to become actively involved in international linking activities were highlighted - including the International Council of Local Environmental Initiatives, the International Union of Local Authorities, United Towns Organisation and the Towns and Development Consortium. The new UK Local Agenda 21 guidelines on North/South Linking for sustainable development were also highlighted, as were the new range of information packs and case studies produced by the Local Government International Bureau.

Amongst other recommendations the following matters were proposed to the UK Local Agenda 21 Steering Group for follow-up action:

1.   New guidelines on international co-operation and North/South partnerships with developing counties (produced by the Local Government International Bureau and funded by the ODA) should be distributed to UK environmental co-ordinators via a future mailing from the Local Government Management Board.

2.   Local government organisations should be encouraged to participate in the September 1995 IULA World Congress, in the Hague, which will focus on international co-operation in the local government sector - and in the UK conference on local government co-operation with South Africa scheduled for March 2/3 1995.

3.   UK local authorities should be encouraged to revive their twinning and friendship links with a view to promoting partnerships for Sustainable Development and international co-operation on Local Agenda 21 activities.

4.   At the European level, action should be taken to ensure that the Council of European Municipalities and Regions, the European Commission, the Council of Europe Congress of Local and Regional Authorities of Europe, United Towns Organisation and other similar bodies actively extend the scope and promote the effectiveness of LOCAL AGENDA 21 initiatives via international co-operation.

5.   Local authorities in Europe should be encouraged to support the European Sustainable Cities and Towns Campaign initiated by the City of Aalborg, the European Commission and ICLEI in May 1994.

6.   At Global level the local government international associations (including IULA) should work in co-operation with the International Council for Local Environmental Initiatives (ICLEI) to:

✪   promote specific programmes, campaigns and networks with a focus on action for Sustainable Development;

✪   draw the attention of the UN and the Commission on
     Sustainable Development to the part played by local gov-
     ernment in implementing action on Agenda 21 at local
     level;

✪   co-ordinate local government input to the 1996 UN
     "Cities Summit" (HABITAT II) conference in Istanbul (and
     other relevant UN Conferences and programmes).

CASE STUDY ONE-URBAN ENERGY STRATEGIES, ADELAIDE, SOUTH AUSTRALIA
LEON BYASS, MEP AUSTRALIA, ADELAIDE

The Strategy focused on the district of New Haven and aims to:

✪ promote design-for-climate (passive energy) housing

✪ demonstrate affordable alternative energy technology applications onto mass housing estates, particularly geothermal plant and solar units;

✪ promote the purchase of 5 and 6 star rated energy consuming appliances;

✪ assist home owners energy and cost-saving strategies through green mortgage extension options on affordable house and land packages with major leading institutions;

✪ trial with the private sector and utilities remote meter reading;

✪ demonstrate new approaches to streetscape and public open space safety and security through high efficiency, low energy, environmentally friendly street lighting;

✪ through extensive monitoring demonstrate that significant energy use and CO2, reductions can be achieved cost effectively and that some alternative energy technologies are already cost effective.

Program Measurement

Performance measures will be tied to commercial success and will include:

✪ at least 75% of all houses designed-for-climate;

✪ household networked energy use reduced by 30%;

✪ up to 30% household energy supplied by renewables;

✪ major bank support for green mortgage extension options;

✪ CO2 emissions per household reduced by 3 ton p.a.

Partners include:

✪ the SA Housing Trust, a national firm of architects, three private sector builders, and the MFP in designing to better meet the prevailing climate;

✪ private sector manufacturers of appliances such as geothermal plant providing domestic hot water, heating and cooling, and domestic solar units;

✪ manufacturers of cooking appliances, washing machines, fridges etc;

✪ two major banks on funding of renewable technologies;

✪ various parties on streetscape and public open space lighting issues;

The New Haven Village Project

The New Haven Village development will comprise 65 low-rise, medium to high density dwellings in the lower price range on a 2 hectare site adjacent to an urban railway station, shopping centre and public park. The project will test MFP design concepts as well as national AMCORD URBAN guidelines for housing development under the Commonwealth's Green Street program. Houses, streetscapes and urban infrastructure will be more people oriented and more environmentally friendly.

While the South Australian Housing Trust is managing the subdivision, the development remains speculative. A number of private and public sector organisations are joining together to demonstrate various initiatives including better design for climate, energy management strategies and the application of alternative energy strategies.

The first display homes at New Haven Estate are programmed for completion in December 1994. The house and land packages are expected to sell for under $120,000.

The energy management and renewable energy strategies contribute to achieving reduced energy use, an increase in the use of renewable technologies in mass housing and, obviously, a reduction of CO2 emissions. They are in line with national and state energy strategies and would provide a visible commitment by Governments in this area. More importantly, however, they will provide the public with a show case that is both practical and costed that developers, builders and householders can afford to copy.

A comprehensive monitoring programme was designed to measure the scheme's success.

NORTH/SOUTH PARTNERSHIPS FOR SUSTAINABLE DEVELOPMENT (NORTH/SOUTH AND SOUTH/NORTH EXCHANGE OF EXPERIENCE)

MEGA CITIES INNOVATIONS FOR URBAN LIFE

Professor Sneha Palnitkar, All India Institute of Local Self Government, Bombay, India.

The long urgency of urban problems especially in mega cities demands immediate and creative policy responses. The traditional top down policies and programmes of the past three decades have not been that successful, and sometimes counter productive. While experts are debating, community-based organisations and local governments are proving that alternative approaches formulated at neighbourhood level can simultaneously begin to regenerate the environment, alleviate poverty, decentralise authority in their city and empower women and minorities.

The cities are and always have been the source of innovations and new ideas. There is enough creative energy in cities today to address urban challenges but there are few mechanisms available to channel these forces into the policy making process or to multiply the effects of approaches that work. There is thus a compelling need to discover alternative approaches that make better use of several urban innovations in the world and create multiplier effects with scarce financial resources. In order to address challenges of sustainable urban development in todays world it is very essential to view the world's cities as a huge research laboratory generating urban management experiments some of which could be identified and replicated. The Mega Cities Project was initiated in 1987 with the goal of shortening the time lag between ideas and their implementation by a transfer process of urban innovation amongst worlds largest mega cities. The project combines theory and practice in its search for successful approaches to improving the conditions of urban life. The Mega Cities approach is based on collaborative efforts among the various sectors to increase efficiency in finding urban innovations and multiplying them for the greatest impact. For the past 6 years the Mega Cities Project has developed an active network of co-ordinating teams in 17 of the worlds largest mega cities, 13 of which are in the developing countries. Each team follows the mega cities procedure and methodology which is the basis for successful participation and co-ordination throughout the network of cities. The project has three inter-related aspects:

1. an investigation, documentation and analysis of successful urban innovation currently under way in mega cities throughout the world.

2. a search for the next generation of urban innovations i.e. promising new ideas, approaches, prototypes not yet implemented but with potential to address urban problems,

3. the development of theoretical understanding about conditions in which urban innovations arise, how they overcome the myriad of obstacles to implementation (political aspects, financial constraints and existing practices) and once implemented how they can be replicated and transferred.

In order to understand how to catalyse urban innovations and how to reduce the time lag between ideas and implementation, serious research is needed on the generation, implementation and transfer of urban innovation. The mega cities project has developed the following three-part research agenda.

1. Generation: Where do innovative ideas come from? What motivates the search for innovative policies and programs? What sector or combination of sectors (public, private, voluntary) generates which types of innovations, and with what frequency? What conditions within the groups, agency, or urban context stimulate or impede innovation? What types of cities generate which types of innovations?

2. Implementation and impact: What are the conditions for successful implementation? How do innovations overcome the political, financial, cultural and technological obstacles to implementation? What factors affect successful evolution from pilot project to full-scale program? How does the process of implementation differ among policy areas, sectors, types of innovation, and urban settings? What is the significance, scope and nature of the innovation's impact on affected citizens and institutions?

3. Diffusion: How does innovation transfer occur? How do economic, political, demographic, and socio-cultural differences among cities affect the transfer process? What is the relationship of the source of innovation to the successful transfer of innovation? What modes of communication and institutional forms could be ideal for ongoing urban interchange?

The Mega Cities Project has reached a milestone in its organisational development and some of the aspects of the mega cities commitment can be listed as follows:-

Principles and Values

✪   The Mega Cities Mission is: to reduce the time lag between urban innovations and their implementation.

✪   Mega Cities aims to transform urban policy toward a socially just, environmentally sustainable, politically participatory, and economically vital city of the 21st century.

✪   The Mega Cities network is composed of local partnerships of urban leaders from every sector who see their cities as centres of hope and opportunity and are committed to making them work.

✪   Mega Cities is committed to collaborative processes within the organisation and in the organisation's work with local and global community.

✪   Mega Cities' focus is not on problems but on solutions.

✪   Mega Cities works to enable cities to learn from each others "success stories" through innovation transfer from South to North, and South to South as well as the more common North to South.

COMMONWEALTH LOCAL GOVERNMENT FORUM (CLGF)

Over the years local governments in many counties have demonstrated a very high degree of effectiveness in the delivery of urban services at the local level. Provision of urban services such as, water supply, waste water treatment, fire protection, solid waste management, traffic and transportation planning, environmental planning and others have achieved a structure that allows for participation and highlights accountability. By their very closeness to the people local governments within most Commonwealth countries are bonded to achieve transparency in the management of resources. This fact is becoming more and more recognised and we are encouraged by the importance accorded to local authority initiatives in support of UNCED's Agenda 21. There is a growing awareness and acceptance of the crucial importance of local government in the pursuit and successful achievement of sustainable urban development.

Commonwealth Local Government Forum (CLGF) was established in the year 1994. The forum is the youngest member in the Commonwealth family which would definitely provide the natural framework for the promotion and achievement of democratic values as well as effective governance at the local level in Commonwealth countries. The promotion of local democracy and decentralised, participatory government is an important element in ensuring good governance. The new Forum, which is drawn from all regions of the Commonwealth, will make an important contribution towards this goal.

The CLGF plans to involve to incorporate the organisation of several regional policy events, research activities pertaining to capacity building and activities to promote local government within the Commonwealth family. It is also intended to consolidate networks to provide a broad-based platform for major stackholders in local government. The Local Government International Bureau, in England, has significantly contributed towards the establishment of the Forum as the latest member of the Commonwealth. The objective of formulating the Forum is to build on similarities within commonwealth countries, the strong and effective local government where participation and democratic values are the base for the provision of effective urban services for sustainability.

Local government need not be seen as a threat by the central government, local government is a means to achieve a higher quality of life for citizens. Waste water treatment, garbage disposal, revenue generation, planning of urban life, urban infrastructure maintenance are the day to day preoccupation of local government to co-ordinate their action, support their efforts and promote their visibility and their recognition is an essential contribution that the Forum hope to make.

It was these considerations and accordingly a movement throughout the world towards decentralisation of government which promoted the formation of Commonwealth Local Government Forum. The CLGF wishes to promote local democracy and participation by providing a network for national and local government associations. It offers a platform for meetings and exchanges particularly between elected councillors; chief executives and specialised professional experts in the field. In future CLGF is going to expand to link up networks of related professional associations and even large municipal authorities. The idea of Commonwealth network got under way with the help of the Commonwealth Secretariat and its Management Training Services Division. Consultations also took place with the Commonwealth Parliamentary Associations and others.

The CLGF is headed today by Jacques Jobian, the International Director of the Federation of Canadian Municipalities and chairperson of the Steering Committee. The promotion of local democracy and decentralisation, and participatory government are important aspects ensuring good governance.

The Commonwealth Local Government Forum which is drawn from all the regions of commonwealth countries will definitely make an important contribution towards this goal and foster decentralisation and democracy.

CITYNET

In recent decades the large scale deterioration of living conditions for people in metropolitan and new metropolitan areas in Asia and the Pacific are attracting great attention amongst urban planners and policy makers. They have become increasingly aware that any country regardless of its level of urbanisation must treat urban development strategies and planning seriously and thereafter strengthen its urban functions. Urban areas can contribute substantially to national development if their growth is effectively managed and closely linked to national development objectives. Many cities around the world are encouraged in sister-city relationships which are primarily for cultural exchange. Recently however many cities have been seeking to exchange more substantial information such as operational schemes, technology transfer in urban planning and management, and capacity building. It is becoming increasingly evident that organised co-operation with non-governmental organisation and community-based organisation can effectively contribute to the improvement of urban management in big cities.

The Regional Network of Local Authorities for the Management of Human Settlements (CITYNET) was established to promote the exchange of expertise and experience amongst local authorities and NGOs in cities of Asia and the Pacific by expanding the concept of bilateral relationship to a multilateral network through technical co-operation on local and grassroots level to overall development and international understanding. CITYNET implements technical training activities, joint applied research documentation and dissemination of urban development experiences, a data bank and newsletter. CITYNET strengthens the institutional base at the local grassroots level, it enables cities to more effectively manage urbanisation and settlement development and to share and exchange technology and technical know-how. CITYNET also offers opportunities for internationalising participating cities. Recognising CITYNET as an efficient vehicle for human resource development among local authorities as well as for its role in the promotion of regional co-operation, the United Nations Development Project (UNDP) is generously supporting a large number of CITYNETs activities.

United Nations Economic and Social Commission for Asia and

the Pacific (ESCAP) provide technical assistance to CITYNET in formulating its work programme, project proposals and implementing activities designed to achieve objectives common to ESCAP and CITYNET.

THE INTERNATIONAL UNION OF LOCAL AUTHORITIES, IULA

The International Union of Local Authorities (IULA) is the world -wide organisation of local governments which was founded in 1913. (The aims of the IULA is to strengthen local government to defend its interest in the international field, governmental organisation to raise the standard of urban services provision and to integrate the international exchange of information and professional experts between local and regional authorities). The IULA-ASPAC section of the IULA work effectively for its members to express their concepts and define programmes on a regional basis. To enable them to do so the IULA-ASPAC region section have been established with the six regions namely North America, Latin America, Europe, Eastern Metropolitan and Middle East Africa.

The IULA-ASPAC founded in 1989 is a non-profit organisation of IULA having its own status and enjoying the official recognition of the Government of Indonesia. The main objectives of the IULA-ASPAC are in line with the basic policies of IULA to promote local autonomy and strengthen government and establish its human resources through regional sections. A number of IULA-ASPAC Centres of local government training and development were established under the umbrella of the IULA-ASPAC Section and these centres have come instrumental in achieving the objective of strengthening local government, and human resources in the Asian and Pacific region. The Centres have been the training delivery arm of the IULA-ASPAC Section. There are four main aims of the strategy as stipulated in the IULA-ASPAC Constitution.

1. to promote the affiliation with the IULA-ASPAC and other organisations in the region that direct their effort towards the promotion of local government.

2. to operate one or more Asian or Pacific Centre for Local Government Training and Development.

3. to enhance the exchange of information among members for the benefit of local government in the Asian and Pacific region.

4. to encourage the concept of participation in local affairs through the use of various media approaches.

INTERNATIONAL COUNCIL FOR LOCAL ENVIRONMENTAL ISSUES (ICLEI):

This international environmental agency of local government was established in 1990 at the World Congress for Sustainable Future. Its prime objectives are to help local authorities around the world, to increase their capacity to prevent environmental problems before they happen, respond effectively to problems when they arise and enhance the built environment at the local level. ICLEI approaches involve integrating and assisting local governments to share ideas, programmes and technology,

research and develop new management solutions. ICLEI helps local governments to meet these challenges in a creative and concrete manner by building capacity within city governments to respond to urban environmental challenges. ICLEI also maintains the information and technical exchange where members can find information about special innovative or effective environmental programmes that municipalities have adopted to protect their environment. This information is specially designed to be practically used in everyday practices of environmental management. The process of ICLEI to serve as an international environmental agency for local governments began with the establishment of Charter Committee in 1990 which is constituted by prominent leaders in local government including elected members of local governments, heads of the national association of local government and local government training institutions from all over the world. ICLEI is strategically positioned to apply knowledge and experience generated through the work of this network to start the world's major local government organisation and especially the national association of local government which constituted IULA. Through its formal association with IULA, ICLEI is in a good position to effectively integrate local government environmental initiatives in international environmental strategies.

NORTH/SOUTH AND SOUTH/NORTH EXCHANGE OF EXPERIENCES.

Sustainable urban development requires that developmental achievements should not be short lived, they should last well into the future. It involves paradigmatic change which is difficult to bring about unless many people get involved. Today, in the urban management field, several national and international networks are in operation working for sustainability in urban development. Public attention, all over, has been focused, as never before, on global warming, stratospheric ozone depletion, pollution, forest destruction, scarcity of various urban amenities and other environmental issues. We have also become more aware of the impact of external as well as internally controlled development policies and practices. The goal of sustainability requires that all countries rethink their policies and activities with respect to their impact on ecology and economic development. One of the greatest challenges faced by urban development is to ensure that cities and towns remain both economically and environmentally sustainable.

Successful implementation of various strategies are largely dependent on mutual co-operation and a good information network. It is possible to achieve positive results on urban management issues, particularly by developing meaningful and workable partnerships with all the current networks involved. Working with other networks to achieve common goals i.e. sustainable urban development would play a key role in the urban management field in approaching broad-based urban development. While we could achieve much on our own strength we would secure even greater success by using others' resources to harness the resources experience and knowledge of each of these partnership members.

Today this is the world of inter-dependence, this is the world where internationalisation of issues, ideas, information and personnel has already occurred. It is the world which is interlinked through various international networks and it is in this extremely inter-linked and interdependent world that we have to face the question of holding together.

Problems of urban poverty, unemployment, environmental programmes, ill health, urban degradation etc. are urban problems which can be solved by applying singular solutions. These are all complex urban problems which are amenable to multi-dimensional solutions from multiple perspectives and strategies. Clearly, current approaches and perspectives have not worked to that effect. One of the ways to approach these urban problems is to approach them from the perception of 'collaboration' by bringing existing networks together to attain a new approach to solve these problems. Collaboration, rather than competition and indifference may help us a great deal with management of such urban problems. Thus today collaboration provides additional ways of enlarging mechanisms that can acquire importance in order to pursue their mission in a long term, and sustainable manner. Therefore, collaboration and partnership amongst existing networks to solve some of the pressing urban problems of our times are essential. It is very difficult to provide a single or simple definition of collaboration, however we have to develop some new kind of format of working together on specific issues and then define such collaborations.

Collaboration involves the common goal that various networks work together to solve complex urban problems. Each network collaboration has a concrete boundary in time and space and can work around the specific urban problem. However, to create effective workable partnerships, it is important to recognise the differences and limitations of each partner in the network. Today all these networks have institutional and organisational frameworks, expertise and data-base. They can form the basis of new appropriate partnerships. Partnerships should create a climate in which other partnerships can grow. We must move from the independent to integration. Only then will there be true partnership which will mean breaking new ground. However, it is essential to build up a framework and clear understanding in this connection.

It is important to look at the city development from a more positive view point. We must try to make cities more sustainable and try to improve the quality of life for citizens. If sustainable urban development is to mean anything at all, it will have to involve good workable partnerships with sustainability as the feature. Expert knowledge of those who have been involved in creating and working in partnerships must be widely and broadly shared. Working through existing networks, we have seen that there is a comprehensive knowledge available and if we can harness it properly a lot can be achieved.

The following areas require attention to develop co-operation amongst existing international networks:

1. Improve the quality and effectiveness of existing networks for sustainable urban development.

2. Identify opportunities for new areas of co-operation amongst existing networks with similar objectives.

3. Encourage flexibility and co-operation.

4. Recognise the importance of each network and value each partner's contribution.

5. Develop co-operation and co-ordination among existing networks and see that networks also benefit themselves.

6. Existing networks must develop a new, appropriate form of partnership and should not be exploited but should create the climate in which other network partners can grow and develop.

INTEGRATED ENERGY STRATEGIES FOR URBAN AREAS
SEMINAR REPORT
The Centre for Sustainable Energy, Bristol City Council and Avon County Council, UK.

The context - climate change and the Earth Summit
Energy was an important element of debate at the Earth Summit in terms of its supply, use and its environmental impacts including climate change, acid rain and nuclear waste.

The richer northern nations have paid much attention to the environmental aspects of sustainable development and little to the issues relating to poverty. For example, the people of the South African townships are looking forward to obtaining decent homes with modern energy services. Does the new South African Government have a sustainable energy strategy that will respond to these needs? - or will they be led down non-sustainable routes by foreign 'aid providers' and multi-national energy supply companies?

The UK is not a model for the South Africans to follow. In Bristol, an outwardly prosperous city, there are still large pockets of people living in relative poverty. In north and south alike, the proportion of people living in poverty is as important an indicator of progress towards sustainable development as the levels of carbon dioxide in the atmosphere.

We are focusing on urban environments. The world trend is for more people to live in cities because of the attraction of a wide range of jobs, resources and services. Many urban dwellers do not have full access to the "good things" cities have to offer, including the services that energy provides.

Case studies of Bristol, UK and Adelaide, Australia are used to illustrate approaches to integrated energy strategies in urban areas.

Building energy efficient housing in Sweden

CASE STUDY TWO- BRISTOL
Trevor Houghton, Centre for Sustainable Energy, CREATE Centre, Bristol.

Bristol Energy and Environment Plan

The Bristol Energy and Environment Plan (BEEP) is Bristol's integrated sustainable energy strategy. This has been based around answering four questions:

The Key Actors - bringing them together

In the diagram, the key actors that we identified are listed. In Bristol most of these organisations were already co-operating through an organisation called the Avon and Bristol Energy Action Campaign. It was through the efforts of this body that European Commission funding for BEEP was secured. However, the representation on this body was only at officer / middle management level. To step up the pace of change and to implement BEEP, a body with higher level representation in member organisations was required, ie director / senior management level.

To this end a new body called the Bristol Environment and Energy Trust (BEET) has been established. BEET has trustees who are board members of companies, heads of NGOs, and heads of the local council directorates. This means that BEET has a way into many of the major institutions in the City of Bristol.

At the working end of BEET are a number of action groups covering areas such as energy, recycling and waste, biodiversity and transport. The officers and technicians who have a good understanding of implementing programmes are represented on these working groups. Between working groups and the Trustees is a steering committee, including BEET's two employees who have an overview of its operation.

Cross sector initiatives of this type are an effective way of achieving concerted action but they also face problems. Chief among these are the conflicting cultures of different types of member organisations. Building tolerance and trust between individuals is an important part of the successful operation of institutions such as BEET.

Barriers to change - the one-stop-shop approach

As shown in the diagram, there are a range of barriers to change. The approach we take is to look at it from the energy users standpoints and to provide a one-stop-shop that will take them over all the main barriers in one go. We are putting forward the concept of what we call the Energy Club; this is an energy service company or ESCO serving the domestic energy user. The role of the Energy Club is to:

✪ involve participation of energy users in the club as 'members' of the club with some influence over how it operates

✪ provide financial services to members in the form of low interest / no interest loan packages for investments in energy facilities

✪ provide a comprehensive range of energy services to members including total energy packages, discounts on goods and services (achieved through bulk purchase), organising contractors / installers etc.

The services provided to owner occupiers and social housing tenants would be different because of the legal differences in tenure and the credit standing of householders.

The financial services of the Energy Club are backed by some of the money now available from the UK private energy companies. There are now regulatory requirements placed on UK electricity and gas companies to invest in demand side measures.

Transport And Energy in Bristol

Transport accounts for approximately 25% of energy use in Bristol with many associated environmental impacts.

Avon County Council, a member of BEET, is the regional authority for the area and is responsible for transport. The Council drew up a Transport Plan in 1993 and 1994. It contains a specific target of minimising CO2 emissions from transport to only a 13% increase by the year 2023. This is an ambitious target bearing in mind the high projected traffic levels in a city with one of the highest levels of car ownership in Europe.

The Transport Plan includes an integrated approach to developing public transport facilities including a new Light Rapid Transit system. There are a number of measures to discourage car use. Like all energy management issues, the Transport Plan also relies on promoting behavioural changes. Overall its implementation depends on the co-operation of the UK Government which in a number of matters does not share the same transport priorities.

Land Use Planning and Energy in Bristol

Bristol City Council is the local authority which has the main powers of controlling development in the area. The Council is also a member of BEET and in 1993 developed a local land use development plan which recognises its effects on energy use. It contains specific measures to reduce energy use in new buildings in development applications. It also attempts to direct developments which by their nature and position to other facilities in the city will minimise the need to travel.

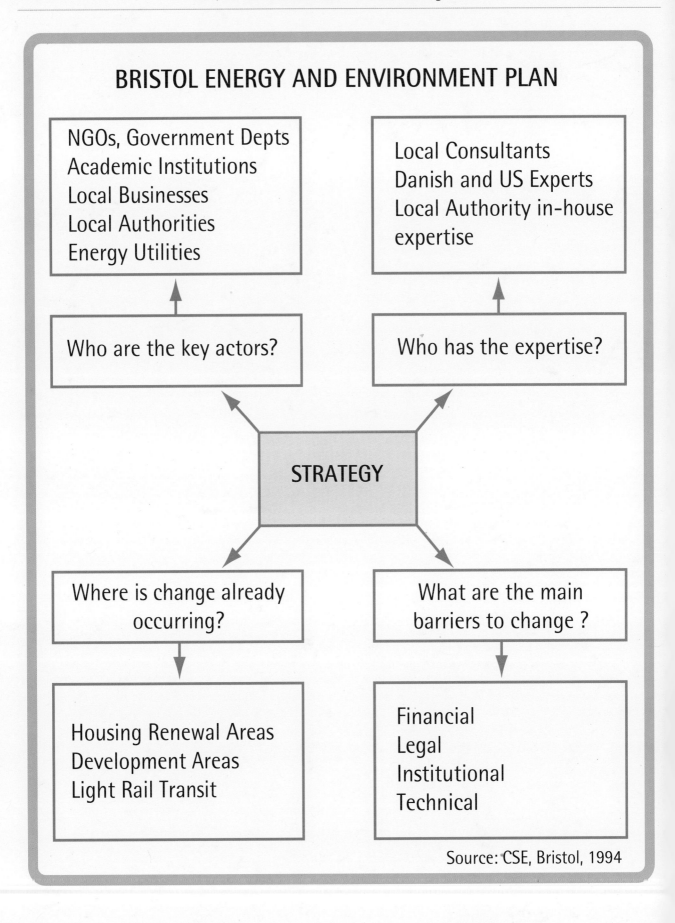

BRISTOL ENERGY AND ENVIRONMENT PLAN

NGOs, Government Depts
Academic Institutions
Local Businesses
Local Authorities
Energy Utilities

Local Consultants
Danish and US Experts
Local Authority in-house expertise

Who are the key actors?

Who has the expertise?

STRATEGY

Where is change already occurring?

What are the main barriers to change ?

Housing Renewal Areas
Development Areas
Light Rail Transit

Financial
Legal
Institutional
Technical

Source: CSE, Bristol, 1994

DELEGATES LIST

LOCAL AUTHORITIES

ARGENTINA
JORGE JOSE CASTELLS
MUNICIPAL BUENOS AIRES
CONCEJAL, PERU 13D,
BUENOS AIRES,
REP ARGENTINA
ARGENTINA

AUSTRALIA
ALDERMAN
CHRISTOPHER DOUGLAS
ADELAIDE CITY COUNCIL,
URBAN PLANNING
CONSULTANT, 55 SYMONDS
PLACE, ADELAIDE, AUSTRALIA
5001 AUSTRALIA

GRAHAM ADAMS
ADELAIDE CITY COUNCIL
GPO BOX 1047,
ADELAIDE,
AUSTRALIA 5001

MS SUZIE HERZBERG
ADELAIDE CITY COUNCIL
URBAN PLANNING
CONSULTANT,
TOWN HALL GPO BOX 2252,
ADELAIDE, 5001 AUSTRALIA

BERNIE COTTER
MUNICIPAL CONSERVATION
ASSOCIATION VICE
PRESIDENT, C/O 12 BARNEY
ST, DOWNER, CANBERRA ACT
2602, AUSTRALIA

PRESIDENT WAYNE WESCOTT
MUNICIPAL CONSERVATION
ASSOCIATION, 247 FLINDERS
LANE, MELBOURNE,
AUSTRALIA

GREG HEYS
NEWCASTLE CITY COUNCIL
COUNCILLOR, 5 LOVELL
PARADE, SHORTLAND NSW
2307 AUSTRALIA

DEPUTY LORD MAYOR
HENRY TSANG
SYDNEY CITY COUNCIL
TOWN HALL, GEORGE STREET
SYDNEY, NSW 2000,
AUSTRALIA

LEON BYASS
MFP AUSTRALIA
ADELAIDE, AUSTRALIA

AUSTRIA
KARL NEIDERL,
AMT FUR UMWELSCHUTZ
DER STAETT GRAZ ECO PROFIT
GRAZ, GREISGRASS 11
A-8001 GRAZ AUSTRIA

BELGIUM
JULIETTE DE VILLERS
COMMUNDE D'ANDERLECHT
ADMINISTRATION
COMMUNALE D'ANDERLECHT
DU TERRITOIRE, PALACE DU
CONSEIL, 1070 ANDERLECHT,
BRUSSELS BELGIUM

BRAZIL
MUNICIPAL MAYOR,
ANDERS WILLY TRINDADE
BELEM PARA CITY
PUBLIC HEALTH SECRETARY,
TRAVESSA MAURITY 1361,
BELEM PARA, BRAZIL

ALFREDO SIRKYS
PREFEITURA DA CIDADE
DO RIO DE JANEIRO
ENVIRONMENTAL SECRETARY,
RUA AFONSO CAVALCANTI
455 1247, RIO DE JANEIRO,
BRAZIL

PATRICIA ANA KRANZ
PREFEITURA DA CIDADE DO
RIO DE JANEIRO,
INTERNATIONAL
COOPERATION OFFICIAL, RUA
AFONSO CAVALCANTI 455
2247, RIO DE JANEIRO,
BRAZIL

PAULA CARMO
PREFEITURA DA CIDADE DO
RIO DE JANEIRO
ENVIRONMENTAL
COOPERATION COORDINATOR,
RUA AFONSO CAVALCANTI
455 1247, RIO DE JANEIRO,
BRAZIL

FERREIRA JOAO LUIZ
SALVADOR PREFEITURE
MUNICIPAL
AV SATA SATEMBRO 89 38
AIDAR, SALVADOR, BRAZIL

MAYOR PAULO MALUF
SAO PAULO BRAZIL
MR REYNALDO EMYGDIO DE
BARROS
SAO PAULO
C/O DR ALINDO PHILLIPI JR,
SECRETARIA DO VERDE O DO
MEIO AMBIENTE, PMSP - AV
PAULISTA 2073 - CONJUNTO
NACIONAL, PISO SUPERIOR,
SAO PAULO, BRAZIL

MR WERNER E ZULAUF
SAO PAULO
C/O DR ARLINDO PHILIPP
JNR, SECRETARIA DO VERDE E
DO MEIO AMBIENTE, PMSP
AV PAULISTA 2073,
SAO PAULO, BRAZIL

CANADA
RASHEDA NAWAZ
CITY OF OTTAWA
CHAIR OF HEALTHY
SUSTAINABLE COMMUNITIES,
12 HYDE PARK WAY, NEPEAN
ONTARIO, CANADA

DR PRATIBHA METHA
ICLEI
C/O ICLEI, CITY HALL,
EAST TOWER 8TH FLOOR,
TORONTO, CANADA

COUNCILLOR JOAN KING
METRO TORONTO,
TORONTO, CANADA

WILLIAM LAUTENBACH
MUNICIPALITY OF SUDBURY
REGIONAL DIRECTOR OF
PLANNING & DEVELOP.,
PO BOX 3700 STATION "A",
SUDBURY PROVINCE,
ONTARIO P3A 5W5, CANADA

DALE TURVEY
REGION OF
HAMILTON-WENTWORTH
COMMISSIONER OF
TRANS/ENV SERVICES, 330
WENTWOTH STREET NORTH
HAMILTON, ONTARIO,
CANADA

CHINA
MR RUAN JIQING
WUHAN COUNCIL WUHAN
CHINA

MS MAI FAN LI
WUHAN COUNCIL WUHAN
CHINA

DEPUTY MAYOR HUA
FANG CHEN
WUHAN MUNICIPAL
GOVERNMENT
WUHAN CITY, 130 YANJIANG
AVE, WUHAN CHINA, 430014

CZECH REPUBLIC
ZDENEK MEISNER
MUNICIPALITY OF PRAGUE
ARCHITECT, KOSTELNI 8/360,
PRAGUE CZECH LAND
CZECH REP

MIROSLAV GREGOR
PARDUBICE COUNCIL
CHIEF OF FINANCIAL AND
STRATEGY DEPT.,
PERNSTYNSKE NAM 1,
PARDUBICE, CZECH REP

DENMARK
ERIK MOLLER
CITY OF AALBORG
PROJECT OFFICER
VESTERBRO 14, BOX 765,
AALBORG, DENMARK

KAJ KJAER
CITY OF AALBORG MAYOR
VESTERRO 14, 9000
AALBORG, DENMARK

MR JAN IPLAND
CITY OF AALBORG
CITY ARCHITECT,
VESTERBRO 14, 9000
AALBORG, DENMARK

PREBEN LASSEN
COPENHAGEN COUNTY
COUNCIL
COUNCILLOR,
STATIONSPARKEN 27
DK-2600, GLOSTRU,
COPENHAGEN, DENMARK

ECUADOR
DR ARALDO VIDAL
QUITO CITY COUNCIL
QUITO CITY
COUNCIL MEMBER,
MUNICIPALIDAD DE QUITO,
ASESORIA, QUITO, ECUADOR

FIJI
LORD MAYOR MANOA DOBUI
SUVA CITY
SUVA CITY COUNCIL
GPO BOX 176,
SUVA, FIJI

ANARE GUKILAU
SUVA CITY COUNCIL
COUNCILLOR, GPO BOX 176,
SUVA, FIJI

ARVIND PARMAR
SUVA CITY COUNCIL
ASSISTANT DIRECTOR
ENGINEERING SVS, GPO BOX
176, SUVA, FIJI

FINLAND
PEKKA JALKANEN
ASSOCIATION OF FINNISH
LOCAL AUTHORITIES
MANAGER OF
ENVIRONMENTAL AFFAIRS,
TOINGN LINJA 14 00530,
HELSINKI, FINLAND

KARI SILFVERBERG
HELSKINKI CITY
COORDINATOR FOR
INTERNATIONAL
COOPERATION,
STURENKATU 25 00510,
HELSINKI, FINLAND

FRANCE
AGBESSI MARIE
COMMUNAIRE URBAINE LILLE
CHARGEE DE FORMATION,
CHATEAU DALLE DUMONT, BP
15 59117 WERVICQ-SUD,
FRANCE

ISABELLE ROMAN
CONSEIL REGIONAL DE HAUTE
NORMANDIE
ENV. CONSEILLER
TECHNIQUE, 25 BD
GAMBETTA BP, 1129-76174,
RONEN, FRANCE

GERMANY
DR PETER HELLER
FREIBURG MUNICIPALITY
UMWELT-BURGERMEISTER
RATHAUS, RATHAUSPLATZ
2-4, FREIBURG D-79098,
GERMANY

LADY MAYOR
MRS BEATE WEBER
HEIDELBERG CITY
RATHAUS, MARKTPLATZ 10,
POSTFACH, 105520 D-69045,
HEIDELBERG, GERMANY

INDIA
MR CHAVAN
BARODA MUNICIPAL CORP.
RAJMAUEL ROAD, BARODA
GUJARAT, INDIA

MAYORESS NIRMALA
SAMANT PRABHAVALKAR
BOMBAY MUNICIPAL
CORPORATION
MAYORESS OF BOMBAY
(MUMBAI)
MUNICIPAL CORPORATION
OFFICER, MAHAPALIKA
MARG.FORT., MUMBAI,
400 028 INDIA

KIRON SAKAR BAROI
MUNICIPAL CORPORATION OF
GTR BOMBAY
ADDITIONAL MUNICIPAL
COMMISSIONER, MUNICIPAL
HEAD OFFICES, MAHAPALIKA
MARG., BOMBAY, 400 001
INDIA

IRELAND (NORTHERN)
COUNCILLOR
ARCHIE MCKELVEY
BANBRIDGE DISTRICT
COUNCIL
19 EDENVALE AVENUE,
BANBRIDGE
NORTHERN IRELAND

IRELAND (SOUTHERN)
COUNTY COUNCILLOR
JACK LARKIN
FINGAL COUNTY COUNCIL
46049 UPPER O'CONNELL
STREET, DUBLIN, IRELAND

COUNTY COUNCILLOR
JOAN MAHER
FINGAL COUNTY COUNCIL
46-49 UPPER O'CONNELL
STREET, DUBLIN, IRELAND

COUNTY COUNCILLOR
MICHAEL O'DONOVAN
FINGAL COUNTY COUNCIL
46-49 UPPER O'CONNELL
STREET, DUBLIN, IRELAND

JAPAN
MR TAKASHI YAMASHIRO
KANAGAWA PREFECTURE
CHIEF ENVIRONMENT POLICY
DIVISION, KANAGAWA
PREFECTURE, JAPAN

MR SATOSHI NAKAZONO
KITAKYUSHU CITY
JAPAN

MR HISAO OGAWA
SAITAMA PREFECTURE
SENIOR ADMINISTRATOR,
ENVIRONMENTAL DEPT.,
SAITAMA PREFECTURE,
JAPAN

MR IWAZO INOUE
SAITAMA PREFECTURE
EXECUTIVE DIRECTOR,
POLLUTION CENTRE,
SAITAMA PREFECTURE,
JAPAN

MR TATSUSHI ARAI
YAMANASHI PREFECTURE
ADMINISTRATIVE DIVISION
FOR ENVIRONMENT,
YAMANASHI PREFECTURE,
JAPAN

MR TSUTOMU NISHITANI
YAMANASHI PREFECTURE
TECHNICAL DIRECTOR
ENVIRONMENTAL
DEPARTMENT, YAMANASHI
PREFECTURE, JAPAN

JORDAN
MANSOUR ABU DALHOUM
MUNICIPALITY OF AMMAN
DIRECTOR OF FOOD AND ENV
CONTROL, SWAILEH PO BOX
132, AMMAN, JORDAN

MOHAMMED KISWANI
MUNICIPALITY OF AMMAN
PROJECT ENGINEER, ALJOFEH
P O BOX 132, AMMAN,
JORDAN

MOHAMMED NAJDAWI
MUNICIPALITY OF AMMAN
DIRECTOR OF PROFESSIONS
AND ADS DEPT,
IM AL-SUMMAG,
PO BOX 749, AMMAN,
JORDAN

SULTAN KHLAIFAT,
MUNICIPALITY OF AMMAN,
UNDER SECRETARY, SWAILEH
PO BOX 132 AMMAN,
JORDAN

KENYA
DICK WAWERU
NAIROBI CITY
NAIROBI, KENYA

SARAH AJWANG
NAIROBI CITY
NAIROBI, KENYA

ZIPPORAH WANDERA
NAIROBI CITY
NAIROBI, KENYA

MALAWI
NICHOLAS NGWIRA
MZUZU CITY COUNCIL
TOWN CLERK AND CHIEF
EXECUTIVE, P O BOX 1,
MZUZU, MALAWI

MAURITIUS
KRISHMA KISTMEN
PAMPLEMOUSSES RIVIERE DE
REMPART COUNCIL,
CHAIRMAN,
ROYAL ROAD, MAPOU,
PAMPLEMOUSSES RIV DU
REMPART, MAURITIUS

SHEIK ABDOOL RAHIM
HOSSEINALLY,
PAMPLEMOUSSES RIVIERE DU
REMPART COUNCIL,
DEPUTY SECRETARY,
ROYAL ROAD, MAPOU,
PAMPLESOUSSE RIV DU
REMPART, MAURITIUS

AWOTAR PREM
THE BLACK RIVER DISTRICT
COUNCIL CHAIRMAN
VILLAGE HALL ROAD, FLIC EN
FLAC, MAURITIUS

MEXICO
FERNANDO MENENDEZ-
GARZA
MEXICAN CITY GOVT
ORGANISATION EXECUTIVE
SECRETARY, PLAZA DE LA
CONSTITUCION NO. 1, 3ER
PISO, COL. CENTRO,
MEXICO, D.F.

NAMIBIA
MR A DU PLESSIS
WINDHOEK COUNCIL
CITY PLANNER, P O BOX 59,
WINDHOEK, NAMIBIA

MR SWART
WINDHOEK COUNCIL
CHIEF TOWN AND REGIONAL
PLANNING, PRIVATE BAG
13289, WINDHOEK, NAMIBIA

NETHERLANDS (THE)
BERT BOVENKERK
DEN HAAG–THE HAGUE
MANAGER DEPT OF
ENVIRONMENTAL AFFAIRS,
POSTBUS 19350, THE HAGUE,
NETHERLANDS

NEW ZEALAND
ANN MAGEE
WAITAKERE CITY COUNCIL
MANAGER STRATEGY AND
DEVELOPMENT, PRIVATE BAG
93109, HINDERSON,
WAITAKERE CITY,
NEW ZEALAND

LYNN JONES
WAITAKERE CITY COUNCIL
COORDINATION AND
PROJECTS MANAGER,
PRIVATE BAG 93109,
HENDERSON,
WAITAKERE CITY,
NEW ZEALAND

N B LEWTHWAITE
WELLINGTON CITY COUNCIL
MANAGER ENVIRONMENT &
RESOURCE MGMT SVS,
ENVIRONMENTAL COUNCIL
OFFICES, 101 WAKEFIELD ST,
PO BOX 2199, WELLINGTON,
NEW ZEALAND

PAPUA NEW GUINEAU
BOB KIKI
NATIONAL CAPITAL
DISTRICT COMMISSION
COMMISSIONER, P O BOX
7270, BOROKO NCD,
PORT MORESBY,
PAPUA NEW GUINEA

DAVID UNAGI
NATIONAL CAPITAL DISTRICT
COMMISSION
MAYOR
P O BOX 7270, BOROKO NCD,
PORT MORESBY,
PAPUA NEW GUINEA

FRANCIS MUGUGIA MR
NATIONAL CAPITAL DISTRICT
COMMISSION
SENIOR EXECUTIVE STAFF, P O
BOX 7270, BOROKO NCD,
PORT MORESBY,
PAPUA NEW GUINEA

PERU
MAYOR LUIS
QUERRERO FIGUEROA
CAJAMARCA CITY
JR DE LA CRUZ DE PIEDRA
613, CAJAMARCA, PERU

OSCAR ELISEO MADELIUS
RODRIGUEX
MUNICIPAL PROVINCIAL
DE CALLAO
REGIDOR PROVINCIAL, JR
SUPE 521 SANTA MARINA
SUR CALLAO, CALLAO, PERU

PHILLIPINES
ANA ALFONSO
CEBU CITY GOVERNMENT
PROGRAM DIRECTOR - HILLY
LAND COMMISSION, 4TH
FLOOR CITY HALL BUILDING,
CEBU CITY, PHILIPPINES

RENE SANAPO
CEBU CITY GOVERNMENT
SECRETARY TO THE MAYOR,
OFFICE OF THE MAYOR, CEBU,
PHILIPPINES

SAUL JOHN
CEBU CITY GOVERNMENT
CITY ADMINISTRATOR,
OFFICE OF THE MAYOR,
CEBU CITY, PHILIPPINES

MR LUIS VILLAFUERTE
CAMARINES SUR
FORMER GOVENOR,
PHILLIPINES

POLAND
JADWIGA KOPEC
CITY OF GDANSK
HEAD DEPT OF
ENVIRONMENTAL
PROTECTION, UL NOWE
OGRODY 8/12, 80-958
GDANSK, POLAND

KAZI MIERZ POREBSKI
WARSAW REGION
LOCAL PARLIAMENT
CHAIRMAN
PL. BANKOWY 3/5 00-950,
WARSAW, POLAND

WITOLD SIELEWICZ
WARSAW REGION
LOCAL PARLIAMENT
MEMBER, PL. BANKOWY 3/5
00-950, WARSAW, POLAND

PORTUGAL
DEPUTY LORD MAYOR
MR RUI GODINHO
LISBON MUNICIPALITY
PRACA DO MUNICIPIO 1194
LISBON, PORTUGAL

RUSSIA
VLADAMIR NAZIN
PERM CITY HEAD OF
ADMINISTRATION OF KIROV
DISTRICT, KIROVOGRADSKAYA
STR 33, PERM RUSSIA

ALEXEI VICTOROVICTH
MARTINOV
ST PETERSBURG
CHIEF EXPERT OF EXTERNAL
AFFAIRS CTTEE, SMOLHY ST
PETERSBURG 193060, RUSSIA

ALEXEI LEONIDAITCH KUDRIN
ST PETERSBURG
CITY COUNCIL
DEPUTY CHAIRMAN OF ST
PETERSBURG, SMOLHY ST
PETERSBURG 193060, RUSSIA

ANATOLY ALEXEIVITAN
LIKHTIN
ST PETERSBURG
CITY COUNCIL DEPUTY HEAD
OF LOCAL ADMINISTRATION,
SMOLHY ST PETERSBURG
193060, RUSSIA

SAUDI ARABIA
ADEL BADAWI
ALMADINAH MUNICIPALITY
P O BOX 4663, ALMADINAH,
KSA, SAUDI ARABIA

AWAD HADI
ALMADINAH MUNICIPALITY
HEALTH ENV. GENERAL
ADMIN MGR, P O BOX 2611,
ALMADINA KSA,
SAUDI ARABIA

SCOTLAND
ALISON CAMERON
ABERDEEN DISTRICT COUNCIL
TWINNING OFFICER, TOWN
HOUSE, BROAD STREET,
ABERDEEN, SCOTLAND

WILLIAM FRASER
ABERDEEN DISTRICT COUNCIL
CHAIRMAN, INTERNATIONAL
COMMITTEE, TOWN HOUSE
BROAD ST, SCOTLAND

ROSEMARY MCKENNA
COSLA SENIOR
VICE-PRESIDENT,
ROSEBERY HOUSE,
9 HAYMARKET TERRACE,
EDINBURGH, SCOTLAND

COUNCILLOR
JULIA STURROCK
DUNDEE DISTRICT
21 CITY SQUARE, DUNDEE,
SCOTLAND

ALISON SILK
DUNDEE DISTRICT COUNCIL
21 CITY SQUARE,
DUNDEE, SCOTLAND

EDWIN REAVLEY
EDINBURGH SCOTTISH OFFICE
ASSISTANT SECRETARY
ENVIRONMENT DEPARTMENT,
83 PRINCESS STREET,
EDINBURGH, SCOTLAND

ALISON TRAINER
GLASGOW CITY COUNCIL
POLICY DEVELOPMENT
OFFICER, CITY CHAMBERS,
GLASGOW G2 1DU, SCOTLAND

COUNCILLOR
TONY McCARTNEY
GLASGOW CITY COUNCIL
CITY CHAMBERS, GLASGOW
G2 1DU, SCOTLAND

SLOVAKIA
MRS OLGA PETKOVA
CITY OF BRATISLAVA
DIRECTOR DEPARTMENT,
HLBUKA 2, 812 35
BRATISLAVA,
SLOVAK REPUBLIC, SLOVAKIA

VICE LORD MAYOR
PETER BENUSKA
CITY OF BRATISLAVA
CHIEF ARCHITECT, DIPL. ING
ARCH PRIMACIALNE NAM 1,
814 99 BRATISLAVA,
SLOVAKIA

SLOVENIA
LORD MAYOR JOZE STRGAR
CITY ASSEMBLY SLOVENIA
MESTNI TRG 1, 61000
LJUBLJANA, SLOVENIA

SOUTH AFRICA
DAVID BRADLEY
CITY OF CAPE TOWN
DEPUTY CITY ENGINEER
(SERVICES), P O BOX 1694,
CAPE TOWN, SOUTH AFRICA

GILL BOLTON
CITY OF CAPE TOWN
ASSISTANT CITY
ADMINISTRATOR, PO BOX 298,
CAPE TOWN,
SOUTH AFRICA

GUY BODDINGTON
CITY OF CAPE TOWN
PRINCIPAL PLANNER - ENV.
MANAGEMENT GP, CITY
PLANNER DEPT, BOX 1494,
CAPE TOWN, SOUTH AFRICA

PETER DE TOLLY
CITY OF CAPE TOWN
DEPUTY CITY PLANNER,
P O BOX 1694, CAPE TOWN
5000, SOUTH AFRICA

TOLLY DU TOIT
CITY OF CAPE TOWN
DIRECTOR OF
ENVIRONMENTAL HEALTH,
PO BOX 2810,
CAPE TOWN 8000,
SOUTH AFRICA

DR DEBRA ROBERTS
CITY OF DURBAN
MANAGER ENVIRONMENT,
P O BOX 680, DURBAN 4000,
SOUTH AFRICA

YASMIN VAN SCHIANDING
JOHANNESBURG CITY
COUNCIL
DIRECTOR ENVIRONMENTAL
HEALTH, PB 1477,
JOHANNESBURG 2000,
SOUTH AFRICA

SOUTH KOREA
JUNG HOON KIM
KWACHON CITY
RESEARCHER, DEPT OF
URBAN PLANNING, SEOUL
DEVELOPMENT INST., 171
SAMSUNG-DONG, KANGNAM
GU, SEOUL, SOUTH KOREA

TONG-KI WOO
SEOUL CITY GOVERNMENT
RESEARCH DIRECTOR OF
SEOUL DEVELOPMENT, 171
SAMSEONG-DONG,
KANGHAM-GU, SEOUL
135-090, SOUTH KOREA

SPAIN
JORDI BORJA
CITY OF BARCELONA
COMMISSIONER FOREIGN
AFFAIRS, PLACA SANT JAUME
2, BARCELONA, SPAIN

KENTY RICHARDSON
GOVERNMENT OF CATALONIA
COORDINATOR INTERNAL
AFFAIRS, AV DIAGONAL 525,
08029 BARCELONA, SPAIN

ANTONIO ALARCON
METROPOLITANA AREA
BARCELONA
CARRER 62, NUM 420
SECTOR A, ZONA FRANCA,
BARCELONA, SPAIN

SRI LANKA
MR L SARATH GUNAPALA
SILVA
COLOMBO MINICIPAL
COUNCIL
MEMBER OF THE COUNCIL
COLOMBO MUNICIPAL
COUNCIL, TOWN HALL
COLOMBO-07, SRI LANKA

K T D MALLANAARACHCHI
COLOMBO MUNICIPAL
COUNCIL
SUPERINTENDENT ENGINEER,
PROFESSIONAL AFFAIR
CORDINATOR, COLOMBO
MUNICIPAL COUNCIL, TOWN
HALL COLOMBO-07,
SRI LANKA

MR H J M S PORERA
COLOMBO MUNICIPAL
COUNCIL
MEMBER OF THE COUNCIL,
COLOMBO MUNICIPAL
COUNCIL, TOWN HALL,
COLOMBO - 07 SRI LANKA

ST LUCIA
A AUGUSTE
CASTRIES
CITY COUNCIL
PRESIDENT
CLGA, CASTRIES CITY
COUNCIL, PEYNIER ST.
CASTRIES, ST LUCIA

SWEDEN
TOMMY MANSSON
ENVIRONMENTAL ADVISORY
COUNCIL
DEPUTY DIRECTOR, MINISTRY
OF ENVIRONMENT, S-10333
STOCKHOLM, SWEDEN

KERSTIN SVENSON
GOTENBURG CITY BOARD
CITY COMMISSIONER FOR
THE ENV.
KOMMUNSTYRELSEN, S-404
82, GOTENBURG, SWEDEN

CHRISTINA RAMBERG
GOTHENBORG CITY BOARD
ENVIRONMENTAL PLANNING
DIRECTOR, BOX 360, S-40125,
GOTHENBURG, SWEDEN

LARS BERGGRUND
GOTHENBURG CITY BOARD
SENIOR COMPREHENSIVE
PLANNER, STADSBYGGNAD-
SKONTORET BOX 2554,
S-40317, GOTHENBURG,
SWEDEN

LISA SUNDELL
GOTHENBURG CITY BOARD
LOCAL AGENDA 21 PROJECT
LEADER. AGENDA 21,
STADSKANSLIET S-404 82,
GOTHENBURG, SWEDEN

EVA GRUNDELIUS
SWEDISH ASSOCIATION OF
LOCAL AUTHORITIES
HEAD OF SECTION FOR
HOUSING URBAN &
REGIONAL PLANNING AND
ENVIRONMENT, BOX 6538
UMEA, SWEDEN

LINDA FIDJELAND
SWEDISH ASSOCIATION OF
LOCAL AUTHORITIES
BIOLOGIST MSC, 118 82
STOCKHOLM, SWEDEN

TANZANIA
LORD MAYOR
KITWANA KONDO
DAR ES SALAAM CITY
COUNCIL, HILL ROAD NO 16,
DAR ES SALAAM, P O BOX
9084, TANZANIA

TRINIDAD & TOBAGO
DR VICTOR KING
TRINIDAD & TOBAGO ASSOC.
37 HONECROFT ROAD,
LONDON SE26 5QN, UK

THAILAND
MS MAEY-ING AMARANGKUL
CHIANG MAI
MUNICIPAL COUNCIL CITY
CLERK, CHIANGMAI
MUNICIPAL OFFICES, MUNAG
CHIANG MAI 5000, 5030,
THAILAND

TURKEY
MS AYDAM BULCA ERIM
GREATER ANKARA
MUNICIPALITY
MEMBER BOARD OF
CONSULTANTS, GUNES SOKAK
NO 6/1, TURKEY

UGANDA
LORD MAYOR
MICHAEL ODWAR
GULU MUNICIPAL COUNCIL
P O BOX 140, GULU, UGANDA

A J BYANDALA
KAMPALA CITY COUNCIL
DEPUTY TOWN CLERK,
P O BOX 417, KAMPALA
UGANDA

GORDON RWESIGYE
KAMPALA CITY COUNCIL
CITY ENGINEER, P O BOX 417
KAMPALA, UGANDA

UK
ANDREA BAILEY
AVON COUNTY COUNCIL
ENVIRONMENTAL OFFICER,
P O BOX 46, MIDDLEGATE
WHITEFRIARS,
LEWINS MEAD, UK

COLIN FUDGE
BATH CITY COUNCIL
DEPARTMENT OF
ENVIRONMENTAL SVS, BATH
CITY COUNCIL,
ABBEY CHAMBERS, UK

SARAH KIRKPATRICK
BEDFORD BOROUGH COUNCIL
ENVIRONMENTAL
DEVELOPMENT OFFICER,
TOWN HALL, ROOM 556,
BEDFORD, MK40 1SJ, UK

MS REGINA DUGGAN/CLLR
JANE SLOWEY
BIRMINGHAM CITY COUNCIL,
HEAD OF ENV. AND
STRATEGIC PLANNING, 67
CURZON STREET,
BIRMINGHAM B4 7DH, UK

COUNCILLOR JACK FOSTER
BOLTON METROPOLITAN
BOROUGH COUNCIL
CHAIRMAN OF PLANNING
AND ENGINEERING SVS,
TOWN HALL, BOLTON,
BL1 1RU, UK

RAY JEFFERSON
BOLTON METROPOLITAN
BOROUGH COUNCIL
DIRECTOR PLANNING AND
ENGINEERING SVS,
TOWN HALL, BOLTON,
BL1 1RU, UK

JIM METCALF
BURY METROPOLITAN
BOROUGH COUNCIL
BOROUGH PLANNING
OFFICER, CRAIG HOUSE,
BANK STREET, BURY, UK

NORMAN DOOTSON
BURY METROPOLITAN
BOROUGH COUNCIL
ENVIRONMENTAL HEALTH
MANAGER
CRAIG HOUSE, BANK STREET,
BURY BL9 5ES, UK

CLLR SHAUN TOPHAM/PAM
WARHURST
CALDERDALE BOROUGH,
NORTHGATE HOUSE, HALIFAX
HX1 1UN, UK

CLLR TONY MELLOR
CALDERDALE BOROUGH
NORTHGATE HOUSE, HALIFAX
HX1 1UN, UK

CLLR STEWART GREENWOOD
CALDERDALE BOROUGH
COUNCIL
NORTHGATE HOUSE,
HALIFAX HX1 1UN, UK

MR KEITH ALDRIDGE
CALDERDALE BOROUGH
COUNCIL
SENIOR MANAGER,
NORTHGATE HOUSE, HALIFAX
HX1 1UN, UK

MR STEVE BHOWRICK
CALDERDALE BOROUGH
COUNCIL
ENVIRONMENTAL
COORDINATOR, NORTHGATE
HOUSE, HALIFAX HX1 1UN,
UK

CARMEL EGAN
CAMBRIDGE CITY COUNCIL
POLICY OFFICER,
THE GUILDHALL, CAMBRIDGE
CITY COUNCIL, CAMBS UK

SUE WOODSFORD
CAMBRIDGE CITY COUNCIL
ENVIRONMENTAL EDUCATION
& PUBLICITY OFF.,
CHIEF EXECUTIVE'S DEPT,
CAMBRIDGE, UK

BRET WILLERS
CARDIFF CITY COUNCIL
ENVIRONMENTAL POLICY
COORDINATOR, ROOM 229,
CHIEF EXECS DEPT,
CARDIFF, UK

BERNARD PAYNE
CHESHIRE COUNTY COUNCIL
CHIEF PLANNING OFFICER.
ENVIRONMENTAL
STRATEGIES, COMMERCE
HOUSE, HUNTER ST, CHESTER
CH1 2QP, UK

H JONES
CHESHIRE COUNTY COUNCIL
CHIEF ENVIRONMENTAL
PROTECTION OFFICER,
ENVIRONMENTAL PLANNING,
COMMERCE HOUSE, HUNTER
STREET, CHESTER, CH1 2QP,
UK

DAVID COUNSELL
CLEVELAND COUNCIL GROUP
LEADER - ENVIRONMENTAL
MANAGEMENT, P O BOX 77,
GURNEY HOUSE, GURNEY ST,
MIDDLESBROUGH,
CLEVELAND, TS1 1JJ, UK

BOB KING
CLEVELAND COUNTY
COUNCIL ENVIRONMENTAL
INITIATIVES OFFICER,
PO BOX 77, GURNEY HOUSE,
GURNEY STREET,
MIDDLESBOROUGH,
CLEVELAND, TS1 2QH, UK

COUNCILLOR J M STEPHEN
CLEVELAND COUNTY
COUNCIL
VICE CHAIRMAN OF COUNTY
COUNCILS ENV. AFFAIRS SUB
COMMITTEE, P O BOX 100A,
MUNICIPAL BUILDINGS,
MIDDLESBOROUGH,
CLEVELAND, TS1 2QH, UK

COUNCILLOR
MARGARET LANCASTER
COVENTRY CITY COUNCIL
4TH FLOOR BROADGATE
HOUSE, COVENTRY CV1 1NH,
UK

PENNY DUGGAN
COVENTRY CITY COUNCIL
HOUSING AND
ENVIRONMENTAL SERVICES
BROADGATE HOUSE,
BROADGATE, COVENTRY
CV1 1NH, UK

COLIN EDWARDS
CREWE AND NANTWICH
BOROUGH COUNCIL
HEAD OF ENVIRONMENTAL
HEALTH, DELAMERE HOUSE
DELAMERE STREET, CREWE,
UK

COUNCILLOR
RICHARD JESSOP,
DARTFORD BOROUGH
COUNCIL
CIVIC CENTR, HOME
GARDENS, DARTFORD, KENT,
DA1 1DR, UK

MICHAEL PRATT
DARTFORD BOROUGH
COUNCIL ENVIRONMENTAL
HEALTH OFFICER, CIVIC
CENTRE, HOME GARDENS,
DARTFORD KENT, DA1 1DR, UK

LEADER
DERBYSHIRE COUNTY
COUNCIL
DERBYSHIRE COUNTY
COUNCIL, COUNTY OFFICES,
MATLOCK, DERBYSHIRE, UK

MAGGIE BISHOP
DERBYSHIRE COUNTY
COUNCIL
ENVIRONMENT POLICY
OFFICER, COUNTY OFFICES,
MATLOCK, DERBYSHIRE,
DE4 3AG, UK

SUNETHRA MENDIS
DONCASTER METROPOLITAN
BOROUGH COUNCIL
PLANNER, DIRECTORATE OF
PLANNING, DANUM HOUSE,
ST. SEPULCHRE GATE,
DONCASTER, UK

PETER RODGERS
EAST HAMPSHIRE DISTRICT
COUNCIL
LEADER OF THE COUNCIL,
PENNS PLACE, PETERSFIELD,
HANTS, GU31 4EX, UK

COUNCILLOR DAVID HALL
EAST SUSSEX CC COUNTY,
PLANNING DEPT, SOUTHOVER
HOUSE, SOUTHOVER ROAD,
LEWES, BN7 1YA, UK

COUNCILLOR GARY GRIFFITHS
EAST SUSSEX COUNTY
COUNCIL
CHAIR OF ENV. POLICY
PANEL, SOUTHOVER HOUSE,
SOUTHOVER ROAD, LEWES,
EAST SUSSEX, UK

SIMON HICKMOTT/STEVE
ANKERS
EAST SUSSEX COUNTY
COUNCIL GROUP
MANAGER/CHIEF ENV.
PLANNER ENVIRONMENTAL
SERVICES, SOUTHOVER
HOUSE, SOUTHOVER ROAD,
LEWES, EAST SUSSEX, UK

SIMON KULARATNE
FYLDE BOROUGH COUNCIL
34 MORETON DRIVE,
STAINING, BLACKPOOL, UK

ARTHUR GILBERT
HIGH PEAK BOROUGH
COUNCIL
CHAIR ENVIRONMENTAL
SERVICES,
4 ST MARYS RD, GLOSSOP,
DERBYSHIRE, UK

CRAIG BOXSHALL/GILLIAN
OGDEN
HULL CITY COUNCIL,
PLANNERS, GUILDHALL,
HULL, UK

T WILKINSON/J HAYNES/
C PEACH
HUMBERSIDE COUNTY
COUNCIL
ENVIRONMENTAL OFFICER,
TECHNICAL SVS DEPT,
BEVERLEY,
NORTH HUMBERSIDE,

STEVE GILBERT
KENT COUNTY COUNCIL
ENVIRONMENTAL
PROGRAMME MANAGER,
SPRINGFIELD, MAIDSTONE,
ME14 2LX, UK

MARGARET SLOANE
KIRKLEES METROPOLITAN
COUNCIL
ISIS COORDINATOR
ENVIRONMENT UNIT, 23
ESTATE BUILDINGS, RAILWAY
STREET, HUDDERSFIELD, UK

COUNCILLOR ERIC LAWSON
KIRKLEES METROPOLITAN
COUNCIL
ENVIRONMENT UNIT,
23 ESTATE BUILDING,
RAILWAY STREET,
HUDDERSFIELD, UK

COUNCILLOR FRETWELL
KIRKLEES METROLPOLITAN
COUNCIL
ENVIRONMENT UNIT, 23
ESTATE BUILDING, RAILWAY
STREET, HUDDERSFIELD, UK

COUNCILLOR JOHN HARMAN
KIRKLEES METROPOLITAN
COUNCIL
LEADER
TOWN HALL
RAMSDEN ST, HUDDERSFIELD,
HD1 2TA, UK

COUNCILLOR MIKE BOWER
KIRKLEES METROPOLITAN
COUNCIL
ENVIRONMENT UNIT,
23 ESTATE BUILDING,
RAILWAY STREET,
HUDDERSFIELD HDI IJY, UK

FIONA GLOVER
KIRKLEES METROPOLITAN
COUNCIL
ENVIRONMENT OFFICER,
ENVIRONMENT UNIT, 23
ESTATE BUILDINGS,
HUDDERSFIELD, HDI 1JY, UK

PHILIP WEBBER
KIRKLEES METROPOLITAN
COUNCIL
HEAD OF ENVIRONMENT
UNIT, 23 ESTATE BUILDINGS,
HUDDERSFIELD, HD1 1JY, UK

ROS GILLAN
KIRKLEES METROPOLITAN
COUNCIL
ENVIRONMENT OFFICER,
ENVIRONMENT UNIT,
23 ESTATE BUILDINGS,
HUDDERSFIELD, HDI 1JY, UK

COUNCILLOR LOUISE ELLMAN
LANCASHIRE COUNTY
COUNCIL
CHIEF EXECUTIVE'S/CLERKS
DEPT, CHRISTCHURCH
PRECINCT, COUNTY HALL,
PRESTON, LANCS, UK

DEREK A TAYLOR
LANCASHIRE COUNTY
COUNCIL
HEAD OF POLICY PLANNING
DEPARTMENT, EAST CLIFF,
COUNTY COUNCIL,
PRESTON, PRI 3EX UK

GRAEME BELL
LANCASHIRE COUNTY
COUNCIL
COUNTY PLANNING OFFICER,
EAST CLIFF OFFICES,
PRESTON, UK

GRAHAM PINFIELD
LANCASHIRE COUNTY
COUNCIL
HEAD OF ENVIRONMENTAL
POLICY UNIT, PLANNING
DEPARTMENT, EAST CLIFF
OFFICES, PRESTON, PRI 3EX,
UK

WILLIAM HORSFALL
LANCASHIRE COUNTY
COUNCIL
PRINCIPAL ENVIRONMENT
OFFICER, PLANNING
DEPARTMENT, EAST CLIFF
OFFICES, PRESTON, PR1 3EX,
UK

IAN LINDLEY
LEICESTER CITY COUNCIL
NEW WALK CENTRE,
WELFORD PLACE, LEICESTER,
LE1 62G, UK

JIM KERSEY
LEICESTERSHIRE COUNTY
COUNCIL
TEAM LEADER POLICY, P & T
COUNTY HALL, GLENFIELD,
LEICESTER, LE3 8RJ, UK

TREVOR WATSON
LEWES DISTRICT COUNCIL
RECYCLING OFFICER, 32 HIGH
STREET, LEWES, EAST SUSSEX,
BN7 2LX, UK

MICHAEL GEORGE MANUEL
LONDON BOROUGH OF BRENT
ENVIRONMENTAL POLICY
MANAGER, 6TH FLOOR BRENT
HOUSE, ENVIRONMENTAL
SERVICES, WEMBLEY HIGH
ROAD, WEMBLEY, MIDDLESEX,
UK

ALEXANDRA SHIPLEY
LONDON BOROUGH
OF CROYDON
ROOM 7-10, TABERNER
HOUSE, PARK LANE,
CROYDON UK

TONY COLMAN
LONDON BOROUGH
OF MERTON
LEADER, CROWN HOUSE,
LONDON ROAD, MORDEN,
SM4 5DX, UK

FRANCES APPLIN
LONDON BOROUGH
OF REDBRIDGE
ENVIRONMENTAL
COORDINATION OFFICER,
LYNTON HOUSE, 255-259
HIGH ROAD, ILFORD, ESSEX,
1G1 1NY, UK

PAULINE MOORE
LONDON BOROUGH
OF REDBRIDGE
ENVIRONMENTAL STRATEGY
OFFICER, LYNTON HOUSE,
255-259 HIGH ROAD, ILFORD
ESSEX, IGA 4NY, UK

COUNCILLOR GRAHAM TOPE
LONDON BOROUGH
OF SUTTON
LEADER OF SUTTON COUNCIL,
LEADERS OFFICE, CIVIC
OFFICES, ST NICHOLAS WAY,
SUTTON, SURREY, UK

COUNCILLOR PAUL BURSTOW
LONDON BOROUGH
OF SUTTON
CHAIRMAN ENVIRONMENTAL
SVS COMMITTEE, 114 GROVE
ROAD, SUTTON, SURREY,
SMI 2DD, UK

GRAHAM DEAN
LONDON BOROUGH
OF SUTTON
SENIOR PLANNER,
ENVIRONMENTAL SVS DEPT,
24 DENMARK ROAD,
CARSHALTON, SURREY, UK

ALISON STOPHER
MANCHESTER CITY COUNCIL
SUSTAINABILITY TEAM,
ROOM 3030, TOWN HALL
EXTENSION, ENVIRONMENTAL
PLANNING DEPARTMENT,
MANCHESTER, M60 2LA, UK

ANDREW SHORT
MANCHESTER CITY COUNCIL
ASSISTANT DIRECTOR
ENVIRONMENTAL PLANNING
DEPARTMENT, TOWN HALL
EXT, MANCHESTER, UK

DR TED KITCHEN
MANCHESTER CITY COUNCIL
CITY PLANNING OFFICER
ENVIRONMENTAL PLANNING
DEPARTMENT, TOWN HALL
EXTENSION, MANCHESTER,
M60 2LA, UK

NICK CLIFFORD
MANCHESTER CITY COUNCIL
SUSTAINABILITY TEAM, ROOM
3030, ENVIRONMENTAL
PLANNING DEPARTMENT,
TOWN HALL, MANCHESTER
M60 2LA, UK

PHIL JOBLING
MANCHESTER CITY COUNCIL
HEAD OF STRATEGY GROUP,
ENVIRONMENTAL PLANNING
DEPARTMENT, TOWN HALL
EXTENSION, MANCHESTER,
M60 2LA, UK

RICHARD LEWIS
MANCHESTER CITY COUNCIL
ENVIRONMENTAL PLANNING
DEPARTMENT, TOWN HALL
MANCHESTER, M60 2LA, UK

SINCLAIR MCLEOD
MANCHESTER CITY COUNCIL
CITY ENGINEER AND
SURVEYOR, P O BOX 488,
TOWN HALL, MANCHESTER,
UK

STEVE MYCIO
MANCHESTER CITY COUNCIL
DIRECTOR OF HOUSING,
TOWN HALL EXTENSION,
MANCHESTER, UK

GRAHAM JEFFS
MENDIP DISTRICT COUNCIL
CHIEF EXECUTIVE, CANNARDS
GRAVE ROAD, SHEPTON
MALLET, SOMERSET, UK

NORMA UNDERWOOD
MENDIP DISTRICT COUNCIL
PROJECT OFFICER, CANNARDS
GRAVE ROAD, SHEPTON
MALLET, BA4 5BT, UK

RUTH ALLEN
MENDIP DISTRICT COUNCIL
ENVIRONMENTAL INITIATIVES
OFFICER, CANNARDS GRAVE
RD, SHEPTON MALLET,
SOMERSET, UK

COUNCILLOR
MARGARET HALL
NORTH TYNESIDE DISTRICT
COUNCIL
MEMBERS SERVICES, TOWN
HALL, HIGH STREET EAST,
WALLSEND, TYNE WEAR, UK

KENNETH WILSON
NORTH TYNESIDE DISTRICT
COUNCIL
SENIOR PLANNER, GRAHAM
HOUSE, WHITLEY ROAD,
BENTON, NEWCASTLE UPON
TYNE, UK

COUNCILLOR
BARRIE JACKSON
NOTTINGHAM CITY COUNCIL
COUNCIL HOUSE,
NOTTINGHAM, UK

COUNCILLOR DAVID POOLE
NOTTINGHAM CITY COUNCIL
COUNCIL HOUSE,
NOTTINGHAM, UK

COUNCILLOR JOHN PECK
NOTTINGHAM CITY COUNCIL
COUNCIL HOUSE,
NOTTINGHAM, UK

DAVID JONES
NOTTINGHAM CITY COUNCIL
SENIOR ENGINEER,
LAWRENCE HOUSE, TALBOT
STREET, NOTTINGHAM,
NG1 5NT, UK

JOHN JOHNSON
OLDHAM METROPOLITAN
BOROUGH COUNCIL
CHAIR ENVIRONMENTAL
HEALTH, 49 DALTON STREET,
FAILSWORTH, MANCHESTER,
UK

LISA BARKER
OLDHAM METROPOLITAN
BOROUGH COUNCIL
SENIOR ENVIRONMENTAL
HEALTH OFFICER, NORTH
HOUSE, 130 ROCHDALE
ROAD, OLDHAM, UK

AMANDA DE GONVILLE
MORRISON
OXFORD CITY COUNCIL
ENVIRONMENTAL POLICY
OFFICER, ST ALDATES
CHAMBERS, ST ALDATES,
OXFORD, UK

COUNCILLOR TATTERSALL
READING BOROUGH COUNCIL
READING BOROUGH COUNCIL
- UK ENVIRONMENT SVS,
CIVIC CENTRE, READING, UK

PETER BULMER
READING BOROUGH COUNCIL
COMMUNITY
ENVIRONMENTAL
COORDINATOR,
ENVIRONMENTAL SERVICES,
CIVIC CENTRE, READING, UK

DAVID DAVIDSON
ROCHDALE METROPOLITAN
BOROUGH COUNCIL
ASST DIRECTOR
ENVIRONMENTAL DEPT, PO
BOX 32, TELEGRAPH HOUSE,
BAILLE STREET, ROCHDALE,
OL1 1JH, UK

MOHAMMED ISHAQ
ROCHDALE METROPOLITAN
BOROUGH COUNCIL
CHIEF EXECUTIVES
DEPARTMENT, TOWN HALL,
ROCHDALE, UK

PETER MCNULTY
ROCHDALE METROPOLITAN
BOROUGH COUNCIL
SENIOR PLANNING OFFICER,
P O BOX 32, TELEGRAPH
HOUSE, BAILLIE ST,
ROCHDALE, OL16 1JH, UK

ROGER BALDRY
ROCHDALE METROPOLITAN
BOROUGH COUNCIL
CHIEF EXECUTIVE'S
DEPARTMENT, TOWN HALL,
ROCHDALE, UK

BENJAMIN WALLSWORTH
SALFORD CITY COUNCIL
CHAIRMAN OF
ENVIRONMENTAL PROT.
CTTEE, SALFORD CIVIC
CENTRE, CHORLEY ROAD,
SWINTON, UK

TONY STRUTHERS
SALFORD CITY COUNCIL
CITY TECHNICAL SERVICES
OFFICER, SALFORD CIVIC
CENTRE, CHORLEY ROAD,
SWINTON, UK

STEVE BYERS
SHEFFIELD CITY COUNCIL
ENVIRONMENTAL POLICY
COORDINATOR,
ENVIRONMENTAL
PROTECTION UNIT, TOWN
HALL CHAMBERS, BARKERS
POOL, SHEFFIELD, UK

TIM ROGERS
SHEFFIELD CITY COUNCIL
ASSISTANT PRINCIPAL
ENGINEER, 2-10 CARBROOK
HALL ROAD, SHEFFIELD, UK

LEONARD RAWLINGS
SLOUGH BOROUGH COUNCIL
BOROUGH DEVELOPMENT
OFFICER, TOWN HALL, BATH
ROAD, SLOUGH, BERKS, UK

STEVE PRICE SOUTH
SHROPSHIRE DISTRICT
COUNCIL
ENVIRONMENTAL SERVICES
OFFICER, STONE HOUSE,
CORVE STREET, LUDLOW,
SY8 1DG, UK

NIGEL BACHMANN
SOUTHAMPTON CITY
COUNCIL
ENVIRONMENTAL POLICY
OFFICER LOCAL PLANS
SERVICES, DIRECTOR OF
COMMUNITY SVS, CIVIC
CENTRE, SOUTHAMPTON, UK

ANDREW CHRISTELOM
STAFFORDSHIRE COUNTY
COUNCIL
ENVIRONMENT OFFICER,
PLANNING AND ECONOMIC
DEV DEPT, COUNTY
BUILDINGS, STAFFORD, UK

BOB CHRISTIE
STOCKPORT METROPOLITAN
BOROUGH COUNCIL
ENVIRONMENTAL
COORDINATOR, TECHNICAL
SVS, HYGARTH HOUSE, TOWN
HALL, STOCKPORT, SK1 3TT, UK

CHRISTOPHER BAMBER
STOKE ON TRENT
CITY COUNCIL
SENIOR PLANNING OFFICER,
DEPT OF LEGAL PROPERTY
AND ADMIN, PO BOX 636,
CIVIC CENTRE, GLEBE STREET,
STOKE ON TRENT, STAFFS, UK

COUNCILLOR JEAN EDWARDS
STOKE ON TRENT
CITY COUNCIL
C/O MISS POWELL, PO BOX
631, CIVIC CENTRE, GLEBE
STREET, STOKE ON TRENT,
STAFFORDSHIRE, UK

COUNCILLOR
PAULINE ANN SHAW
STOKE ON TRENT
CITY COUNCIL
C/O MISS POWELL
P O BOX 631, CIVIC CENTRE,
GLEBE STREET, STOKE ON
TRENT, STAFFORDSHIRE, UK

COUNCILLOR JOHN SILVESTER
SURREY HEATH BOROUGH
COUNCIL DIRECTOR OF
PLANNING & COMMUNITY
SERVICE, SURREY HEATH
HOUSE, KNOLL ROAD,
CAMBERLEY, SURREY,
GU13 8AN, UK

COUNCILLOR MARTIN CATON
SWANSEA CITY COUNCIL
83 WEST CROSS AVENUE,
WEST CROSS, SWANSEA, UK

TAFF ELY BOROUGH COUNCIL
UK 11 MILL STREET,
PONTYPRIDD,
MID GLAMORGAN, UK

GLEN ROUTLEDGE
TAMESIDE METROPOLITAN
BOROUGH COUNCIL
PLANNING OFFICER,
PLANNING AND
ENGINEERING DEPT, COUNCIL
OFFICES, WELLINGTON ROAD,
ASHTON U LYNE, OL6 6DL, UK

CHRISTOPHER WORTHINGTON
THAMESDOWN BOROUGH
COUNCIL
SENIOR ECONOMIC
DEVELOPMENT OFFICER, CIVIC
OFFICES, EUCLID STREET,
SWINDON, SN1 2JH, UK

LINDA JOSEPH
TRAFFORD METROPOLITAN
BOROUGH COUNCIL,
PRINCIPAL ENVIRONMENTAL
DEVELOPMENT OFFICER, DEPT
OF ENV. AND LEISURE,
TRAFFORD TOWN HALL,
TALBOT ROAD, STRETFORD,
M32 OYZ, UK

BRIAN JAMIESON
VALE ROYAL BOROUGH
COUNCIL
VICE CHAIRMAN -
ENVIRONMENTAL & TECH.
CT, ENVIRONMENTAL AND
HOUSING SERVICES, WYVERN
HOUSE, THE DRUMBER,
WINSFORD, CHESHIRE, UK

RICHARD HALLOWS
VALE ROYAL BOROUGH
COUNCIL
HEAD OF ENVIRONMENTAL
SERVICES, ENVIRONMENTAL
AND HOUSING SERVICES,
WYVERN HOUSE,
THE DRUMBER, WINSFORD,
CHESHIRE, UK

RON GOODIER
VALE ROYAL BOROUGH
COUNCIL
CHAIRMAN ENVIRONMENTAL
& TECHNICAL CTTEE,
ENVIRONMENTAL AND
HOUSING SVS, WYVERN
HOUSE, THE DRUMBER,
WINSFORD, CHESHIRE, UK

COUNCILLOR A FROGGATT
WARRINGTON BOROUGH
COUNCIL
PALMYRA HOUSE,
PALMYRA SQUARE, NORTH
WARRINGTON, WA1 1JH, UK

COUNCILLOR M GREENSLADE
WARRINGTON BOROUGH
COUNCIL
PALMYRA HOUSE,
PALMYRA SQUARE, NORTH
WARRINGTON, WA1 1JH UK

M FLOYD
WARRINGTON BOROUGH
COUNCIL
ENVIRONMENTAL AUDIT
OFFICER, PALMYRA HOUSE,
PALMYRA SQUARE, NORTH
WARRINGTON, WA1 1JH, UK

GARY HAROLD
WIGAN METROPOLITAN
BOROUGH COUNCIL
GROUP LEADER,
ENVIRONMENTAL PLANNING,
CIVIC BUILDINGS, NEW
MARKET STREET, WIGAN,
WN1 1RP, UK

MRS JEAN MELVILLE
WILTSHIRE COUNTY COUNCIL
CHIEF EXECUTIVES DEPT,
COUNTY HALL, TROWBRIDGE,
WILTS, UK

NOEL TOSTEVIN
WILTSHIRE COUNTY COUNCIL
C/O MRS J WHITE, ROOM
246, CHIEF EXECUTIVES DEPT,
COUNTY HALL, TROWBRIDGE,
UK

PETER DENTON
WILTSHIRE COUNTY COUNCIL
COUNTRYSIDE OFFICER,
PLANNING AND HIGHWAYS
DEPT, COUNTY HALL,
TROWBRIDGE, WILTS, UK

BOB COLE
WINCHESTER CITY COUNCIL
HEALTH AND SAFETY OFFICER,
CITY OFFICES, COLEBROOK
STREET, WINCHESTER, SO23
9LJ, UK

DENISE LONSDALE
WINCHESTER CITY COUNCIL
MANAGEMENT SUPPORT
OFFICER, CX UNIT, CITY
OFFICES, COLEBROOK STREET
WINCHESTER, HANTS,
SO23 9LJ, UK

COUNCILLOR JOHN ROWLEY
WOLVERHAMPTON
METROPOLITAN BOROUGH CLL
CHAIR, PLANNING AND ENV.
COMMITTEE, CIVIC CENTRE,
ST PETERS SQUARE,
WOLVERHAMPTON, UK

KEITH KIRBY/SUSAN LEIGH
WOLVERHAMPTON
METROPOLITAN BOROUGH CLL
HEAD OF STRATEGIC
PLANNING, OFFICE OF THE
CHIEF EXECUTIVE AND POLICY
COORDINATOR, CIVIC CENTRE,
WOLVERHAMPTON, UK

ANDREW LOCKE
WREKIN DISTRICT COUNCIL
DIRECTOR PLANNING &
ENVIRONMENTAL SVS,
PO BOX 212, CIVIC OFFICES,
TELFORD, SHROPSHIRE, UK

COUNCILLOR BRIAN GREEN
WREKIN DISTRICT COUNCIL
PLANNING AND ENV. SVS,
PO BOX 212, CIVIC OFFICES,
TELFORD, SHROPSHIRE, UK

COUNCILLOR DAVID DAVIES
WREKIN DISTRICT COUNCIL
PLANNING AND ENV SVS,
PO BOX 212, CIVIC OFFICES,
TELFORD, SHROPSHIRE, UK

COUNCILLOR
GUYNNE ROBERTS
WREKIN DISTRICT COUNCIL
PLANNING AND ENV. SVS,
PO BOX 212, CIVIC OFFICES,
TELFORD, SHROPSHIRE, UK

COUNCILLOR HENRY CURRAN
WREKIN DISTRICT COUNCIL
PLANNING AND ENV. SVS,
PO BOX 212, CIVIC OFFICES,
TELFORD, SHROPSHIRE, UK

UKRAINE
ELENA CHERNIKOVA
KIEV CITY RESEARCHER,
PRIRECHNAYA 17 KV 322,
KIEV, UKRAINE

LEONID SAMOKHVALOV
KIEV CITY
HEAD OF PUBLIC HEALTH
DIVISION, GORKY STR, 160
KV50 KIEV, UKRAINE

NATALYA POUSTOVIT
KIEV CITY
HEAD-ENVIRONMENTAL
INSTITUTE, KIEV FLDRETSII
STREET, 1/11 KV 43, KIEV,
UKRAINE

ONISHCHENKO YURIK
KIEV CITY
HEAD OF ADMINISTRATION
DEPARTMENT, KIEV
SAKSAGANSKY STR 69, KV14
KIEV, UKRAINE

VICTORIVA MELENTUEVA
KIEV CITY
HEAD OF CITY
ADMINISTRATION
DEPARTMENT, RUSH KIM STR
KV1, KIEV, UKRAINE

USA
DAVID CROCKETT
CHATTANOOGA CITY COUNCIL
CITY COUNCILMAN
DISTRICT 3, ROOM 111, CITY
HALL 100 E. 11TH ST.,
CHATANOOGA, TENNESSEE,
USA

MARTHA RUTHERFORD
CHATTANOOGA CITY COUNCIL
CITY COUNCIL WOMEN
DISTRICT 6, ROOM 111, CITY
HALL 100 E., 11TH ST.
CHATTANOOGA, USA

YVES MIKHOL
DEPARTMENT OF
ENVIRONMENT
NY CITY
DEPT OF ENVIRONMENT
PROTECTION, 59-17
JUNCTION BOULEVARD,
CORONA NY 11368, USA

WALES
ALAN MORRIS
CLWYD COUNTY COUNCIL
ENVIRONMENTAL
CO-ORDINATOR,
CHIEF EXECUTIVE'S DEPT,
SHIRE HALL, MOLD, CLWYD,
CHESHIRE, CH7 6NB, WALES

ZIMBABWE
MAYOR J T MALINGA
BULAWAYO CITY COUNCIL
COUNCILLOR
ZIMBABWE

MR M M NDUBIWA
BULAWAYO CITY COUNCIL
TOWN CLERK AND CHIEF
EXECUTIVE
ZIMBABWE

MR ZENZO NSIMBI
BULAWAYO CITY COUNCIL
INTERNATIONAL/
COMMERCIAL SECTOR,
ZIMBABWE

MS VIVIAN S NEUBE
BULAWAYO CITY COUNCIL
CITIZEN SECTOR
ZIMBABWE

MS S MPOFU
CITY OF BULAWAYO
PUBLIC RELATIONS OFFICER,
MUNICIPAL BUILDINGS,
BULAWAYO, ZIMBABWE,

DR TIZIRAI SWATA
CITY OF HARARE
ALDELMAN
12 SHANSAN ROAD,
MOUNT PLEASANT,
HARARE, ZIMBABWE

EDWARD CHIVALVEA MUTERO
CITY OF HARARE
TOWN CLERK/CHIEF
EXECUTIVE, P O BOX 990,
HARARE, ZIMBABWE

JUNIOR MUZONDIWA
CITY OF HARARE
COUNCILLOR
RESS MALVERN ROAD,
HARARE, ZIMBABWE

MAYOR CHARLES TAWENGWA
CITY OF HARARE
MAYOR
BOX 990, HARARE,
ZIMBABWE

ORGANISATIONS

BELGIUM
MARINA ALBERTI
EUROPEAN COMMISSION
DG XI ENVIRONMENT
NUCLEAR SAFETY AND CIVIL
PROTECTION
BRUXELLES
BELGIUM

JOKE VAH ASSCHE
FREE UNIVERSITY BRUSSELS
RESEARCHER
LAARREEKLAAM NO3
LOGO BRUSSELS
BELGIUM

CANADA
JEB BRUGMAN
ICLEI
SECRETARY GENERAL
ICLEI WORLD SECRETARIAT
CITY HALL EAST TOWER
8TH FLOOR TORONTO
CANADA

MICHAEL MANOLSON
ICLEI
ASSISTANT SECRETARY
GENERAL
CITY HALL
TORONTO M5H 2N2
CANADA

DR P. MEHTA
ICLEI
DIRECTOR MODEL
COMMUNITIES PROGRAMME
ICLEI,
CITY HALL
TORONTO M5H 2N2
CANADA

COLUMBIA
EDGARD MONCAYO
MISION SIGLO XXI
DIRECTOR
MISION SIGLO XXI
CARRERA 10 N0 9-30
INT 2 AA 93597
COLUMBIA

MARGARITA PACHERO
ENVIRONMENTAL STUDIES
INSTITUTE,
NATIONAL UNIVERSITY
OF COLUMBIA,
BOGOTA, COLUMBIA

DENMARK
JAN WOOLHEAD
CIBU
CHAIRMAN
GULDERGSGADE 8 ITV
2200 COPENHAGEN N
DENMARK

ECUADOR
MR JAIME VALENZUELA
IULA
LATIN AMERICAN SECTION
PROJECT DIRECTOR
QUITO
ECUADOR

JOERG-WERNER HAAS
PGU GTZ
SENIOR ADVISOR
CASILLA 17-17-1449
QUITO
ECUADOR

FRANCE
JOHN CELECIA
UNESCO
DIVISION OF ECOLOGICAL
SCIENTISTS
MAB+ THE BIO SYSTEM
PROGRAMME
UNESCO
FRANCE

MISS PONS
UTO PARIS
PROJECT OFFICER
22 RUE D'ALSACE
92350
LEVALLOIS PERRET
FRANCE

MR NOWERSZTERN
UTO PARIS
PROJECT MANAGER
22 RUE D'ALSACE
92350
LEVALLOIS PERRET
FRANCE

GIANFRANCA GABBIA
TESTORE
UTO-PARIS
PROJECT OFFICER
82 RUE D'ALSACE
92532 LEVALLOIS PERRET
FRANCE

ALAIN LE SAUX
WORLD ASSOCIATION OF THE
MAJ METROPOLISES
1 AURIF 215
RUE DE VARGIRARD 75 AD
PARIDS CEDEX 15
FRANCE

GERMANY
GIANLUCA SOLERA
TECHNICAL UNIVERSITY
BERLIN
PHD STUDENT
ILO TU BERLIN
FRANKLINSTRASSE
28/29 10587 BERLIN
GERMANY

INDIA
MS SNEHA PALNITKAR
ALL INDIAN INST. OR LOCAL
SELF GOVT.
STHANIKRAJ BHAVAN, CD
BARFAEA MARG
ANDHERI (WEST)
INDIA

HANSA PATEL
LOCAL SELF GOVERNMENT
INSTITUTE
DIRECTOR
PRESIDENT WOMEN AND
CHILD DEVELOPMENT
NEHRU BHAVAN
RAJMAHEL ROAD
BARODA
INDIA

MS SANDHYA
VENKATESWARAN
RESEARCH CONSULTANT
30 FEROZESHAH ROAD
APARTMENT B-3
NEW DELHI 110 00
INDIA

INDONESIA
HAFIZ FATCHURRAHMAN
IIMO/BKS-AKSI
SECRETARY GENERAL OF IIMO
GEDUNG PEM.DKI JARKARTA
BLOCK G
LT.22 J1.MERDEKA SELATAN
8-9 JARKARTA 10110
INDONESIA

AGUSTINUS D SABAKODI
INTER INDONESIAN
MUNICIPALITIES ORG
DEPUTY SECRETARY GENERAL
OF IIMO
GDG PEM DKI JAKARTA
BLOCK G LT 22 J1
MERDEKA SELATAN 8 -9
JARKATA 10110
INDONESIA

JAPAN
KENJI KAWASAKI
ALL JAPAN MUNICIPAL
WORKERS UNION
MEMBER OF JICHIRO
TOYONAKA CITY EMP UNI
ROKUBANCHO 1
CHIYODA-KU
TOKYO JAPAN

MITSURU TANAKA
ALL JAPAN MUNICIPAL
WORKERS UNION
MEMBER OF JIRCHIRO
KAWASAKI CITY EMP.UNI
ROKUBANCHO 1
CHIYODA-KU
TOKYO JAPAN

MS TASUO DEGUCHI
ALL JAPAN MUNICIPAL
WORKERS UNION
STAFF OF POLITICAL AFFAIRS
DEPT JICHIRO
HEADQUARTERS
ROKUBANCHO 1
CHIYODA-KU JAPAN

CHRISTAIN SEMONSEN
ICLEI
MANAGING DIRECTOR
ICLEI ASIAN SECRETARIAT
JAPAN OFFICE GEF
LIKURA BUILDING4-9-7 AZA-
BODAI JAPAN

MR YASUKO TAKAMASU
TOKYO BROADCASTING
DEPUTY VICE PRESIDENT
INTERNATIONAL AFFAIRS
TOKYO JAPAN

NETHERLANDS
JOHANNES P JUFFERMANS
ENVIRONMENTAL PRESS
THE SMALL EARTH
POSTBUS 151
5280 AD BOXTEL
THE NETHERLANDS
NETHERLANDS

GRETHA VAN DER WEST
SME
PROJECT MANAGER
PO BOX 13030
3505 LA UTRECHT
NETHERLANDS

NORWAY
KNUT H RAMTVEDT
LOCAL ENVIRONMENTAL
INITIATIVES
COMMUNICATION SYSTEMS
MANAGING DIRECTOR
BRYGGERIVEIEN 2
POSTBOKS 229
N-J601 NORWAY

SLOVAKIA
MILOSLAVA PASLOVA
MINISTRY OF ENVIRONMENT
SENIOR PLANNING OFFICIAL
HLBUKA 2
812 35 BRATISLAVA
SLOVAKIA

SOUTH KOREA
DR YOO JAE HYUN
KOREA ECONOMIC JUSTICE
INST.
25-1 CHONERO 5-6A
CHONGRO-GU
SEOUL
SOUTH KOREA

PROFESSOR KIM KWI
SEOUL NATIONAL UNIVERSITY
103 SEODUN-DONG
SUWOM
KOREA
SOUTH KOREA

SWEDEN
LARS KARKBERG
BOPLATS 96
ASSISTANT UNDER SECRE-
TARY
MINISTRY OF ENVIRONMENT
AND NAT. RESOURCE
S-10333 STOCKHOLM
SWEDEN

TURKEY
AHMET OZER
SOUTH EASTERN ANATOLIA
REGION MUN UNION
GENERAL SECRETARY
GEVRAN CAD 30/1
DIYARBAKIR
TURKEY

UK
CHRIS BAINES
PO BOX 35
WOLVERHAMPTON
WEST MIDLANDS
WV1 4XS

CHRIS CHURCH
UNA
3 WHITEHALL COURT
LONDON
SW1A 2EL

PAUL DUTTON
ASSOCIATION METROPOLITAN
AUTHORITIES
CORPORATE POLICY OFFICER
35 GREAT SMITH STREET
LONDON
SWIP 3BJ
UK

DAVID GEE
WBMG
24 BROMWOOD ROAD
LONDON
SW11 6HT

JOHN HILTON
ASSOCIATION OF GTR MCR
AUTHS-AGMA
CHAIRMAN - GREATER
MANCHESTER PLANNING
& TRANSPORTATION
COMMITTEE AGMA
SECRETARIAT
NEW TOWN HALL
LIBRARY STREET
WIGAN
WN1 1NN
UK

ROGER LEVETT
CAG MANAGEMENT
CONSULTANTS
ENVIRONMENTAL TEAM
LEADER
ANTORIA HOUSE
262 HOLLOWAY ROAD
LONDON
UK

JOE RAVETZ
CENTRE FOR EMPLOYMENT
RESEARCH
RESEARCH CO-ORDINATOR
16 PARK ROAD
TODMORDEN
LANCS
UK

LES NEWBY/STEVE CHARTER
ENVIRON
TEAM LEADER PLANNING &
RESEARCH
PARKFIELD
WESTERN PARK
HINCLEY ROAD
UK

PETER STANWAY
GOVERNMENT OFFICE NORTH
WEST
REGIONAL ENVIRONMENTAL
CONTACT
ROOM 1308 SUNLEY TOWER
PICCADILLY PLAZA
MANCHESTER
UK

STUART DONALDSON
GOVERNMENT OFFICE
NORTHWEST
DEPUTY ENVIRONMENTAL

CONTACT OFFICER
ROOM 1308 SUNLEY TOWER
PICCADILLY PLAZA
MANCHESTER
UK

JACK MCBANE
GROUNDWORK FOUNDATION
TRUST DEVELOPMENT
ADVISER
85/87 CORNWALL STREET
BIRMINGHAM
UK

JANE MORRIS
LGMB
LOCAL AGENDA 21 PROJECT
OFFICER
ARNDALE HOUSE
ARNDAL CENTRE
LUTON
UK

COUNCILLOR KEN BODFISH
LOCAL GOVERNMENT
INTERNATIONAL BUREAU
LGIB - UK
35 GREAT SMITH STREET
LONDON
UK

COUNCILLOR MCOMMICK
LOCAL GOVERNMENT
INTERNATIONAL BUREAU
LGIB - UK
35 GREAT SMITH STREET
LONDON
UK

JOHN ARNOLD
LOCAL GOVERNMENT
INTERNATIONAL BUREAU
PROJECT OFFICER
35 GREAT SMITH STREET
LONDON SW1P 3BJ
UK

JUDITH BARTON
LOCAL GOVERNMENT
INTERNATIONAL BUREAU
EDITOR CIS
35 GREAT SMITH STREET
LONDON
SW1P 3BJ
UK

PAUL BONGER
LOCAL GOVERNMENT INTER-
NATIONAL BUREAU
DIRECTOR
35 GREAT SMITH STREET
LONDON SW1P 3BJ

PETER SLITS
LOCAL GOVERNMENT
INTERNATIONAL BUREAU
DEVELOPMENT OFFICER
35 GREAT SMITH STREET
LONDON
UK

VERNON SMITH
LOCAL GOVERNMENT
INTERNATIONAL BUREAU
DEVELOPMENT
CO-OPERATION ADVISER
35 GREAT SMITH STREET
LONDON
UK

DR DAVID GOODE
LONDON ECOLOGY UNIT
SENIOR ECOLOGIST
BEDFORD HOUSE
125 CAMDEN HIGH STREET
LONDON NW1 7JR
UK

ANDREW PHILIP ANDERSON
LONDON TRANSPORT
ORGANISATION
SENIOR TRANSPORT PLANNER
LT PLANNING
55 BRADWAY
LONDON
SW1H OBD
UK

DR JAMES MCEVOY
NATIONAL RIVERS AUTHORITY
RESEARCH AND
DEVELOPMENT OFFICER
RICHARD FAIRCLOUGH
HOUSE
KNUTSFORD ROAD
ARRINGTON
CHESHIRE
UK

ED CHMARA
PRINCE OF WALES BUSINESS
LEADERS FORUM
DEVELOPMENT MANAGER
EASTERN EUROPE
5 CLEVELAND PLACE
ST JAMES'S
UK

MAZHAR HUSSAIN
SALFORD UNIVERSITY
STUDENT ENVIRONMENTAL
RESOURCES UNIT
NEWTON BUILDING
UNIVERSITY OF SALFORD
MANCHESTER
M5 4WT
UK

DAVID PASTEUR
UNIVERISTY OF BIRMINGHAM
SENIOR LECTURER
DEVELOPMENT ADMIN
GROUP
SCHOOL OF PUBLIC POLICY
UNIVERSITY OF BIRMINGHAM
BIRMINGHAM
B15 2TT
UK

SUSAN KIDD
UNIVERSITY OF LIVERPOOL
LECTURER
LIVERPOOL UNIVERSITY
DEPT OF CIVIC DESIGN
PO BOX 147
LIVERPOOL
UK

USA
PETER SMITH
FOUNDATION FOR GLOBAL
COMMUNITY
CO-ORDINATOR
130 WASHINGTON STREET
NEWTON
MASSACHUSETTS 02158
USA

ALIOUNE BADIANE
UMP AFRICA
C/O THE WORLD BANK
1818 HIGH STREET
NW WASHINGTON
DC 20433
USA

NANCY SKINNER
GLOBAL SOLUTION TO
GLOBAL POLLUTION
DIRECTOR
GLOBAL SOLUTIONS TO
GLOBAL SOLUTIONS
1429 BANKCROFT WAY
BERKELEY
USA

MR COSTIS TOREGAS
ICLEI
PRESIDENT OF PUBLIC
TECHNOLOGY INC
WASHINGTON DC
USA

JOHN CRADDOCK
MUNCIE WATER QUALITY
BUREAU
DIRECTOR
5150 W KILGORE AVE
MUNCIE
USA

NEA CARROLL
SUSTAINABLE SEATTLE
METRICENTRE YMCA
909 4TH AVENUE
SEATTLE
USA

MS ZEHRA AYDIN
UNITED NATIONS
COMMISSION ON SUST.DEV.
SECRATARIAT
UNITED NATIONS
NEW YORK
10017
USA

VENEZUELA
JAIME ALBERTO MONJE
FUNDATACHIRA
DIRECTOR OF URBAN AND
HOUSING RESEARCH
DEPARTMENT OF ARCHITEC-
TURE
EDIFICIO COMPLETO FERIAL
FINAL AVENIDA
ESPANA
SAU CRISTOBAL-TACHIRA
VENEZELA

INDEX

Page references in italics refer to figures or photographs.

Aalborg, environmental action plans 75
Aalborg Charter (European Charter for
 Sustainable Cities and Towns 18, 20, 69
Aalborg Conference (European Conference
 on Sustainable Cities and Towns) 20, 69-70, 102, 120
Abidjan, urban environmental management 165
accountability, role of local authorities 23, 24
Accra (Ghana) 165
Action 21 *see* Agenda 21
action plans 73
 in Lancashire 159-61, *162*
 setting up of *108*, 116
  in Sao Paolo 142
  in Wellington 143
 in the UK 33-8
action points, 'Manchester 100' 7
Adelaide, energy stragegies 221
Africa, Senegal and Cote D'Ivoire, urban
 environmental management 164-66
African Institute of Urban Management (IAGU) 164
Agenda 21 9
 Chapter 28 9, 18
 coordination 22
 local-international links 81
 references to local government in 20, 24
 reporting process 22
 and the UN process 22
air pollution *see* pollution, air
Amsterdam, transport policies 215, 216
Asia, CITYNET 223-4
atmosphere, pollution in *see* pollution, air
auditing 73, 84, *85*, *90*, 155
 in Lancashire *157-62*
 of policy assessments 76, 145
 record sheets for *91-5*
 in Wellington 145
Australia 20
 Adelaide, energy stragegies 221
 information exchange and reporting 167
 levels of government 30
 Local Conservation Strategy 30, 31
  Municipal Conservation
  Association (MCA) 30, 32, 167
 national Local Agenda 21 program 30-2
 New Haven Village Project 221
 St. Kilda 74
  information gathering 167
Austria 20
 Graz, pollution prevention using
  ECOPROFIT 174-*7*
awareness *see* education

Barcelona, link with Leicester 219
Berkley, economic development strategy 171-3
Bogota, model process 42-3
Boston (USA) 74
Brazil
 Sao Paulo *25*

environmental action plan 142
environmental problems 142
Rapid Urban Environmental Assessment 165
Bristol Environment and Energy Trust (BEET) 227
Bristol [U] under[u] United Kingdom
British Columbia, Round Tables 132
Brooking Institute, 2050 project 23
Brooklyn 130
Brown Agenda, Thailand 56
Brundtland Commission 49, 188-9
budgeting *see* funding
Buga (Columbia) 43
buildings
 energy efficient, in Wellington 145
 and the environment, in Chiang-Mai 60
 grime 6
buses, in Sao Paulo 25
businesses
 environmentally responsible 33, 171, 210-11
 financial incentives 211
 involvement with 61
  in Berkley 171, 172
 and poverty in Harare 63
 see also industries
businessmen, training of 55

Cajarmarca *see under* Peru
Canada
 British Columbia, Round Tables 132
 Hamilton-Wentworth 48
  policy integration 75
  sustainable development project 48-52
  Vision 2020 49-50, 51, 75
 Ottawa
  funding 76
  policy integration 75
 Toronto, childcare 120
carbon dioxide
 in Kawasaki *151*
 public informed of levels 67
 reduction 18
  in Heidelberg 67
Cardiff *see under* United Kingdom
Caribbean, growth in GNP *42*
cars
 governmental attitudes to 18
 pollution from, in Sao Paulo 25
 restricted in Amsterdam 215
 see also traffic; transport
case studies, initiatives *see under* local authorities
Castlefield (Manchester) *7*
CFCs, in Kawasaki *151*
Charter Committee 224
Charter for European Cities 18, 20, 69
'Chemical sweep' (Gothenburg) 61
chemicals, hazardous, reduction 61
Chiang-Mai *see under* Thailand
childcare, in Toronto 120
children, in Harare 66
cities
 administrative organisation 102

co-operation between 102, 219, 222,
    see also North-South partnerships
density 200-1
'ecological' 200
economic effects of traffic restriction 215
as ecosystems *114*, 120, 196-7, 200-*4*
effect of peer pressure 23
Environment City Model (UK) 37
information exchange *111*, 117
and innovative ideas 222
Mega Cities Project 222
Model Cities 84
populations 18, 100
poverty and Agenda 21 102, *see also* poverty
'sister' 32, *see also* twinning
and sustainability 69-70, 222
citizens' task force 49
City Summit (UN Conference on Human Settlements -
    1996) 12, 21, *see also* Habitat II Conference
CITYNET 223-4
'Clean out' (Gothenburg) 61
closed-cycle production 174, 175
co-operation
    decentralised 102, 103
    international 55, 103, 121, 222-5
    sustainability through 13, 70, 225
    see also partnerships
collaboration *see* co-operation
Columbia 41
    co-operation with the US 22
    decentralisation 41
    development model 41
    environmental problems 42
    indicators of development 41, *42, 43*
    Local Agenda 21 42-3
    national campaign 42-*4*
    and population growth 41, *44*
    social expenditure 41-2
    urban transition 41, *43*
    urbanisation 41, *44*
Commission on Sustainable Development *see* CSD
Commonwealth Local Government Forum (CLGF) 223
communication, electronic systems, in Australia 31, 32, 167
communities 115
    consultation with 73, 74-5, 96, *97, 108-9*, 115
        in Hamilton-Wentworth 49, 51
        sustainability through 70
        to set priorities 84, *85*
        in the UK 35-7
    deciding sustainability indicators 119, 183, 184, 192
    definition of sustainable 192
    information gathering by 167
    informing *98*
    Model Communities Programme 43, 84, *96-8*
    partnerships with *96*
        in British Columbia 132
        in Japan 133-8
        in Lancashire 158
        and Mendip District Council *131*
        in New York City *130*
        in Wellington 145, 146

target *97-8*
to prioritise service needs 84, *85*, 96, *97*
computer screens 67
conservation, in Wellington 145
conservationism 72
consultation, with communities *see under* communities
Copenhagen, transport policies 214
Cote d'Ivoire, urban environmental management 165
countries, involved with Local agenda 21 20, 27
Coventry, Greening Industry Policy 178
CSD (Commission on Sustainable Development) 20, 22
    and local authorities 23, 24
cycling, in Copenhagen 214

Dakar, urban environmental management 164-5
databases 171
deforestation, combating in Harare 65
Denmark 20
    Aalborg, environmental action plans 75
    car ownership 214
    Copenhagen, transport policies 214
    inter-sessional meetings 22
developing countries
    links with other cities 38, *see also* North-South
        partnerships
    transport problems 218
development
    definition 120
    processes of 72
disease intervention programmes, in Harare 64
diversity, biological, in Harare 65
drainage, problems in Chiang-Mai 59

Earth Day Movement 133
Earth Summit 9, 14
    and Agenda 21 22, 81
    and sustainability 189
East Sussex, businesses and environmental performance 210
EC Directives, Freedom of Access to Environmental
    Information 67
Eco Handbook (Gothenburg) 61
Eco-Audit 176
eco-balancing, in Gothenburg 198-9
eco-ecology 72
ecocyles, and FOCUSED ANALYSIS 205-6
EcoFeedback 37
economic strategies *112*, 118
    alongside environmental protection 210-11
    in Berkley 171-3
    in Coventry 178
    ECOPROFIT in Graz 174-7
economic structure, and environmental problems 166
ECOPROFIT (Graz) 174-*7*
ECOPROFIT II and III 176-7
ecosystems
    urban systems as 74, *114*, 120, 196-7, 200-*4*
        issues 200, *202-4*
        in Wellington 145
education
    at the local level 18
    in Cajamarca 55

in Gothenburg 61
in Harare 66
local authorities' role in 13
in Sao Paulo 25
in the UK 36
see also information; training
electronic communication systems, in Australia 31, 32, 167
employment 118
protection, in Berkley 171, 173
training 172
energy
conservation 118, 205
energy-efficient housing 33, 206
management 67
solar-powered 205
strategies 226
in Adelaide 221
in Bristol 227-*8*
Energy Club 227
environment, components *161*
environmental action plans **see** action plans
Environmental Benefits Programs (EBPs) 130
Environmental Forums 36
environmental health 166
in Harare 64
Environmental Impact Assessments 205
environmental quality profiles *162*
equal opportunities, strategies for 36
ESCAP 223-4
Europe
co-operation with Latin American cities 219
north-south differences 102
sustainability indicators compared 119
sustainable transport policies 214-17
European Campaign for Sustainable Cities and Towns 20, 70, 219
European Charter for Sustainable Cities and Towns (Aalborg Charter) 18, 20, 69
European Commission 219
indicators project 182
European Community Eco-Management and Audit Scheme 210
European Conference on Sustainable Cities and Towns (Aalborg Conference) 20, 69-70
European Economic Community, regional fund 43
evaluations, performance *85*

farmers, training of 55
feedback 84, *85*
Fiji, Suva City, sustainability and funding 76
Finland 20
Focus Groups 36
in Hamilton-Wentworth 49
FOCUSED ANALYSIS 205-6
frameworks, international **see** international frameworks
France
inter-sessional meetings 22
La Rochelle, transport policies 215
Upper-Normandy, businesses and environmental performance 210-11

funding
of Local Agenda 21
in Australia 32
in Cajamarca (Peru) 76-7
in Ottawa 76
in the UK 33
'funding trusts' 32

garages, waste reduction *177*
Germany
Heidelberg
'Action Against Global Climatic Change' 18
city problems 18
initiatives 67-8
Karlsruhe, public transport 215
Global Forum'94 9, 121, 189
Gothenburg *see under* Sweden
governments, commitment to Agenda 21 18
Graz, pollution prevention using ECOPROFIT 174-*7*
Green Agenda, Thailand 56
Green Audit (Lancashire) 122, *124, 157-9*
greenhouse gases 69
Greenpoint/Williamsburg (Brooklyn) 130
Gronigen, transport policies 214
gross national product 185
Group of Four 100-2

Habitat Conference 22, 119
Habitat II Conference 12, 100, 121, 123, 220
and sustainability indicators 119
see also City Summit
Hamilton-Wentworth *see under* Canada
Harare *see under* Zimbabwe
health
packages 55
strategies for 36
in Harare 63-4
in Heidelberg 68
Healthy Cities (WHO) 68
Heidelberg *see under* Germany
housing
energy-efficient 33, 206
in Mancheste 5, 6
shortages in Harare 64
see also slums
Human Settlements, UN Conference on **see** City Summit; Habitat II Conference

ICLEI
European Campaign for Sustainable Cities and Towns 20, 70
Model Communities Programme 43, 84, *96-8*
objectives 24
report on implementation of Local Agenda 21 20-1
response by CSD 24
India 20
public involvement 115
Singraul Region 165
Vrindavan, link with Leicester 219
indicators 188
environmental *162*

sustainability 73, *113*, 119
    chosen by the community 119, 183, 184, 192
    European Commission's indicators project 182
    good 189-90
    in Seattle 183-*91*
    in the UK 38, 119, 192
    using a menu 192
indigenous people
    in Australia *167*
    in Harare 66
industries
    adverse consequences, in Manchester 5
    and air pollution in Harare 65
    benefits of cleaner production 174-*7*
    'Greening Industry' in Coventry 178
    preservation in Berkley 172-3
    projects with 61
    supporting development of 118
    see also businesses
information
    computer screens 67
    electronic systems, in Australia 31, 32
    gathering *111*, 117
    in Germany 67
interpretation 111, 117
    local authorities as providers of 13
    see also education; reporting
initiatives, local authority *see under* local authorities
innovative ideas, for cities 222
integration, policy 73, 75, 76
inter-sessional meetings 22
intergenerational equity 72-3
international co-operation *see under* international
    frameworks
International Council for Local Environmental Initiatives
    see ICLEI
international frameworks 84-95, 123
    international co-operation 55, 103, 121, 222-5
        technology transfer 66
    see also Group of Four; Model Communities
        Programme; networking
International Union of Local Authorities (IULA) 100, 224
    IULA-ASPAC section 224
    World Congress (1995) 219
    see also 'Group of Four'
Istanbul Conference (1996) **see** City Summit; Habitat II
    Conference
IULA *see* International Union of Authorities
Ivory Coast, urban environmental management 165

Jakarta (Indonesia) 165
Japan 20
    administrative reform and local livlihoods 133
    'Earth Charter' 137
    Eco-check 25 134-6
    elements of Local Agenda 21 74
    Jichiro 133
    Kankyo Jichitai *134*, 135, 137
    Kawasaki, environmental administration 147-54
    local government 40
    municipal environmental management 137-8

    national Agenda 21 39
    national Local Agenda 21 program 39-*40*
    seminar with Malaysia 22
    unions 133
Jichiro 133

Kankyo Jichitai *134*, 135, 137
Karlsruhe, public transport 215
Kawasaki City, environmental administration 147-54
Kennedy, Robert F., *quoted* on gross national product 185
King, Martin Luther, Jnr., *quoted* 189
Kotowice (Poland) 165

La Rochelle, transport policies 215
labels, awarded for environmental support 174, 176, 210
Lancashire, environmental information gathering *157-63*
Lancashire Environmental Action Programme (LEAP)
    159-61, *162*
land use
    planning
        in Bristol 227
        in Chiang-Mai 60
        in the UK 33
    reviewed, in Berkley 172
    sustainable 69
Latin America
    growth in GNP *42*
    Sao Paulo (Brazil) *25*
Leicester, international partnerships 219
lifestyles, changing 206
light bulbs, low-energy 67
Local Agenda 21 9, 15
    benefits, Australian viewpoint 31, 32
    and the City Summit 21, *see also* City Summit
    integration with existing processes 73, 75
    local government response 72-3
    mandate 20
    role in the UN process 23-4
    and sustainable development 72
Local Agenda 21 Statement, from Manchester 7
local authorities
    in Britain, birth 5
    and the CSD 23
    initiatives
        in Aalborg (Denmark) 69-70
        in the Cajamarca (Peru) 53-5
        in Chiang Mai (Thailand) 56-60
        in Gothenburg (Sweden) *61-2*
        in Hamilton-Wentworth (Canada) *48*-52
        in Harare (Zimbabwe) *63*-6
        in Hieldelberg (Germany) 67-8
        see also under individual countries
    links
        in Asia and the Pacific 223-4
        in the Commonwealth 223
        to the UN process 23-4
        see also twinning
    a 'major group' in Agenda 21 23, 24
    and national government 43
    networks 62
    numbers involved with Local Agenda 21 20, 27

planning for services *see* Strategic Services Planning Framework
    response to Local Agenda 21 20-1
    spheres of influence 13-14
    strengths 23
    'twinning' **see** twinning
    see also ICLEI; International Union of Local Authorities; local government
local government
    Commonwealth Local Government Forum (CLGF) 223
    and the international context 20
    precondition for sustainability 69
    principles, in Japan 137-8
    referred to in Agenda 21 20, 24
    response to Local Agenda 21 72-3
    setting a good example 102
    see also local authorities
Los Angeles, waste water management plan 84

'major groups' 22, 23
    local authorities as 23, 24
    mentioned in Agenda 21 24
Malaysia, seminar with Japan 22
Man and the Biosphere (MAB) programme 196-7
management systems *57, 58*
    Australia's approach 31
    in Peru 54-5
Manchester *see under* United Kingdom
Manhatten 130
marginalised groups 73, 74
    Mexican Popular Youth 74-5, 78-80
medical services, in Harare 63-4
Mega Cities Project 222
Mendip District Council *131*
Mexico
    'Space for Students' 78
    youth involvement 74-5, 78-80
migration
    rural-urban 102
        in Columbia 41, *43*
        in Harare 63
Model Cities 84
Model Communities Programme (of ICLEI) 43, 84, *96-8*
monitoring *see* auditing
municipalities *see* local government

national campaigns
    for Local Agenda 21 20, 27
        Australia 30-2
        Columbia 41-4
        Japan 39-40
        United Kingdom 33-8
Netherlands 20
    Amsterdam, transport policies 215, *216*
    Gronigen, transport policies 214
networking 103, 225
    and local authorities 13, 62
    sustainable development 32
New York City, community-based programs *130*
New Zealand 20
    Resource Management Act (1991) 143, 146
    Wellington 143

    environmental action plan 143-6
    South Coast Management Plan 145
    'Sustainable City Strategy' 145-6
Newhaven Green Business Initiative 210
NGOs **see** Non-Governmental Organisations
Nicaragua, Masaya, link with Leicester 219
nitrogen dioxide, in Kawasaki *151*
Non-Governmental Organisations (NGOs) 100
    in Harare 66
North Carolina (USA) 74
North-South differences 123, 124
    in Europe 102
North-South partnerships 219-20, 222-5
Norway, inter-sessional meetings 22

OECD Ecological City project 200
ordinances, Kawasaki Fundamental Environmental Ordinance 147-9
Ottawa *see under* Canada
ozone, low-level, public informed of levels 67

Pacific, CITYNET 223-4
Pakistan, Sahiwal, link with Leicester 219
Parish Map projects 37
parks, development, in Cajamarca 55
partnerships 12, 225
    categories of 96
    codes of conduct 96
    marginalised groups 73, 74-5
    North/South 219-20, 222-5
    in the planning framework 84, *85*, *96-7*
    public/private 172
    in the UK 37-8
Peru 53
    Cajamarca 53
        funding 76-7
        importance of unification 77
        initiatives 53-5, 77
Piedmont Peace Project 74
planning
    participatory *96-8*, *see also* consultation; partnerships
    physical, in Gothenburg 198
    town **see** urban planning
'Planning for Real' 36-7
plans
    action **see** action plans
    statutory, and Local Agenda 21 73, 75
    strategic services 84-*7*
pollution
    air
        in Chiang-Mai 59-60
        n Gothenbburg 61
        in Harare 65
        in Lancashire *160*
        in Manchester 5-6
        public informed of levels 67
        in Sao Paulo 25
    economic strategy to prevent, in Graz 174-*7*
    in Kawasaki 147, *151*
    salmon as indicators of 190-*1*
    water in

in Chiang- Mai 59
in Manchester 6
populations
city 18, 100
growth
in Columbia 41, *44*
in Harare 63
poverty 226
and environmental degradation 164, 166
and Local Agenda 21 102
strategies for combatting 36
in Harare 63
priorities
in the planning framework 84, *85*, 96, *97*, *110*, 116
public/professional differences 166
private sector, partnerships with 96
privatisation 74
public involvement *see* communities; education
public opinion, differs from professional priorities 166

Rapid Urban Environmental Assessment (RUEA) 164-6
record sheets, auditing *91-5*
recycling
in Gothenburg 61, *62*
of materials, in industry 172, 174, 175
refrigerants 13
refuse collection 55
in Cajamarca 77
Regional Network of Local Authorities for the Management
of Human Settlements (CITYNET) 223-4
reporting
'state of the environment' *see* auditing
in the UK 38
resources
generation 205-6
local authorities as consumers of 13
Rio Summit *see* Earth Summit
Rochdale, link with Pakistan 219
role models, local authorities as 13
Round Tables 37
in British Columbia 132
model used by Hamilton-Wentworth 49
used in Heidelberg 68
RUEA (Rapid Urban Environmental Assessment) 164-6

St. Kilda (Australia) 74, 167
salmon, environmental indicators *190-1*
Sao Paulo *see under* Brazil
Seattle, indicators chosen by the community 119
Senegal, urban environmental management 164-5
services 72
planning for *see* Strategic Services Planning
Framework
sustainability of 73
sewage treatment, in Harare 65
slums
in Chiang-Mai 60
in Sao Paulo *25*
Smoke Control Orders 5
social equity, and urban sustainability 69, 74
society, 'major groups' 22
South Africa 20

Spain, Barcelona, link with Leicester 219
squatter settlements, in Harare 65
'state of the environment' reporting *see* auditing
Strategic Services Planning Framework 84-*7*
service issues map *89*
service system auditing 84, *90-5*
service system map *88*
sulphur dioxide 61
in Harare 65
public informed of levels 67
Summit Conference on the World's Major Cities
see 'Group of Four'
sustainability
at international level 13-14
at national level 13
defined 69, 184, 188-9
indicators of *see* indicators, sustainability
key principles 189
local action 12-14
monitoring and evaluation 73
and social equity 69
translation into other languages 119
see also sustainable development
sustainable development 23, 72
definition 192
Hamilton-Wentworth initiative *48-52*
and local government 20
local strategies *112*, 118
North/South partnerships 219-20
and privatisation 74
Round Table guidelines in the UK 37
see also sustainability
Sustainable Seattle project 183-91
Sweden 20
FOCUSED ANALYSIS 205-6
Gothenburg
eco-balancing 198-9
initiatives *61-2*
transport policy 214
inter-sessional meetings 22
Switzerland, Zurich, transport policies 215

targets *110*, 116
task force, citizens' 49
Task managers 22
technology transfer, international 66
tender documents 33
Thailand
Chiang-Mai 59
environmental issues 58, *59-60*
ecological threats 56
environmental action plans 56-8
environmental policy 56, 57
Tianjin (China) 165
Toronto, childcare 120
tourism
'green' 36
in Heidelberg 68
town planning *see* urban planning
towns, and sustainability 69-70
Towns and Development Consortium 219
Trade Unions

in Harare 66
in Japan 133
traffic
    controlled in cities
        economic effects 215
        in Manchester 6
    problems in Chiang-Mai *59*
    public support for restriction 215
    see also cars; transport
training
    of businessmen 55
    in closed-cycle production 176-7
    employment 172
    of farmers 55
    see also education
transparency 76, 97
    role of local authorities 23, 24
transport
    Bristol Transport Plan 227
    development plan in Heidelberg 67-8
    in Gothenburg 198, 214
    policies 33
        sustainable policies in Europe 214-17
    prioritisation in Europe 214
    public
        in Harare 218
        in Wellington 143
        in Zurich 215
    and sustainability 69
    in the UK 212-13
    in Wellington 145
    see also cars; traffic
trees
    indigenous forest, in Wellington 145
    planting
        in Cajamarca 77
        in Harare 65
triggers 84
tropical rain forest timber, reduction *151*
Tunis (Tunisia) 165
'twinning'
    of local authorities 32, 38, 62, 219
        in Harare 66
2050 project 23

UNCED (United Nations Conference on the Environment
    and Development) *see* Earth Summit
UNESCO, Man and the Biosphere (MAB) programme 196-7
United Kingdom (UK) 20
    Bristol
        Bristol Environment and Energy Trust (BEET) 227
        energy strategies 227-*8*
    Cardiff
        auditing policy statements 76
        effects of National policy 76
    Coventry, Greening Industry Policy 178
    East Sussex, businesses and environmental
        performance 210-11
    EcoFeedback 37
    Environment City Model 37
    Environmental Impact Assessment (EIA) 38

Global Action Plan 37
Lancashire
    environmental forum *122*
    environmental information gathering *157-63*
    Green Audit 122, *124, 157-9*
    Lancashire Environment Forum 158, *162*
    Lancashire Environmental Action Programme
        (LEAP) 159-61, *162*
Leicester, international partnerships 219
Local Agenda 21 Steering Group 33
local authorities
    commitment 75
    'green' housekeeping 33-6
    Local Agenda 21 Plan 38
    policy integration 76
Manchester
    Castlefield *7*
    and Local Agenda 21 7-8
    Metrolink *4*, 6
    problems associated with industrialisation 5-6
    sustainability 6-7, 12
Mendip Local Agenda 21 *131*
national Local Agenda 21 program 33-8
National Sustainable Development Strategy 33
Rochdale, link with Pakistan 219
sustainability indicators 38, 119, 192
transport system 212-13
United Nations
    and Agenda 21 22
    Commission on Sustainable Development *see* CSD
    Conference on the Environment and Development
        (UNCED) *see* Earth Summit
    Conference on Human Settlements
        (City Summit - 1996) 12, 21
    Development Project (UNDP) 223
    Economic and Social Commission for Asia and the
        Pacific (ESCAP) 223-4
    local government representation 100
    World Commission on Environment and
        Development 188
United States
    Berkley
        Community Energy Services Corporation (CESC)
        172
        economic development strategy 171-3
        industry preservation 172-3
    California, 'Recycling Market Development Zones' 172
    cooperation with Columbia 22
    Los Angeles, waste water management plan 84
    New York City, community-based programs *130*
    public participation 74
    Seattle, indicators chosen by the community 119
    Valdez Principles 137
United Towns Organisation 219
Upper-Normandy, businesses and environmental
    performance 210-11
Urban Energy Management project 67
urban energy strategies *see* energy, strategies
Urban Forum (1992) 121
urban management 70
    Urban Management Programme (UMP) 164

urban planning 117
    and the RUEA methodology 165
    in Wellington 143
urbanisation, in Columbia 41, *44*
utopianism 72

Valdez Principles 137
vision 188
    in Gothenburg 198
    in Wellington 143-4
Vision 2020 49-50, 51, 75

waste 118
    degradation 205, 206
    Eco-check list (Japan) 136
    management
        in Gothenburg 61
        in Harare 65
        in Heidelberg 68
        in Wellington 145
    problems in Chiang-Mai 59
    reduction through cleaner production (Graz) 174-*7*
    in Sao Paulo 25
    see also pollution
water
    cleaning, in Sao Paulo 25
    in Kawasaki *151*
    and poverty 102
    quality
        in Harare 65
        in Manchester 6
    service planning for 84
    waste water management plan, in Los Angeles 84
    see also pollution, water
wealth, urban, relation to environmental problems 166
welfare, strategies for 36
Wellington *see under* New Zealand
West Harlem (Manhatten) 130
women 121
    in Harare 65-6
World Association of Major Metropolises
    see 'Group of Four'
World Cities Forum 100
World Conservation Strategy, Australia's response to 30, 31
World Health Organisation, Healthy Cities 68

youth involvement, in Mexico 74-5, 78-80

Zimbabwe 20
    Harare
        initiatives *63*-6
        public transport 218
Zurich, transport policies 215

Printed in the United Kingdom for HMSO
Dd 0298467 C30 8/95 59226